~a sky longing for memories~

contents

Glossary of Terms

3DCG
3-D computer-generated imagery. While it can accurately create complex shapes and smooth movement, there is a disparity between CG and hand-drawn animated elements that can make it look out of place against backgrounds, so the use of 3DCG is a true test of a director's skills.

Animation Director
The person in charge of keyframe animation on an animated production. Maintains unity of the artwork and determines motion in accordance with production content. Since the keyframes of animated works are created by several animators, the animation director orders corrections or redrawings as needed (or does the correcting himself) to ensure the feel of the animation doesn't change from cut to cut or scene to scene, and to unify the tone and quality of the overall work.

Anti-aliasing
A technique that smooths the zig-zag artifacts ("jaggies") that can develop on the borderline between colors when an image on a monitor is zoomed in. Anti-aliasing fills the jaggies with a color between those of the surrounding pixels to eliminate any sense of incongruity. Too much anti-aliasing results in a loss of image sharpness.

Art Director
The person in charge of creating the background artwork in a work of animation, including establishing the background art and determining the overall feel and aesthetic of the artwork. In animation, it's often the character design that gets talked about, but background art plays a major role in influencing the impression and worldview of an animation.

Background Animation
This refers to either animation elements produced by the colors used for backgrounds, or moving background elements created on animation cels. In the past, as it was necessary to expend the effort to create as many background art elements as required for the number of frames, this technique was not often used due to money and manpower issues. In modern, digital-centric animation, background art textures can be mapped onto 3DCG modeling elements, so the use of background animation has become relatively more commonplace.

Brightness, Value
The brightness of a color. The higher the value (as expressed on a scale from 0 to 100%), the brighter the color; the lower, the darker. 100% produces white, while 0% produces black, and at those extremes "hue" and "saturation" become meaningless. The greater the difference in brightness between elements in the same image, the stronger the contrast.

Cel
Originally referred to celluloid (actually polyacetate) film, but in digital animation this refers to the colorized keyframes and inbetweens data that form the basis of the animated images.

Continuity
A blueprint for a video that, in accordance with a finished screenplay, defines which images are combined at which timestamps, using rough drawings with dialogue, stage directions, etc. Typically drawn up by the director or producer. In live-action film, this is often referred to as a "storyboard."

Cut
A single sequence of images or a movement. A collection of cuts becomes a scene.

Depth of Field
The range of distance that an image is in focus.

Digital Animation
This refers to the technique of creating animation on a computer from data files, which includes nearly every step of production except storyboarding, key frames and inbetweens. This development has resulted in the older technique of photographing cels with film cameras being referred to as "analog animation." The popularization of various types of computer-based video software has led to the rapid evolution of such software.

Digital Ink & Paint
The process of turning the preliminary animation into cels. In previous eras cels were painted by hand by inkers and painters, but these days this phrase refers to the process of scanning the preliminary line art animation, coloring using painting software, and creating cel data.

Effects, FX
Special effects. In previous eras, this referred to the filming or post-production techniques of adding light or smoke by way of transmitted light or airbrushing, with each separate process managed by a craftsman, but in modern digital animation, when the film is created with video software, the effects are added all at once, for the most part.

Flare
"Lens flare," to be precise. An artifact created when the camera is angled directly into a source of light. This is the same phenomenon that is referred to as "halation" in photography. In previous eras this effect was added via airbrushing, but modern software has a function that can produce this effect.

Frame
The range of an image shown on screen. Or, a single segment of film.

Harmony Cel Process
As with animation cels, harmony cels are line art created by the animators that are then colored by the art staff and are used to minimize on-screen incongruity between the cels and the backgrounds. This technique, rarely seen in overseas animation, was developed within the world of Japanese television animation. In Shinkai's works, small objects, daily commodities, and vehicles that are close to the animated characters are mostly drawn on harmony cels.

HSB, HSV
The variables of color expression: Hue, Saturation and Brightness (or Value). One method of determining colors is by changing the levels of each variable. As this is a method of preparation based on the Munsell color solid instead of the RGB-based visualization most often used in computer imaging software, it's more suited

As this is a collection of background artwork used in animation, this book uses terminology and technique names particular to animation production. So that readers whose knowledge of animation techniques may be limited can better understand the contents of this book, these pages offer simple explanations of the technical terms used. The numbers listed with each art image are given as the "cut" numbers used in the actual production so you can get a better sense of what the production of each work was like.

for intuitive color adjustments. Programs or technique manuals may use either "HSB" or "HSV" but the meaning is essentially the same.

Hue

The difference in chromaticity. The 5 primary colors of red, yellow, green, blue and violet plus their intermediate colors make up 12 colors that can be arranged in a circle to create a "color wheel" that expresses a 360° range of colors.

Inbetweens

The frames that fill the gaps in the animation between each key frame to create a series of movements. During animation production, inbetweeners are also responsible for creating clean copies of key frames.

Key Frames

Fundamental artwork, created by the animators in accordance with the storyboard or layouts, which are the basis of any animated work. For anime filmed at 30 frames per second, at most 15 images will be required. A sequence of key frames defines movement.

Layer

The separation of elements in an image onto individual planes. Picture editing software comes with the function that allows the rendering of multiple layers of images, and Shinkai's animated work uses this function to great advantage.

Multiplane

This method adds a phased blur effect to cels or backgrounds to create a 3D perspective. In the era when animation was created on film, the animation elements were placed on planes set at different elevations on a large scaffold above which a camera was set. This technique, first seen in Disney's *The Old Mill* in 1937, could only be used in a large-scale production environment, but digital animation software allows animators to create a pseudo-multiplane effect.

Overlay/Underlay

The artwork that comes before the character cels are painted. Once upon a time they were hand-drawn on drawing paper then cut out for use, but with digital animation, the art is drawn on separate layers, which makes it easy to create.

Photography

In previous eras, each frame would be shot with a stop-motion camera mounted on an imaging table specialized for animation work, but in digital animation, this refers to the process of combining individually-created cels, backgrounds and 3DCG elements with animation software, (in some cases special effects are added) and creating cuts for video signals. Those video signals converted to NTSC or PAL for television broadcast are called "composite video." Individually-photographed cuts are joined using editing software (all of Shinkai's works are edited using Adobe After Effects), then voices, music and sound effects are added to create the finished work.

Pulling

The technique of moving cels or backgrounds left or right during filming. It's simple but very effective. The speed at which an object moves can be modulated by varying the distance the object moves between each frame. In Shinkai's works, the movement of clouds, etc. is created using this method.

Resolution

The numerical value that indicates the maximum display capacity of a monitor or projector. The number of display pixels. The unit of measure is DPI (dots per inch). The larger the screen used to display an image, the greater the required resolution, and therefore the greater the volume of data needed.

RGB

The three primary colors of light. Colors can be determined by modulating the balance of the brightness of Red, Green and/or Blue. As this method of determining colors is easier to control than other methods thanks to simple digitization, it has been used in video signals and computer software for ages. In digital displays, red, green and blue are each assigned 8 bits (in 24-bit color) which logically allows the expression of 16,770,000 colors, but there are ranges of colors created beyond what the human eye can perceive, which makes this difficult to use in art.

Saturation

The vividness of the colors. The greater the intensity the more vivid the color; at lesser intensities the colors appear gray or turbid. The values range from 0 to 100%. While Shinkai's artwork is often referred to as "highly saturated," in actuality he avoids using colors close to their pure forms and instead effectively uses mid-tones, which we hope you can see for yourself in this book.

Scene

A series of cuts within a fixed setting or limited time frame that create a meaningful segment of footage in accordance with the director's intentions.

Still Image

A non-moving cel. Typically used for crowd scenes and the like.

Tracing

The process of tracing over a rough sketch to create the line art for an image. For key frames and inbetweens, this refers to scanning pictures to create line art data that is later colored. Tracing can also refer to the process of creating a general outline for background art from location photographs.

Transmitted Light

A special effect added during the filming process to depict light. Back when animation was shot on film, actual lights were photographed using multiple exposures, but now the effects are added using video software.

■ Bibliography

Tsukioka, S. *Shin Gihou Shirizu 11 Animation* [New Method Series 11 Animation]. Tokyo, Japan: Bijutsu Publishing.

Kuzuoka, H. *Shin Jissen Animation* [New Practical Animation]. Tokyo, Japan: Atelier Bauhaus.

Sano, M. *CG/Dejitaru Eizou Yougo Jiten* [CG/Digital Video Lexicon]. Tokyo, Japan: Aspect, Inc.

Kodera, N., et al. *Dejitaru Bideo Hyojun Gaidobukku* [Guide Book to Standard Digital Video]. Tokyo, Japan: MdN Corporation.

5 Centimeters per Second

a chain of short stories about their distance.

Japanese theatrical release: March 3, 2007
DVD release: July 19, 2007 (JP); March 2008 (USA)
HD DVD, Blu-Ray Disc release: April 18, 2008 (JP)

Best Animated Feature Film, 2007 Asia Pacific Screen Awards
Lancia Platinum Grand Prize, 2008 Future Film Festival

Running time: 63 minutes

Staff:
Original Creator, Screenwriter, Director: Makoto Shinkai
Animation Director/Character Design: Takayo Nishimura
Art Director: Makoto Shinkai
Sound Director: Makoto Shinkai
Music: Tenmon
Producers: Makoto Shinkai/CoMix Wave Films
Background Art: Takumi Tanji, Akiko Majima, Akira Hirosawa, Minako Shimada, Yumi Ishii, Shingo Kanai, Yoshitaka Takeuchi, Kaori Izumiya, Makoto Shinkai
Background Art Assistants: Kenta Nakajima, Tasuku Watanabe, Ayumi Aoki, Mio Hosoya

Act 1: "Cherry Blossom"

Spring–Hometown

This is the town within Tokyo where Takaki and Akari spent their grade school years. The features of their residential neighborhood are shown in the cut where they gaze at the skyscrapers in the city center. The art in Shinkai's works are not just simple background elements; as independent cuts, the structure of scenes that are meant to appeal to the audience's emotions are considered important. Each scene's background coloring and screen composition subtly reveals the state of mind of the characters.

Clouds, considered a signature feature of Shinkai's works, are all drawn by Shinkai himself. "They always end up having similar shapes and colors as the clouds I see in my home prefecture of Nagano. Perhaps that's my personal touch," Shinkai says.

In *The Place Promised in Our Early Days*, the art was very dense, but in *5 Centimeters per Second*, the density of the art was more modulated, creating a more varied on-screen result, and this method allowed "warm" and "cool" scene tones to come directly from the background art. With this difference in mind, if you observe the art of both works, you can pick up on the shift in Shinkai's intentions with regards to the backgrounds.

Akari: Hey, they say it's five centimeters per second.

Takaki: Huh? What is?

Akari: The speed of a falling cherry blossom petal. Five centimeters per second.

Takaki: Really? You know a lot of things like that, Akari.

Akari: Hmm... You know, (*a little happily*) they look just like snowflakes.

Takaki: I guess... Ah, hey! Wait up!

(SFX): *klang klang klang*

Takaki: Ah! (*cut off*) Akari!

Akari: Takaki, I hope we get to see the cherry blossoms together next year, too!

(Excerpt of *5 Centimeters per Second*, Act 1: "Cherry Blossom")

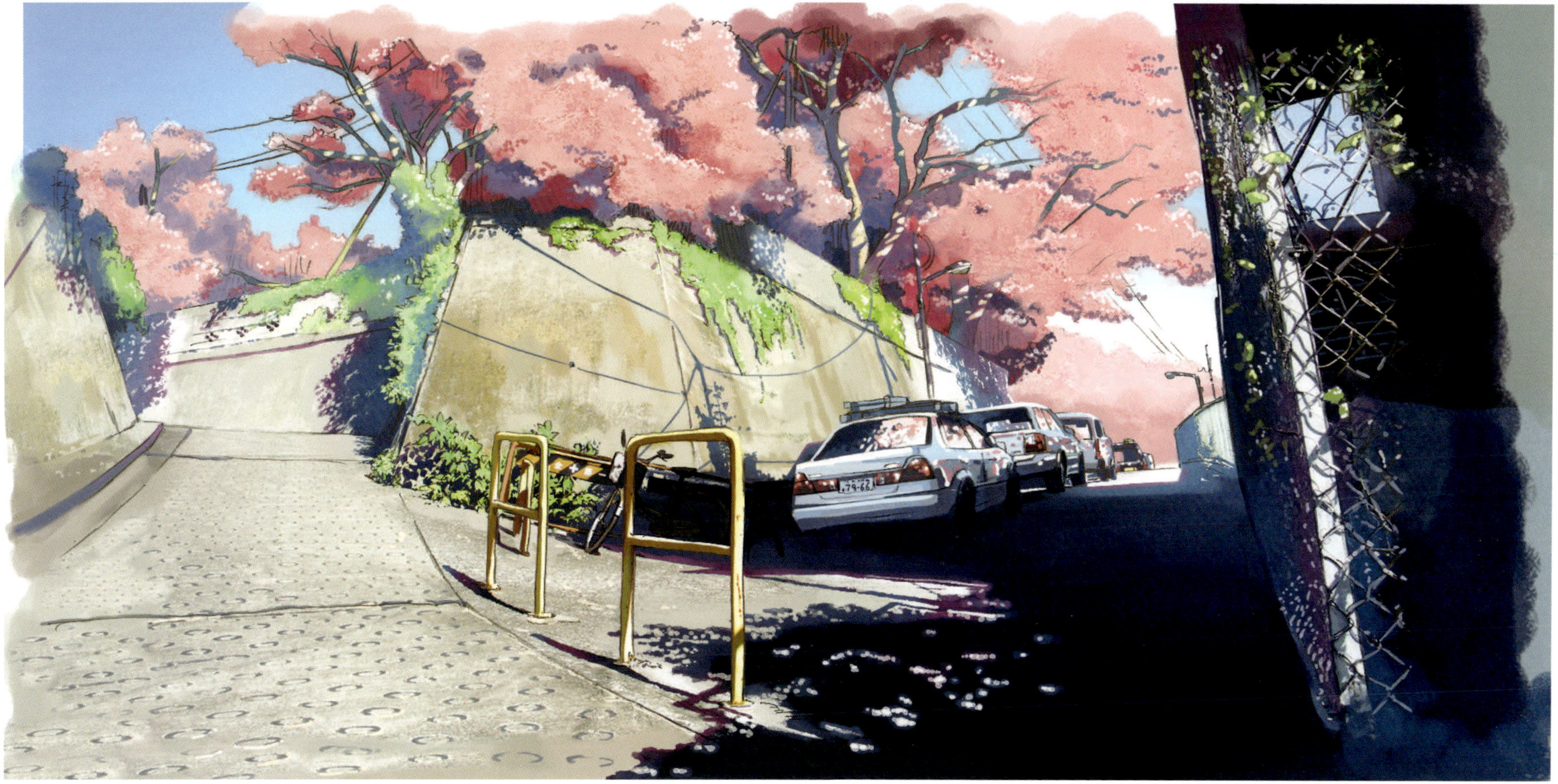

"Cherry Blossom" / CUT_005 / Setting: The road Takaki and Akari take to school

The road Takaki and Akari take to school. This was the first art board created for *5 Centimeters per Second*, used as-is as a cut in the animation. A pencil-drawn rough sketch was scanned then colored using CG. This image is modeled on the grove of trees in front of Sangubashi Station, in western Tokyo.

The final version included animation of Takaki and Akari walking to school under falling cherry blossom petals, and sunlight effects. The far-away car and distant background were processed on a separate layer in order to add lighting effects using imaging software, and the density of the details in the art was toned down in proportion to the results.

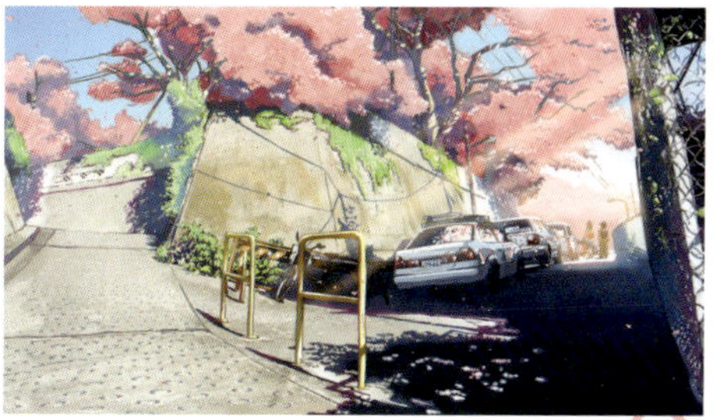

CUT_005 Final Version

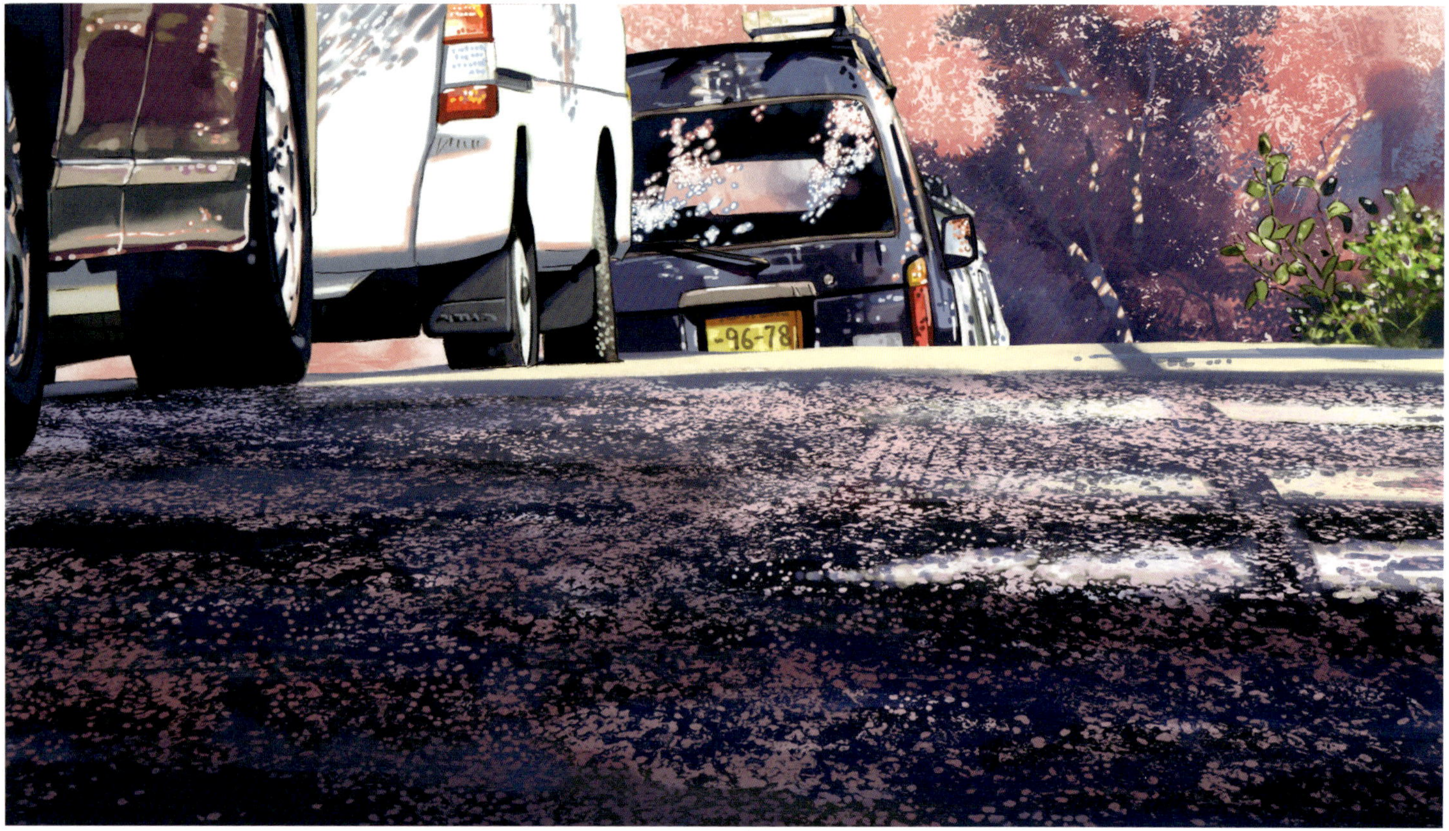

Background art for the cut showing Takaki and Akari's feet as they walk along the street. In the finished film, a blur effect was added, and the cars in the frame were all processed on separate layers. Additionally, a pink halation effect was layered on top to give it a very spring-like tinge.

"Cherry Blossom" / CUT_006 / Setting: The road Takaki and Akari take to school

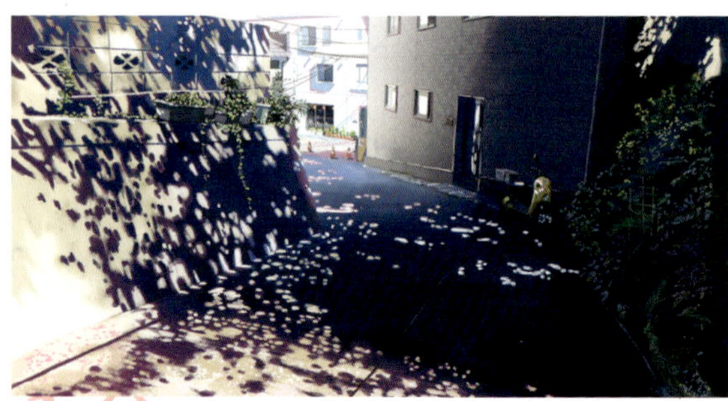

"Cherry Blossom" / CUT_011 / Setting: The road Takaki and Akari take to school

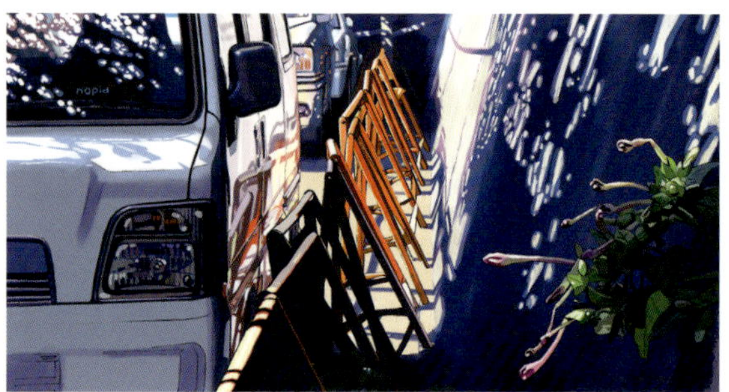

"Cherry Blossom" / CUT_004 / Setting: The road Takaki and Akari take to school

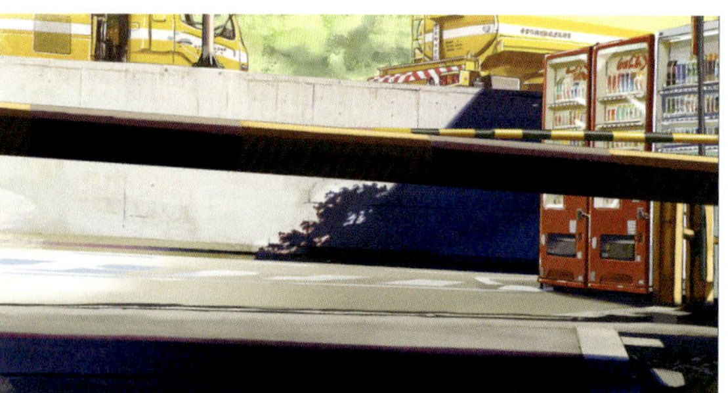

"Cherry Blossom" / CUT_015 / Setting: The road Takaki and Akari take to school

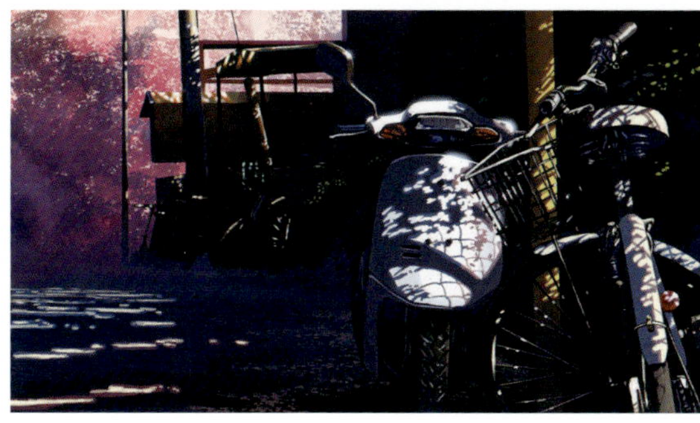

"Cherry Blossom" / CUT_003 / Setting: The road Takaki and Akari take to school

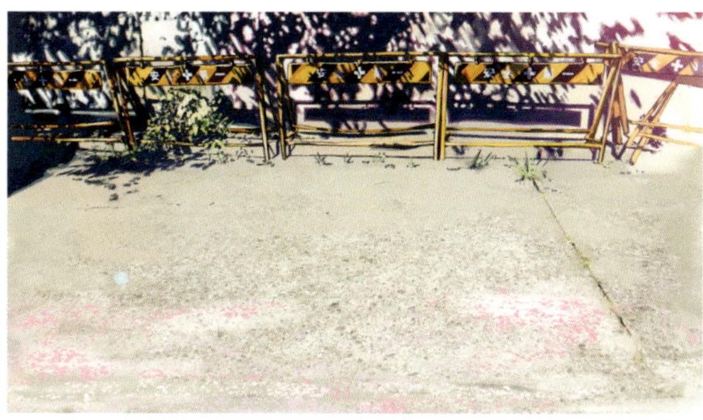

"Cherry Blossom" / CUT_010 / Setting: The road Takaki and Akari take to school

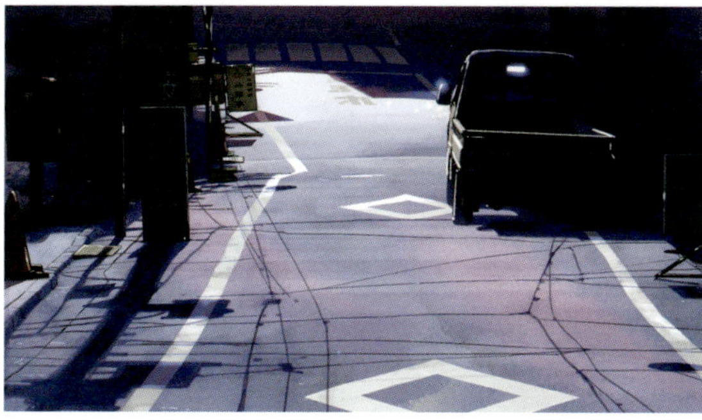

"Cherry Blossom" / CUT_024 / Setting: View of Tokyo

Dead branches reflected in the puddle with cherry blossom petals floating on the surface are lit by sunlight, making a memorable opening shot. The shadows of the tree on the ground and in the water were drawn on separate layers.

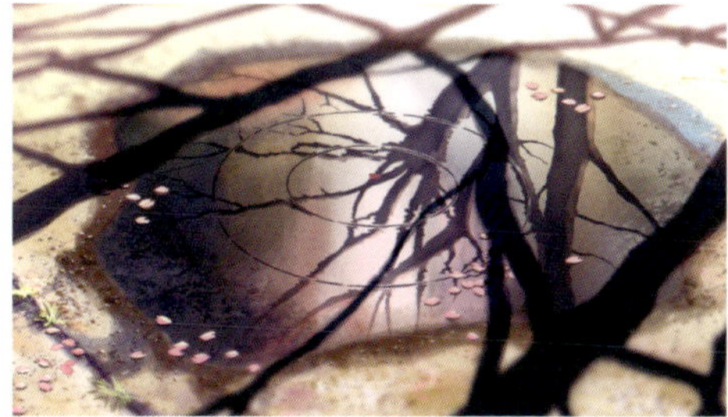

CUT_001 Final Version

This is a cut from the finished film. Animation for ripples on the puddle's surface and falling petals were added. Also, the foreground was sharpened and the background blurred to create a narrow depth of field and a deep feel in the image.

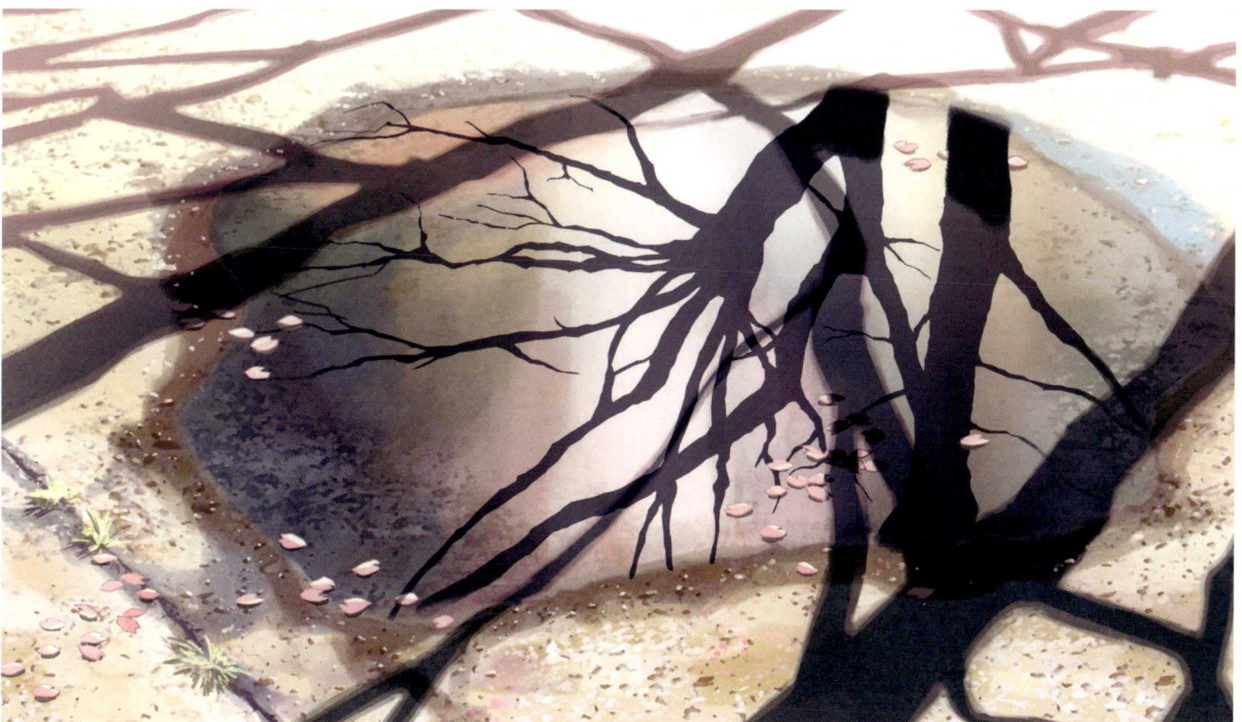

"Cherry Blossom" / CUT_001 / Setting: The road Takaki and Akari take to school

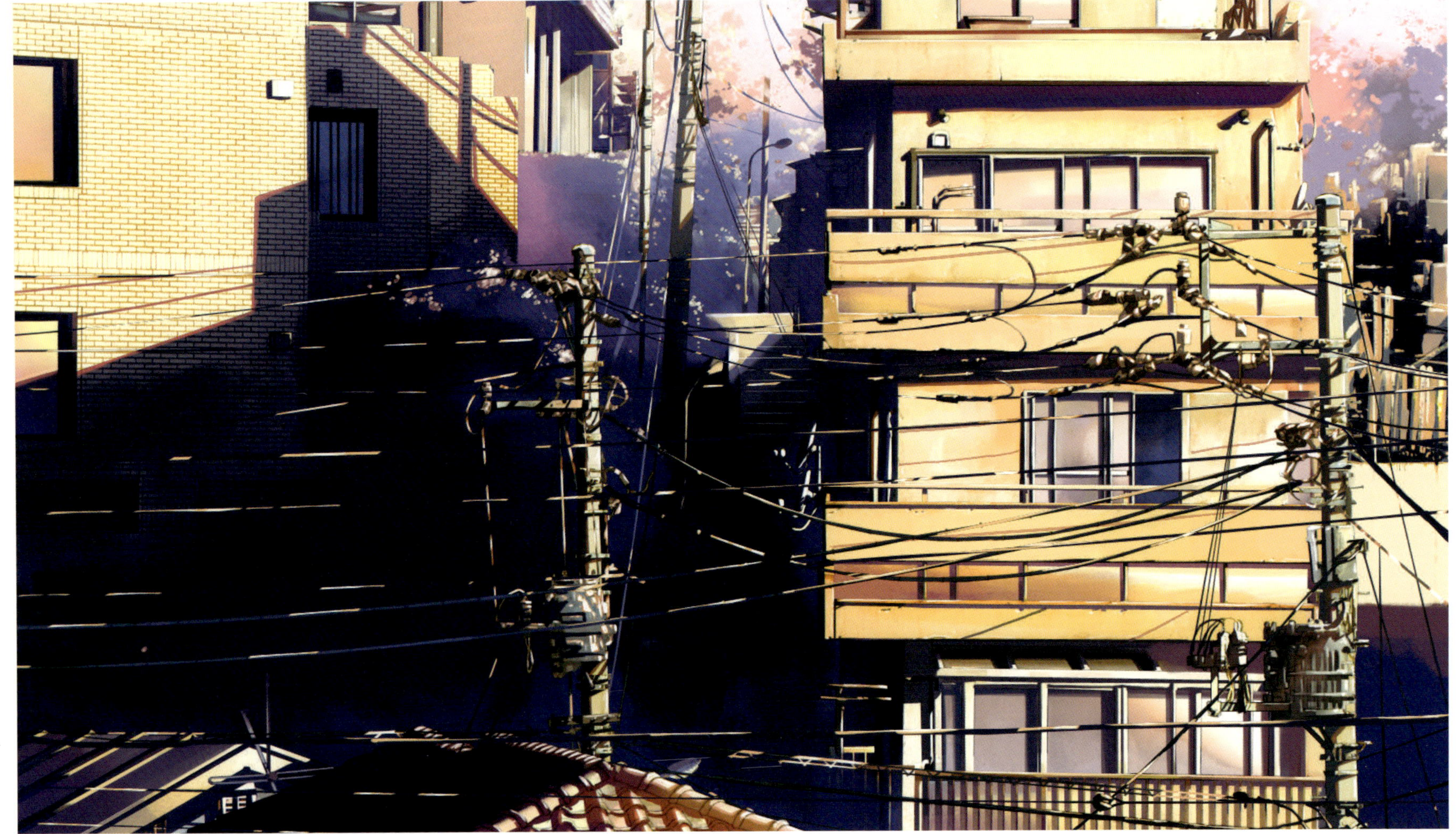

"Cherry Blossom" / CUT_088 / Setting: The road Takaki and Akari take to school

This is the backstreet route Takaki and Akari take to school. The preliminary sketch was made by combining several location photos. By reducing the density of the shadowy parts, this single image leaves a lasting impression.

The Shinto shrine and environs along the route that Takaki and Akari take to school. The color and contrast of the light give off a chilly, early-spring air. Please note the effective use of a wide range of mid-tones. The balance between the colors, with each color decidedly not highly saturated, improves the overall impression of this image.

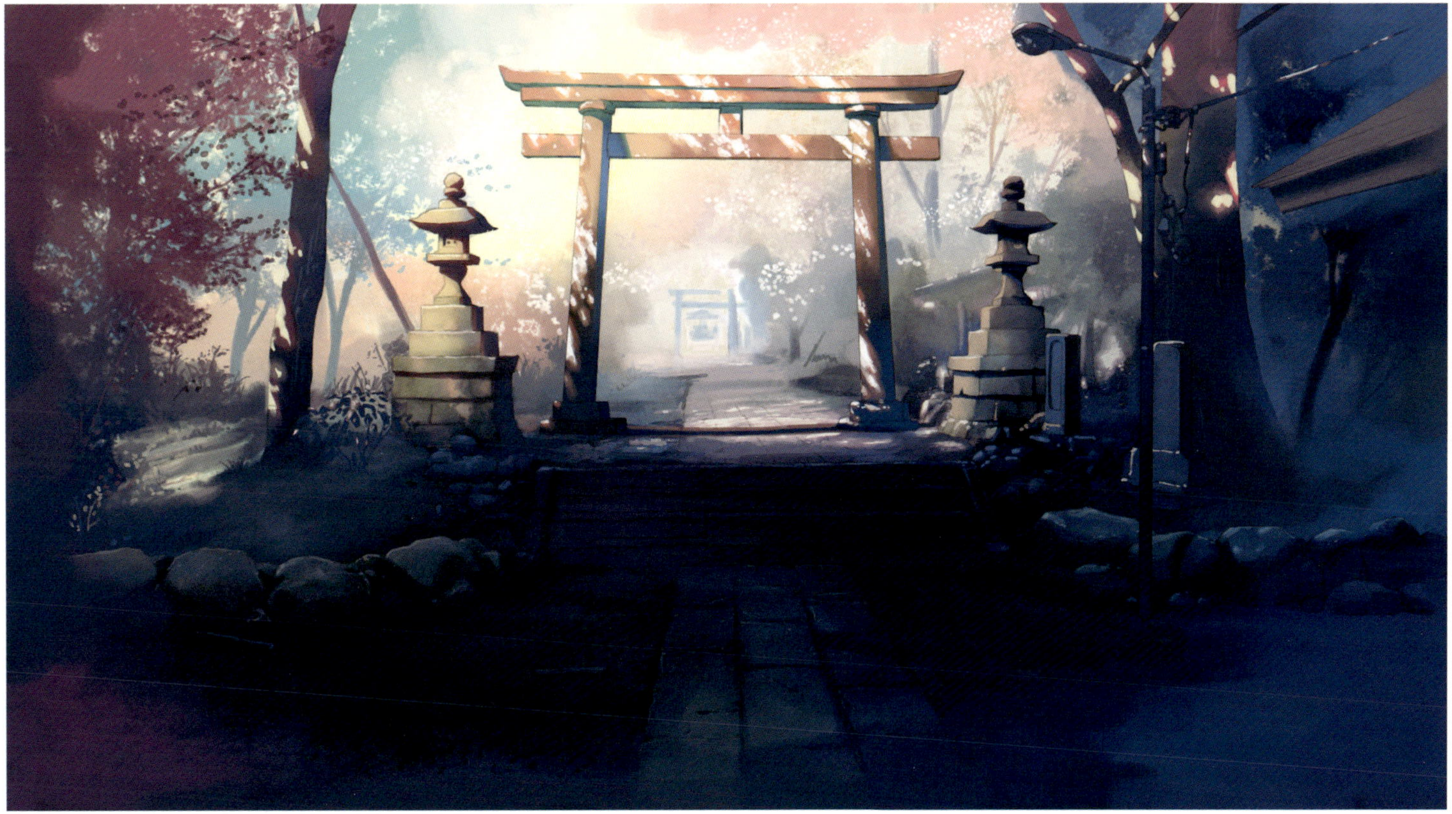

"Cherry Blossom" / CUT_086 / Setting: The shrine on the way to school

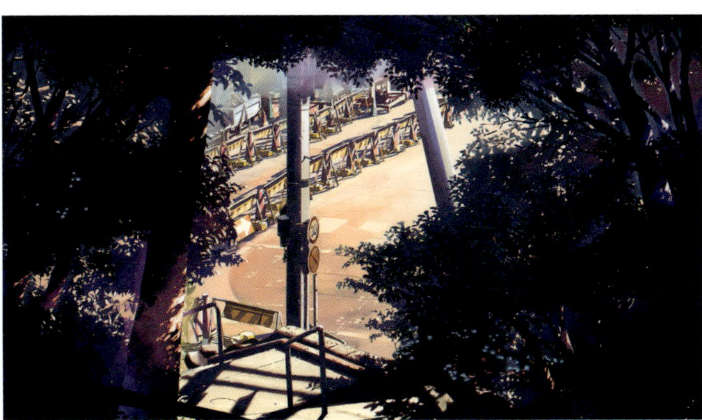

"Cherry Blossom" / CUT_081 / Setting: The shrine on the way to school

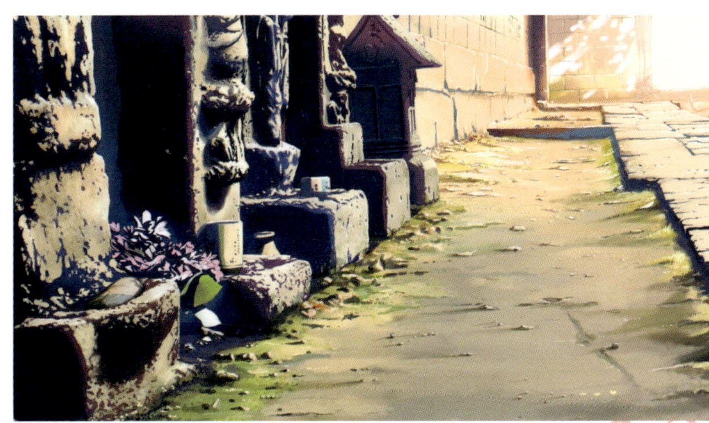

"Cherry Blossom" / CUT_087 / Setting: The shrine on the way to school

We used the residential area around Sangubashi Station as a location. The clouds reflected in the windows of the Tokyo Government Office are pretty. Past the rooftops of the houses, the overpass of the Shuto Expressway #4 Shinjuku Line is visible. By adjusting the heights of the foreground buildings, the sky and the spaces between the cluster of skyscrapers look much nicer.

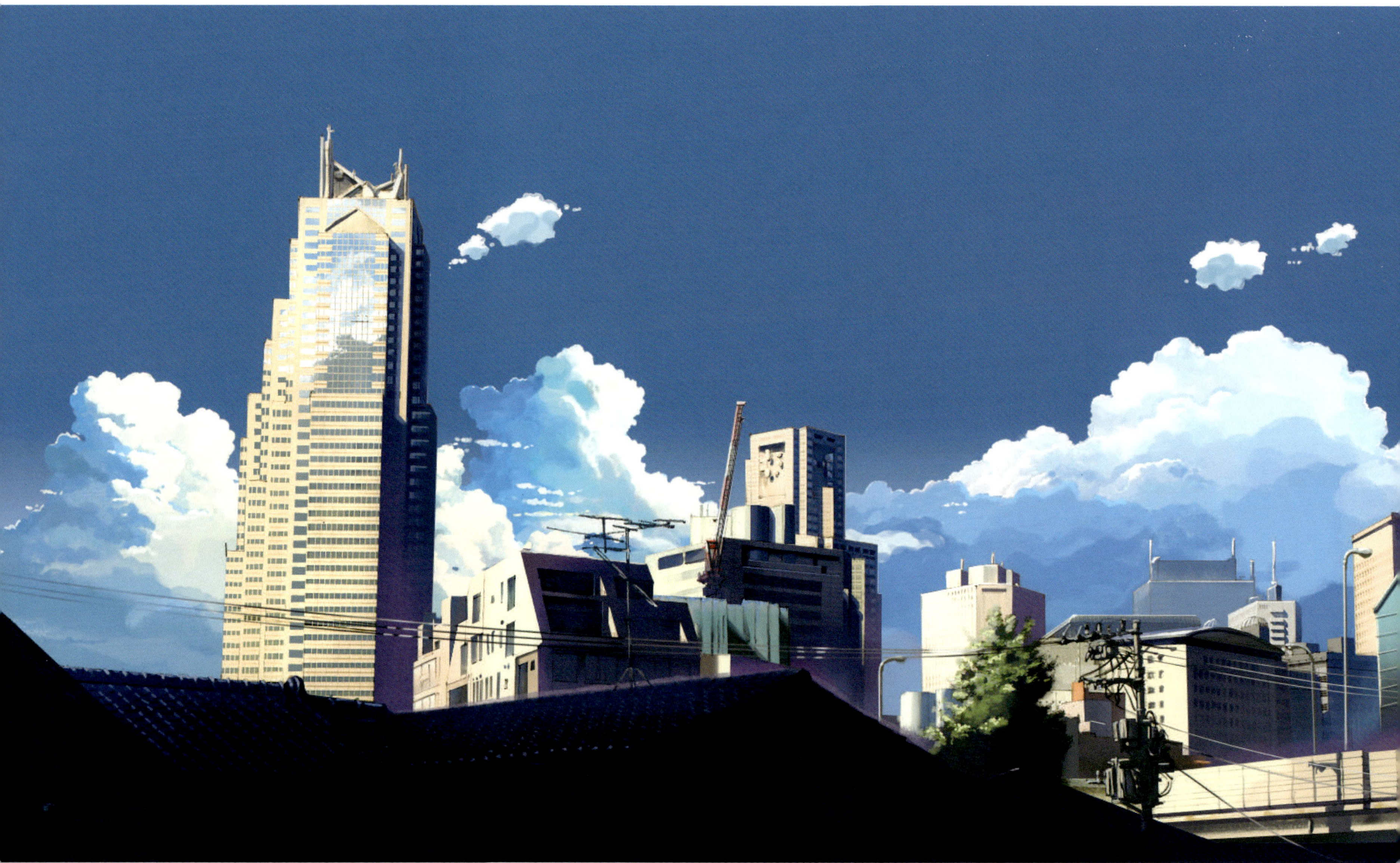

"Cherry Blossom" / CUT_025 / Setting: View of Tokyo

The progress of time shown by early morning scenes, evening scenes, and night scenes are depicted not only by changes in sunlight; the shapes of clouds were also taken into consideration. The phone booth near Akari's house is modeled on a phone booth at the intersection near the Tokyo Horseback Riding Club.

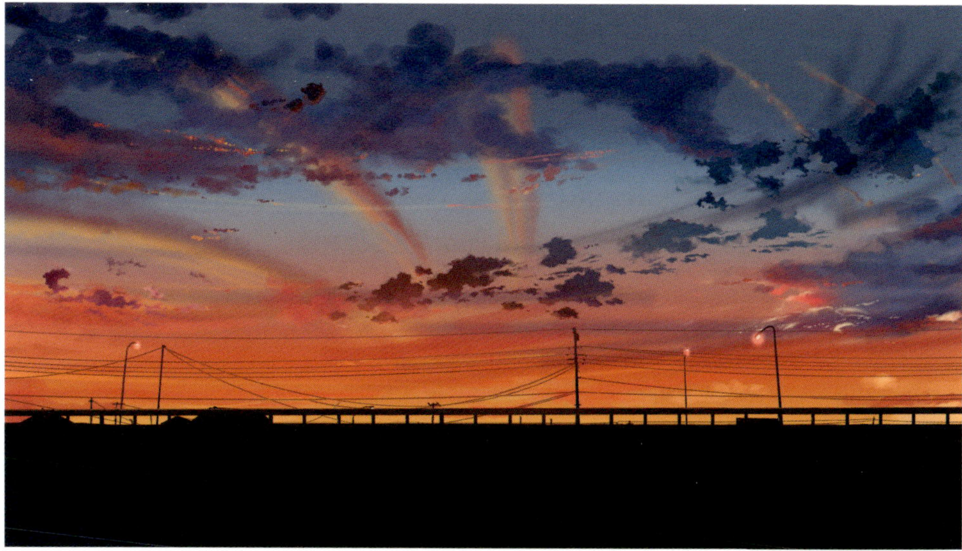

"Cherry Blossom" / CUT_032 / Setting: The road Takaki takes to middle school

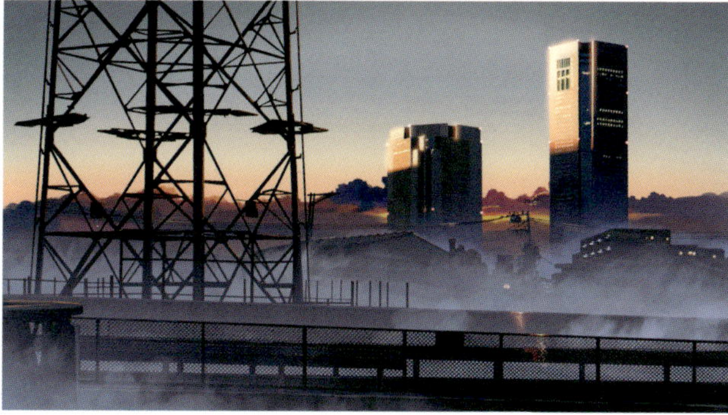

"Cherry Blossom" / CUT_048 / Setting: View of Tokyo

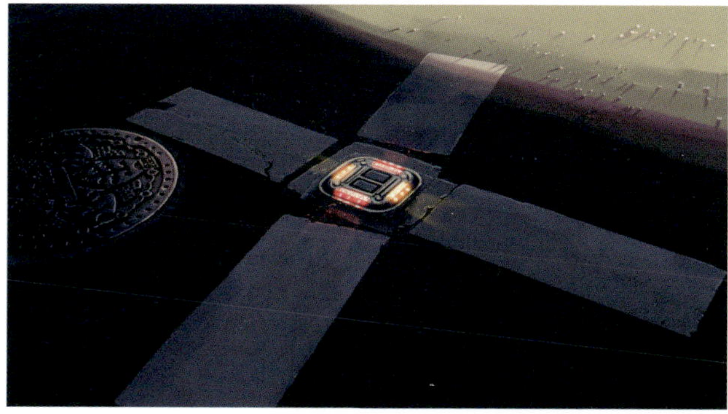

"Cherry Blossom" / CUT_B-14 / Setting: Akari's neighborhood

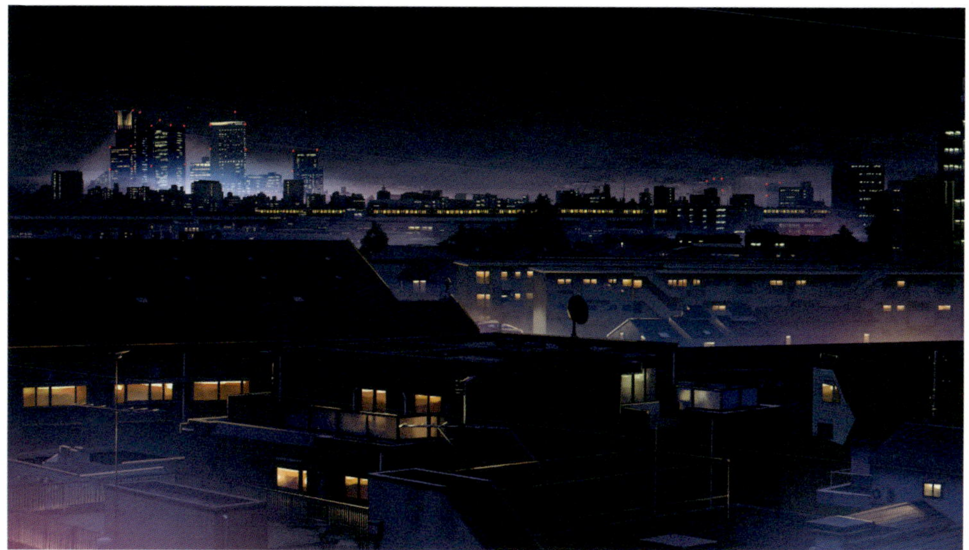

"Cherry Blossom" / CUT_047 / Setting: View of Tokyo

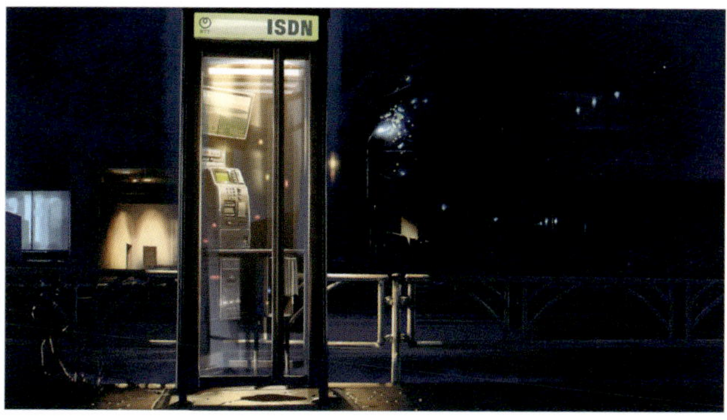

"Cherry Blossom" / CUT_139 / Setting: Phone booth in Akari's neighborhood

Act 1: "Cherry Blossom"

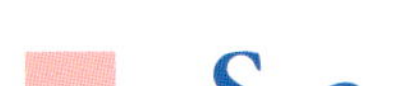

School Buildings

The many complex 3-D objects such as desks and chairs in the classrooms of Takaki and Akari's elementary and middle schools were not created from location photos but were based on 3DCG-rendered line art. To keep it from looking unnatural when they were all neatly lined up, the chairs and desks were all positioned just a bit randomly. In order to prevent a sense of incongruity between the character cels and the backgrounds, the staff created harmony cels for the finished product.

[first section omitted]

Akari: (*monologue*) Dear Takaki; Thank you for writing me back! It made me so happy. It's already well into autumn now and the leaves are turning beautiful colors. The day before yesterday, I pulled out a sweater for the first time this year.

(sfx) *rattle rattle* (*sound of door sliding open*)

Female Student: Tono?

Takaki: Hi...

Female Student: What's that? A love letter?

Takaki: Ah, no, it's not!

Female Student: Heh heh... Sorry for having asked you to do all that.

Takaki: No, it was no problem.

Female Student: Thank you. Hey, are you really transferring to another school?

Takaki: Uh, yeah. At the end of the school year.

Female Student: Where?

Takaki: To Kagoshima. Because of my parents...

Female Student: Really? I'm gonna miss you...

Akari: (*monologue*) Lately I have to get up early for school activities, so I'm writing this letter on the train. I got a haircut the other day. It's so short that my ears show. You probably wouldn't even recognize me.

... I bet you'll change little by little over time, too, Takaki.

(Excerpt of *5 Centimeters per Second*, Act 1: "Cherry Blossom")

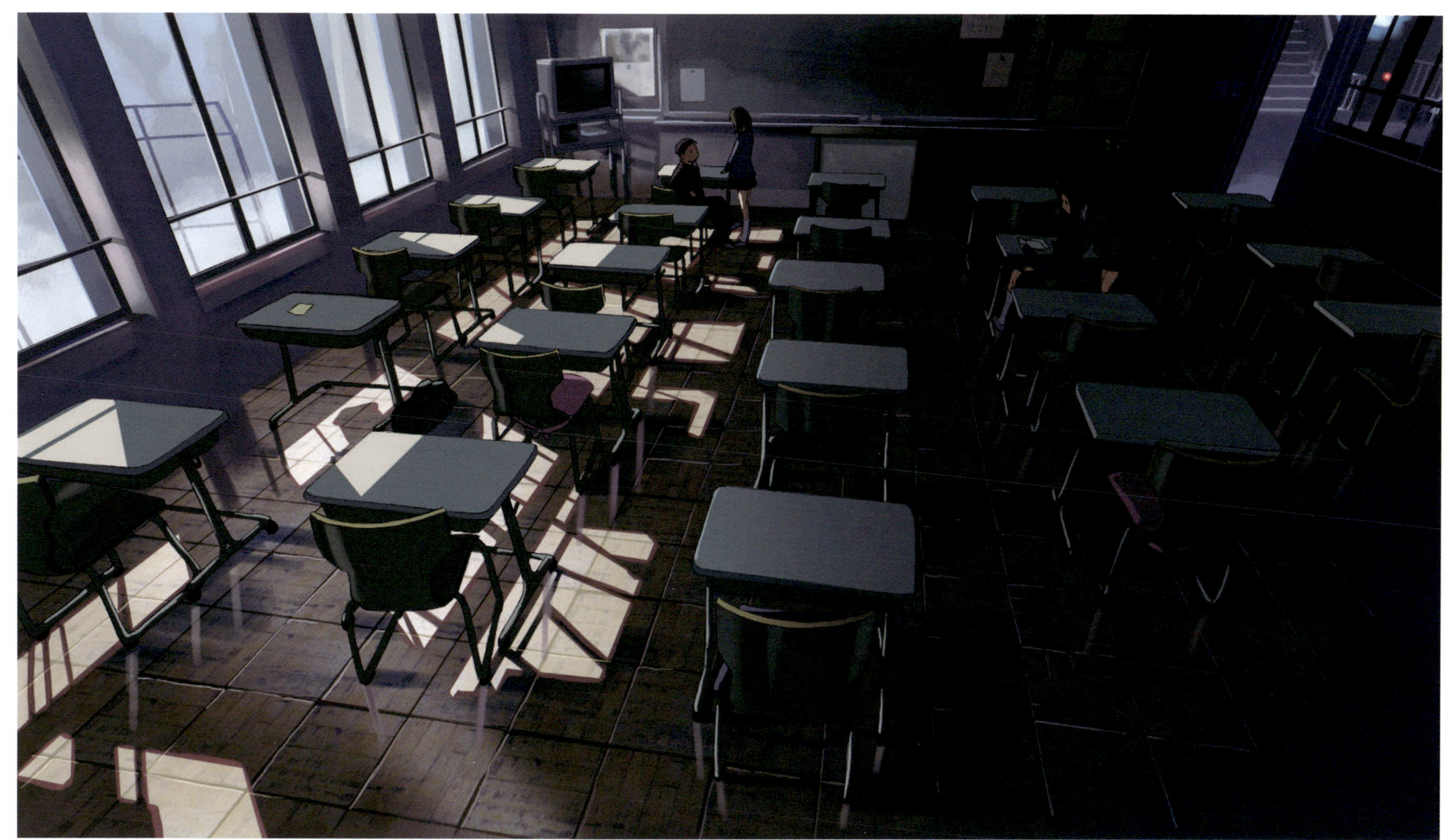

"Cherry Blossom" / CUT_067 / Setting: Middle school classroom

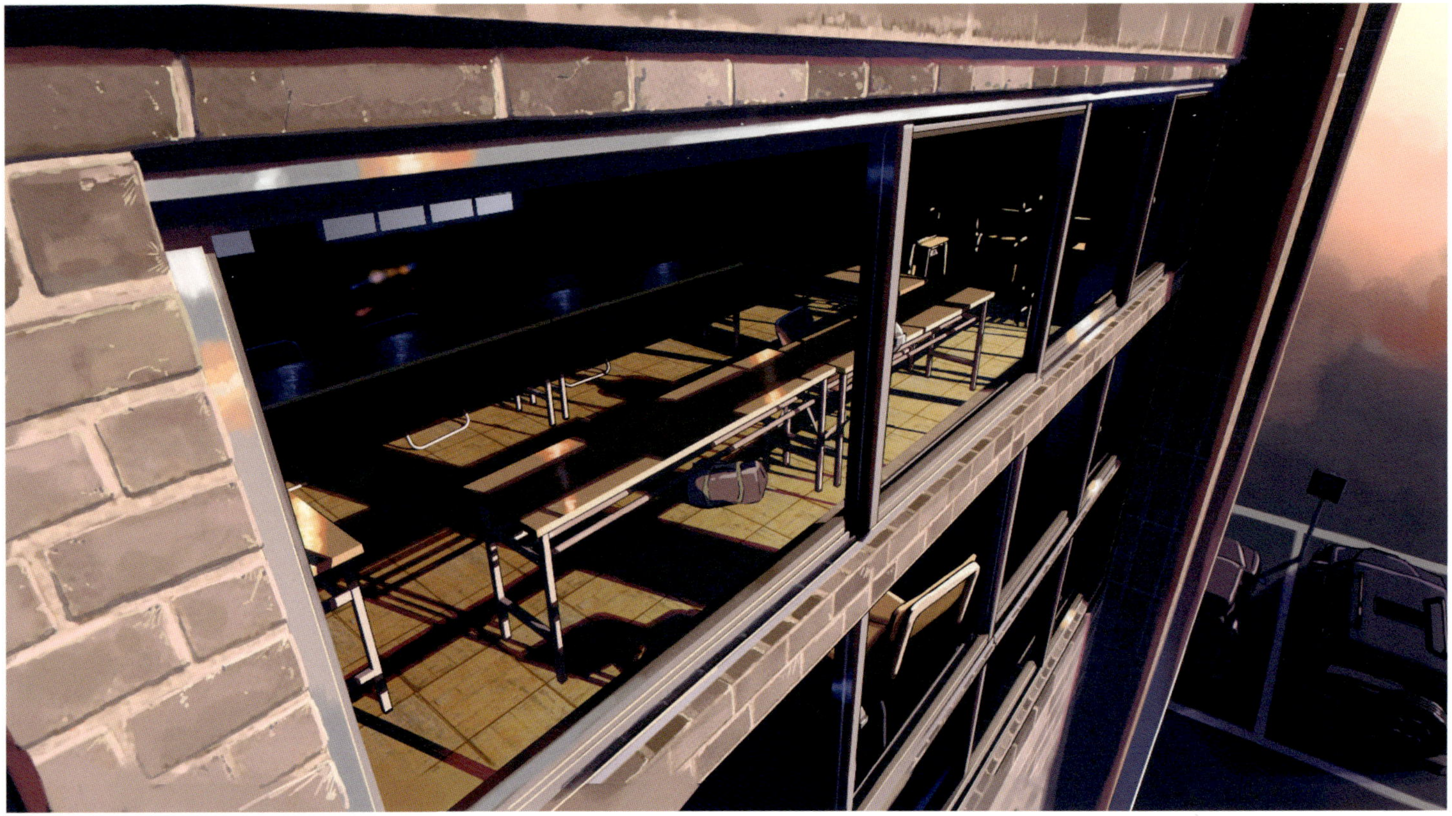

View from outside the window of the students' council room. This sort of technical angle would be difficult to photograph in real life.

"Cherry Blossom" / CUT_038 / Setting: Middle school students' association room

For the cuts with fluorescent lights, instead of having the background art staff draw a halation of the lights reflecting on the ceiling, Mr. Shinkai created the video effects himself. At such times, Mr. Shinkai gave very clear, detailed instructions regarding the content of the images to the art staff. The girls looking out the window are still image cels.

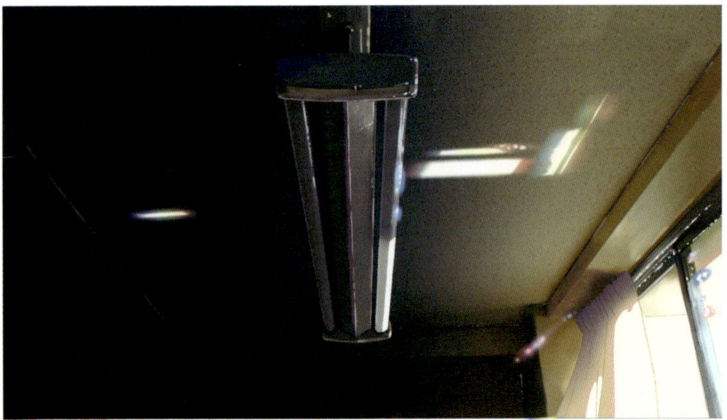

"Cherry Blossom" / CUT_028 / Setting: Middle school classroom

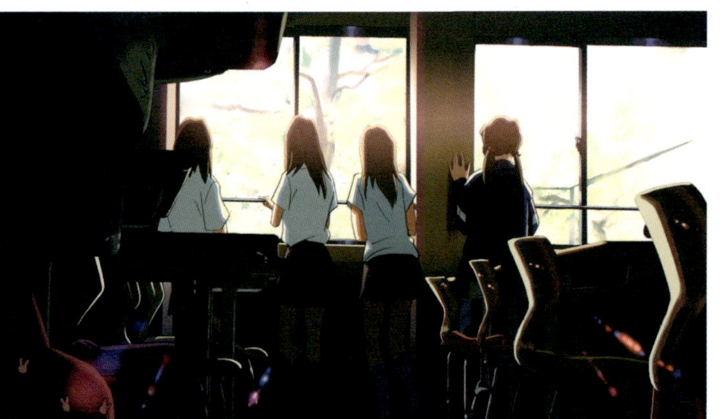

"Cherry Blossom" / CUT_029 / Setting: Middle school classroom

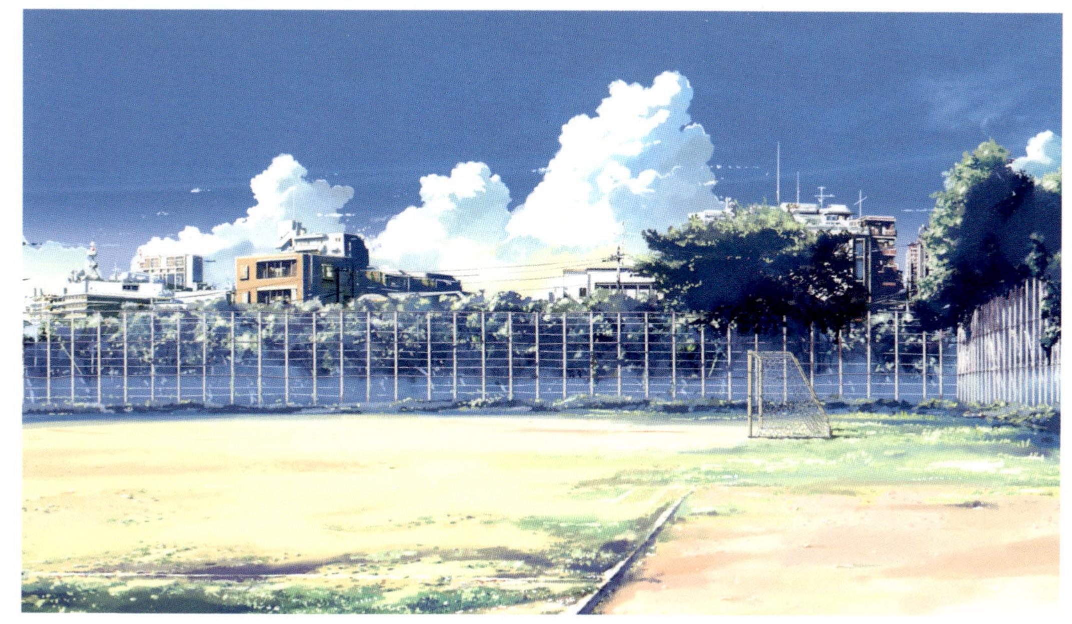

"Cherry Blossom" / CUT_019 / Setting: Middle school sports field

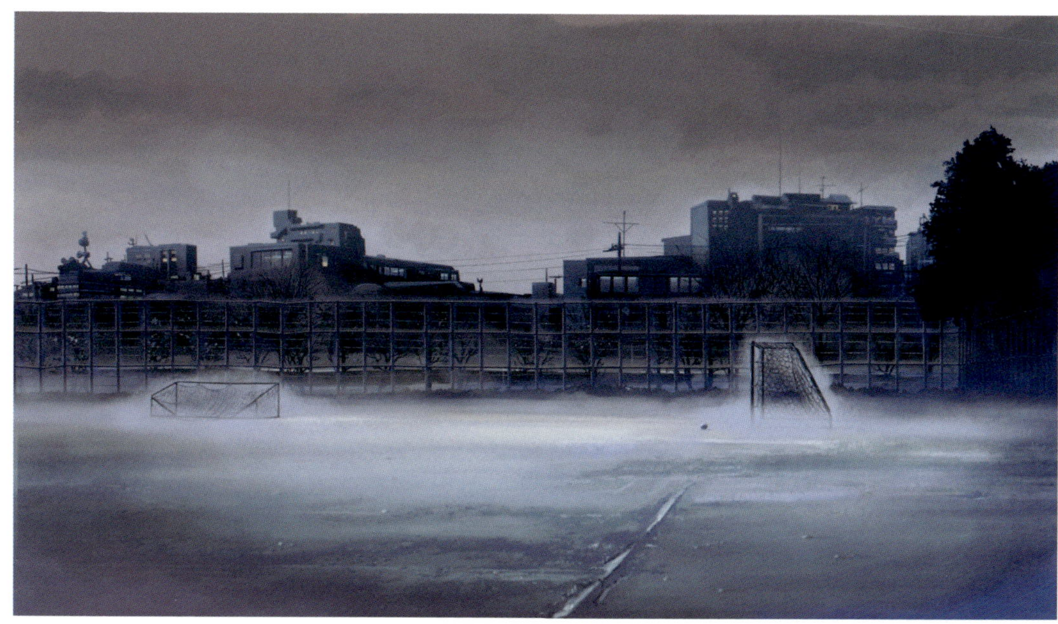

"Cherry Blossom" / CUT_ 060B / Setting: Middle school sports field

This is the field where Takaki's middle school soccer team practices. The summertime day (CUT_019) and early-spring midnight (CUT_060B) cuts were based on the same preliminary sketch. The final version of CUT_060B included animation of falling rain.

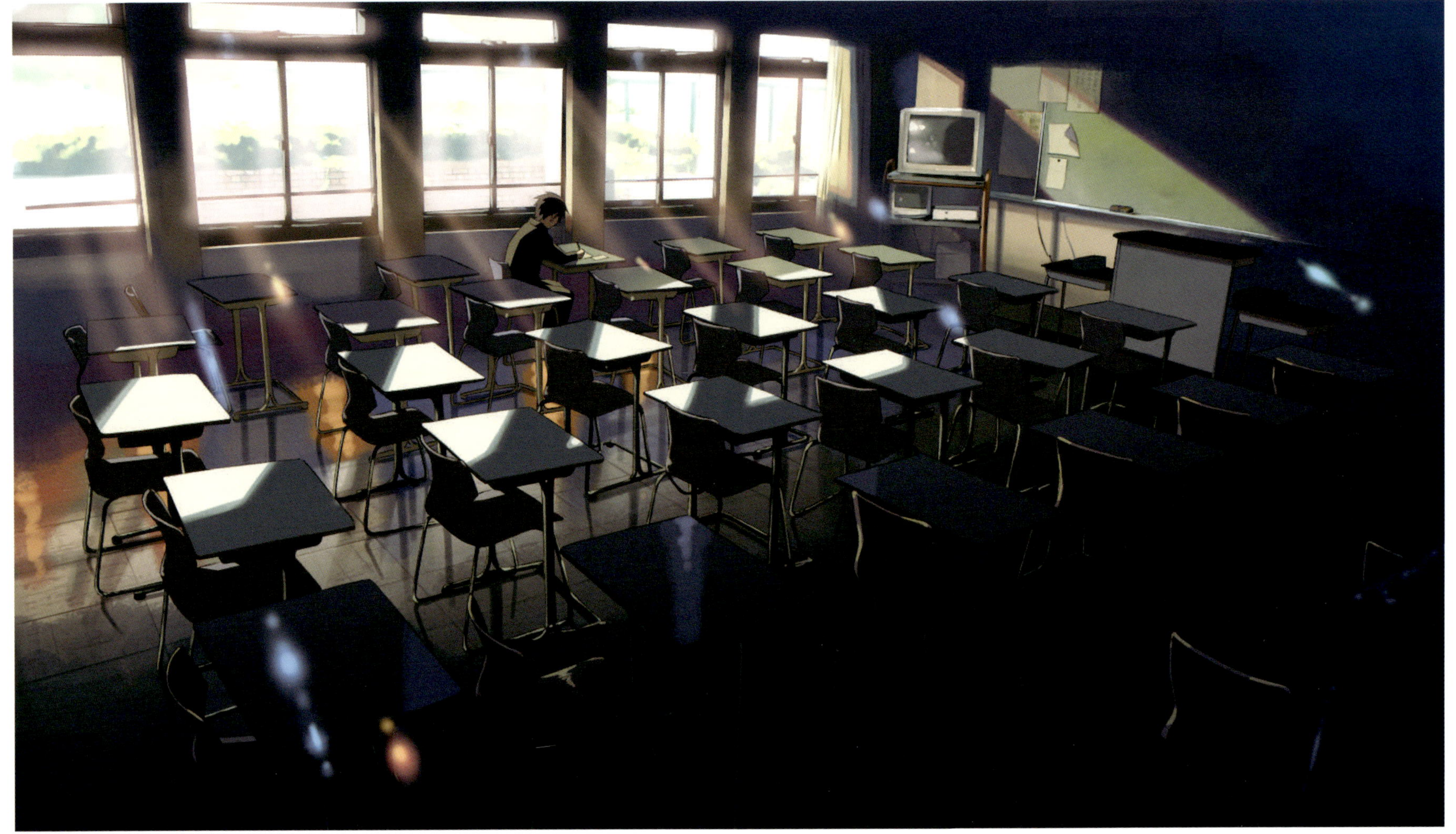

"Cherry Blossom" / CUT_B002 / Setting: Middle school classroom

In the early morning, Takaki writes a letter to Akari. The details are concentrated in the places in the classroom where the light falls, which has the effect of drawing in the viewers' gaze. It's an intricate composition, but the use of 3DCG preserves an accurate perspective.

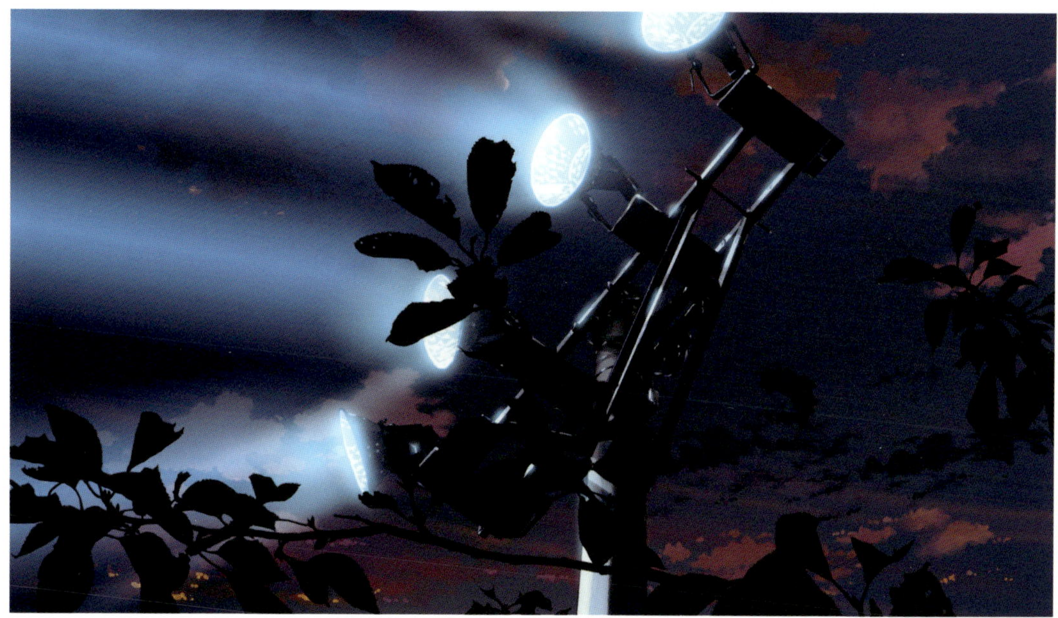

"Cherry Blossom" / CUT_B006-07 / Setting: Middle school sports field

The middle school's schoolyard floodlights. The passage of time from evening to night was depicted using the same base sketch. Branches in the foreground are on a separate overlay layer. It's difficult to see here as the scene is backlit, but the branches and leaves are drawn with plenty of detail.

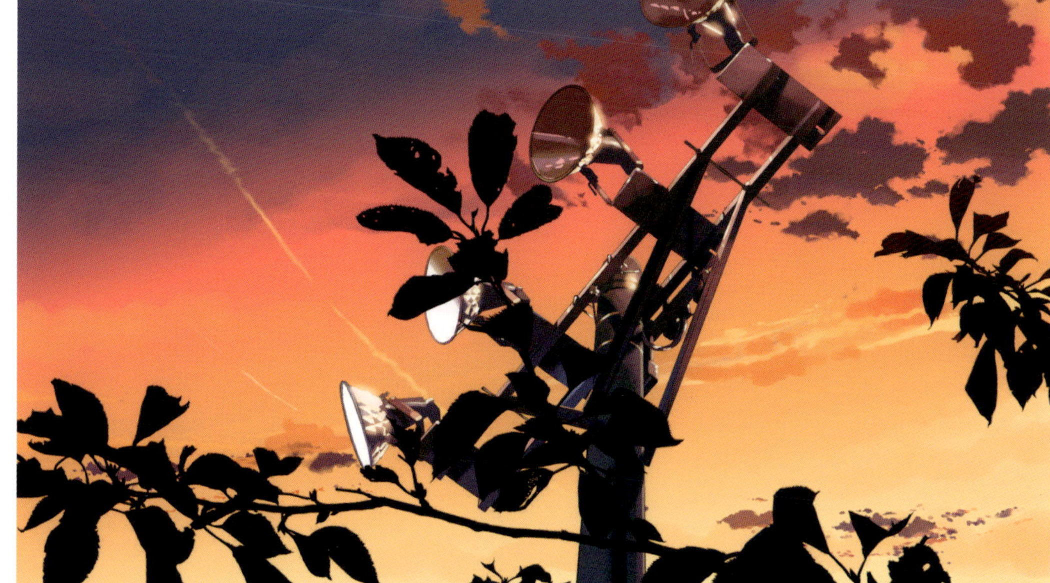

"Cherry Blossom" / CUT_B006-05 / Setting: Middle school sports field

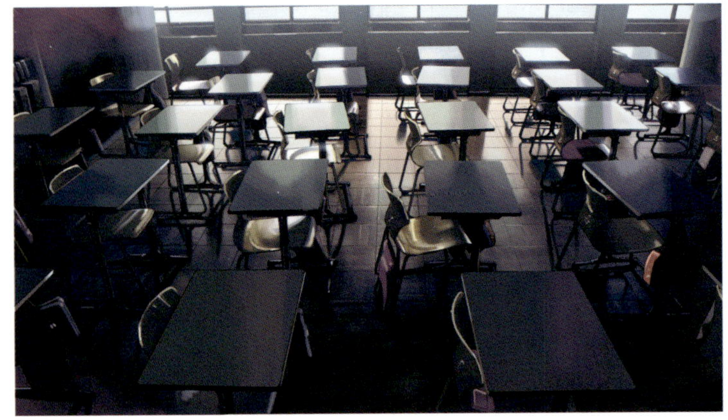

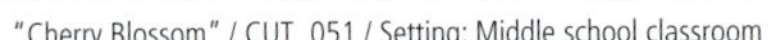

"Cherry Blossom" / CUT_051 / Setting: Middle school classroom

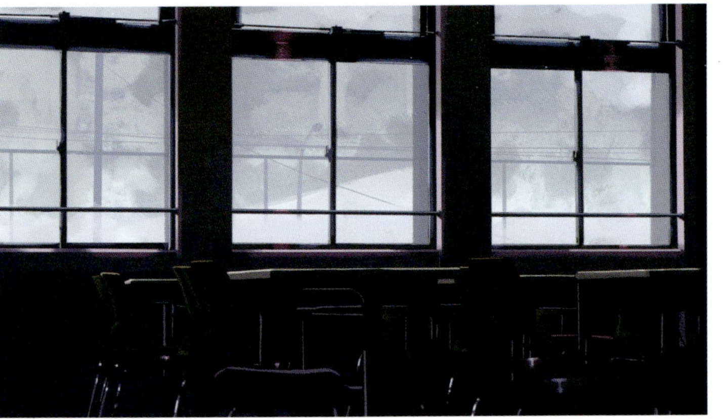

"Cherry Blossom" / CUT_068 / Setting: Middle school classroom

The classroom in late winter. Please note the differences between this version and the summertime version shown on page 18. Cold colors were mainly used here, and the contrast between light and darkness was strengthened, creating a cold, clear atmosphere. For CUT_B010, animation of snow falling outside the windows was added to complete the image.

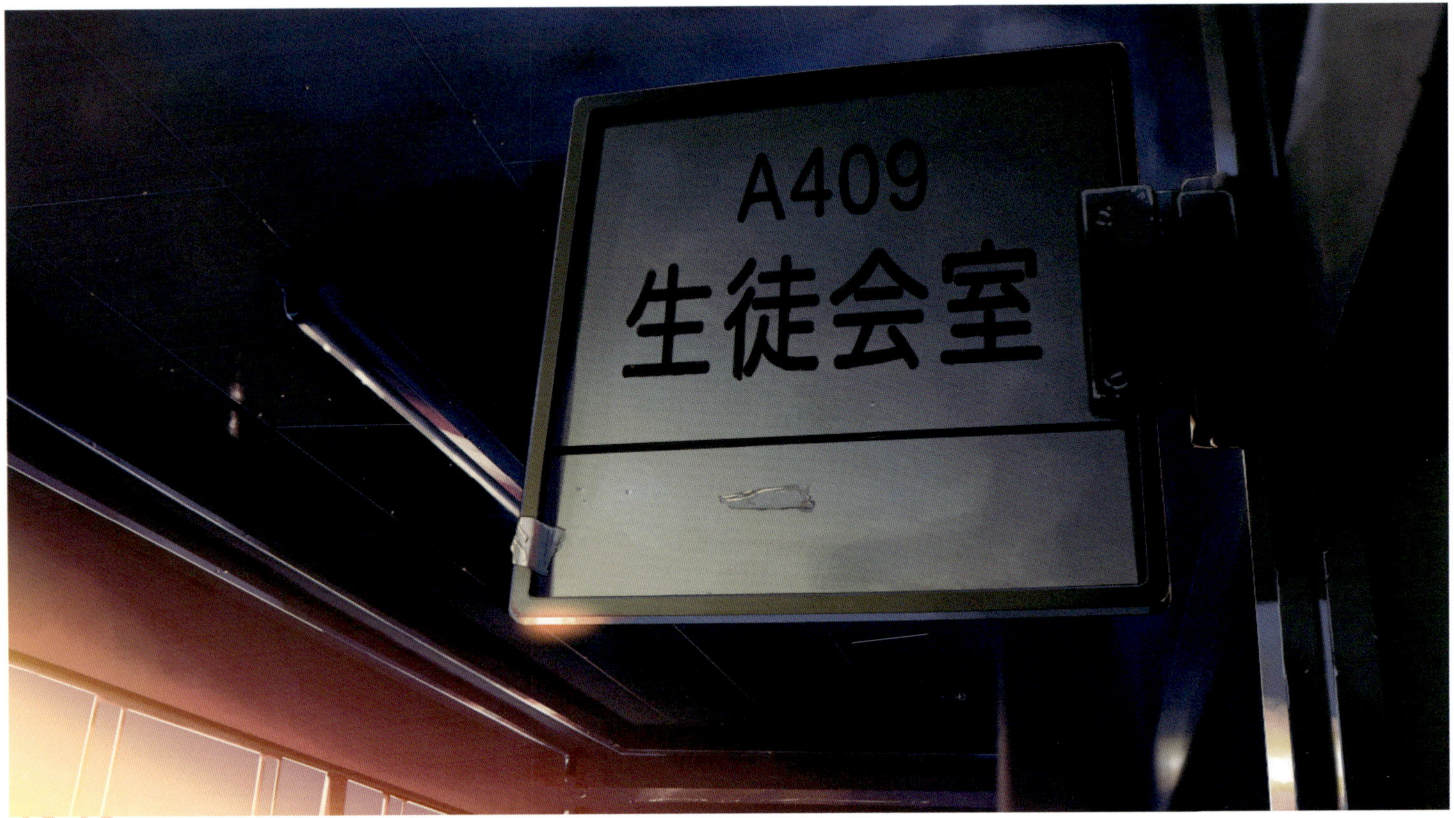

"Cherry Blossom" / CUT_034 / Setting: Middle school hallway

In order to have the room sign in the foreground be the focus, the ceiling and wall in the background were drawn on separate layers.

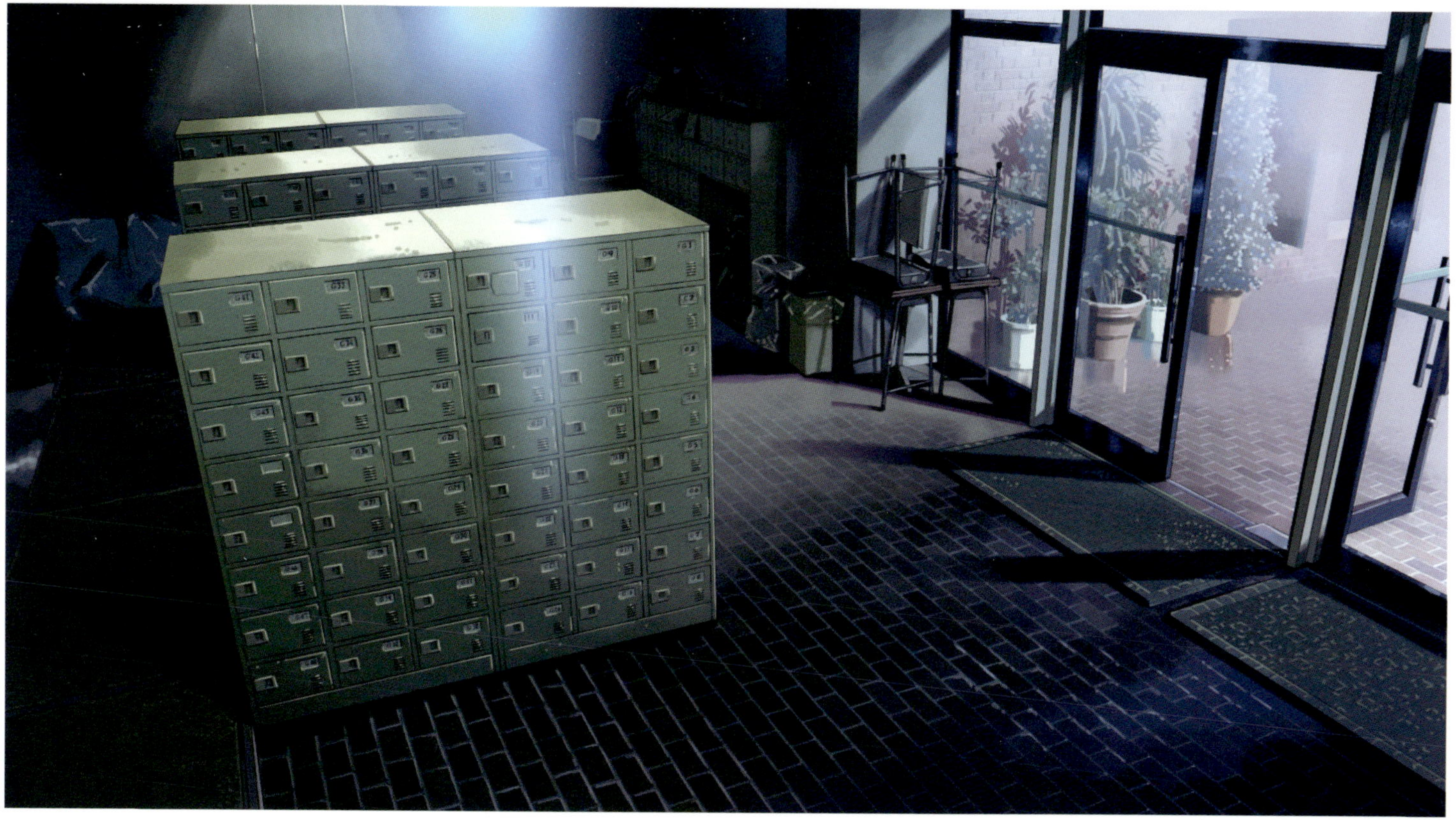

The entryway of Takaki's middle school. In order to emphasize the coldness of the outside air, the entire image is unified with the use of cool tones.

"Cherry Blossom" / CUT_071 / Setting: Middle school entryway

In CUT_069, to allow the animation of Takaki to be added, the outer walls and windows were drawn on one layer and the insides of the classrooms were drawn on another. The final cut included animation of snow.

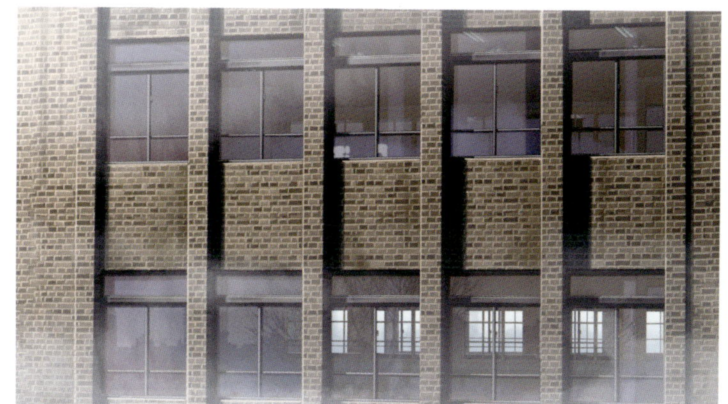

"Cherry Blossom" / CUT_069 / Setting: Middle school building

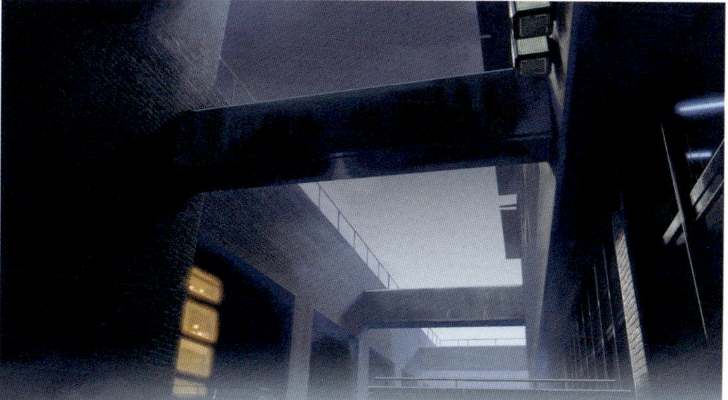

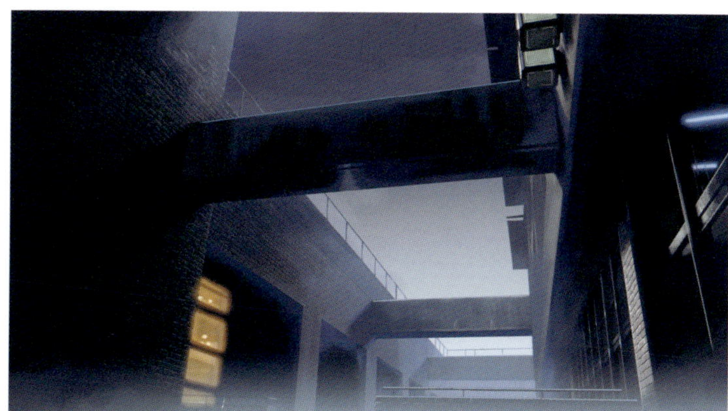

"Cherry Blossom" / CUT_072 / Setting: Middle school entryway

A hallway in Takaki and Akari's elementary school. Here you can see the graduation messages written on the blackboard. Please note how, in order to make the depth more defined, the far part of the hallway was drawn with lower chroma saturation than the classroom in the foreground. This technique uses color to create a sense of perspective. The parts of the image which Takaki and Akari's cels overlapped were not drawn in.

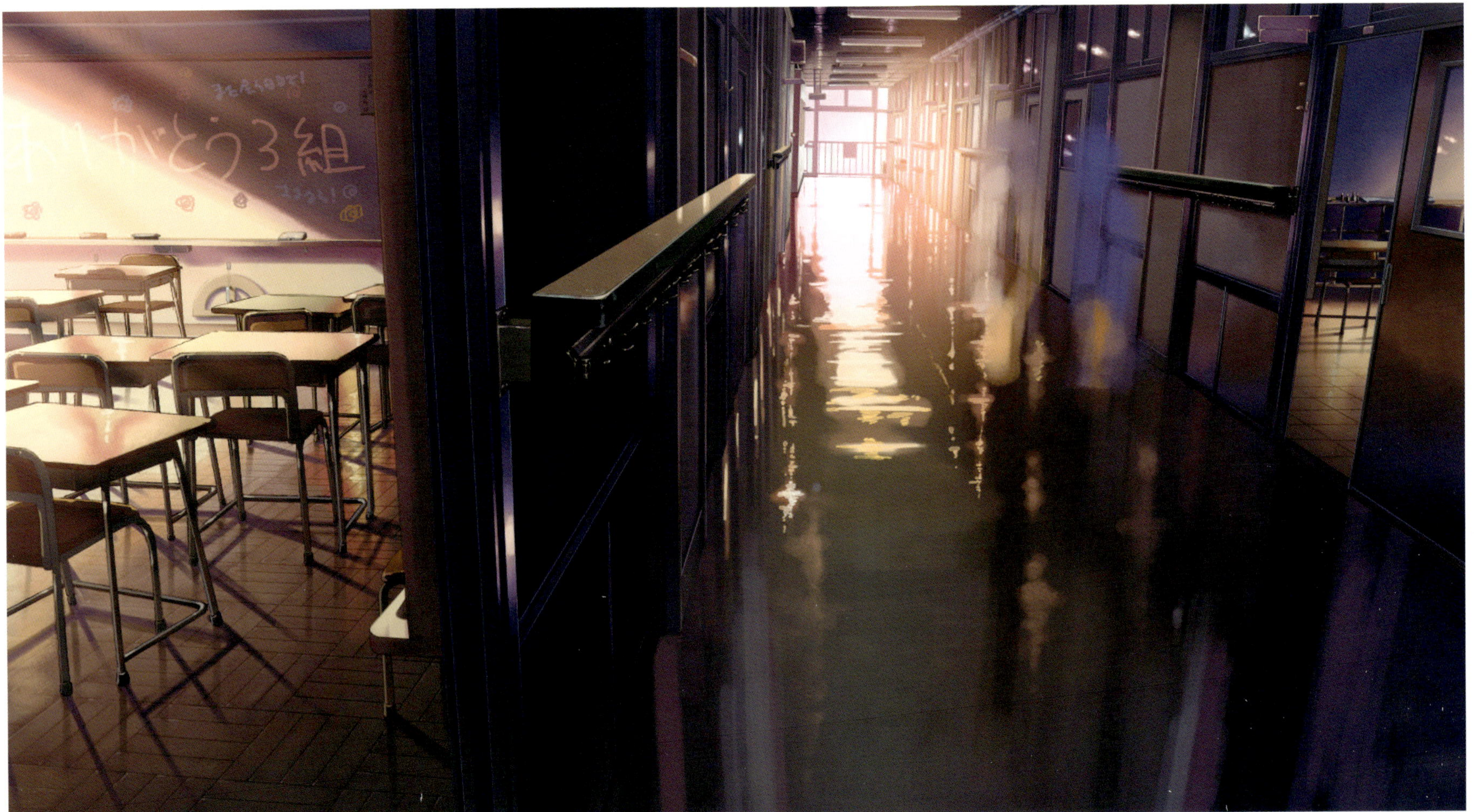

"Cherry Blossom" / CUT_182 / Setting: Elementary school hallway

The elementary school library where Takaki and Akari shared their innermost thoughts and feelings. Every single author name and title on the books in the foreground were drawn by hand.

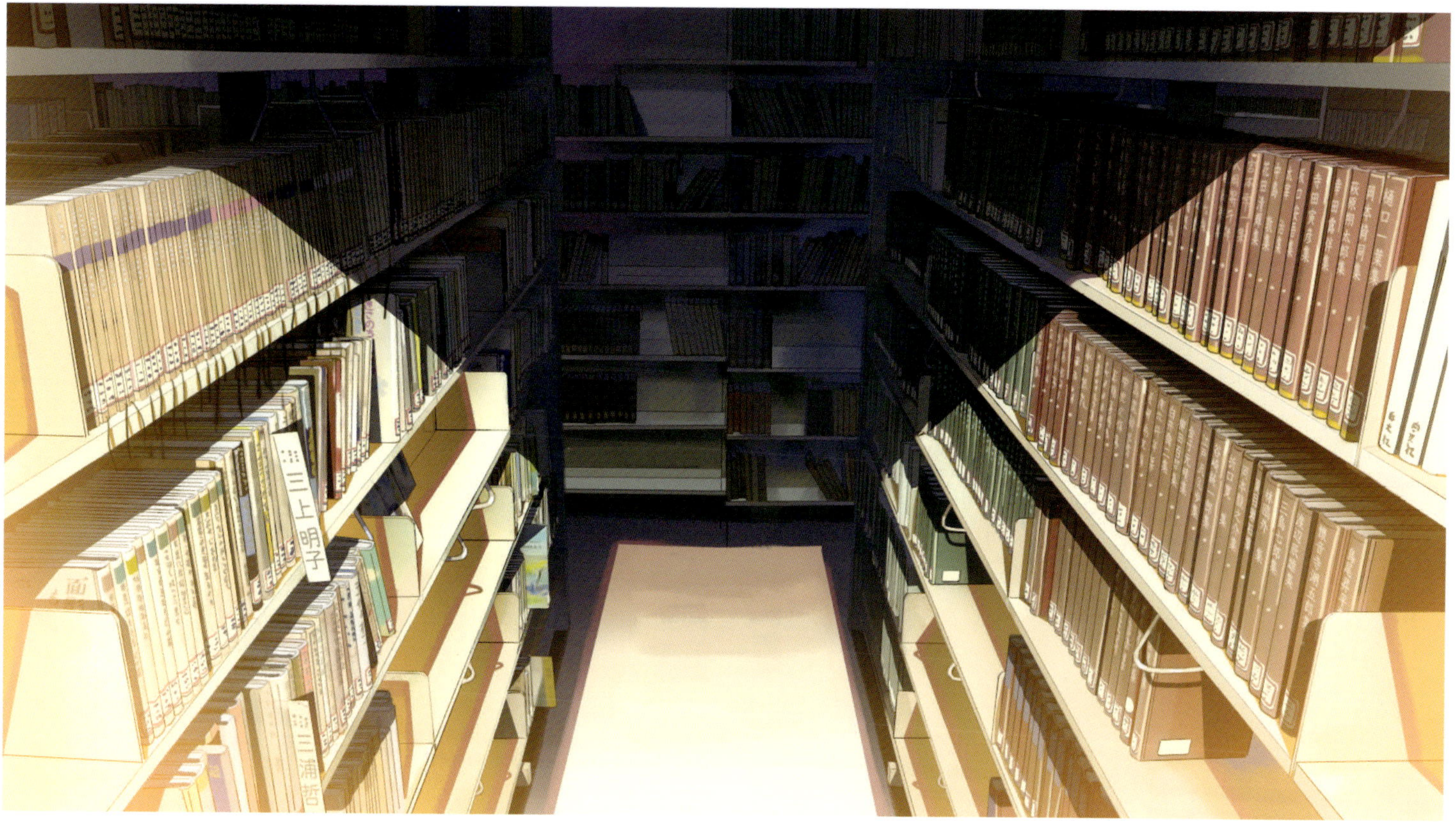

"Cherry Blossom" / CUT_096 / Setting: Elementary school library

Animated curtains and cherry blossom petals were added to CUT_095 to create the finished image. The library book cards showing Takaki and Akari's names listed right after each other also show the actual titles and authors of those books.

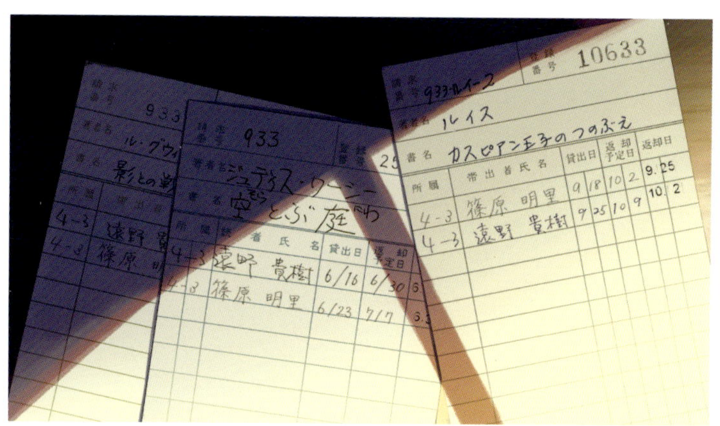

"Cherry Blossom" / CUT_097 / Setting: Elementary school library

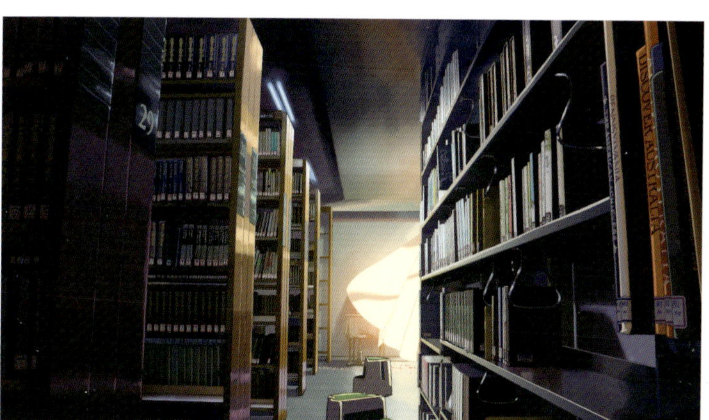

"Cherry Blossom" / CUT_095 / Setting: Elementary school library

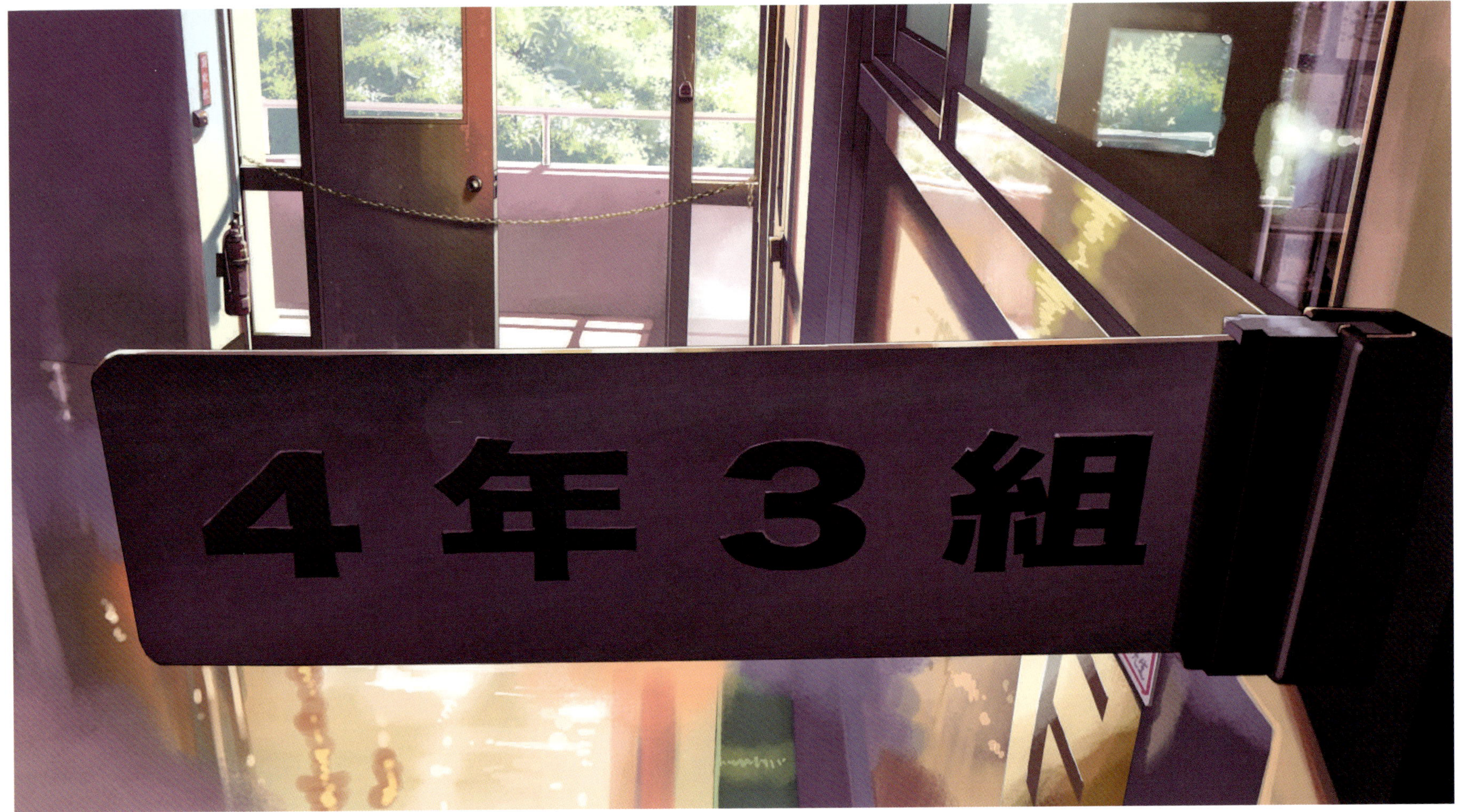

"Cherry Blossom" / CUT_093 / Setting: Elementary school hallway

A classroom sign in Akari's new school. The saturation is not high, but this cut makes it clear that a wide range of hues was used across the entire image. Please note how the space around the door plate draws your eye, and the difference in density of details in the other areas.

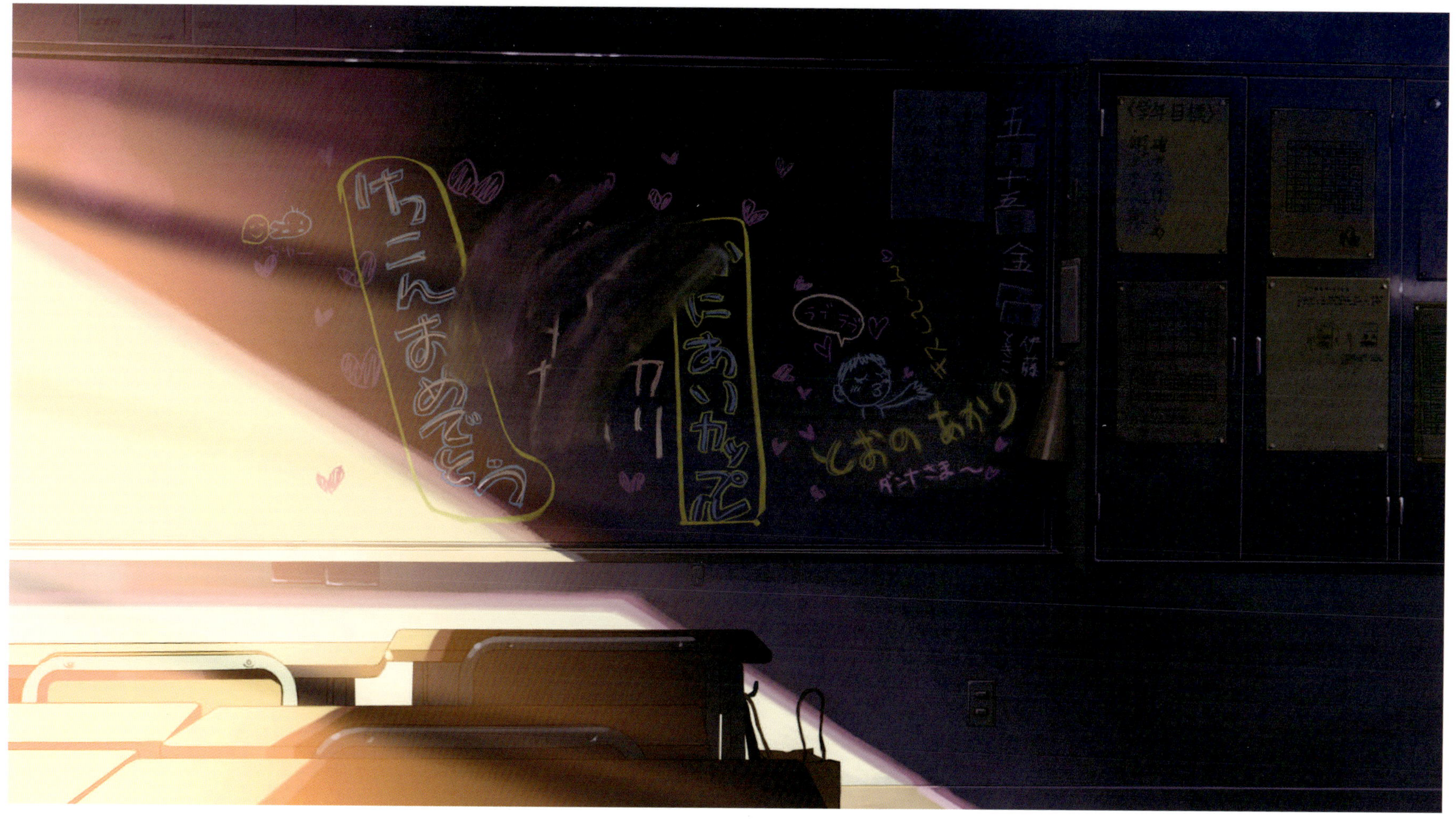

"Cherry Blossom" / CUT_102 / Setting: Elementary school classroom

Other students made fun of Takaki and Akari. This was based on location photos of an elementary school classroom. The words were actually written on the blackboard and photographed, which was then used in the background art. One layer was prepared for the blackboard with the written words, then another layer had the words erased with a chalk eraser, and the layers were revealed or hidden in coordination with Takaki's animated movements.

Act 1: "Cherry Blossom"

The Tono Household

A room within the condominium where Takaki lived from grade school until his second year of junior high (according to the storyboard, this is corporate housing provided by Takaki's father's workplace, Azusa Bank. Judging by the number of mailboxes there are 12 households in the building). Takaki lives with his parents, but as they are rarely depicted in the film their presence is confirmed via newspapers folded on the table and written messages left him by his mother. This had the effect of giving the viewers a more powerful sense of Takaki's loneliness.

Takaki: (*off screen*) ... Transferring schools...?

Takaki: ...But what about Nishi Junior High? (*sounding lost*) After all that work to get accepted...

Akari: They said they'd do the paperwork to get me into the school in Tochigi... I'm sorry.

Takaki: No... There's nothing for you to apologize for, Akari.

Akari: (*off screen; voice coming through the phone receiver*) I told them I wanted to stay with my aunt in Katsushika and commute...

Akari: But they said no, that I would have to wait until I'm older...

Takaki: (*interrupting Akari; sounding impatient as he realizes he can't do anything*) All right!

Takaki: (*off screen; voice coming through the phone receiver*) Don't tell me any more!

Akari: Ah...

Takaki: That's enough.

Akari: Sorry.

Takaki: (*monologue*) I held the receiver so tight against my ear it was like I could feel her pain directly through the phone. But there was nothing I could do.

(Excerpt of *5 Centimeters per Second*, Act 1: "Cherry Blossom")

The Tono household's dining room/kitchen. Takaki's mother leaves messages for him on the whiteboard in the back. Takaki's uniform, bag, and the odds and ends on the table were drawn on harmony cels.

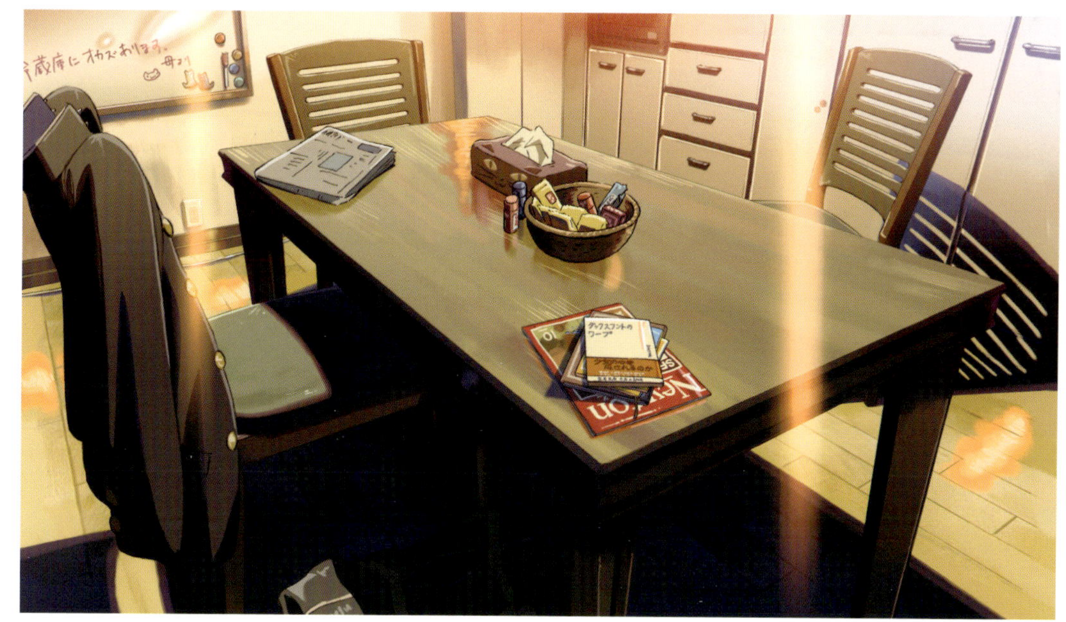

"Cherry Blossom" / CUT_041 / Setting: The Tonos' dining room/kitchen

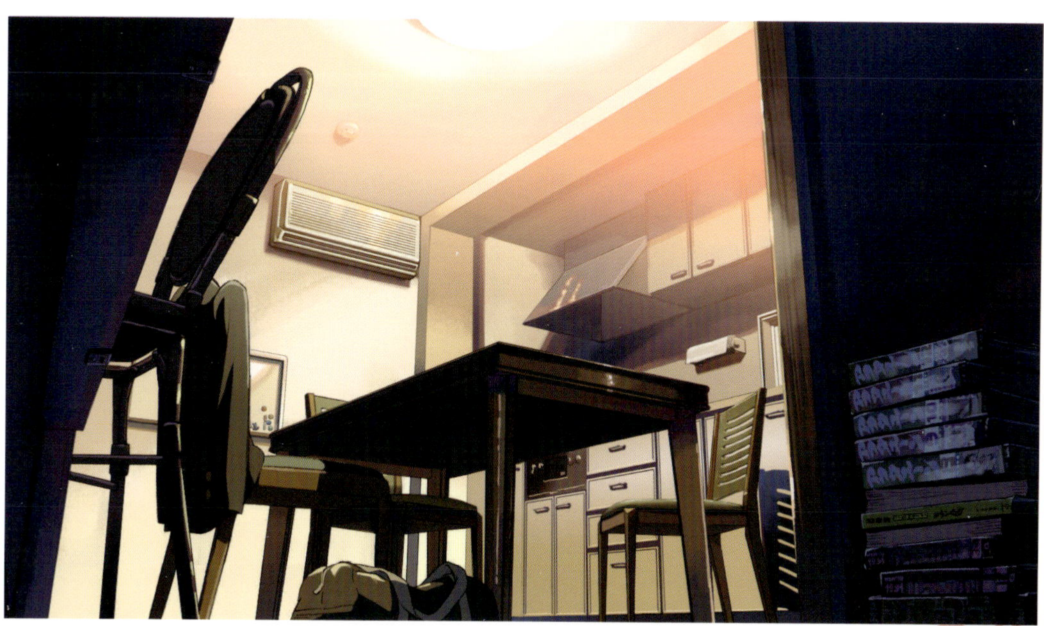

"Cherry Blossom" / CUT_042 / Setting: The Tonos' dining room/kitchen

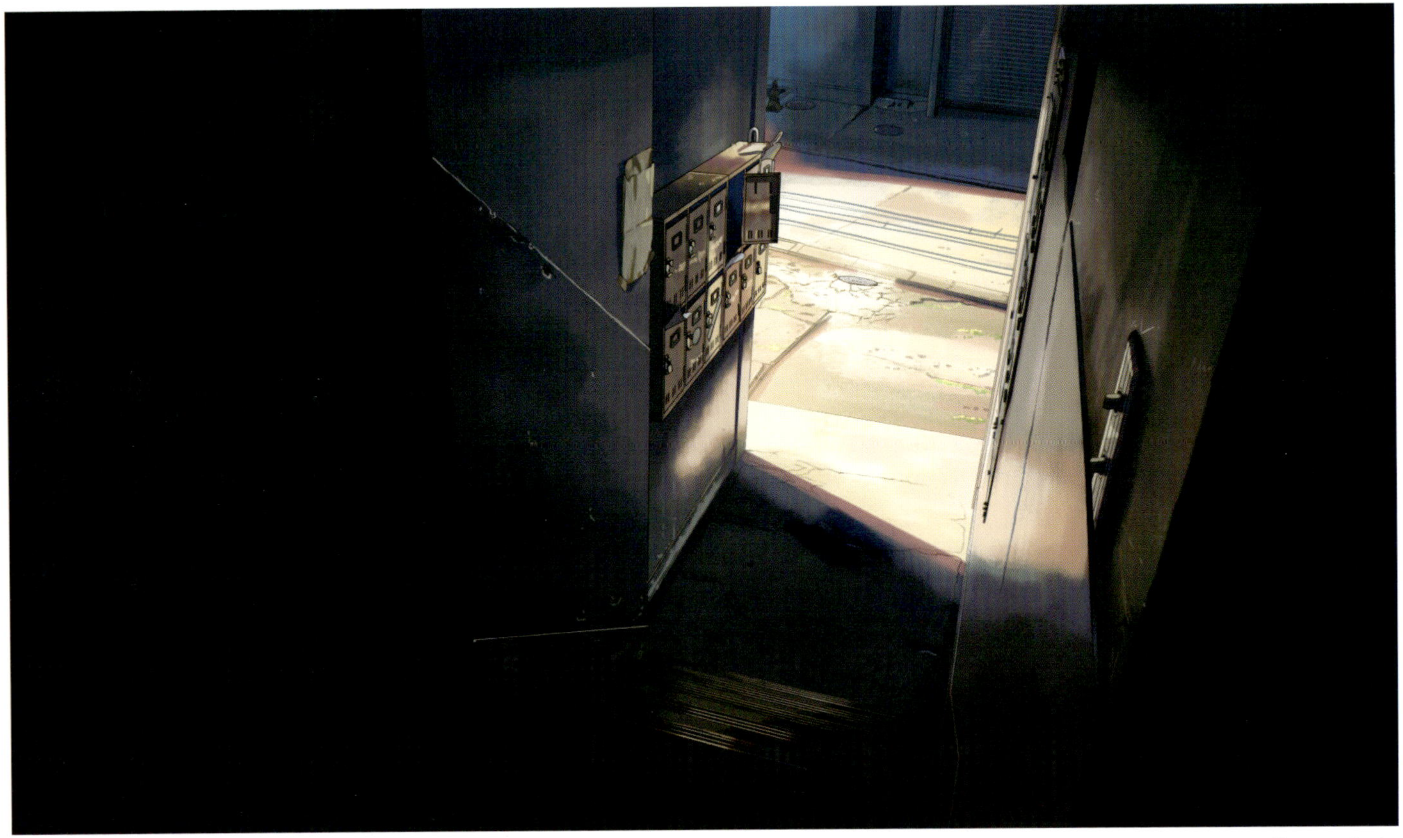

The entrance to the corporate housing where the Tonos live. Judging by the number of mailboxes, the building can accommodate a total of 12 households. Here you can see that Takaki's shadow is painted directly onto the background.

"Cherry Blossom" / CUT_018 / Setting: Entrance to Azusa Bank's corporate housing

The artwork of the tatami mat flooring of Takaki's room is based on actual location photos, with detailed highlights used to draw focus where needed and shadows used to illustrate texture. The pattern along the edges of the matting was carefully hand-drawn.

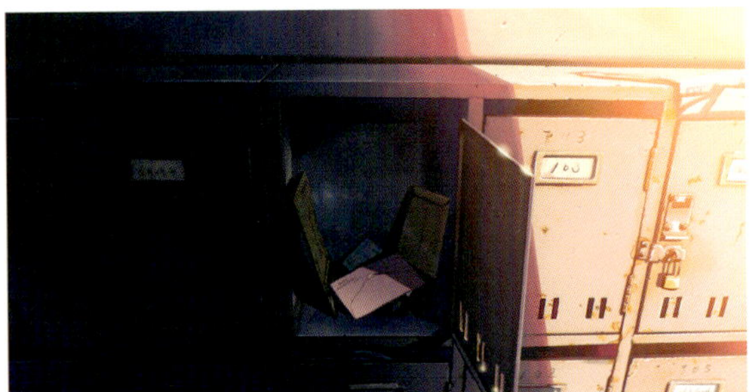

"Cherry Blossom" / CUT_033 / Setting: Entrance to Azusa Bank's corporate housing

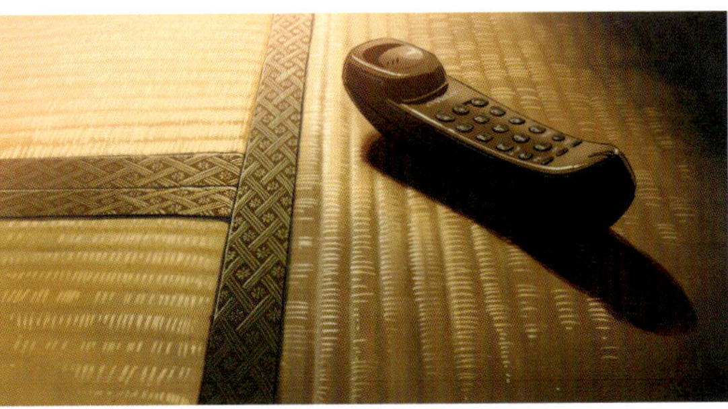

"Cherry Blossom" / CUT_177 / Setting: Tono household: Takaki's room

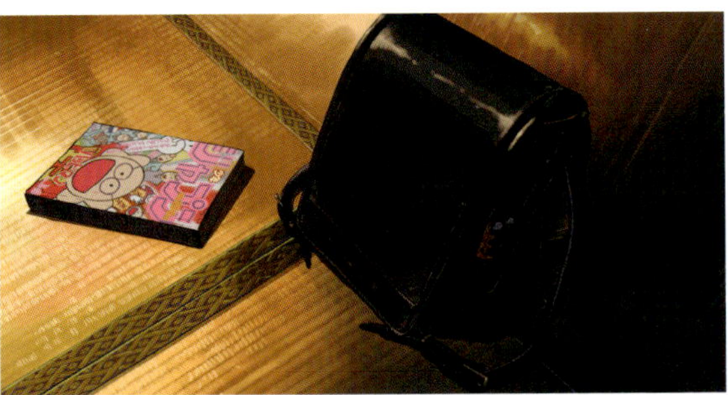

"Cherry Blossom" / CUT_131 / Setting: Tono household: Takaki's room

This is one piece that the background artists created with painstaking care. The book was hand-drawn based on perspective data of an open book. Each letter on the fare table shown in CUT_104 on page 35 was carefully hand-drawn by the background art staff as well.

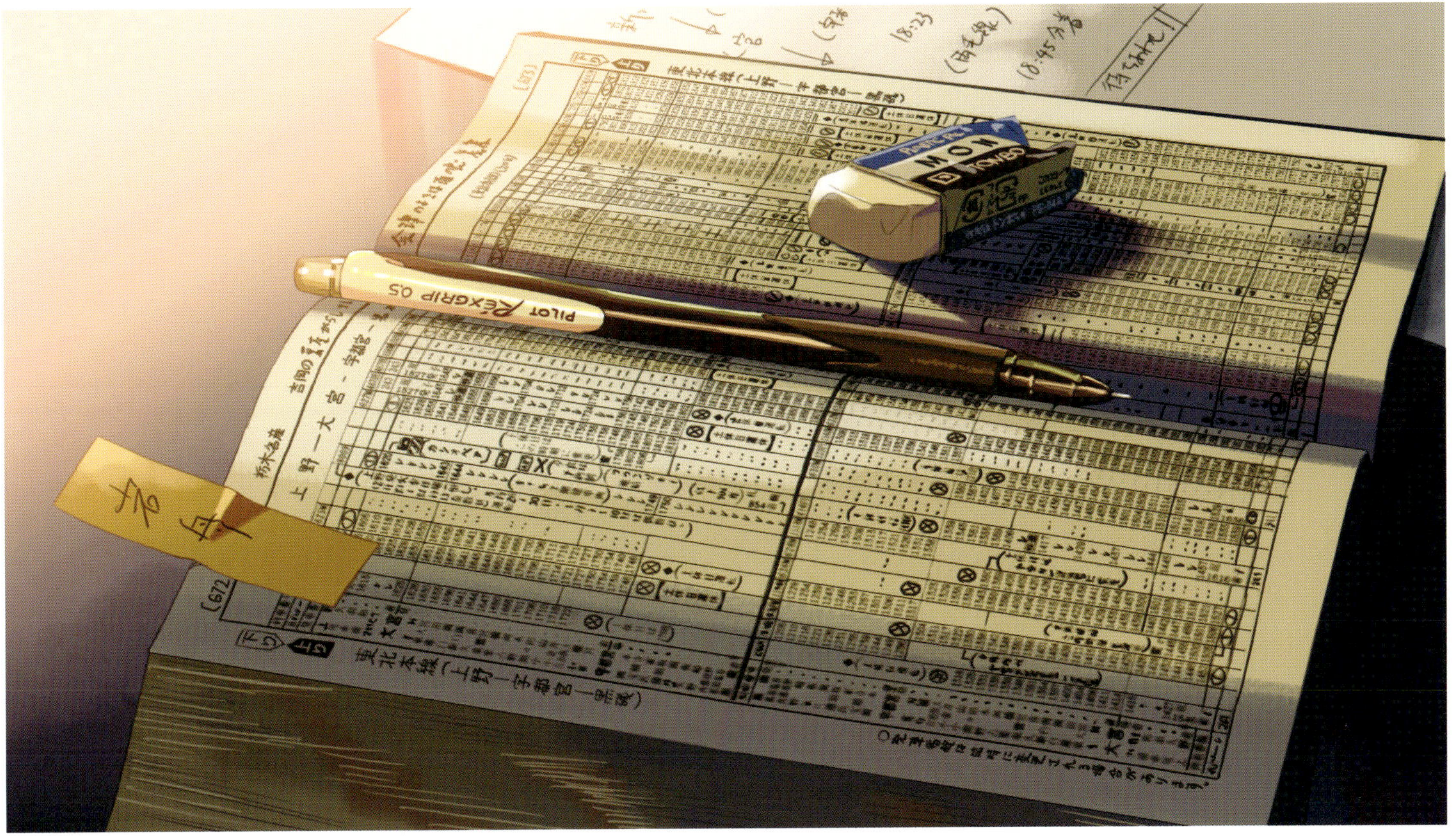

"Cherry Blossom" / CUT_B015 / Setting: The Tono household: Takaki's room

CUT_B017 and CUT_189 are from the same angle and shown at the same time of day, and the emphasis here is on the progress made in preparation for the move as time goes on. The final version of this scene includes Takaki's cel. Also, the photo printed on the cover of the train schedule in CUT_B012 is a shot from *The Place Promised in Our Early Days.*

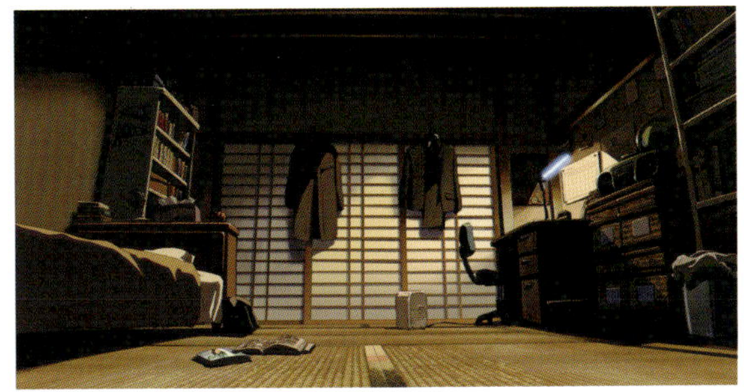

"Cherry Blossom" / CUT_B017 / Setting: The Tono household: Takaki's room

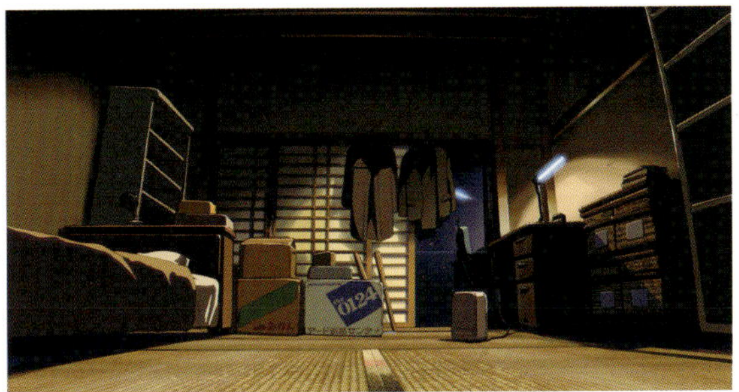

"Cherry Blossom" / CUT_189 / Setting: The Tono household: Takaki's room

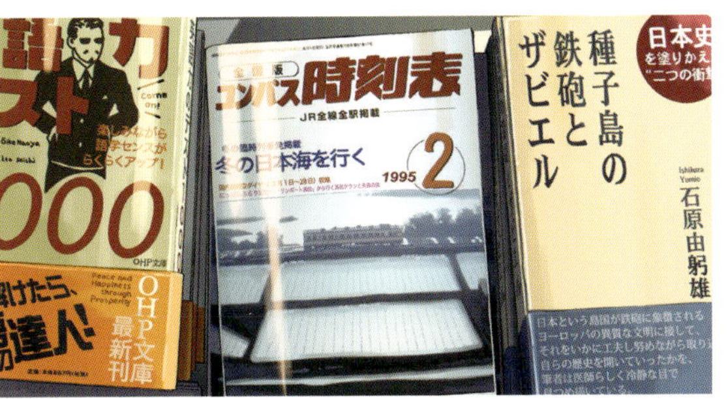

"Cherry Blossom" / CUT_B012 / Setting: A shelf in a bookstore

Act 1: "Cherry Blossom"

Railways

A depiction of railways is already an essential element of Makoto Shinkai's works. In Act 1 of *5 Centimeters per Second*, the railway scenes are all grouped together. The train that Takaki takes to visit Akari is modeled on a Kanto-region private railway and a JR line. The schedule was precisely calculated to show that if one takes the first rapid-service train bound for Kawagoe on the Saikyo Line, it's possible to transfer to a commuter train upon arriving at Omiya Station, for example. Most of the trains were created with 3DCG, and in order to match the background art and character animation, the surface textures used materials created by the background artists.

Takaki: (*monologue*) The terminal station where I switched trains was filled with commuters heading home. Everyone's shoes were soaked with snow and water. The air was chilly, and filled with that certain smell a city has on a snowy day.

Train Station Announcement: Attention all passengers: Utsunomiya-line trains bound for Oyama and Utsunomiya will be arriving 8 minutes behind schedule due to heavy snow. We apologize for any inconvenience...

Takaki: (*monologue*) Until that moment, it had never even crossed my mind that the train might be delayed. Suddenly, I became really worried...

(Excerpt of 5 *Centimeters per Second*, Act 1: "Cherry Blossom")

This angle shows the view of the train tracks heading towards Shinjuku as seen from above Sangubashi. The trains were done in 3DCG, and to unify the shadows cast by the expressway overpass and the bridge, the shapes of those objects were modulated in 3DCG. Also, as not every element could be captured in the same photograph, several location photos were combined to create the base for the image.

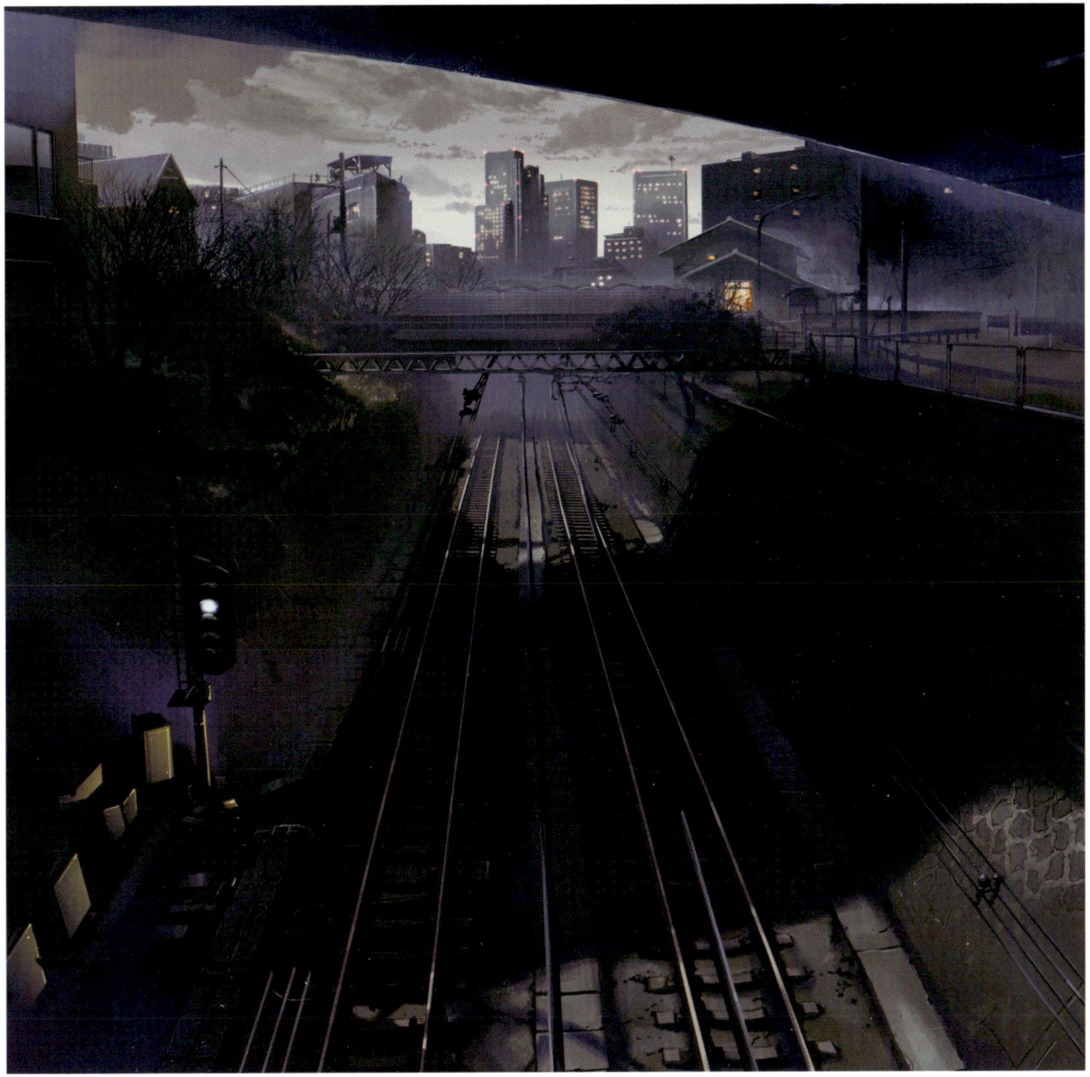

"Cherry Blossom" / CUT_104 / Setting: Takaki's neighborhood

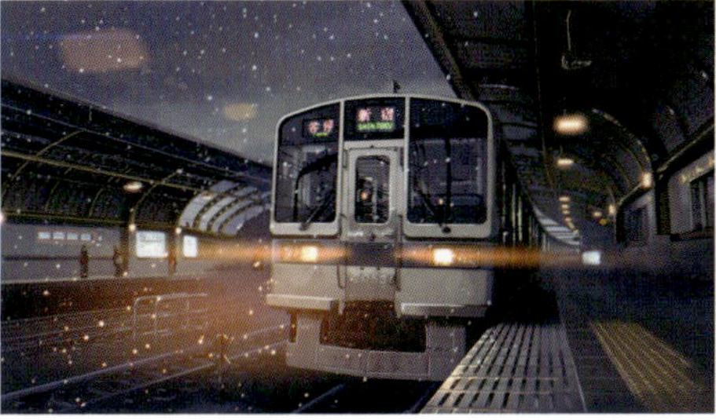

CUT_076 Final Version

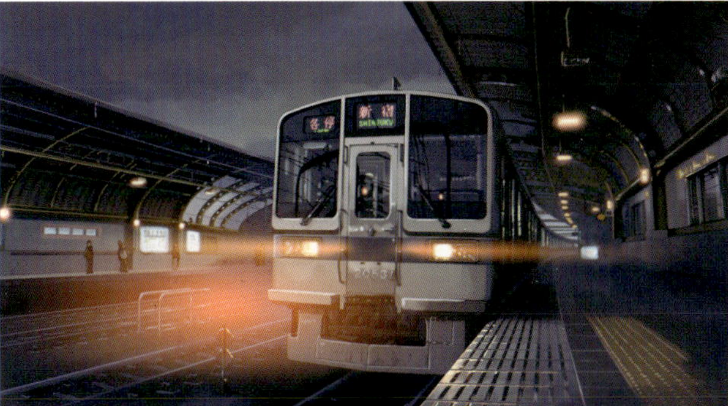

"Cherry Blossom" / CUT_076 / Setting: Private railway train platform

In the cut where the train pulls into the station, video software was used to create the 3DCG elements of the train and animation of falling snow, and lighting effects from the headlights were added to create the finished product.

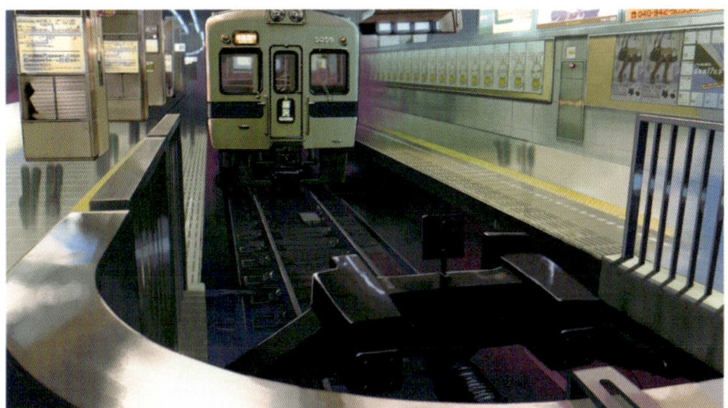

"Cherry Blossom" / CUT_105 / Setting: Private railway train platform

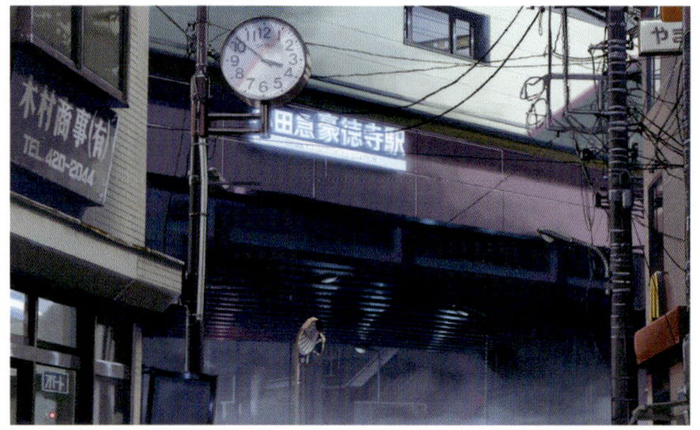

"Cherry Blossom" / CUT_074 / Setting: Private railway station environs

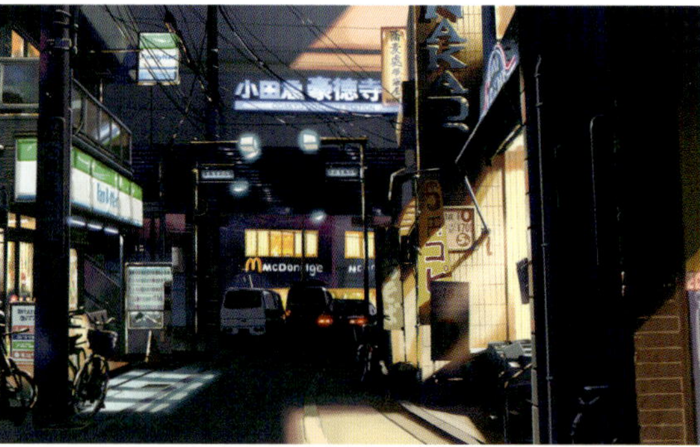

"Cherry Blossom" / CUT_039 / Setting: Private railway station environs

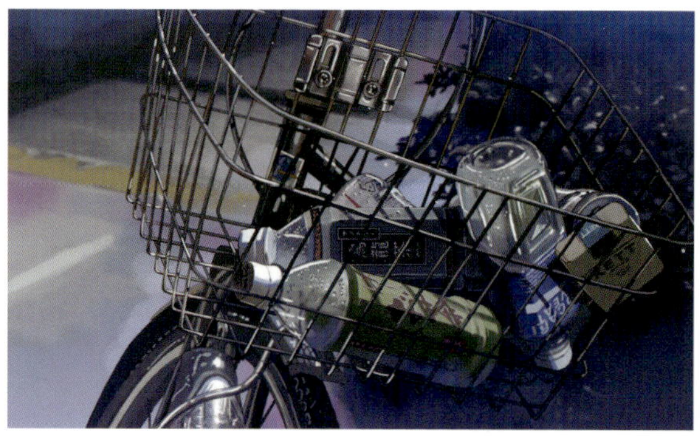
"Cherry Blossom" / CUT_060A / Setting: Private railway station environs

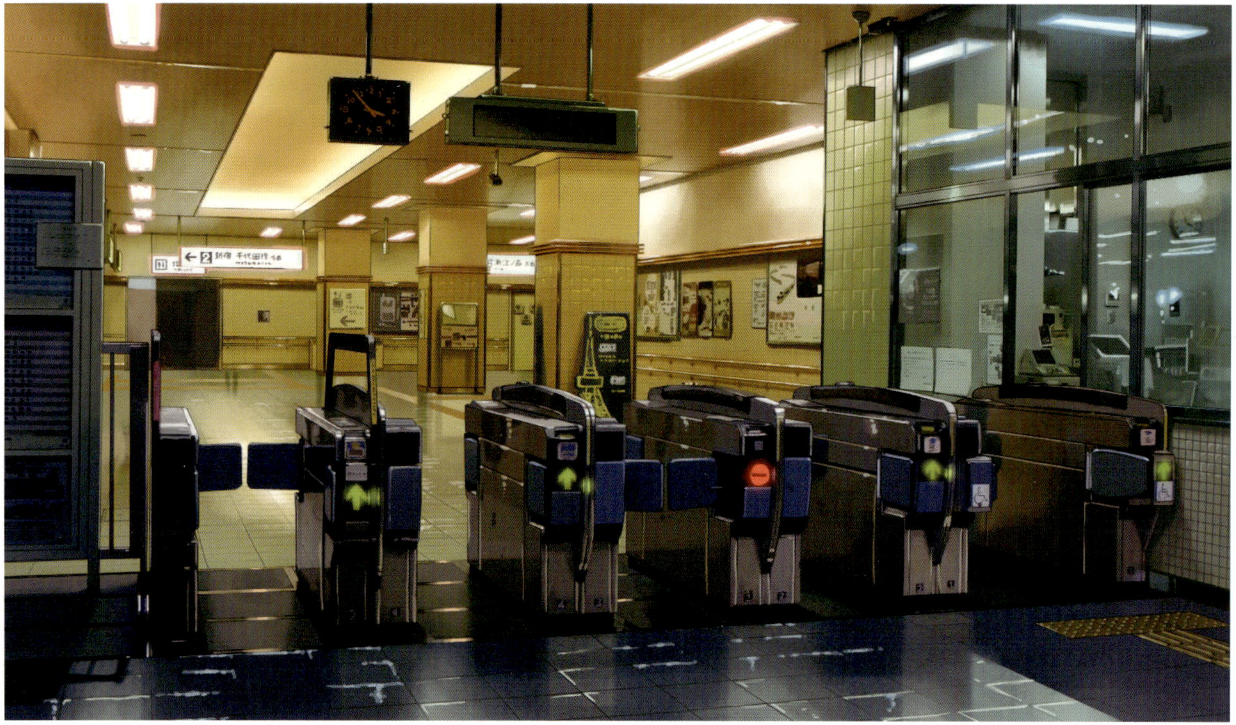

"Cherry Blossom" / CUT_075 / Setting: Private railway turnstiles

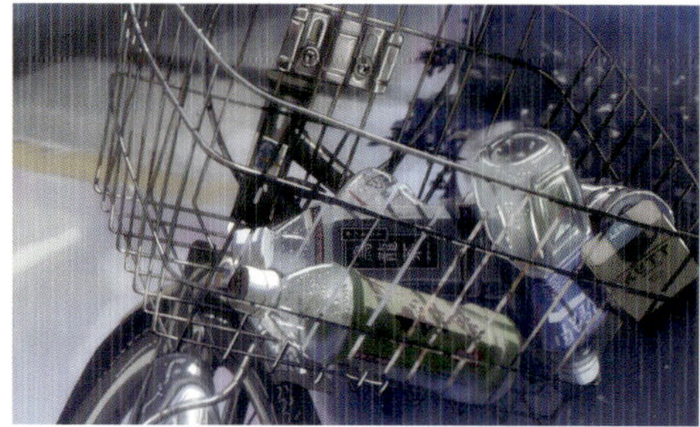
CUT_060A Final Version

Animation of falling rain was added for the final version of CUT_060A.

For the area around the station, these cuts show that only in those places where a great amount of detail was needed is where the management of linework is critical. The area outside the turnstiles is dark and the area inside is light, which allows you to see the co-ordination of density in the artwork.

A bank of train ticket machines at JR Shinjuku Station. As the story takes place in 1994, we researched ticket machines, fare tables and notices from that year for use in the artwork. All of the station names and fares were added by hand.

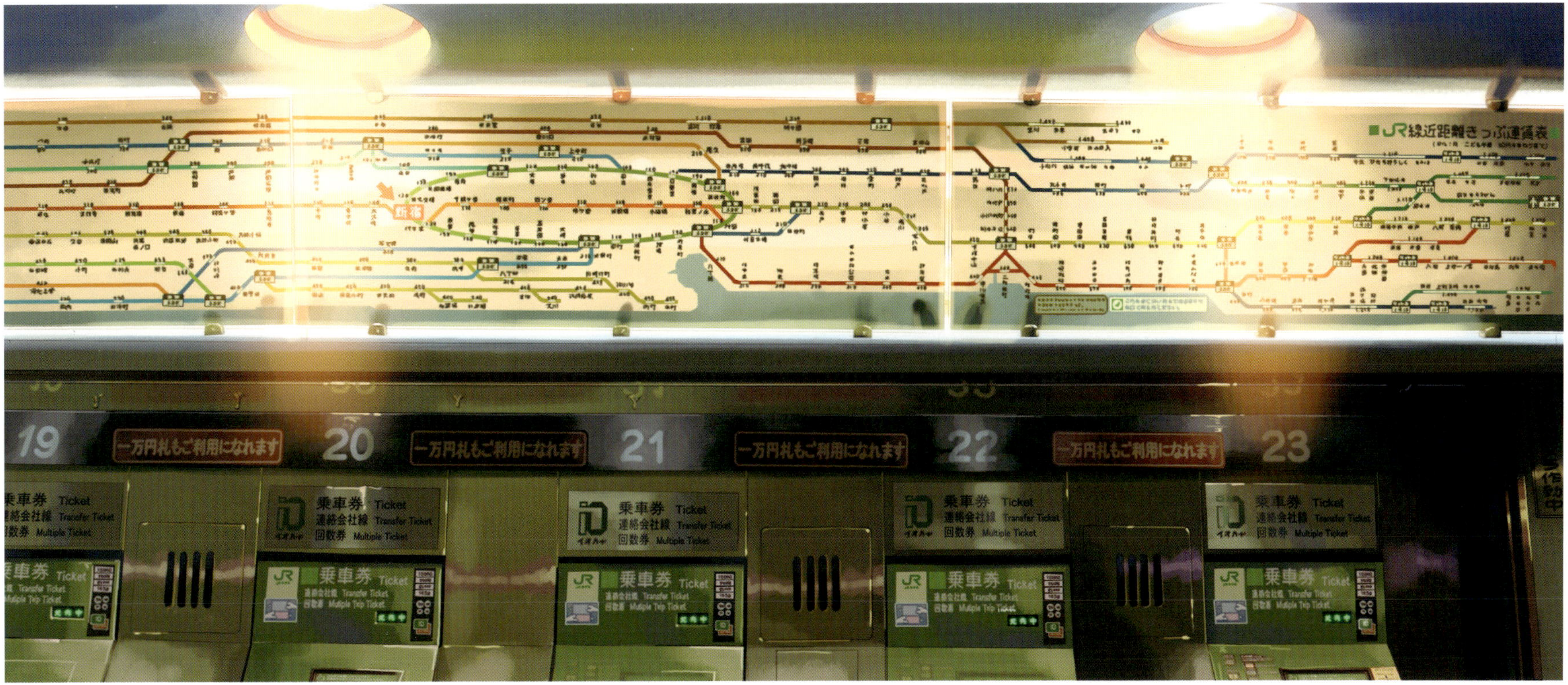

"Cherry Blossom" / CUT_108 / Setting: JR Shinjuku Station ticket machines

The backgrounds weren't mere recreations of location photographs. The time, season, and state of mind of the character(s) were taken into consideration. Mr. Shinkai gave detailed instructions to the artists, and Mr. Shinkai corrected the density and color tones at the final stage himself.

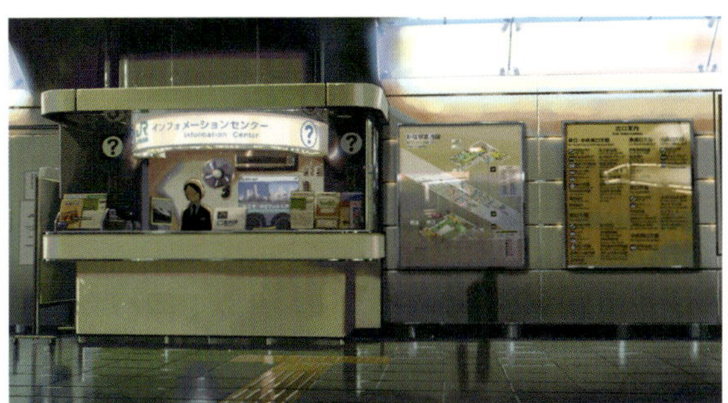

"Cherry Blossom" / CUT_113 / Setting: JR Shinjuku Station concourse

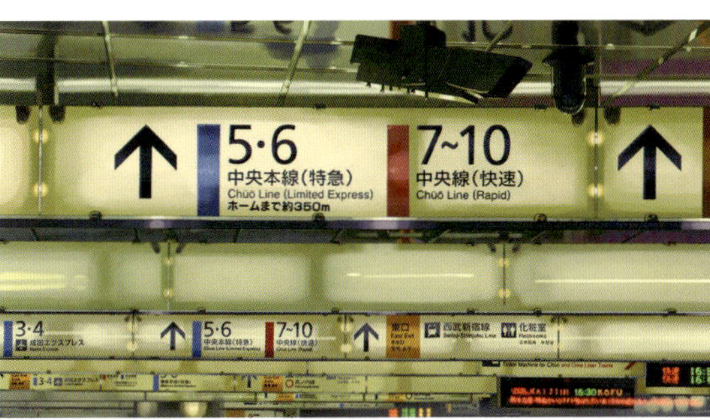

"Cherry Blossom" / CUT_111 / Setting: JR Shinjuku Station passageway

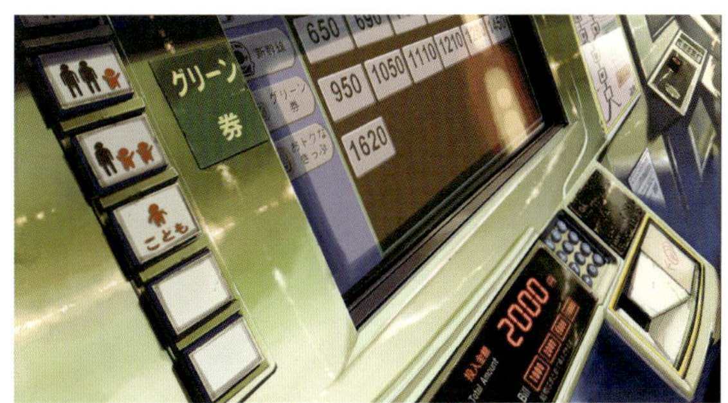

"Cherry Blossom" / CUT_109 / Setting: JR Shinjuku Station ticket machines

The scene where Takaki stands before the mirror in the bathroom in Shinjuku Station uses the same angle as the scene in Act 2: "Cosmonaut" where Kanae works up the courage to confess her feelings for Takaki.

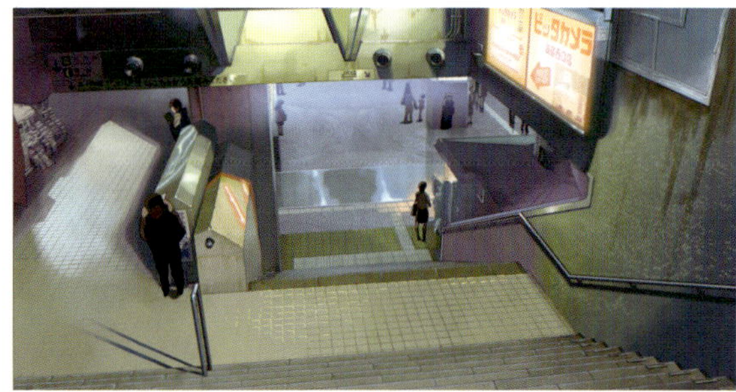

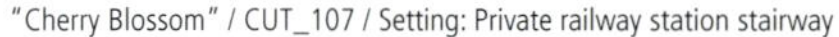

"Cherry Blossom" / CUT_107 / Setting: Private railway station stairway

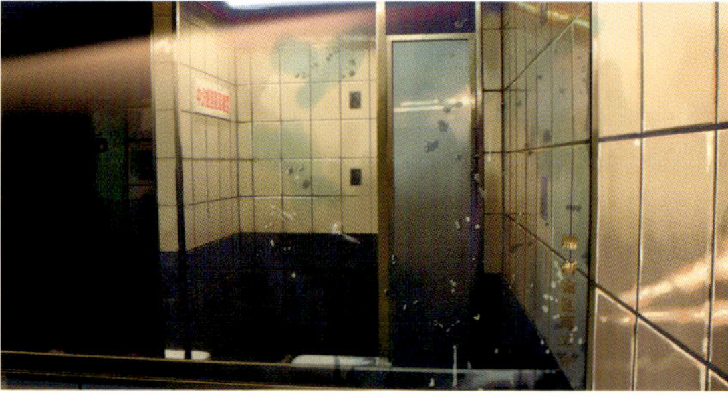

"Cherry Blossom" / CUT_115 / Setting: JR Shinjuku Station bathroom

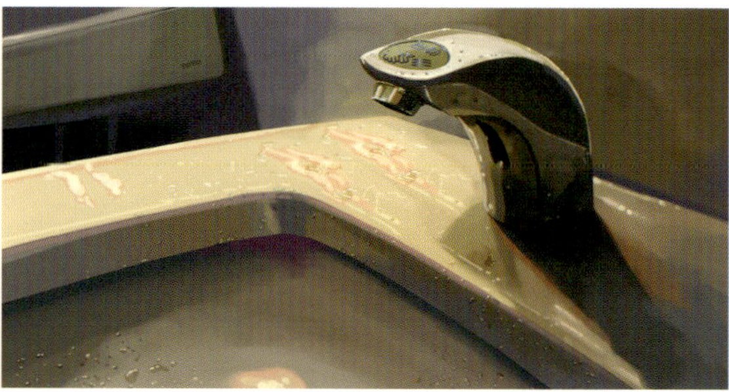

"Cherry Blossom" / CUT_114 / Setting: JR Shinjuku Station bathroom

In cases where words on LED signs are required to change in a scene, the contents of the display panels are prepared on separate layers which were swapped using video software. The 24 x 24 grid of 2-color LED nodes were all precisely drawn. The LED signs in Shinjuku Station also feature prominently in *The Place Promised in Our Early Days*.

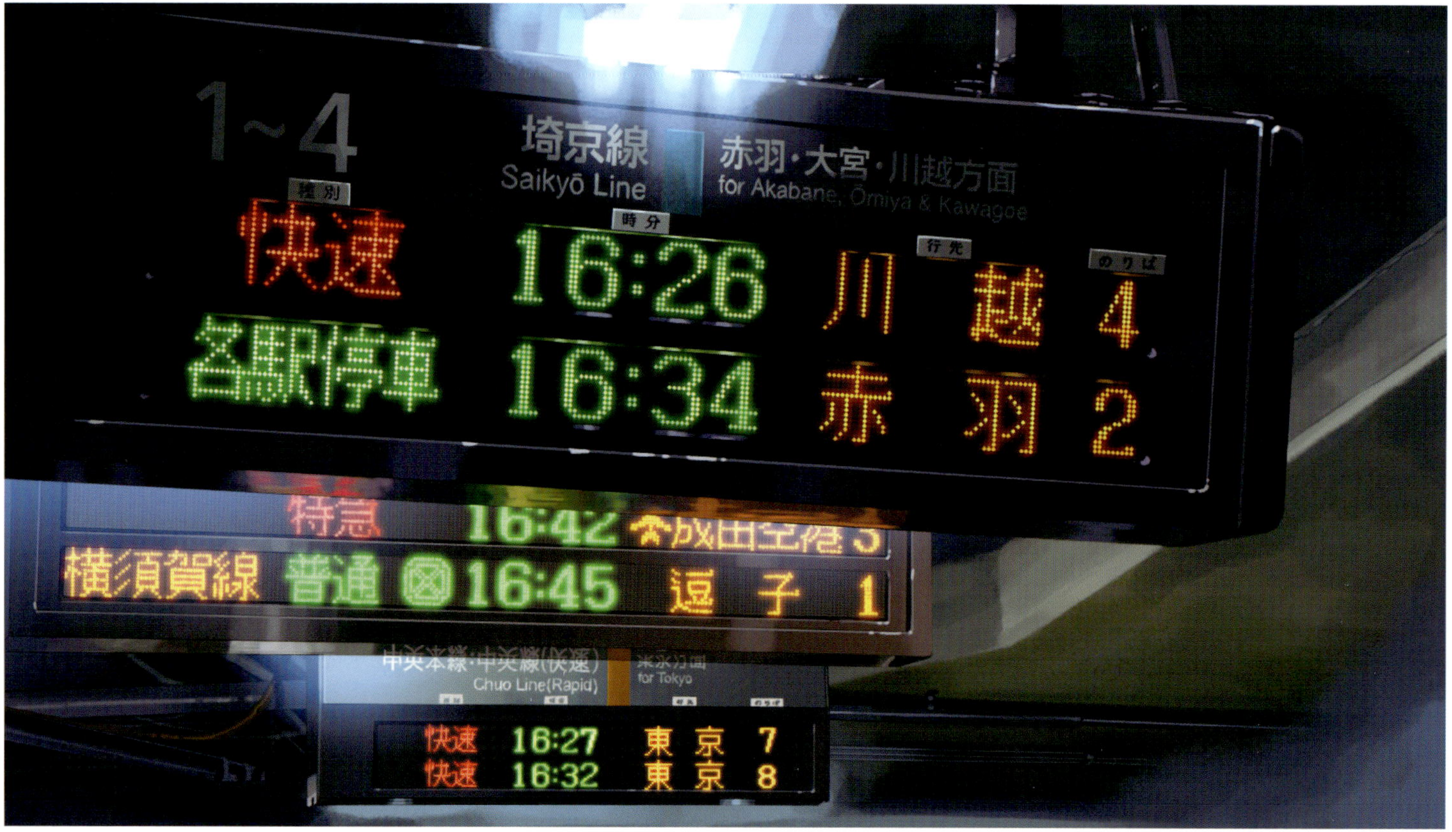

"Cherry Blossom" / CUT_116 / Setting: JR Shinjuku Station passageway

When this train (a Model 205 on the Saikyo Line) was created in 3DCG, in order to match the train to the background, textures drawn by the background artists were used. The train moves through background art subdivided into multiple layers.

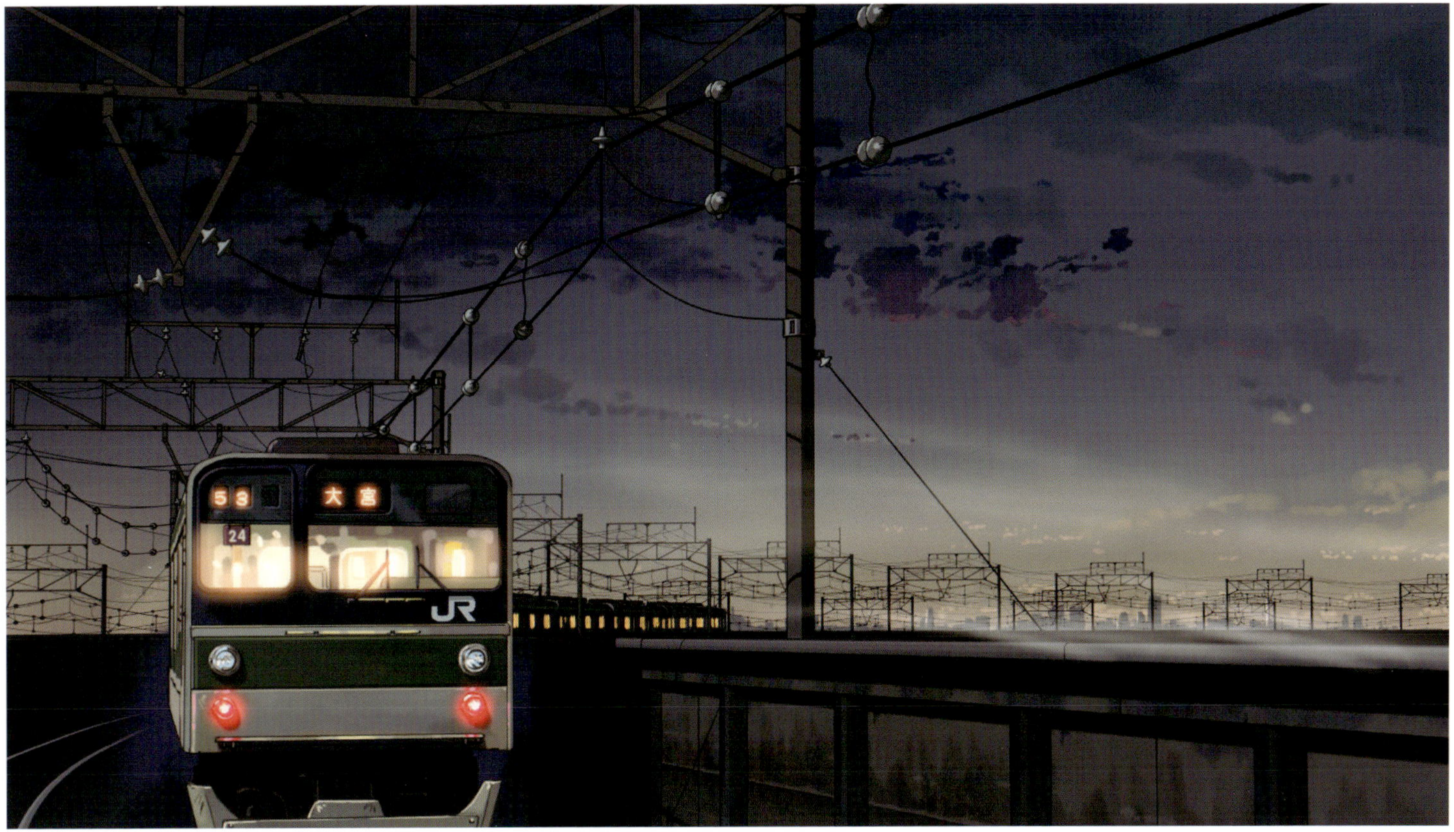

"Cherry Blossom" / CUT_119 / Setting: JR Saikyo Line

In the scene when snow causes delays during rush hour, the interactions between the background elements and the animated elements became more complex. Please also note the separate applications of cool and warm colors.

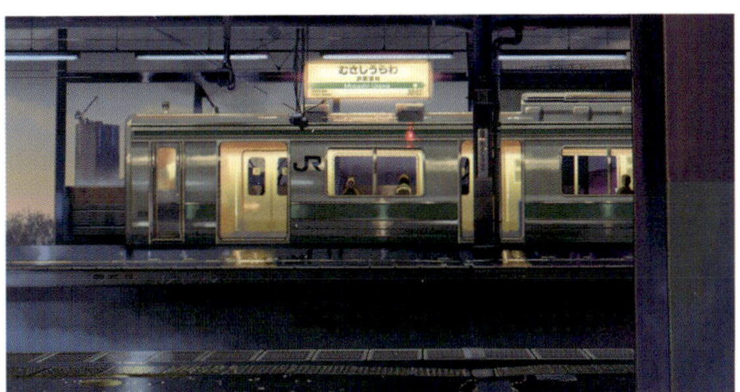

"Cherry Blossom" / CUT_124 / Setting: JR Musashi-Urawa Station platform

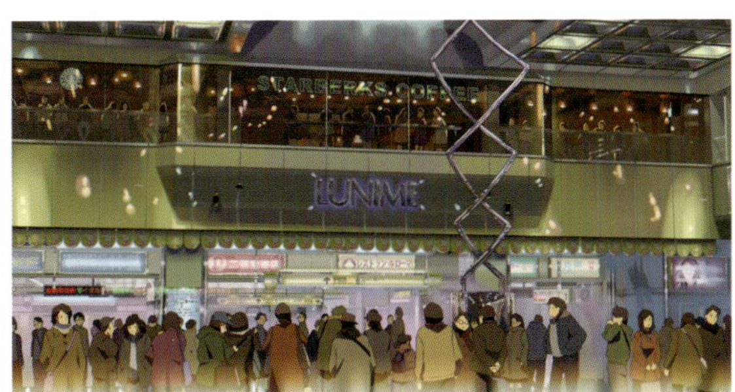

"Cherry Blossom" / CUT_143 / Setting: JR Omiya Station concourse

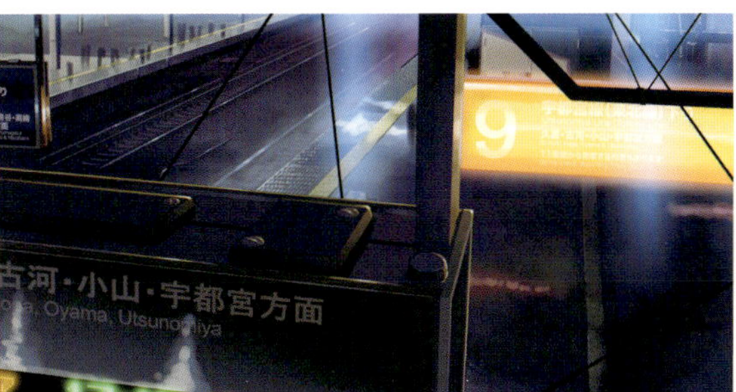

"Cherry Blossom" / CUT_148 / Setting: JR Omiya Station platform

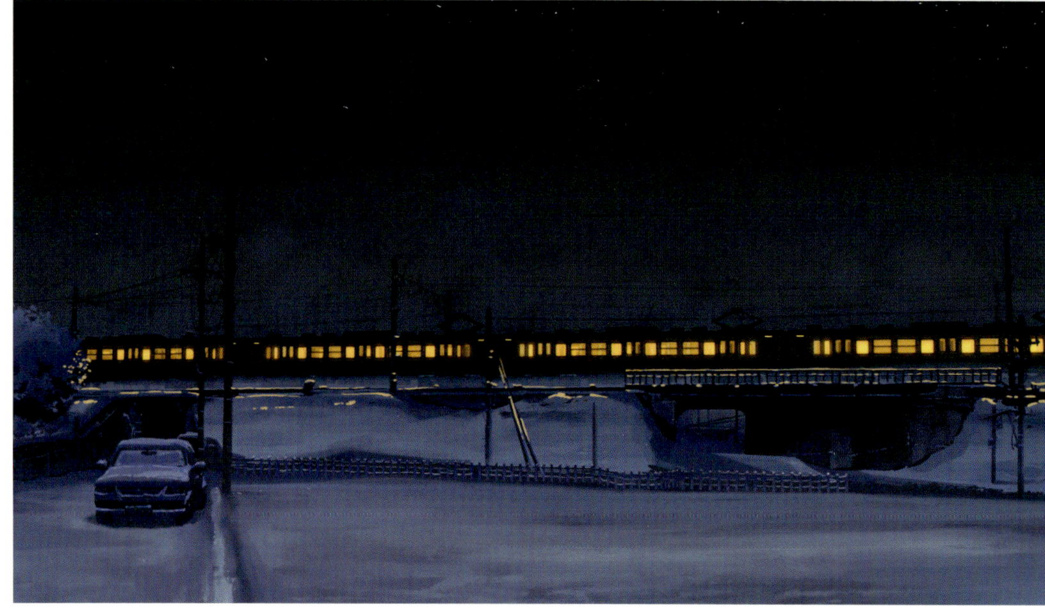

"Cherry Blossom" / CUT_155 / Setting: JR Utsunomiya Line

A train passing through the snow-covered countryside. The train windows show different textures. The warmth of the train interior serves to further illustrate the coldness of the outside air. The final version included animation of snow.

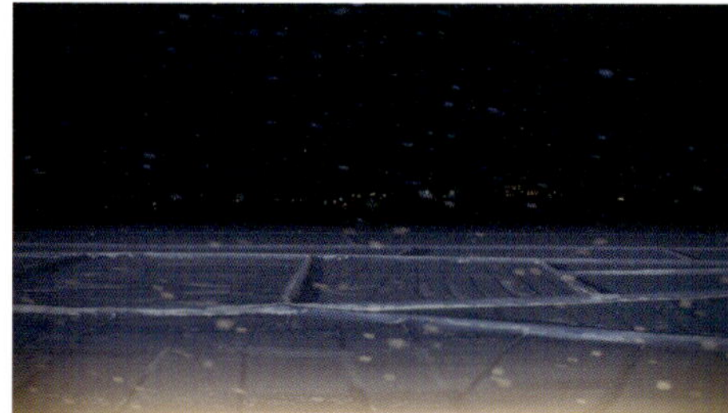

CUT_154 Final Version

For the snow-covered paddy fields seen from the train window in CUT_154, 3DCG was used to create a model with ridges and furrows, onto which the background artists pasted texture data. The city lights in the far distance were drawn on a separate layer, and video software was used to make the lights flicker.

"Cherry Blossom" / CUT_154 / Setting: View from a JR Utsunomiya Line train

A Model 115 train on the Utsunomiya Line pulling into Kuki Station, as seen from the opposite platform. The final version included animation of falling snow. Snow clinging to the train was added to the surface texture of the train.

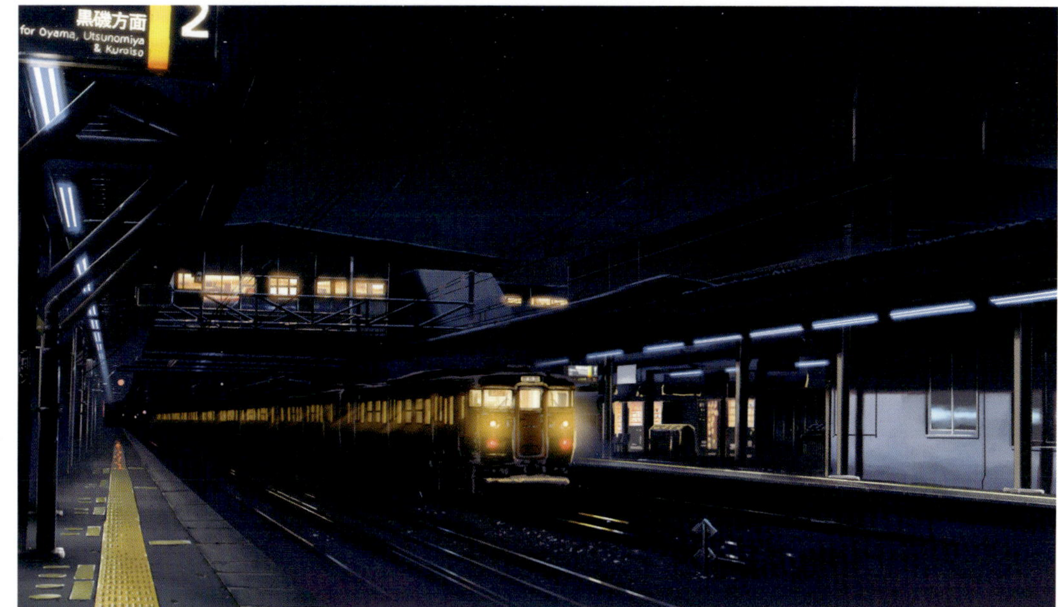

"Cherry Blossom" / CUT_157 / Setting: JR Kuki Station platform

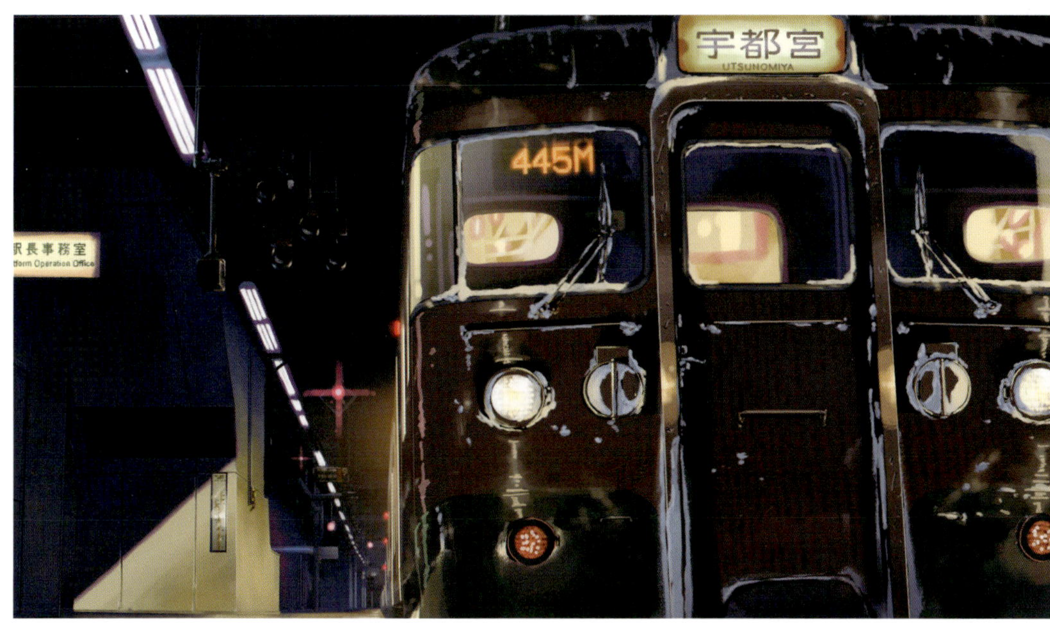

"Cherry Blossom" / CUT_158 / Setting: JR Kuki Station platform

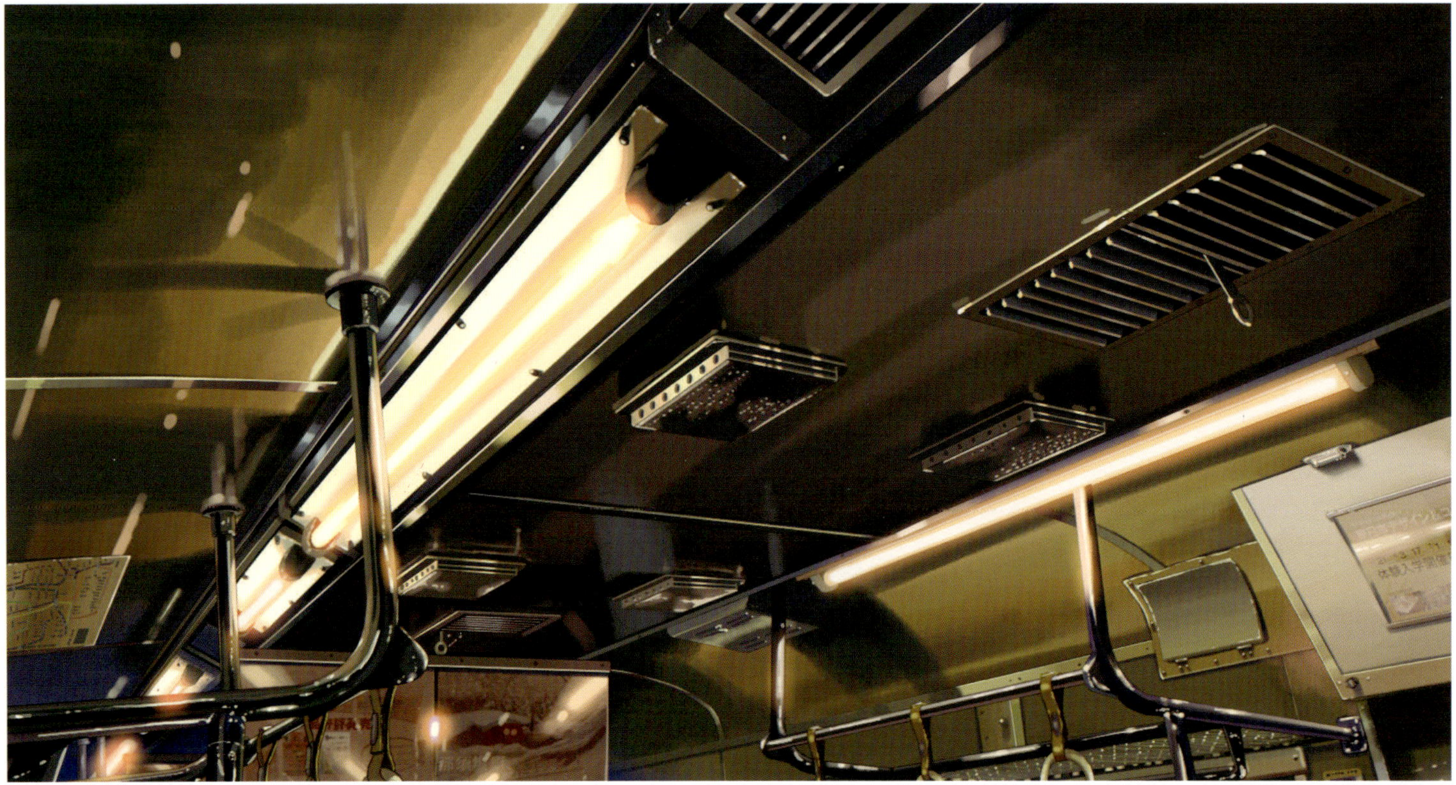

"Cherry Blossom" / CUT_152 / Setting: JR Utsunomiya Line

The interior of a Model 115 train reinforced to withstand cold temperatures and heavy snow that runs on the Utsunomiya Line into snow-bound areas. Takaki took this train from Omiya Station to Oyama Station. As you can see by the backs of the cross seats and the colors of the seats, research on older train cars was done before artwork was created.

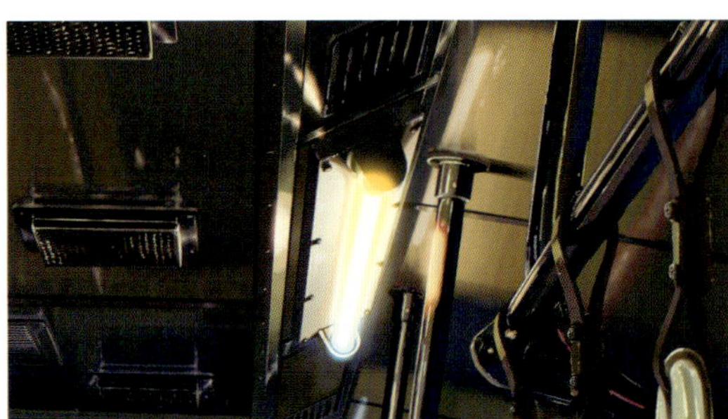

"Cherry Blossom" / CUT_173 / Setting: JR Utsunomiya Line

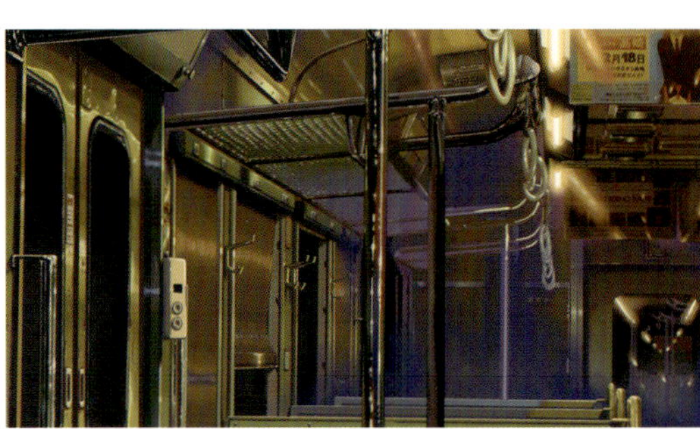

"Cherry Blossom" / CUT_170 / Setting: JR Utsunomiya Line

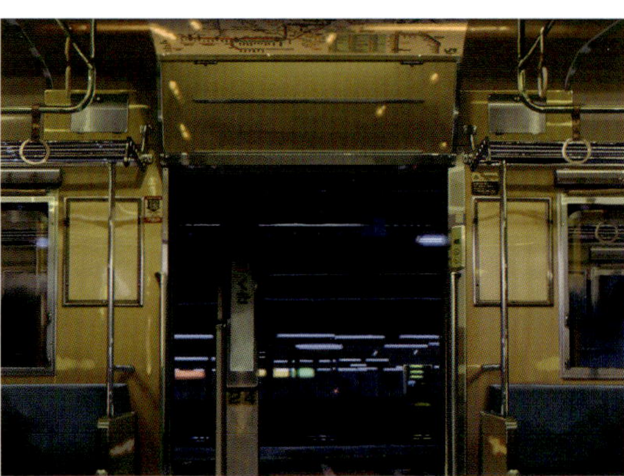

"Cherry Blossom" / CUT_160 / Setting: JR Utsunomiya Line

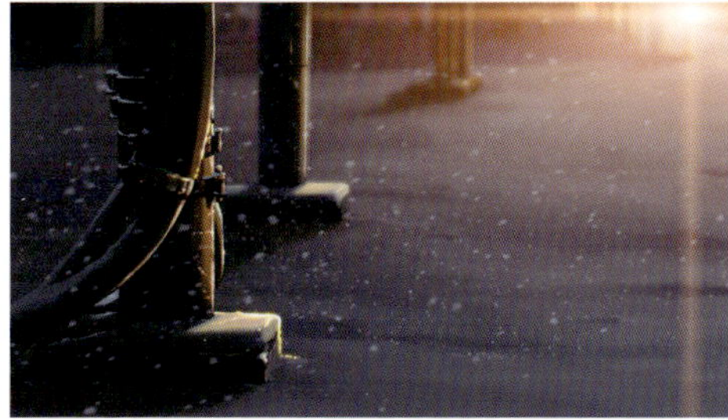

CUT_165 Final Version

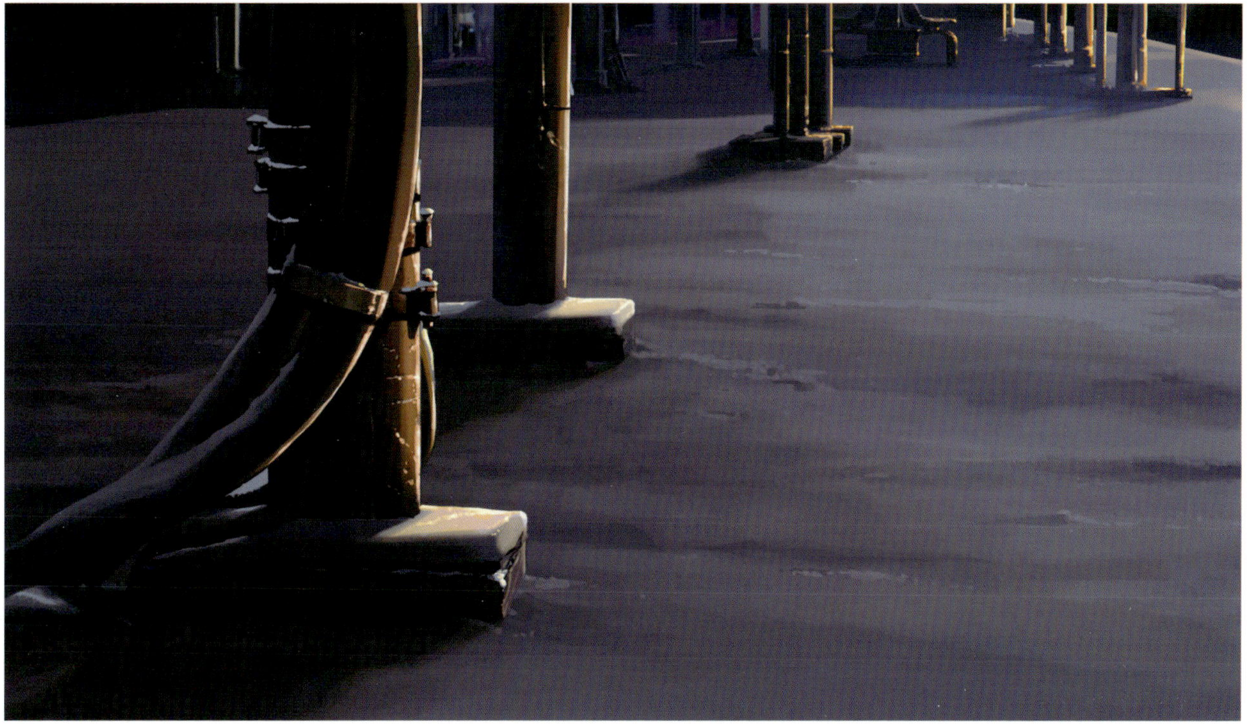

In CUT_165, the platform and poles were drawn on separate layers, and Mr. Shinkai used video software to add a graded multiplane effect to increase the sense of depth in the image. This results in differences in detail rendered in the artwork between the in-focus pole and the rest of the background elements. The final version included lighting effects for the headlights and animation of snow.

"Cherry Blossom" / CUT_165 / Setting: JR Nogi Station platform

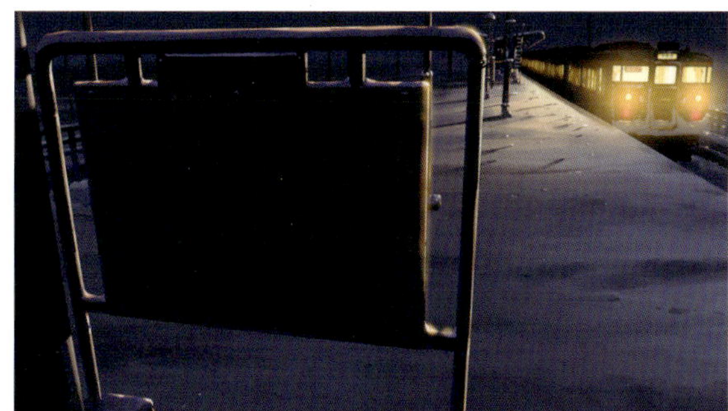

"Cherry Blossom" / CUT_190 / Setting: JR Nogi Station platform

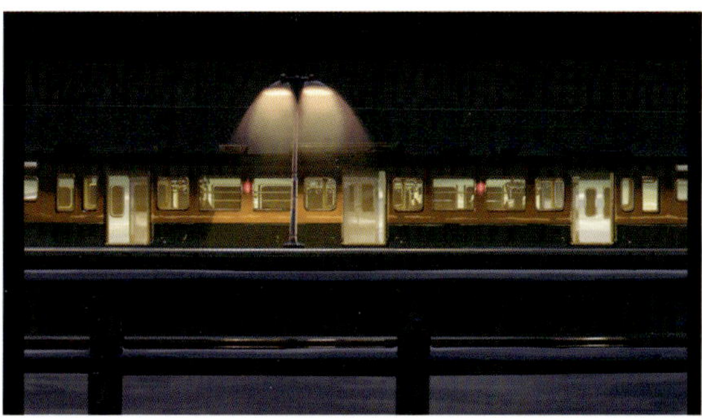

"Cherry Blossom" / CUT_167 / Setting: JR Nogi Station platform

If you compare CUT_157 and 158 on page 39, you'll note the greater amount of built-up snow on the nose of the train in these images. This aspect of the background art was used to illustrate the increase in the strength of the snowstorm once they left the city limits.

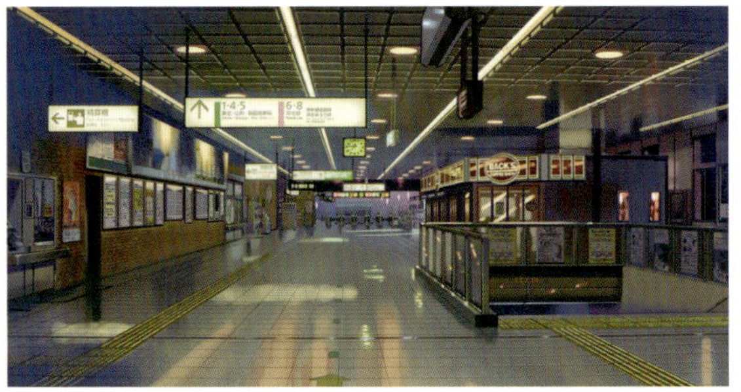

"Cherry Blossom" / CUT_197 / Setting: JR Oyama Station turnstiles

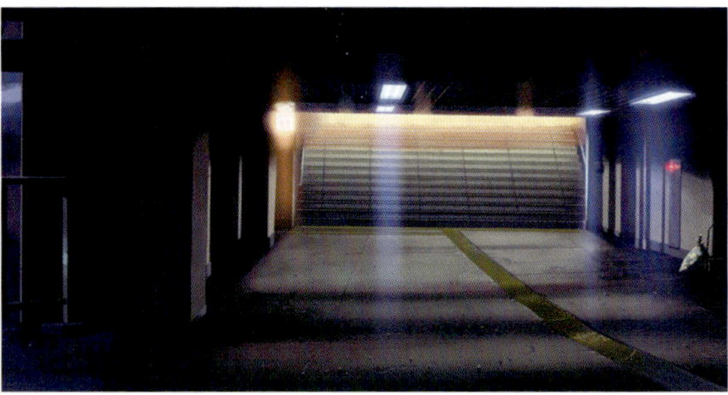

"Cherry Blossom" / CUT_199 / Setting: JR Oyama Station passageway and stairs

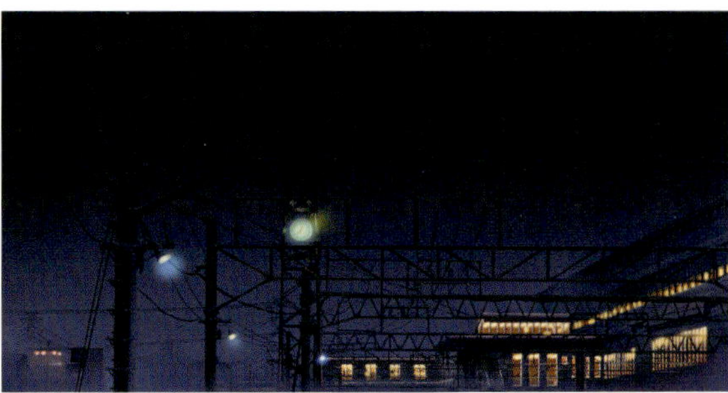

"Cherry Blossom" / CUT_207 / Setting: JR Oyama Station

In Oyama Station, the Ryomo Line platform is located directly below the Tohoku Bullet Train platform. Sound effects were used to recreate that atmosphere.

The snow begins to fall more vigorously, mixing with strong winds to create a snowstorm. In the final version of CUT_195, Mr. Shinkai himself created the animation of the wind lifting up drifts of snow off the platform roof. Twinkling lights in the distance were added to create a detailed rendering.

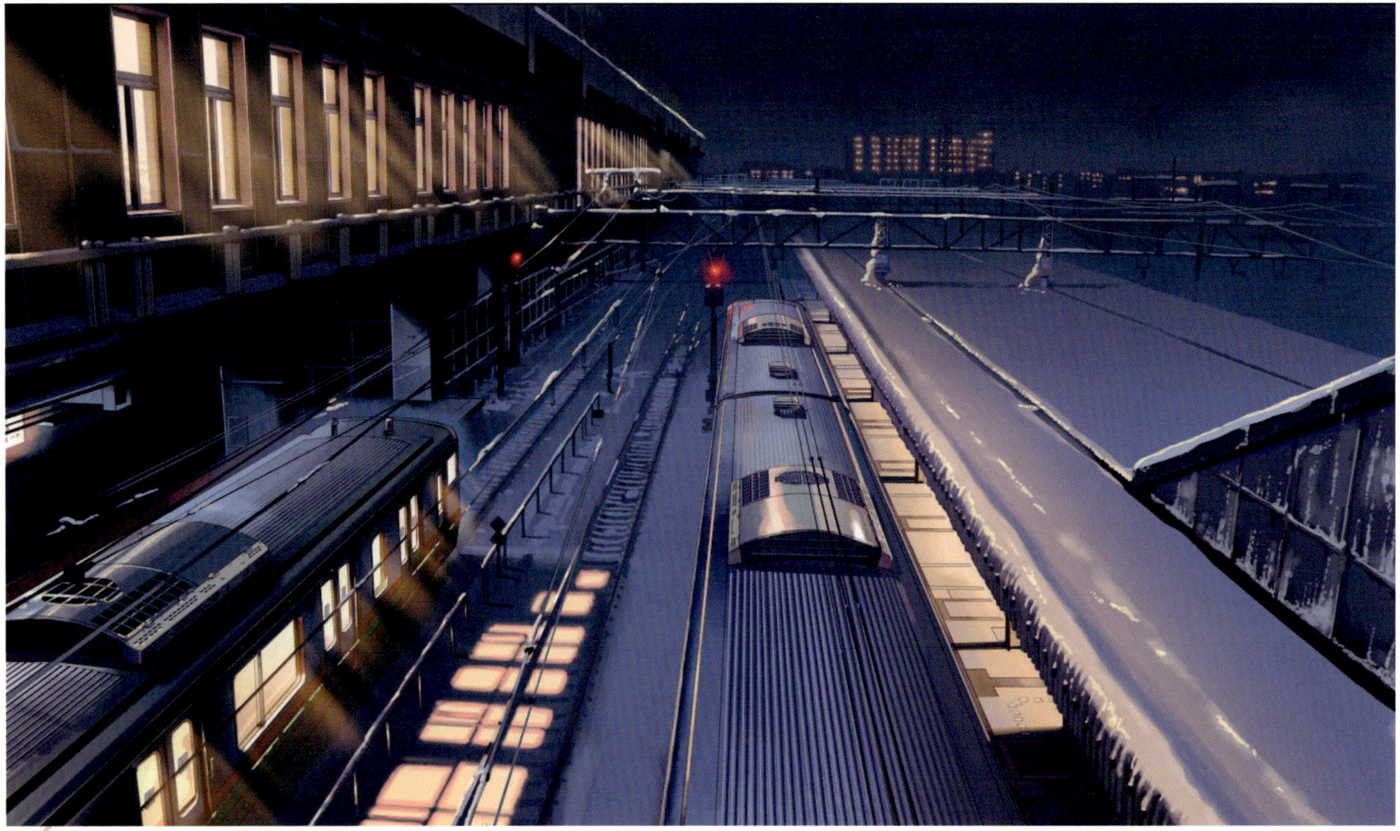

"Cherry Blossom" / CUT_195 / Setting: JR Oyama Station

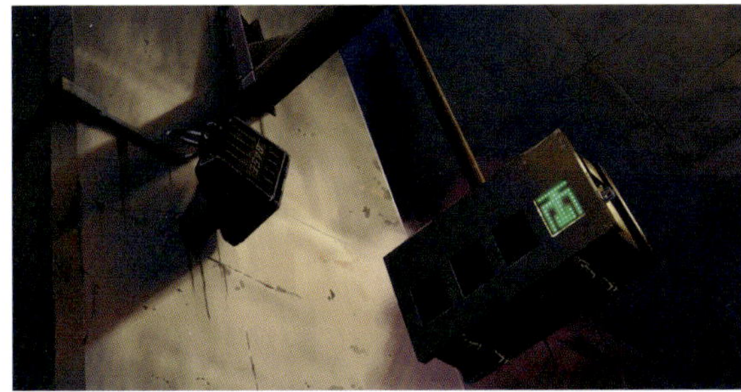

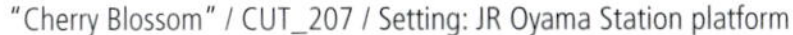
"Cherry Blossom" / CUT_207 / Setting: JR Oyama Station platform

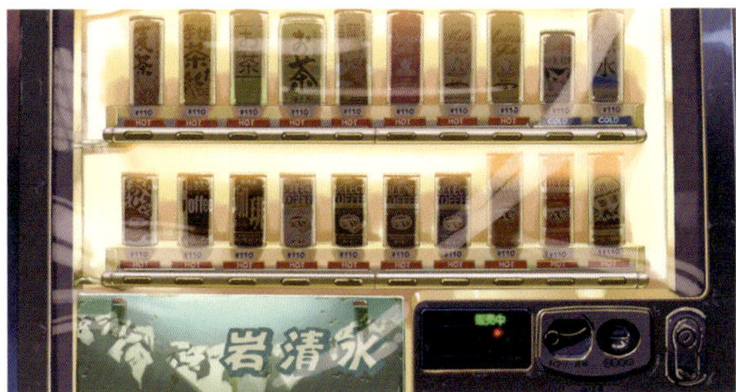

"Cherry Blossom" / CUT_212 / Setting: JR Oyama Station platform

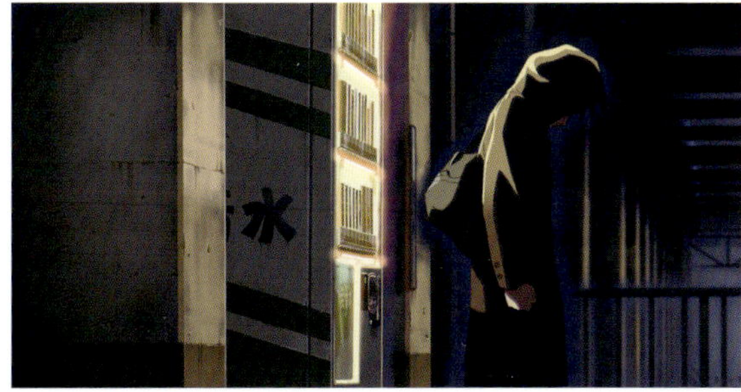
"Cherry Blossom" / CUT_219 / Setting: JR Oyama Station platform

The drink vending machine is based on an actual vending machine on the platform of the Ryomo Line at Oyama Station.

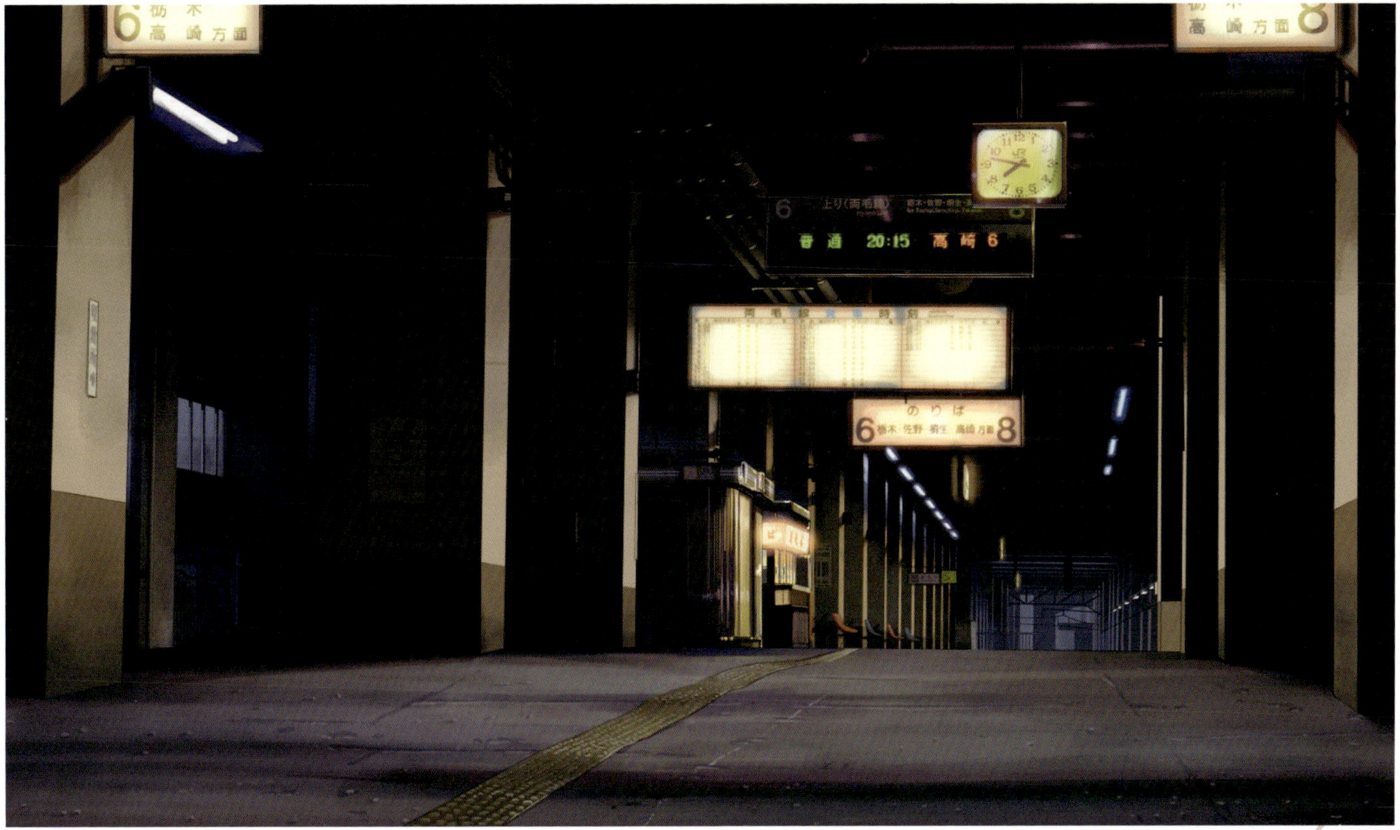

The standing-room-only noodle shop gives off a warm, inviting glow as Takaki fights against the cold and an empty stomach. As the entire platform is depicted in cool tones, this image was designed to naturally draw the viewer's eye.

"Cherry Blossom" / CUT_202 / Setting: JR Oyama Station platform

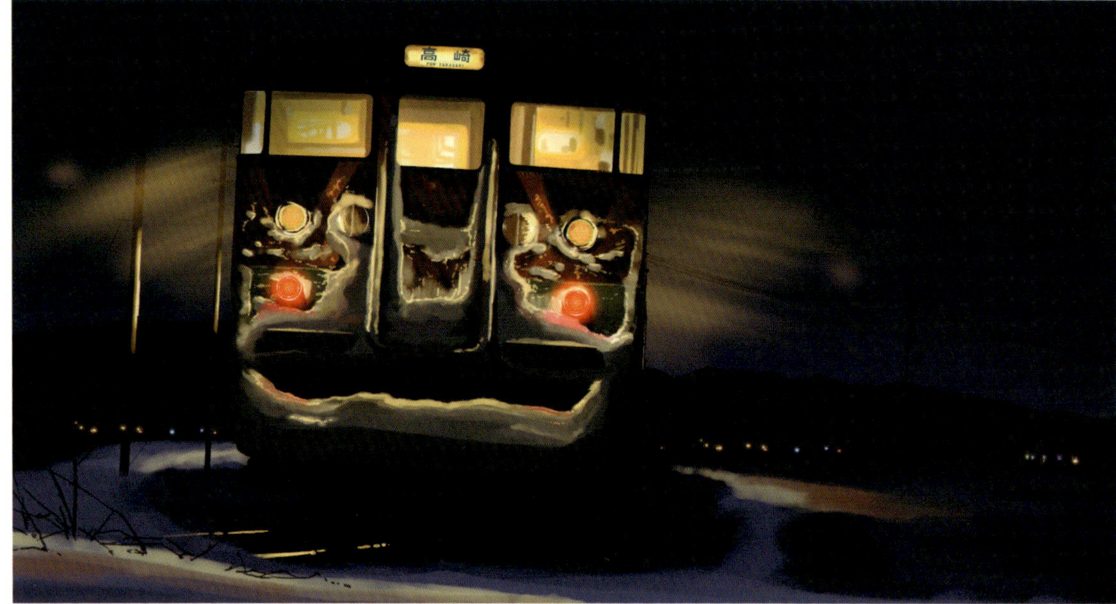

Takaki's train (a Model 115 on the Ryomo Line) as it was stopped in the snow due to disruptions in the train schedules. As the windshield wipers were animated, they're not a part of the background art. The final version included lighting effects for the headlights and animation of falling snow.

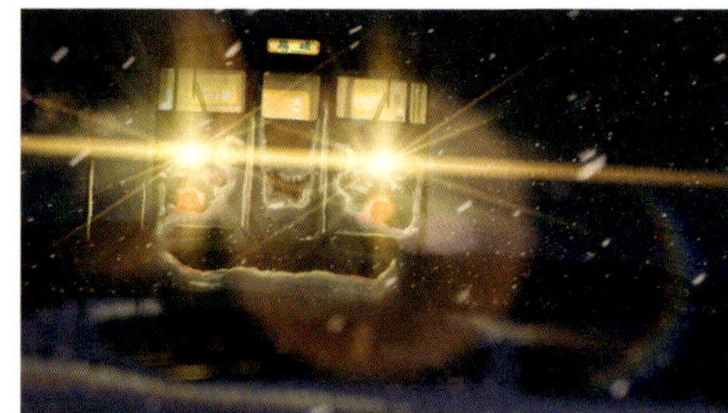

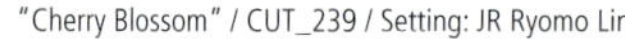

"Cherry Blossom" / CUT_239 / Setting: JR Ryomo Line

CUT_239 Final Version

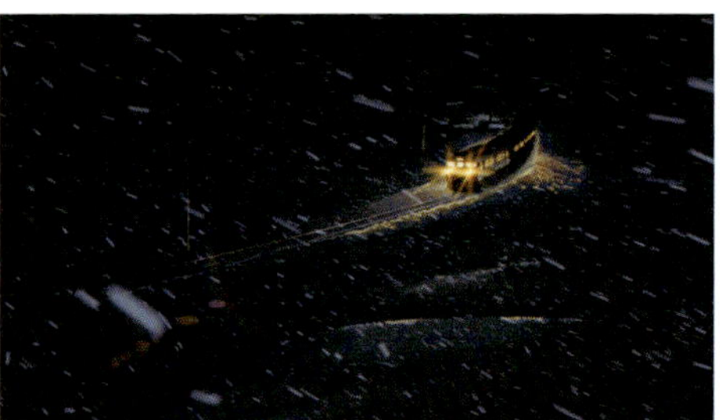

CUT_227 Final Version

In order to illustrate Takaki's loneliness, the background artwork here includes the least amount of detail necessary. When it comes to understanding the intention behind the art direction in *5 Centimeters per Second*, this cut is the best example. The final version included lighting effects for the headlights and animation of falling snow.

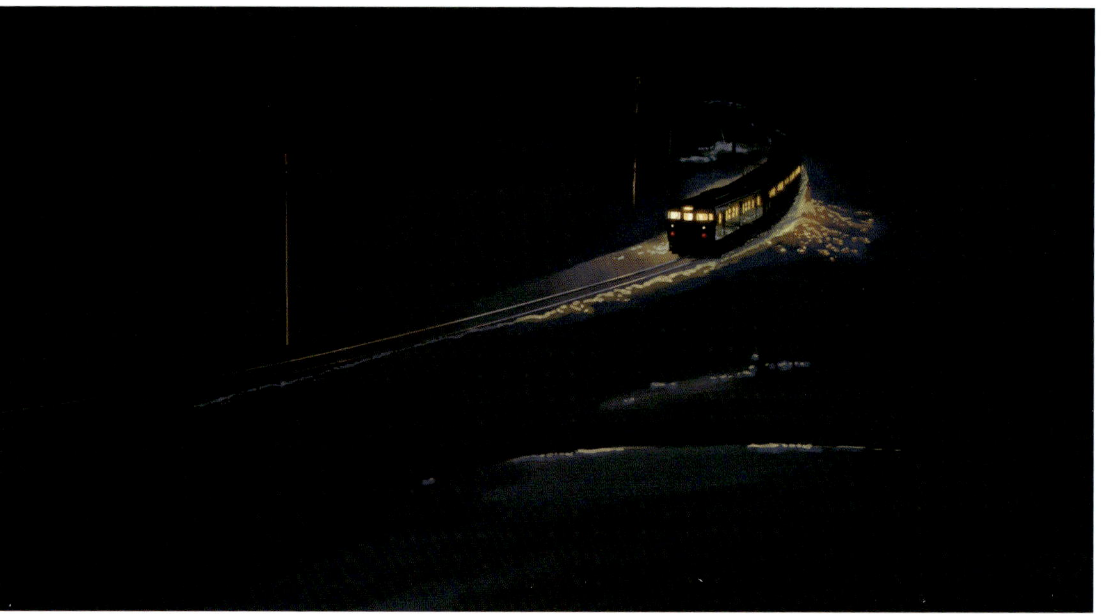

"Cherry Blossom" / CUT_227 / Setting: JR Ryomo Line

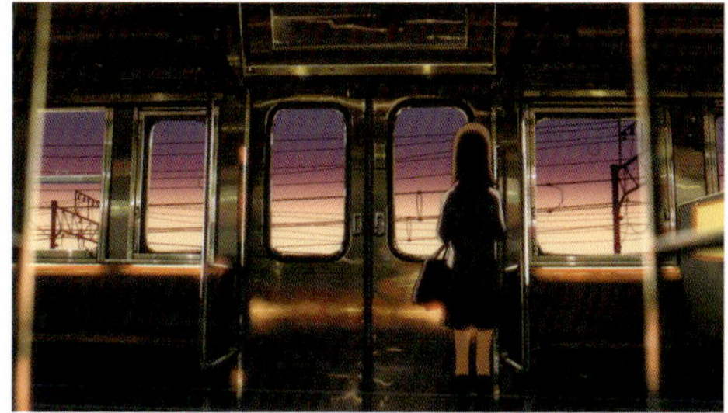

CUT_235 Final Version

Akari on her way to school as seen in Takaki's imagination. The interior of the train car and the sky in the distance are background elements, the animation of the overhead wires passing by outside was created with 3DCG, and the animator added a layer with Akari's cel.

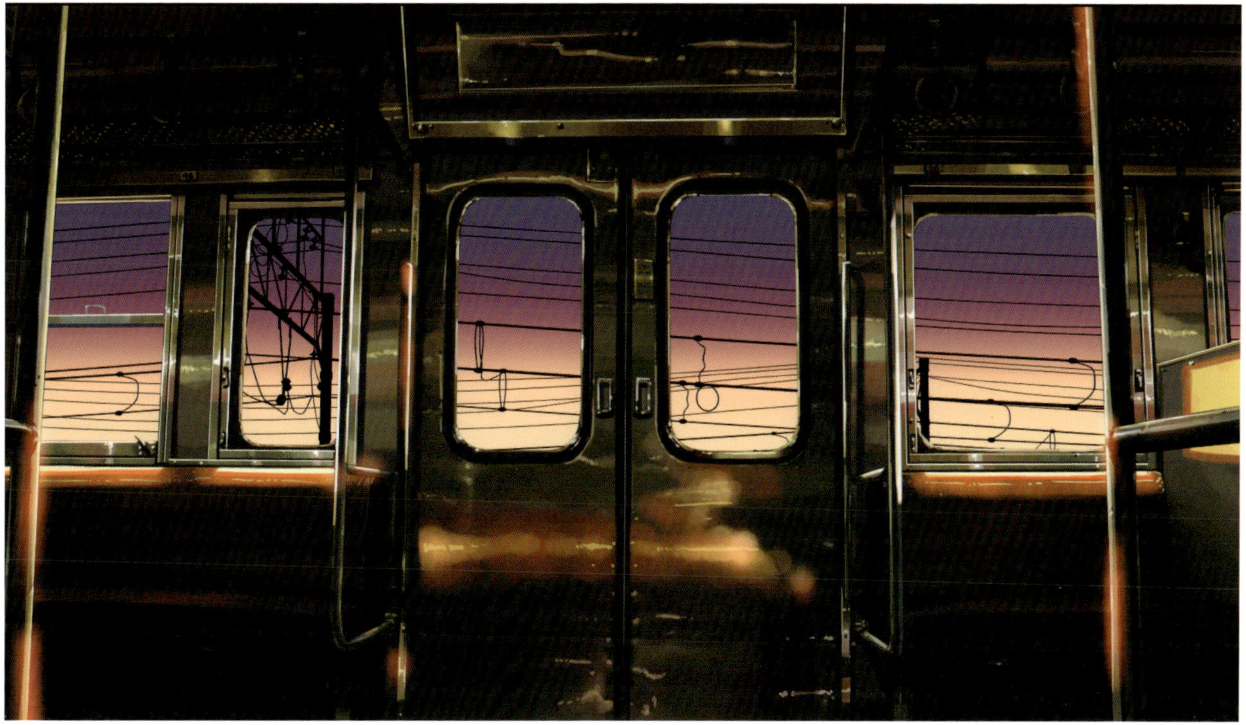

"Cherry Blossom" / CUT_235 / Setting: JR Ryomo Line

For Takaki's wristwatch, reference photos were prepared when deciding the layout, then the watch was rendered in 3DCG and processed with harmony cels. The detailed contents of the display were prepared on a separate layer, and the passage of time was reproduced via animation.

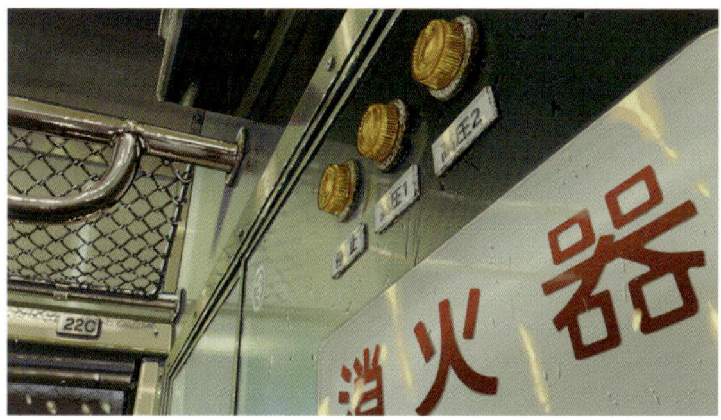

"Cherry Blossom" / CUT_228 / Setting: JR Ryomo Line

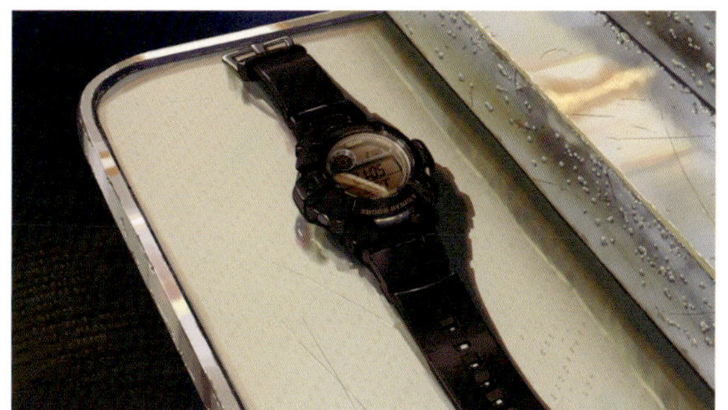

"Cherry Blossom" / CUT_236 / Setting: Takaki's watch inside a JR Ryomo Line train

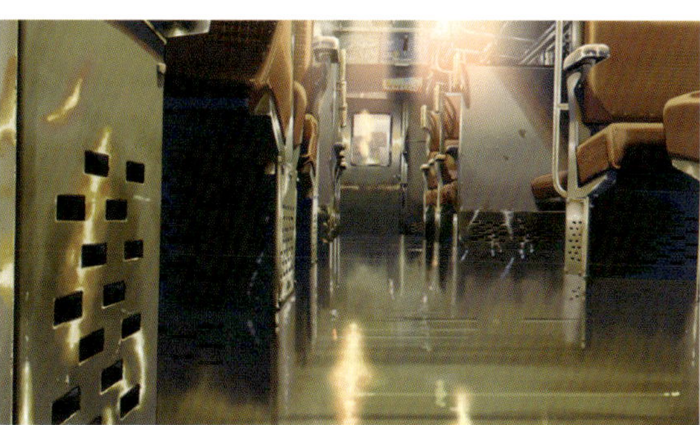

"Cherry Blossom" / CUT_243 / Setting: JR Ryomo Line

Act 1: "Cherry Blossom"

Rendezvous

Takaki and Akari's reunion, illustrated through their thoughts and feelings. Points of warm-tone lighting effects were added to scenery underpinned with blue tones to produce a wintry countryside scene. To symbolize their quiet time together, the animation element of snow in this scene, unlike the snowstorm from before, was designed to fall gently. The main memorable settings were the wooden buildings around Iwafune Station on the JR Ryomo Line and the radiator-heated waiting room, but in 2003 the station was modernized and left unattended, so it now appears very differently than it did in 1994, when the story is set.

Akari: Can you see it? That tree?

Takaki: The one you wrote about in your letter?

Akari: Yes, the cherry tree... Hey, they look like snowflakes...

Takaki: You're right, they do.

Takaki: (*monologue*) At that moment, I felt like I understood things like the existence of eternity, the heart and the soul. I felt as though we had shared all the experiences of my 13 years. And in the next moment... I became unbearably sad.

Sad because I didn't know what to do with Akari's warmth or her soul or what to do with that soul, or how long I should hold onto them. I also came to the realization that we would not be able to stay together. The overwhelming weight of the lives to come and the uncertainty of time hung over us.

But soon, all my fears began to melt away, leaving only Akari's soft lips on mine...

(Excerpt of *5 Centimeters per Second*, Act 1: "Cherry Blossom")

The contrast in colors between the warm lights inside the station and the bluish-white streetlights at the traffic circle serves to emphasize the coldness of the outside air. Also, the soft light that spills out from the turnstiles hints at Akari's presence.

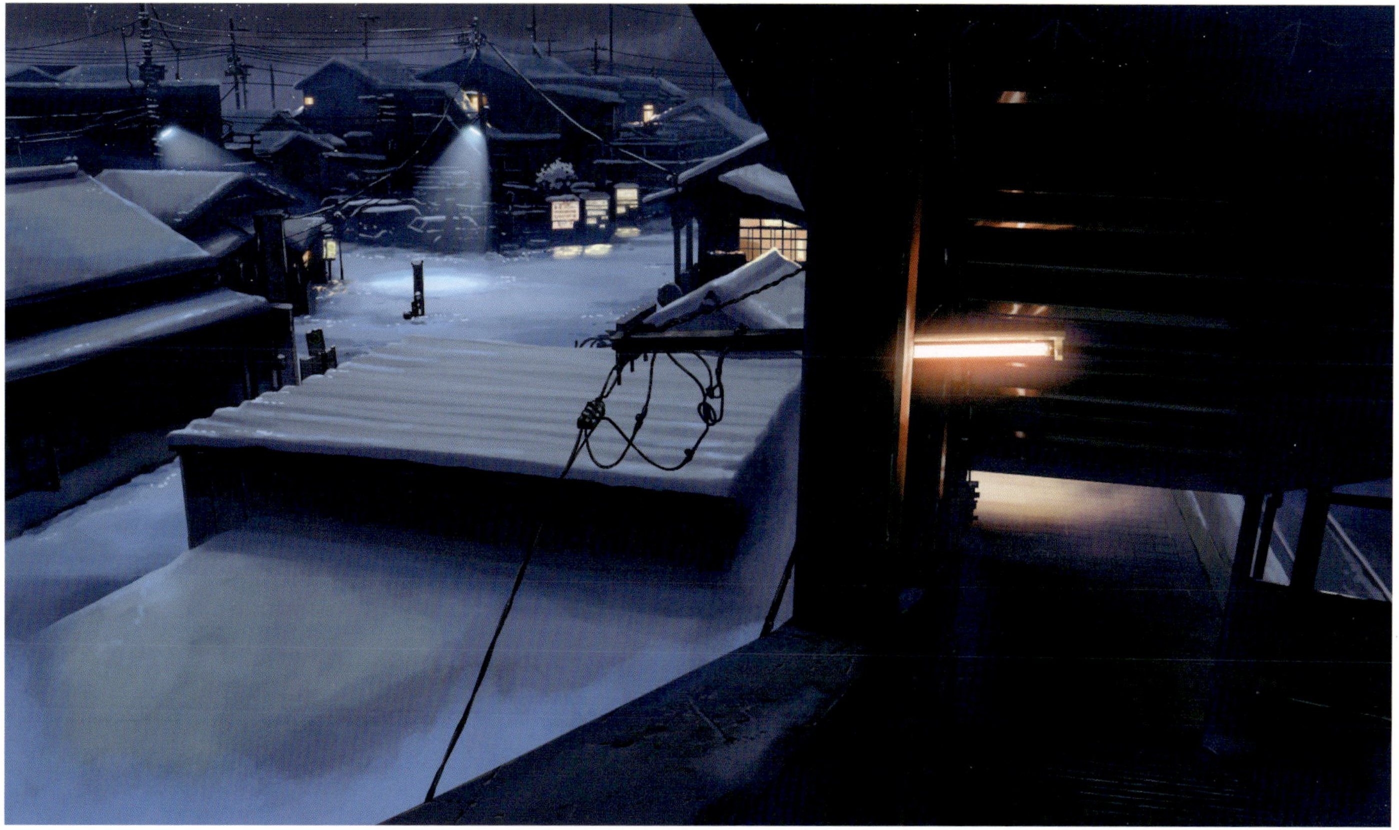

In CUT_249, the poles on the edge of the platform in the foreground and the wall of the overpass were drawn on a separate layer. There is a station name sign under the platform awning in CUT_251. There is a different notice posted at that location in the actual station, but for storytelling purposes it was changed to a station name sign.

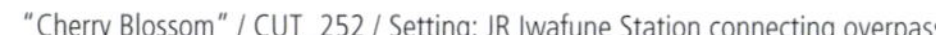

"Cherry Blossom" / CUT_252 / Setting: JR Iwafune Station connecting overpass

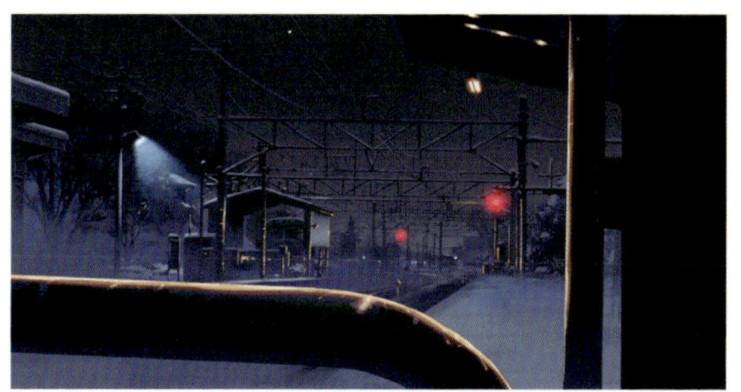

"Cherry Blossom" / CUT_249 / Setting: JR Iwafune Station platform

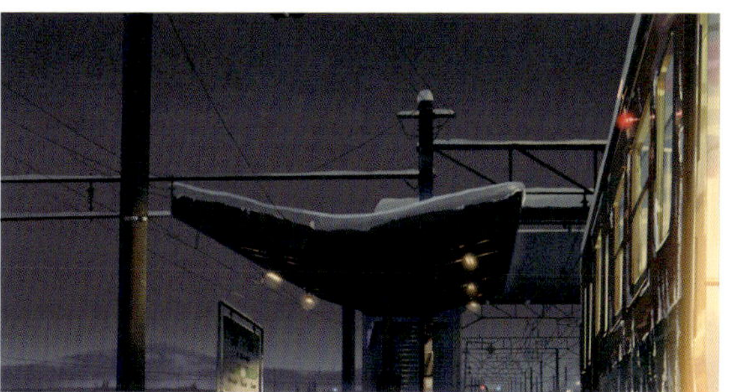

"Cherry Blossom" / CUT_251 / Setting: JR Iwafune Station platform

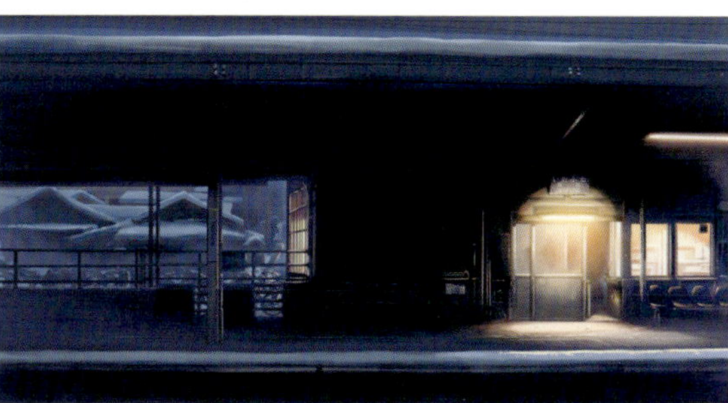

"Cherry Blossom" / CUT_253 / Setting: JR Iwafune Station turnstile

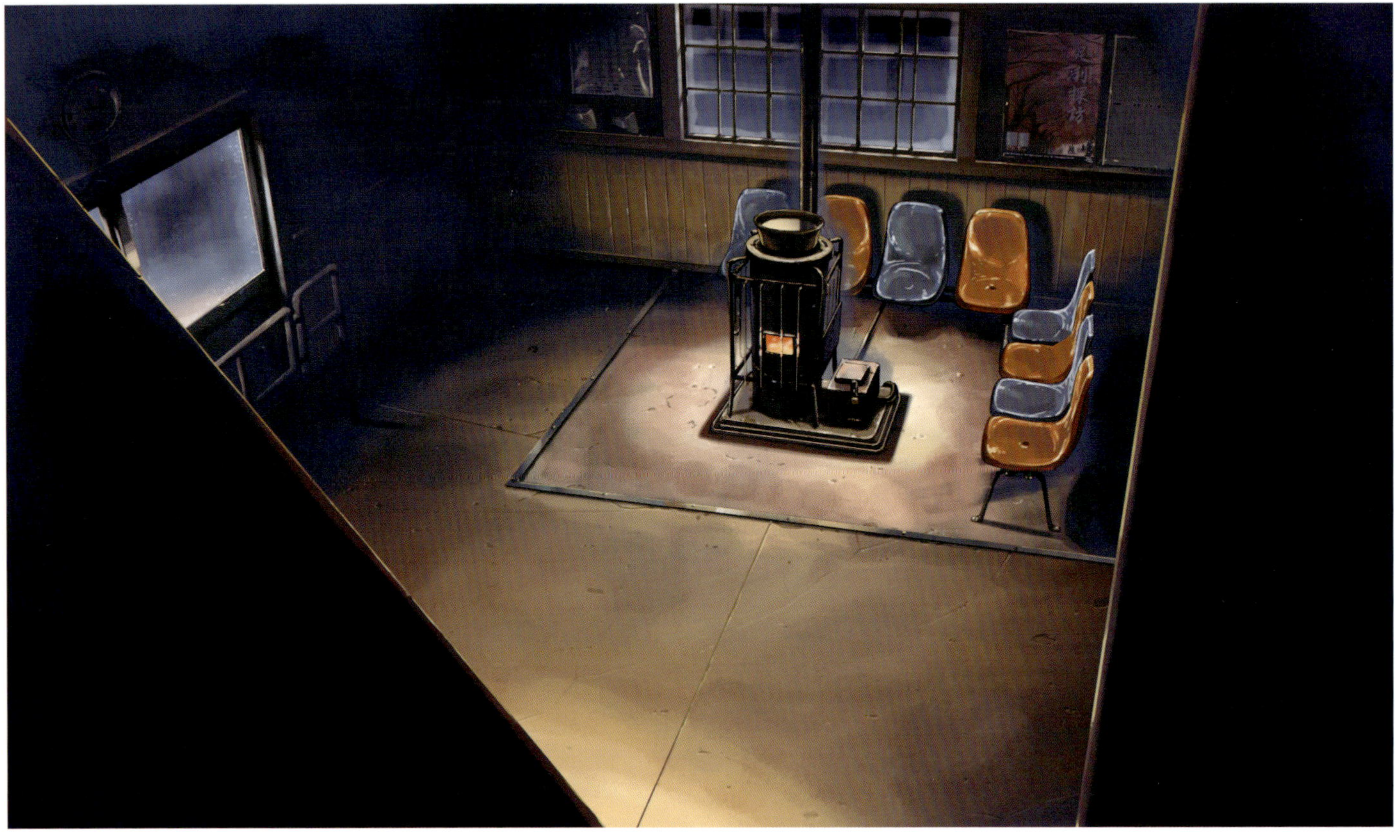

This is the background art for the scene when, after reuniting, Takaki and Akari weep as time stands still. The ceiling joist is on a separate layer, on which a blur effect was added. The interior of the room was drawn in detail by the background artists, and you can see where Mr. Shinkai himself painted the shadows. The waiting room is entirely fabricated.

"Cherry Blossom" / CUT_261 / Setting: JR Iwafune Station waiting room

Mr. Shinkai indicated what Akari's homemade lunch should contain at the storyboard stage. In order to get the colors and positions just right, the staff actually cooked and packed the meal, then photographed it, before using the photo for reference when creating harmony cel elements.

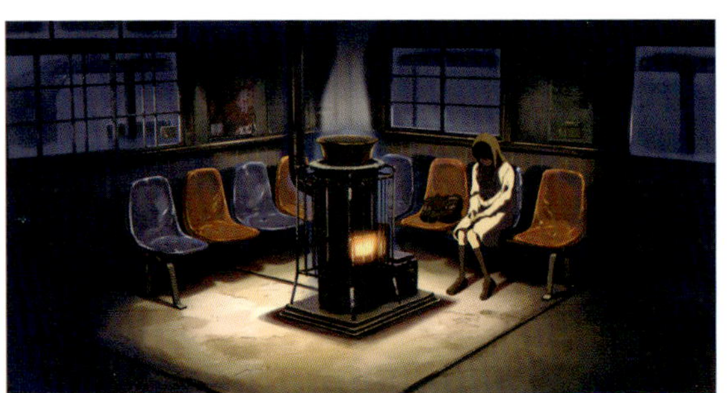

"Cherry Blossom" / CUT_256 / Setting: JR Iwafune Station waiting room

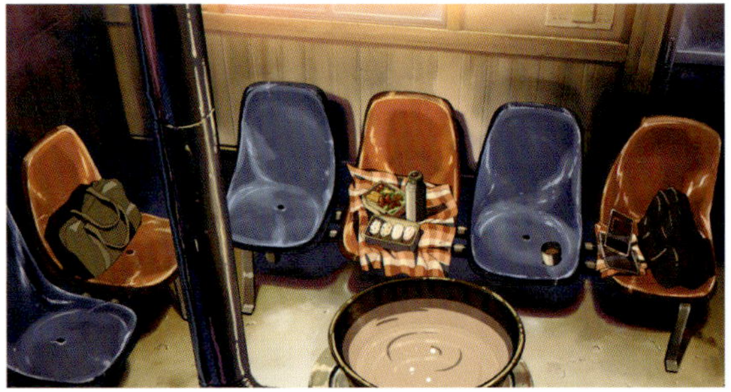

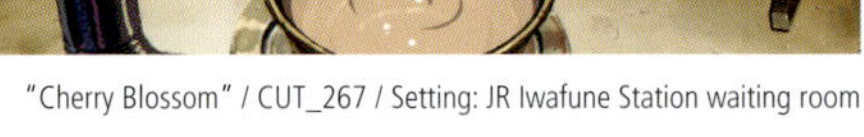

"Cherry Blossom" / CUT_267 / Setting: JR Iwafune Station waiting room

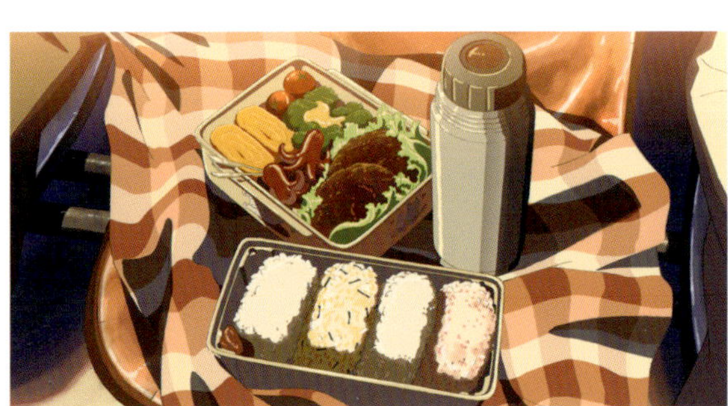

"Cherry Blossom" / CUT_266 / Setting: JR Iwafune Station waiting room

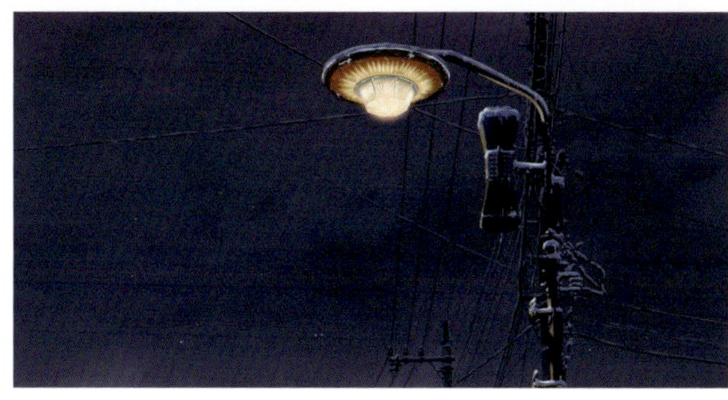

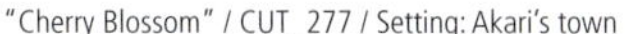
"Cherry Blossom" / CUT_277 / Setting: Akari's town

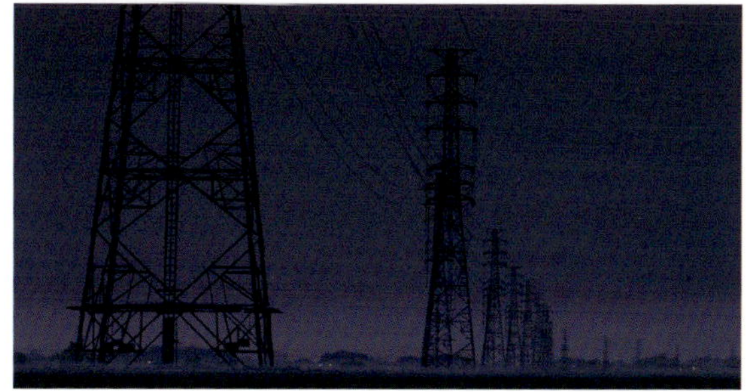
"Cherry Blossom" / CUT_280 / Setting: Akari's town/countryside

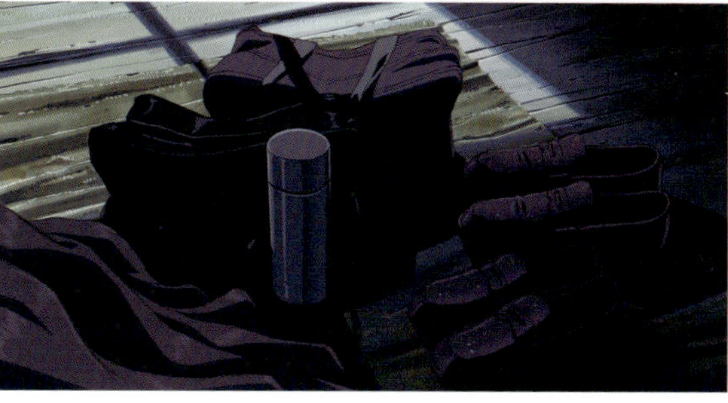
"Cherry Blossom" / CUT_306 / Setting: Akari's town/an old rural barn

This is the background art used in the scene when Takaki and Akari exit the station building. The dim light given off by the vending machines are points of warmth in the overall cool scenery. The lack of detail in the foreground objects makes the image seem that much colder.

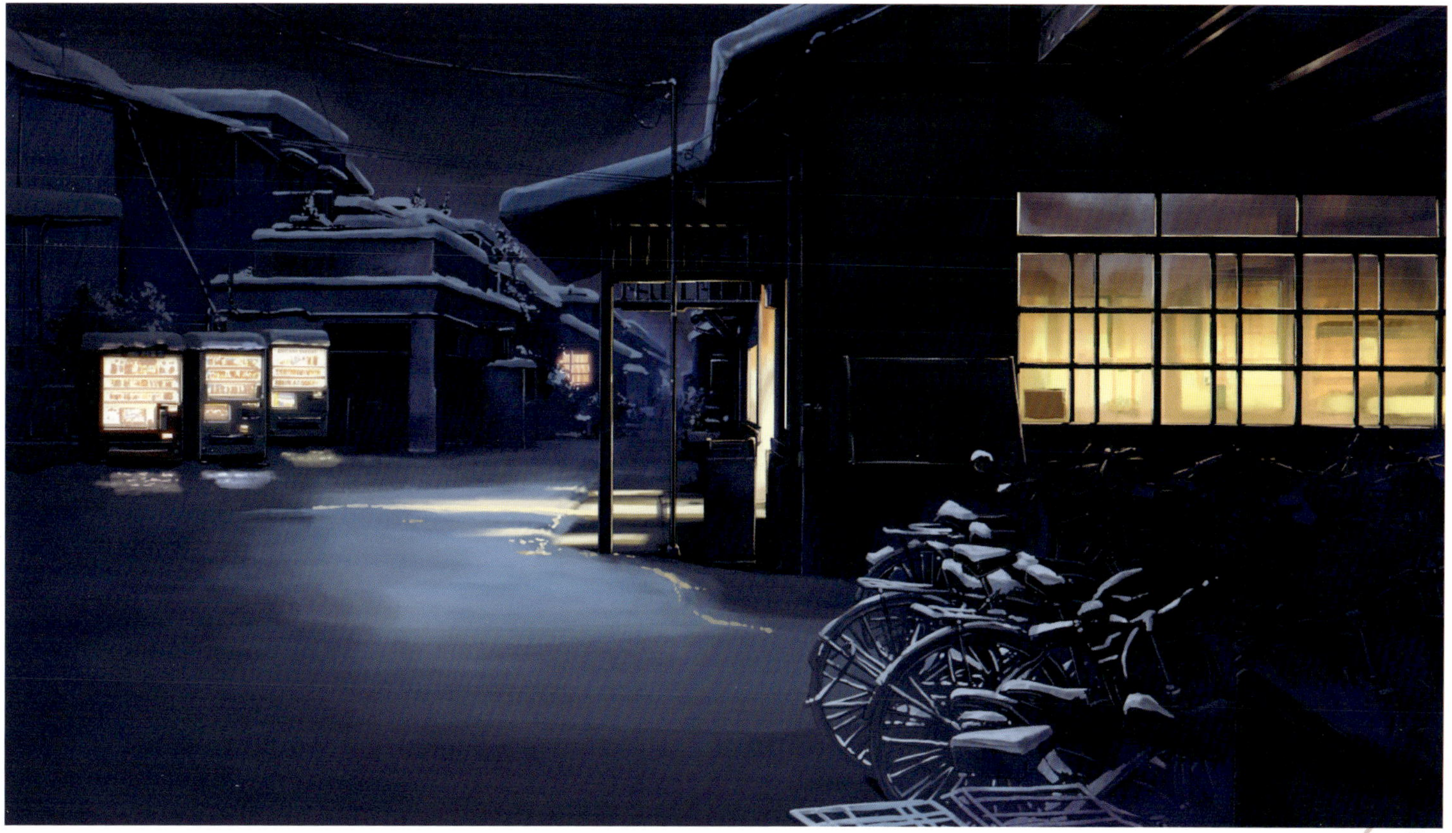

"Cherry Blossom" / CUT_278 / Setting: Akari's town/in front of the train station

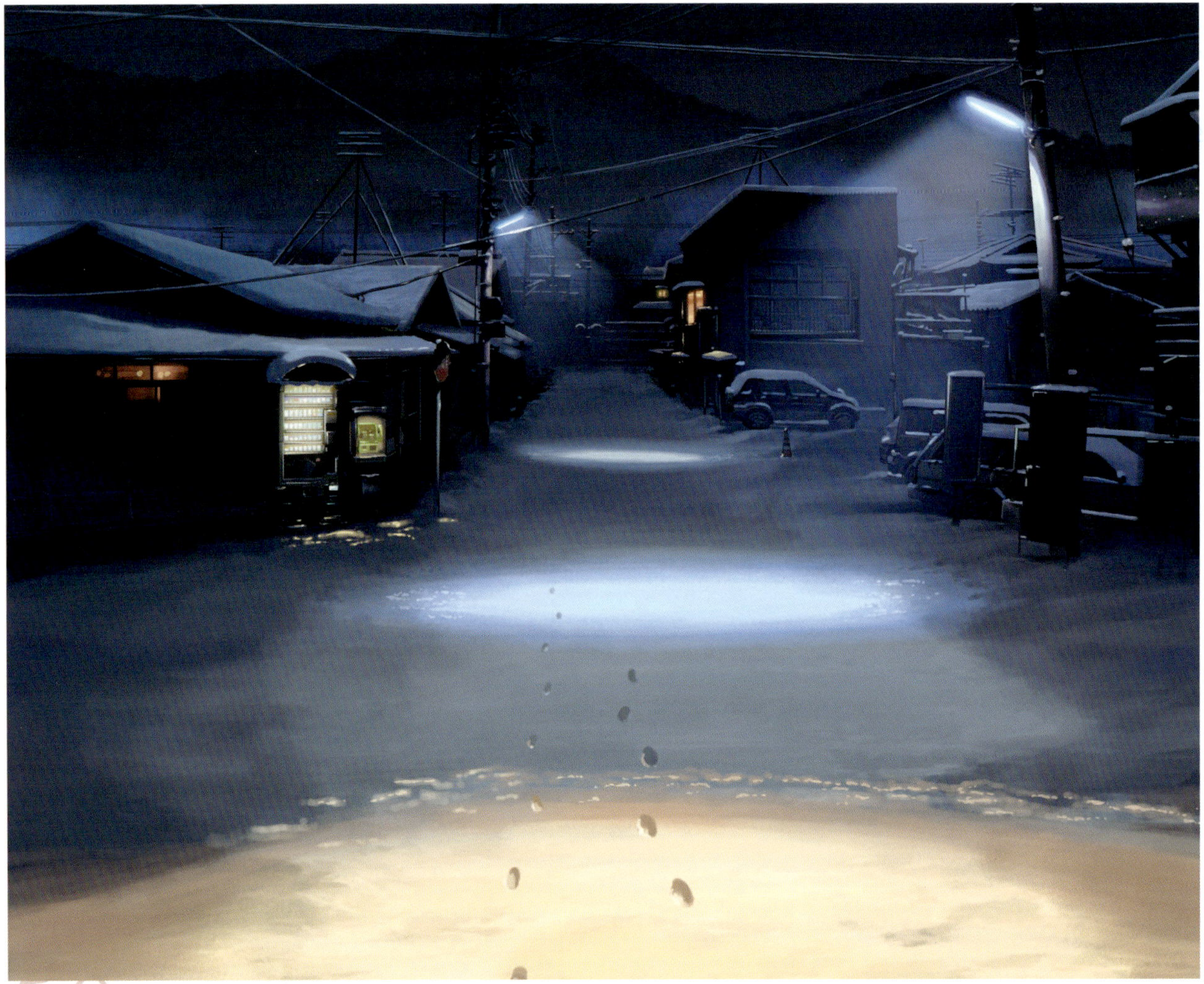

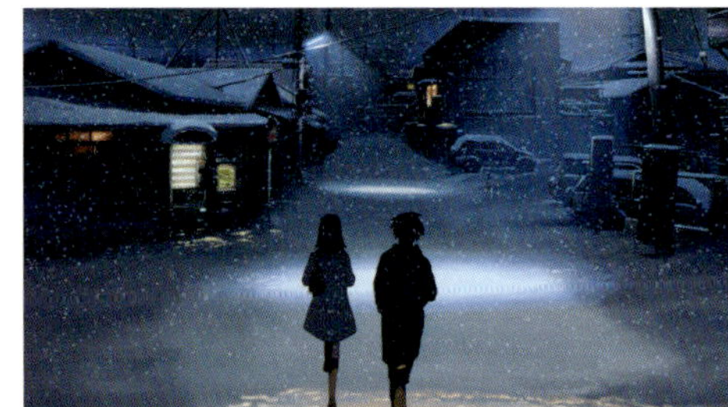

CUT_279 Final Version

Takaki and Akari walking outside of Iwafune Station. This artwork, used on promotional posters, represents the film as a whole. The artwork of the footprints left behind by the characters was drawn on a separate layer, which were revealed in time with the characters' movements. The location photos of Iwafune used for reference were taken at midday during the summer, but the town is depicted here on a winter's night. Several animation elements of falling snow were prepared, and different ones were used depending on the scene. A gently-falling snow was chosen for this scene to depict the quietness of the late hour.

"Cherry Blossom" / CUT_279 / Setting: Akari's town/in front of the train station

The cherry tree in Takaki and Akari's imagination. The final version included animation of falling cherry blossom petals, cels of the pair gazing into each other's eyes, and a soft light flare coming from under their feet. A blur effect was also added to create a soft imaginary scene.

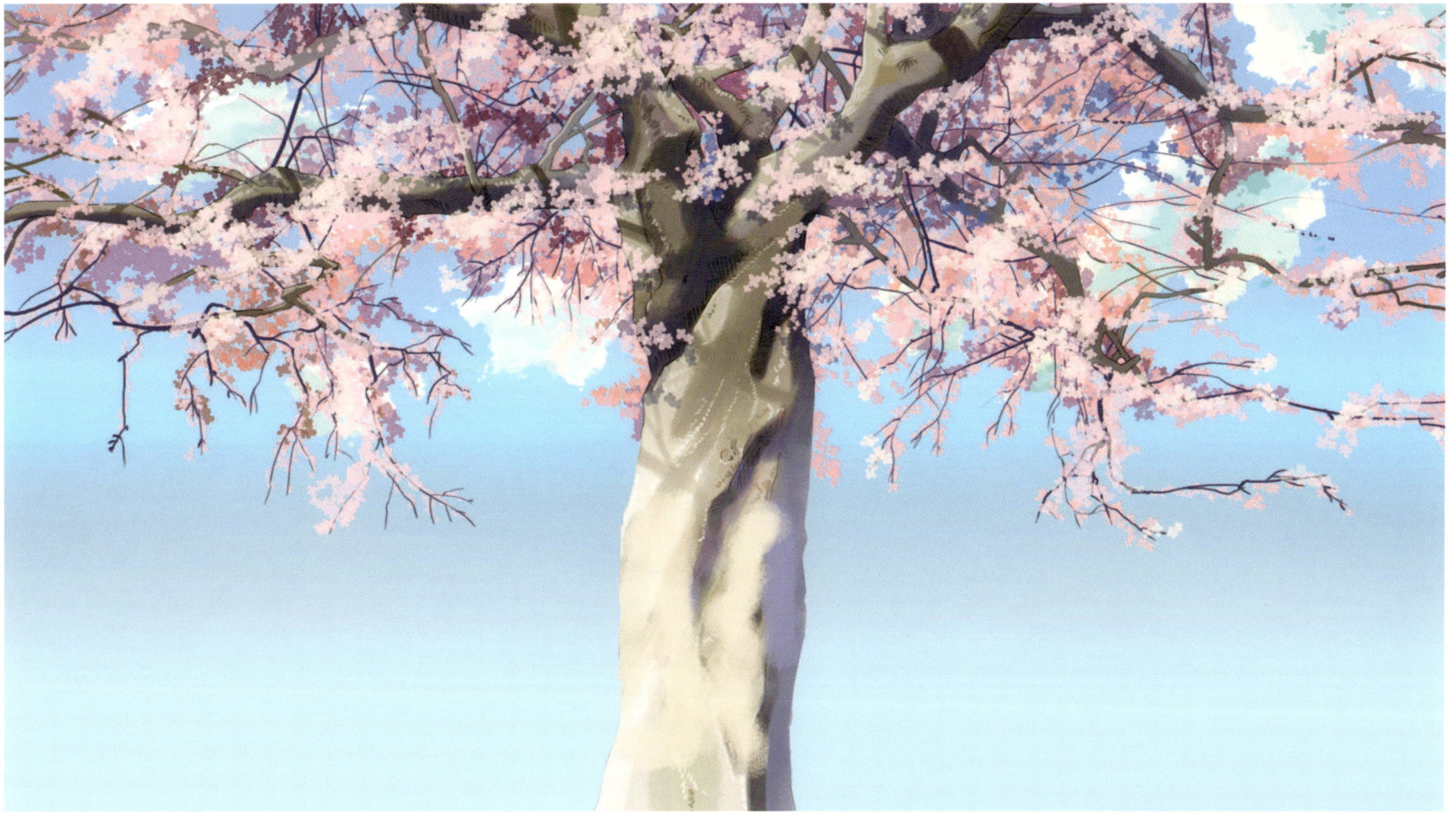

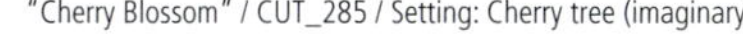

"Cherry Blossom" / CUT_285 / Setting: Cherry tree (imaginary)

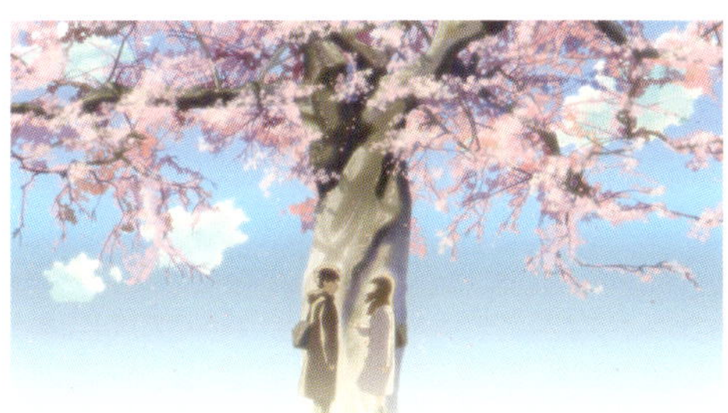

CUT_285 Final Version

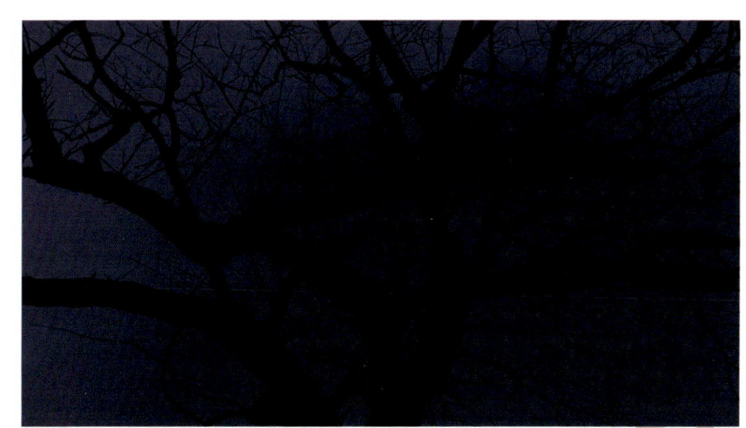

"Cherry Blossom" / CUT_298 / Setting: Cherry tree in Akari's neighborhood

Akari: I... Takaki...

Takaki: (*in a rough, barely-there voice*) Mm...

SFX: *ring ring ring ring* (*train departure bell*)

Akari: Takaki, I think... you'll be okay! I know you will be...!

SFX: *shhff* (*door sliding shut*)

Takaki: Thank you for that... Take care of yourself, Akari! I'll write to you! I'll call!

(Excerpt of 5 *Centimeters per Second*, Act 1: "Cherry Blossom")

Act 1: "Cherry Blossom"

The Morning of Their Separation

The final section illustrating Takaki and Akari's parting. Bathed in gentle morning sunlight, Akari looks poetic as she sees off Takaki's train as it heads down the Ryomo Line tracks. The clusters of white clouds in the blue sky, so different from the snowy skies from the night before, are elements that were used effectively to symbolize Mr. Shinkai's aesthetic. Along with the sadness of parting, they can also sense the hopelessly vast size of the world they are entering. The interior of the Ryoma Line train car is depicted with light tones, and the background art evokes the clear countryside air.

This is the reverse angle of CUT_251 shown on page 47. The final version included animation of Akari seeing off the 3DCG train as it raced away from the station.

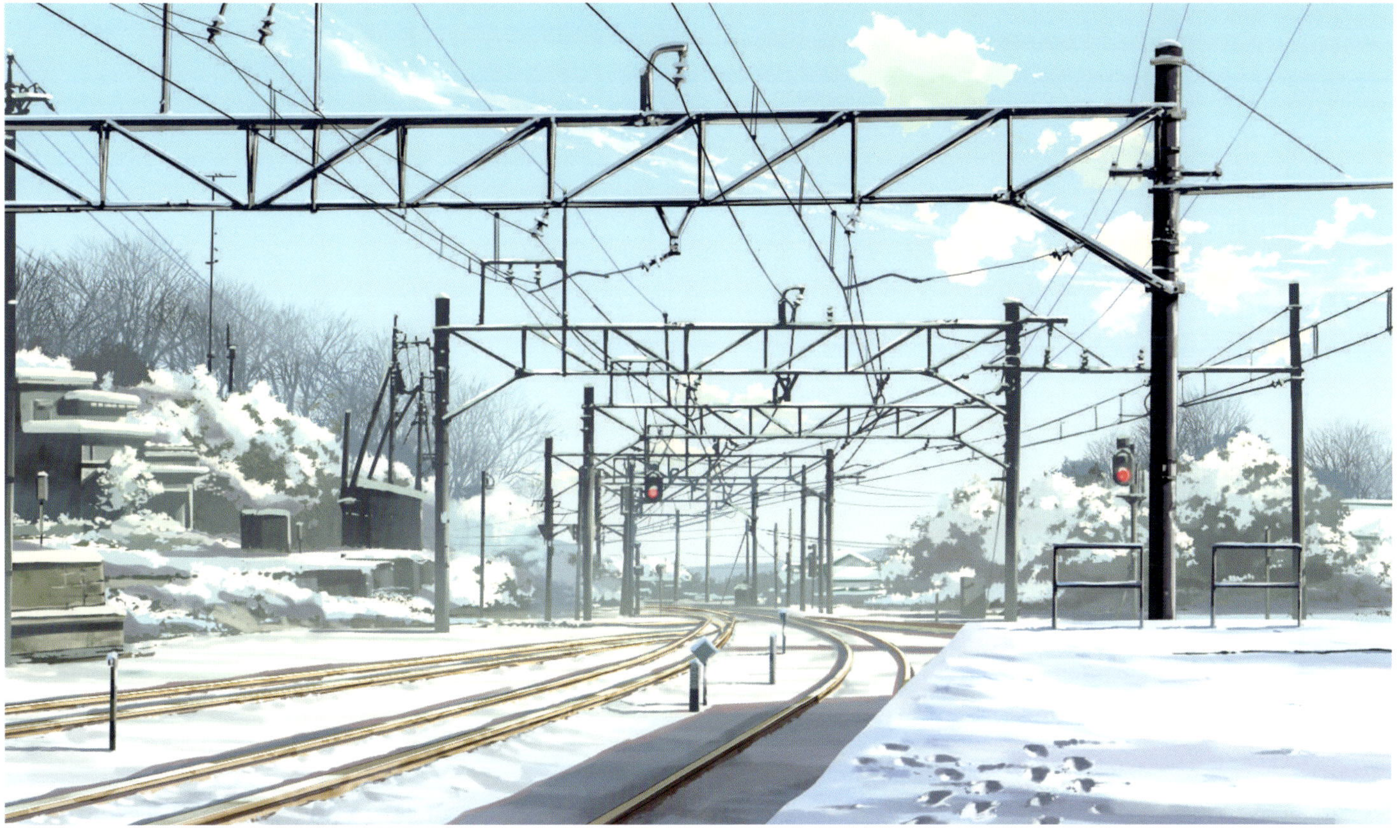

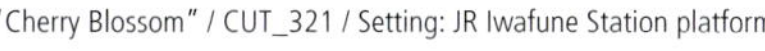

"Cherry Blossom" / CUT_321 / Setting: JR Iwafune Station platform

Takaki and Akari's footprints are part of the background artwork.

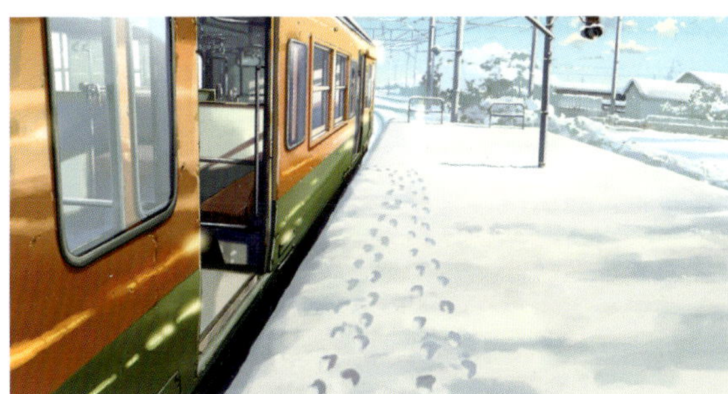

"Cherry Blossom" / CUT_310 / Setting: JR Iwafune Station platform

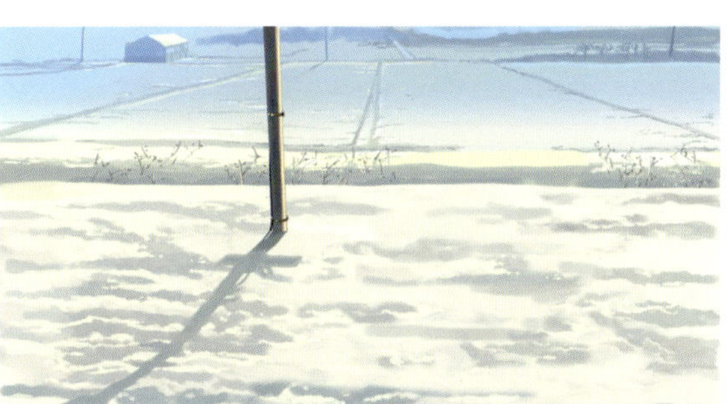

"Cherry Blossom" / CUT_314 / Setting: JR Iwafune Station platform

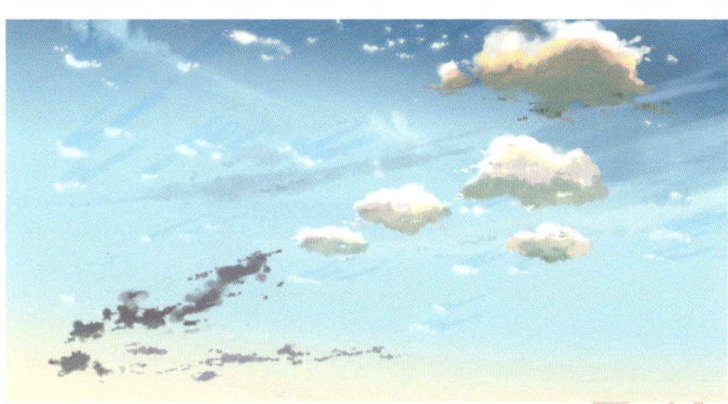

"Cherry Blossom" / CUT_320 / Setting: The sky in Akari's town

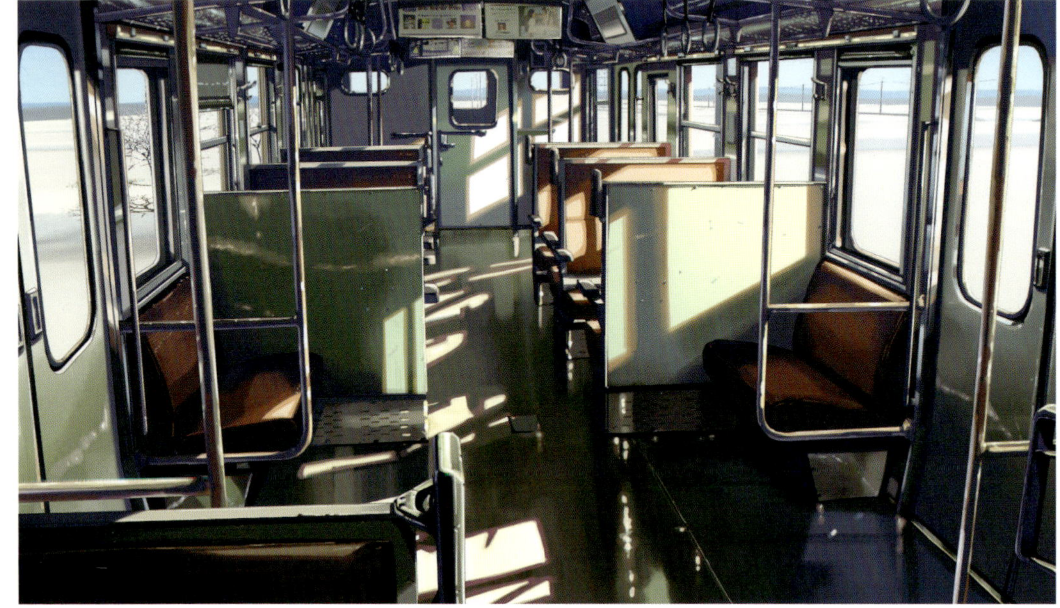

"Cherry Blossom" / CUT_324 / Setting: JR Ryomo Line

The background art elements of the interior of the train car and the scenery passing outside the windows were combined using video software. Since the cel animation of Takaki was placed near the back righthand door of the train, everything before that point was drawn on a separate layer and treated as an overlay.

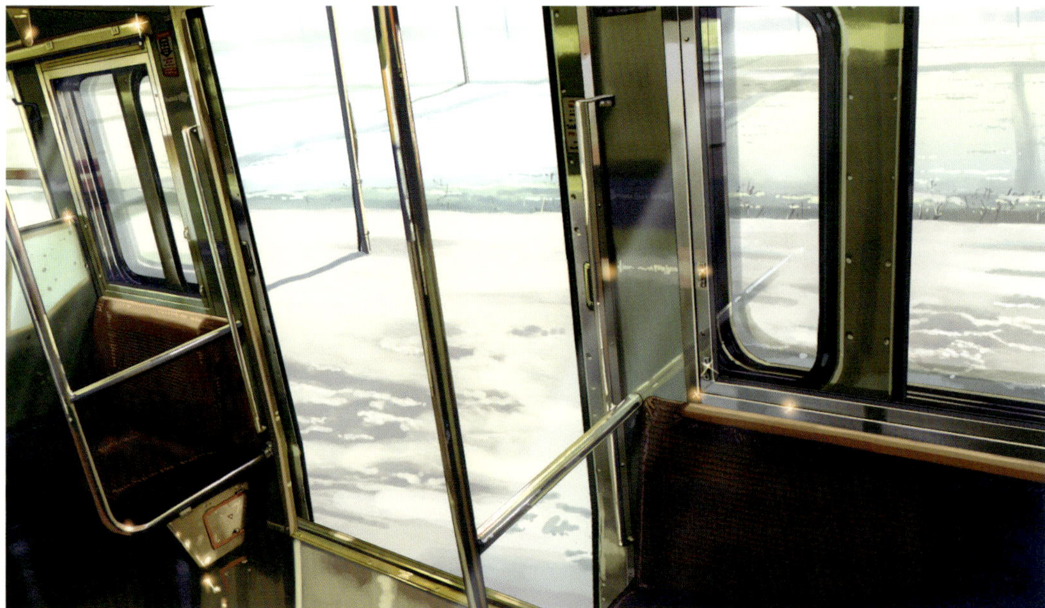

"Cherry Blossom" / CUT_311 / Setting: JR Ryomo Line

The scene where Akari is reading a book on a train platform at dawn had a different layout than the version of Iwafune Station created afterwards, so this platform is considered something from Takaki's imagination. This is why the cherry tree near Akari's house some distance from the station is visible from the train platform.

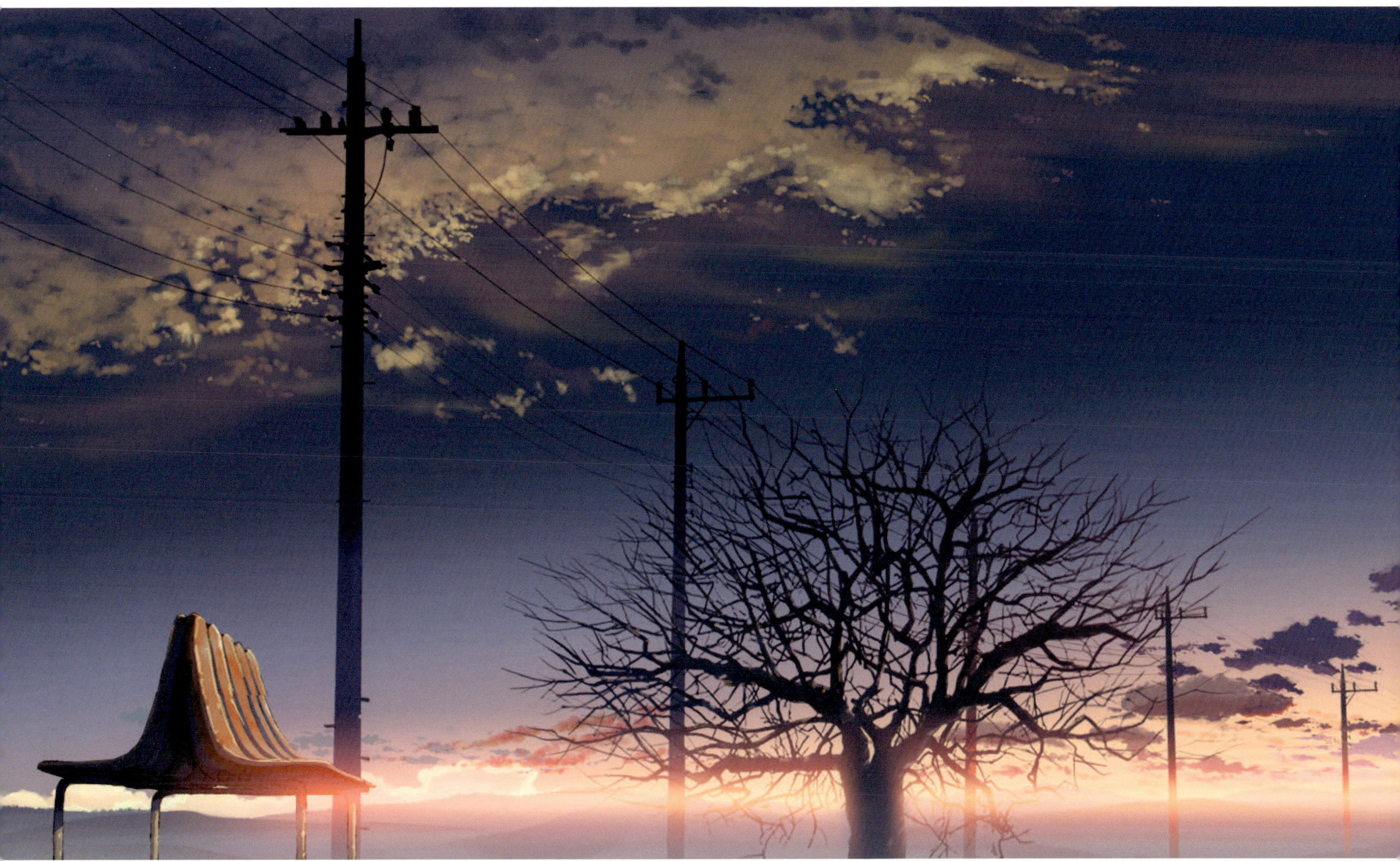

"Cherry Blossom" / CUT_B023 / Setting: A train platform somewhere (imaginary)

Takaki:	Wanna head back together?
Kanae:	(*monologue*) If I was a dog, my tail would have been wagging so hard... my happiness would have been so obvious. I heaved a sigh of relief, thinking it was a good thing I wasn't a dog. And I was amazed how stupid a thought that was, even for me.
	Yet the ride home with Tono made me happy.
	Right from the beginning, Tono seemed somehow different from others. That very day in 8th grade, I fell in love with him. I studied hard because I wanted to go to the same high school as him, and I somehow managed to pass my school's entrance exams.
	The more I see Tono, the more I love him. It's been scary and every day's been painful. But every time I see him, I'm happy. There's nothing I could do about it.

(Excerpt of 5 *Centimeters per Second*, Act 2: "Cosmonaut")

Act 2 : "Cosmonaut"

The Sky That Leads to Her

Act 2 of 5 *Centimeters per Second* is presented from the point of view of Kanae Sumida, a classmate of Takaki at the school he transferred to on Tanegashima. In contrast to Kanae, drawn within the powerful southern island sunlight, Takaki is often shown standing before sunset skies. The imaginary cosmos depicted at the beginning of the act makes the loneliness that Takaki carries within him appear all the more poignant when compared to Kanae, who lives a healthy lifestyle surrounded by lush nature. Makoto Shinkai's attention to detail is seen in the way nature on the southern island of Tanegashima is drawn.

Takaki's imaginary world. Takaki, an enthusiastic reader of fantasy and scientific books since grade school, writes a story on his cell phone featuring a protagonist based on Akari to distract himself from his loneliness. This scene shows the rings of natural satellites floating against the faint morning twilight in the distance. Since the camera pans over this image downward diagonally, the parts of the image not seen on camera are not drawn at all. Animation of two birds flying was added. This scene is reminiscent of *Voices of a Distant Star*.

"Cosmonaut" / CUT_001 / Setting: Takaki's imaginary world

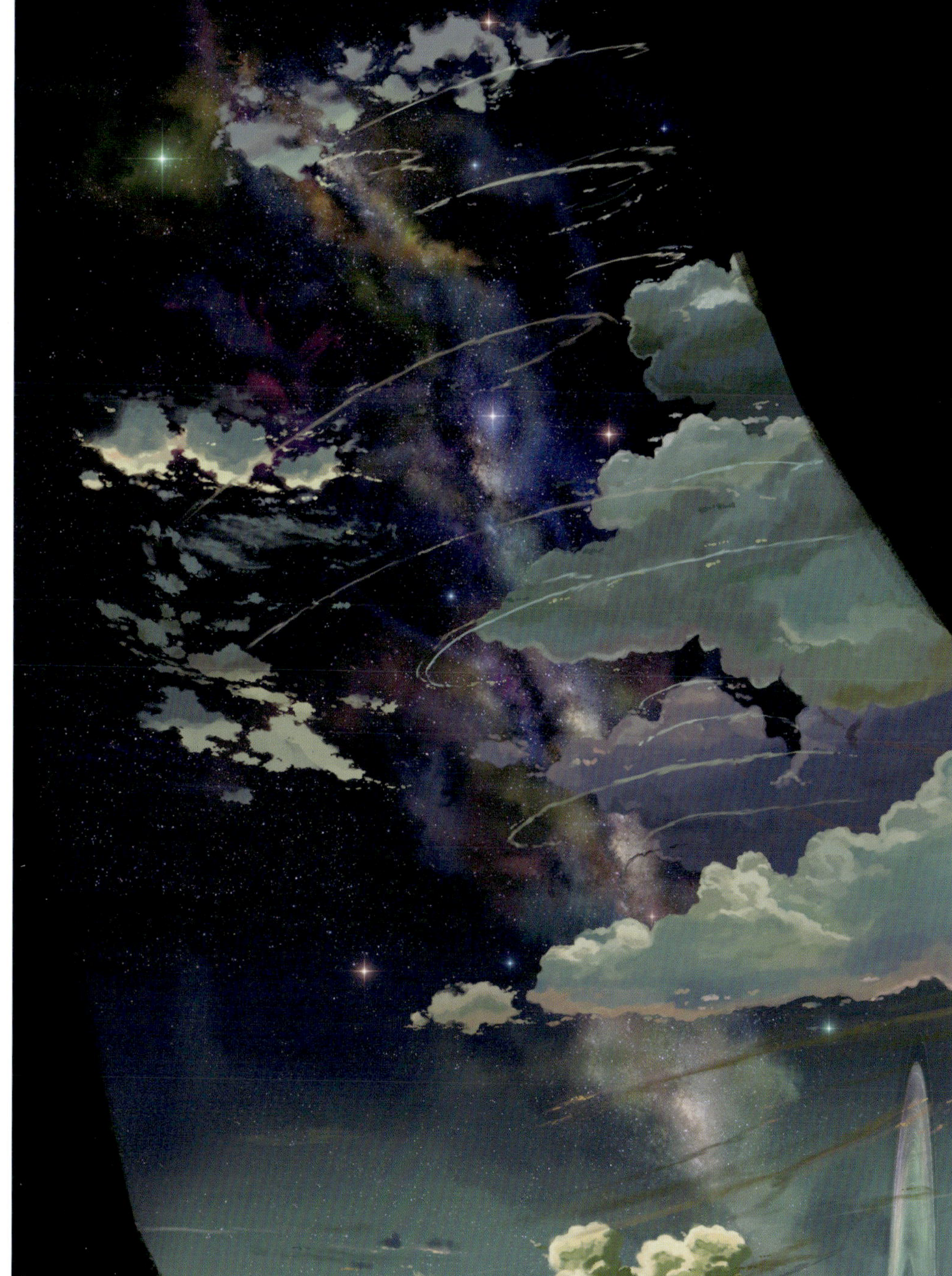

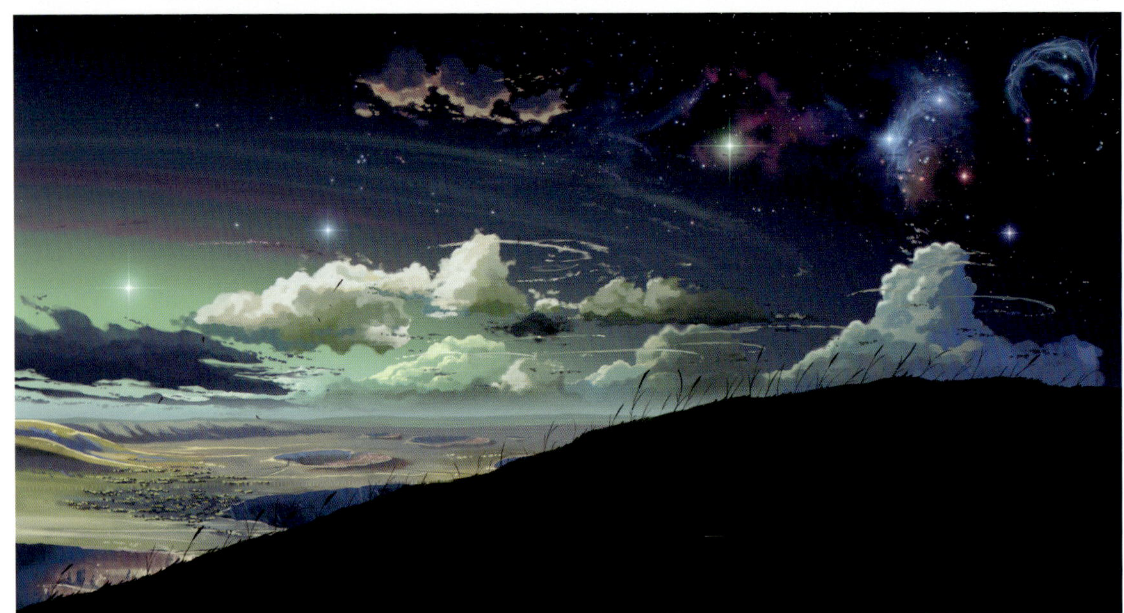

"Cosmonaut" / CUT_003 / Setting: Takaki's imaginary world

A boy and a girl watching the sunrise on an unknown planet. They stand on a plateau modeled on the one that Takaki often visits on Tanegashima. In the distance on this strange planet is a wasteland pitted with many giant craters. This image, which shows the sky's gradation from night to dawn, makes it appear all the more fantastical.

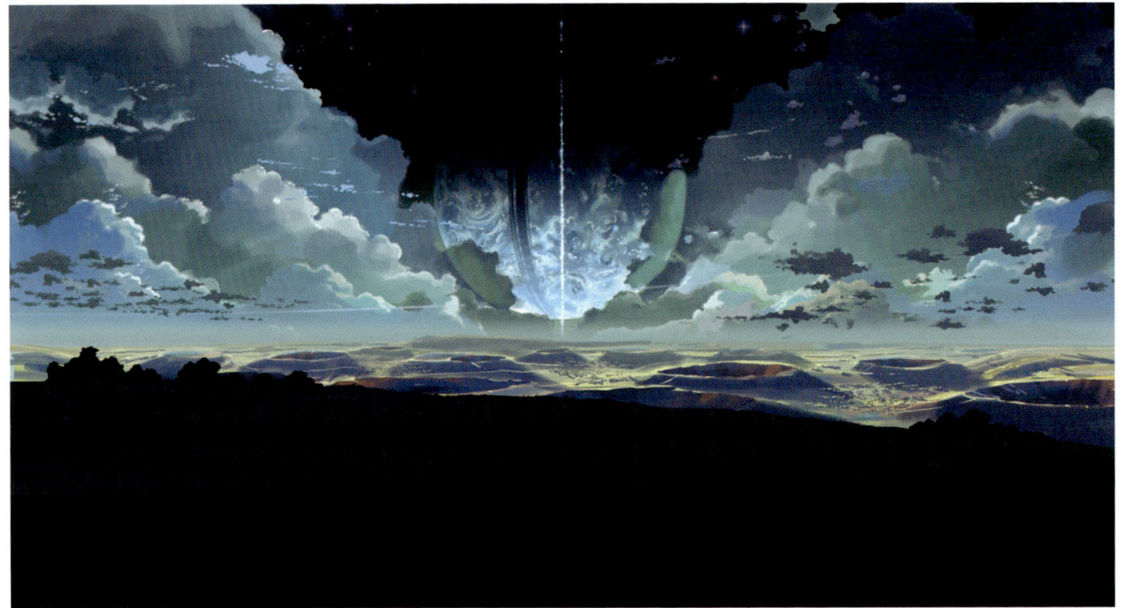

"Cosmonaut" / CUT_005 / Setting: Takaki's imaginary world

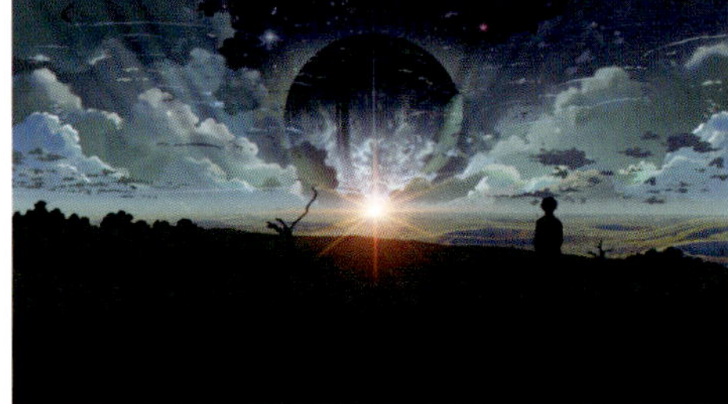

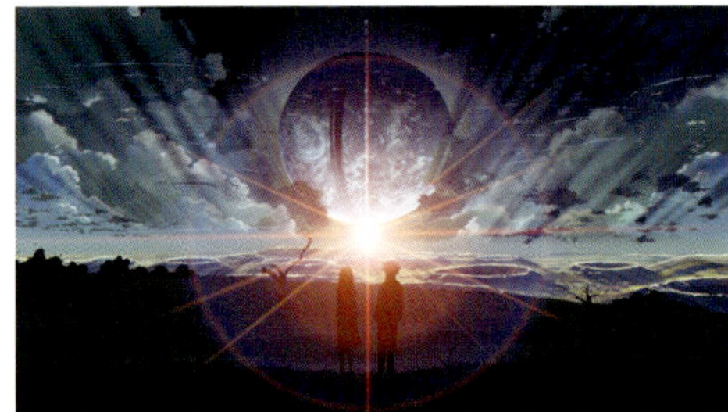

CUT_005 Final Version

Daybreak on a strange world. The sun's rays shine between the ring of satellites and the land in the distance, lighting up the planet. The final version included cels of Takaki and the girl, as well as grasses waving in the wind.

The ring of satellites around the planet shines in the risen sun's rays. The final version included air wavering in the sunlight and animation of a flock of birds flying in the distance.

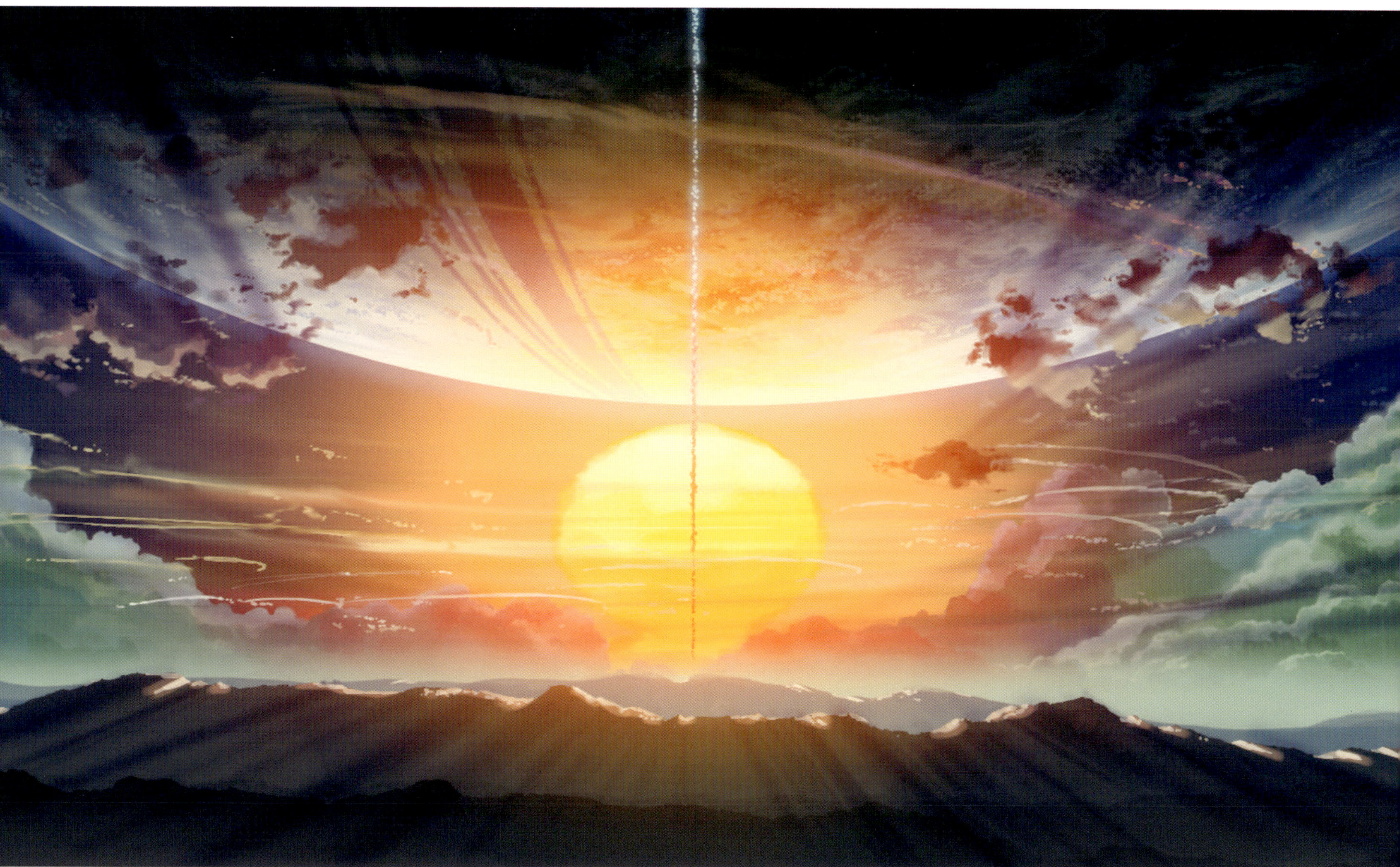

"Cosmonaut" / CUT_009 / Setting: Takaki's imaginary world

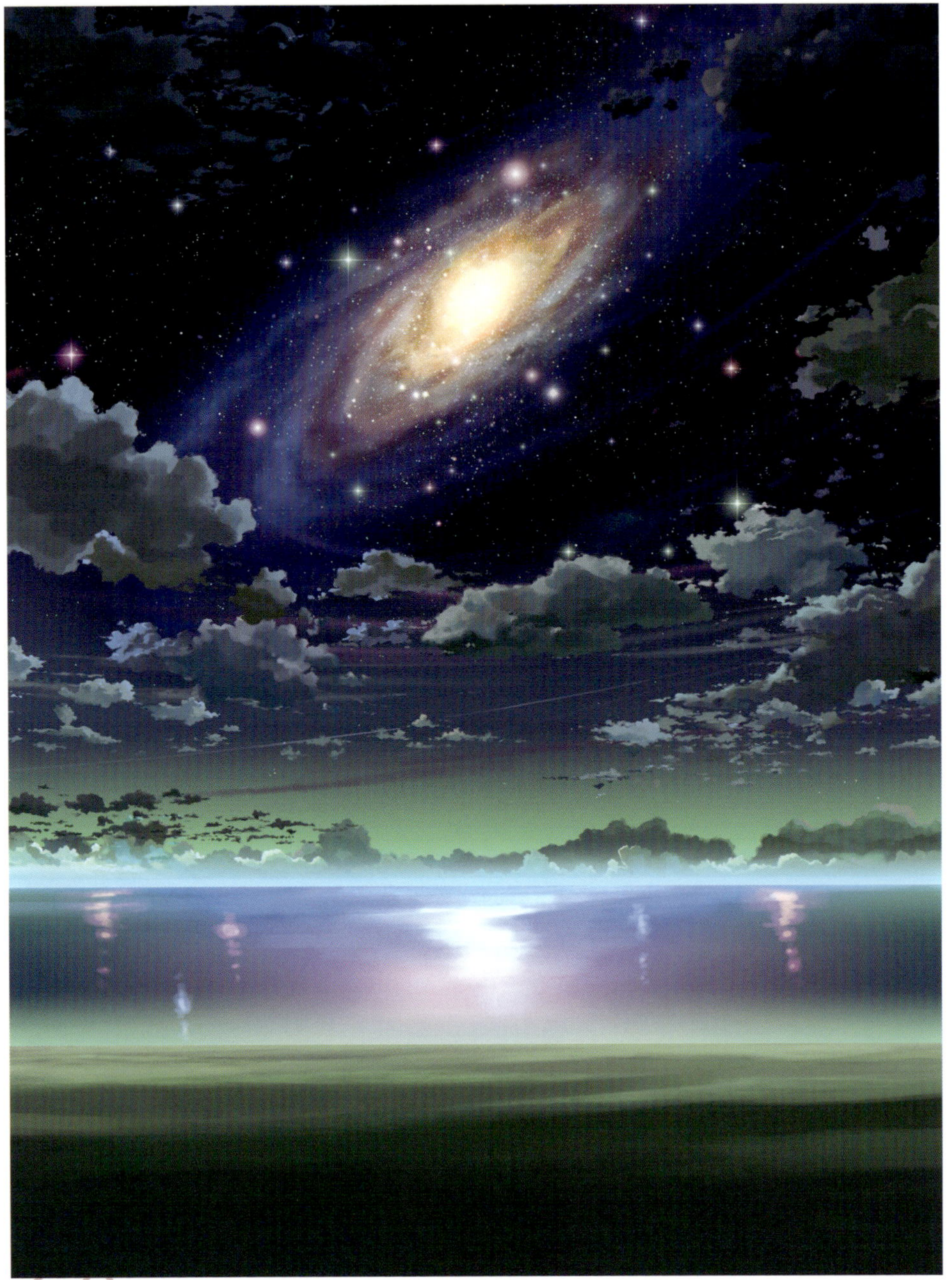

"Cosmonaut" / CUT_168 / Setting: Takaki's imaginary world

Takaki and the girl walking along the shore of the strange planet. A giant spiral galaxy and the light from countless stars are visible above the horizon. On the storyboard for this scene, Mr. Shinkai wrote, "This sort of skyscape must exist somewhere."

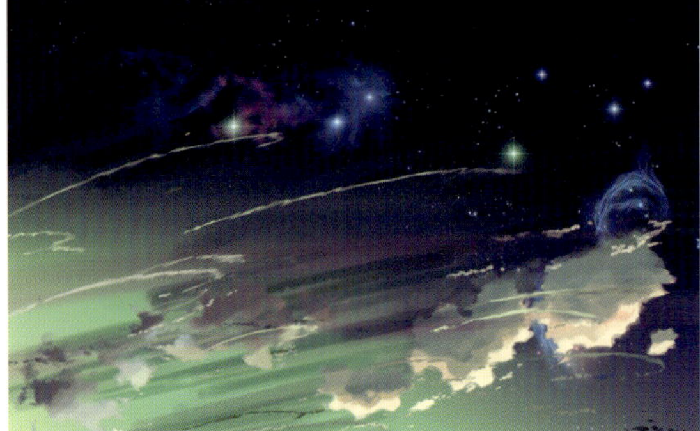

"Cosmonaut" / CUT_284 / Setting: Takaki's imaginary world

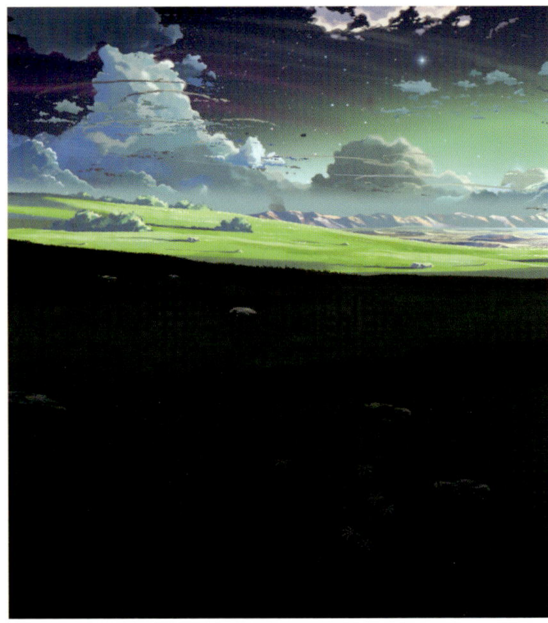

"Cosmonaut" / CUT_287 / Setting: Takaki's imaginary world

CUT_287 was used for the scene where we see, for the first time, the face of the girl on the foreign planet. (Is it Akari?) The camera follows the girl as she stands up, so the shadows of the area where she was sitting are very strong. The area visible when she stands is bright, so the background artwork could be pulled vertically to create the illusion of time passing.

CUT_012 is the background of the title card for Act 2, "Cosmonaut." The plants in the foreground are animation elements. The clouds were drawn on a separate layer, which slide across the sky to create a sense of wind blowing.

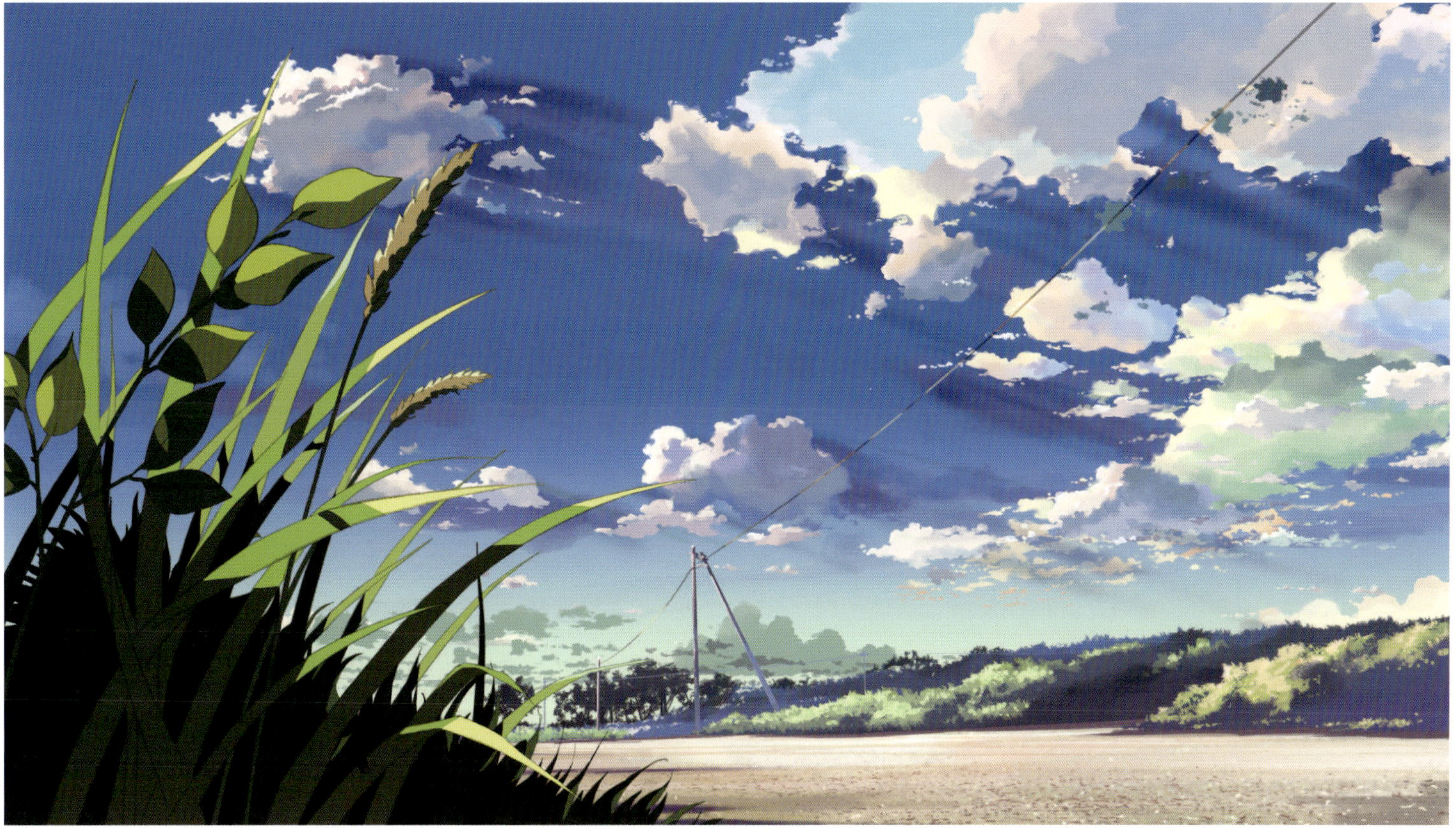

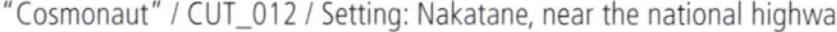

"Cosmonaut" / CUT_012 / Setting: Nakatane, near the national highway

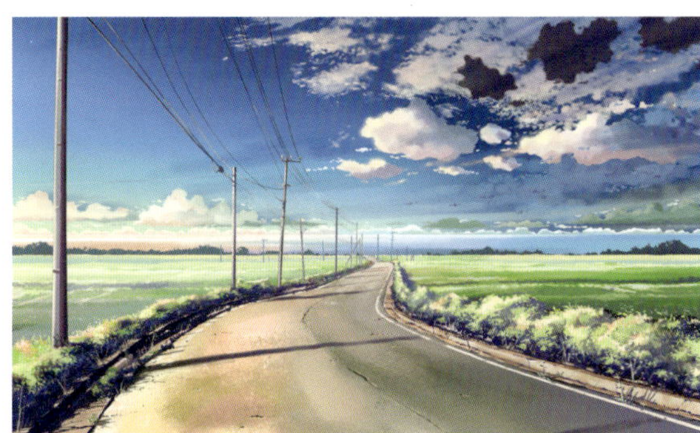

"Cosmonaut" / CUT_013 / Setting: Nakatane, near the national highway

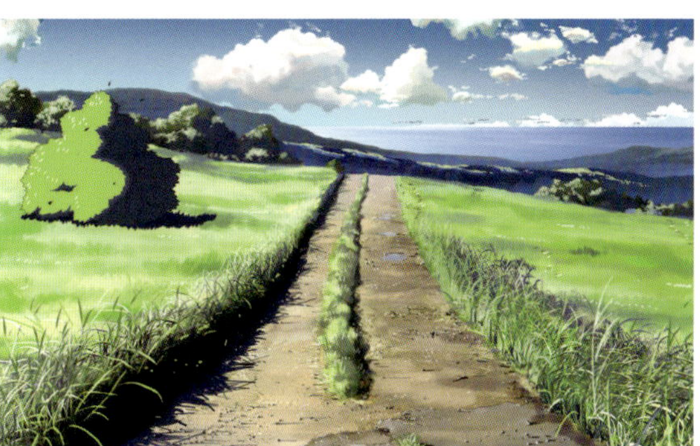

"Cosmonaut" / CUT_175 / Setting: Nakatane, on a back road

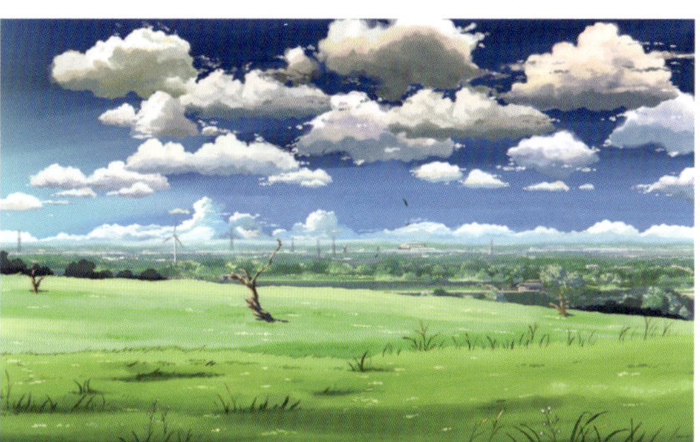

"Cosmonaut" / CUT_178 / Setting: Plateau in Nakatane

Act 2 : "Cosmonaut"

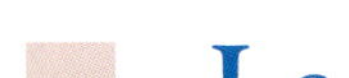

Island Life

Before creating the storyboard for the part of the tale that takes place on Tanegashima, Mr. Shinkai went to the island himself to go location hunting. The kids commuting to school on Super Cub scooters, the surfing club, the Sumidas' dog in the tub were all references to location photos that were incorporated into the story. According to Mr. Shinkai, in order to accentuate the scenery of the southern island, extra care was taken when drawing the greenery. Nakatane High School, a prefectural school in Kagoshima in which much of the action takes place, merged with Minamitane High School in 2008 and is currently called Tanegashima Central High School.

Kanae: (*monologue*) When I get near Tono, I get this tight sensation deep in my chest...

Kanae: (*off screen*) Tono!

Takaki: Sumida? What's up? How'd you know I was here?

Kanae: Heh heh. I saw your scooter, so I stopped by. Is that okay?

Takaki: Yeah. I'm glad you came by. I mean, since we couldn't meet in the parking lot like we usually do.

Kanae: Yeah!

Kanae: (*monologue*) He's so nice. Sometimes it makes me want to cry...

Kanae: (*off screen*) Hey, Tono, are you taking college entrance exams?

Takaki: Yeah, a college in Tokyo.

Kanae: Tokyo? Really... I kinda thought so.

Takaki: Why's that?

Kanae: You just kinda seem like you want go somewhere far away, for some reason.

Takaki: (*sighs softly*) ...How about you, Sumida?

Kanae: Hmm. I don't even know what I'll do tomorrow.

Takaki: Maybe nobody does.

Kanae: Really? Even you?

Takaki: Naturally.

Kanae: But you seem to know exactly what you're doing.

Takaki: That's weird because I don't really. I'm sorta lost all the time. I just do what I can... that's all I can do.

Kanae: Really...? Yeah, you're right.

SFX: *rustle rustle* (*sounds of paper being folded*)

Takaki: Making a plane?

Kanae: Yeah.

(Excerpt of *5 Centimeters per Second*, Act 2: "Cosmonaut")

The road home just after the sun has set; the place where Kanae found Takaki's scooter on the way back from school; finally the plateau Kanae climbs to find Takaki. The progression of the sky from CUT_129 to CUT_130 to CUT_137 shows the transformation from twilight to nighttime.

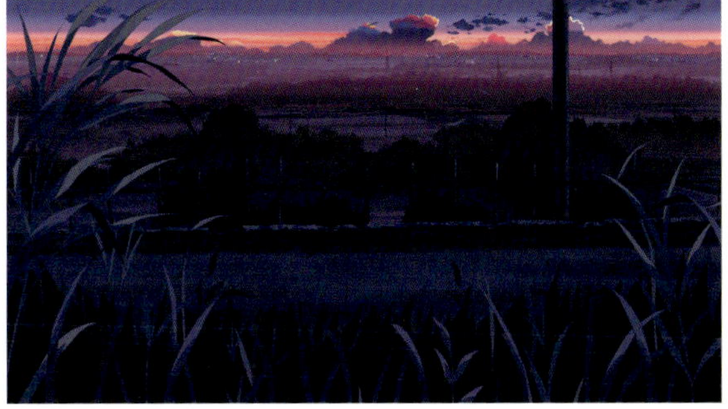

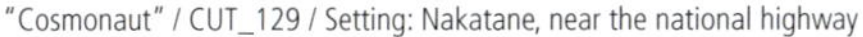

"Cosmonaut" / CUT_129 / Setting: Nakatane, near the national highway

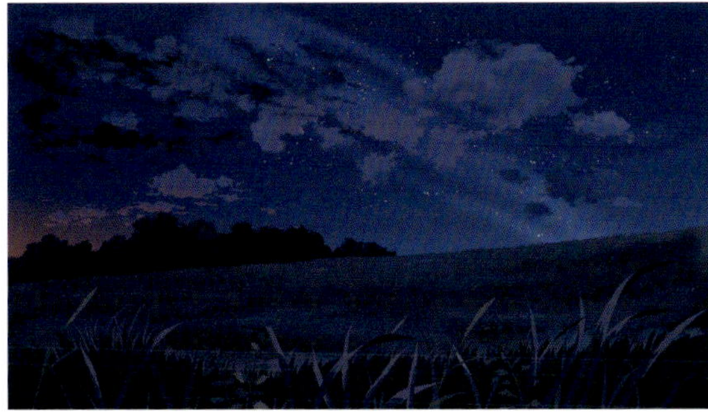

"Cosmonaut" / CUT_130 / Setting: Plateau in Nakatane

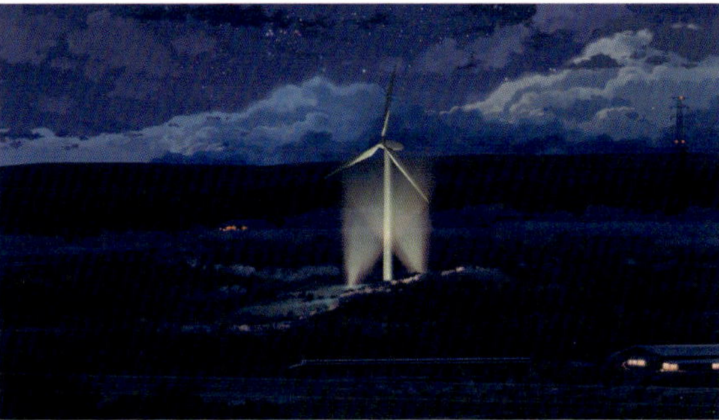

"Cosmonaut" / CUT_137 / Setting: Nakatane, Taiyonosato

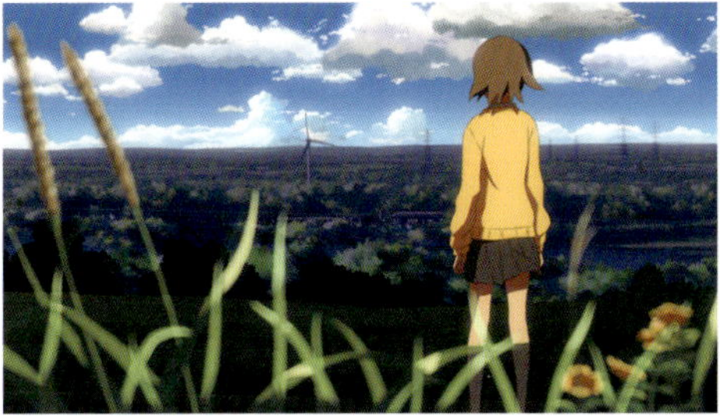

CUT_177 Final Version

Kanae looking down at Taiyonosato in the early morning from the plateau where she speaks with Takaki. The windmills are 3DCG elements, and in order to create a shallow depth of field effect with Kanae in focus, the foreground plants (animated), middle and far backgrounds were all placed on separate layers and given a blur effect. The shadows cast on the ground by passing clouds were created by sliding the shadow colors and making the background art transparent.

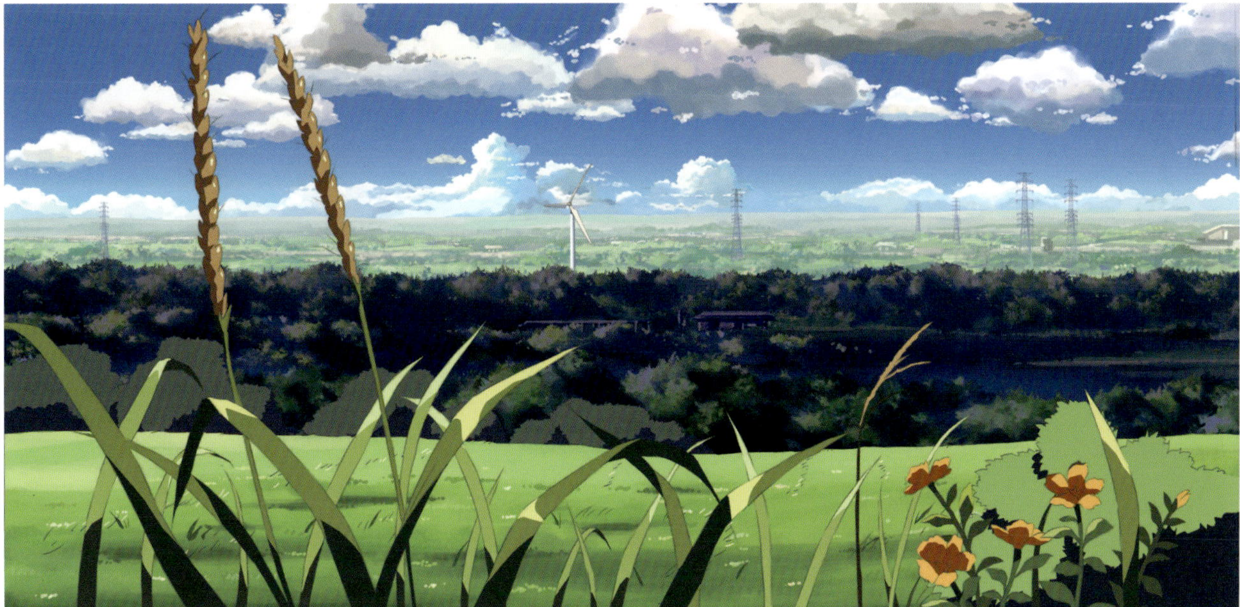

"Cosmonaut" / CUT_177 / Setting: Plateau in Nakatane

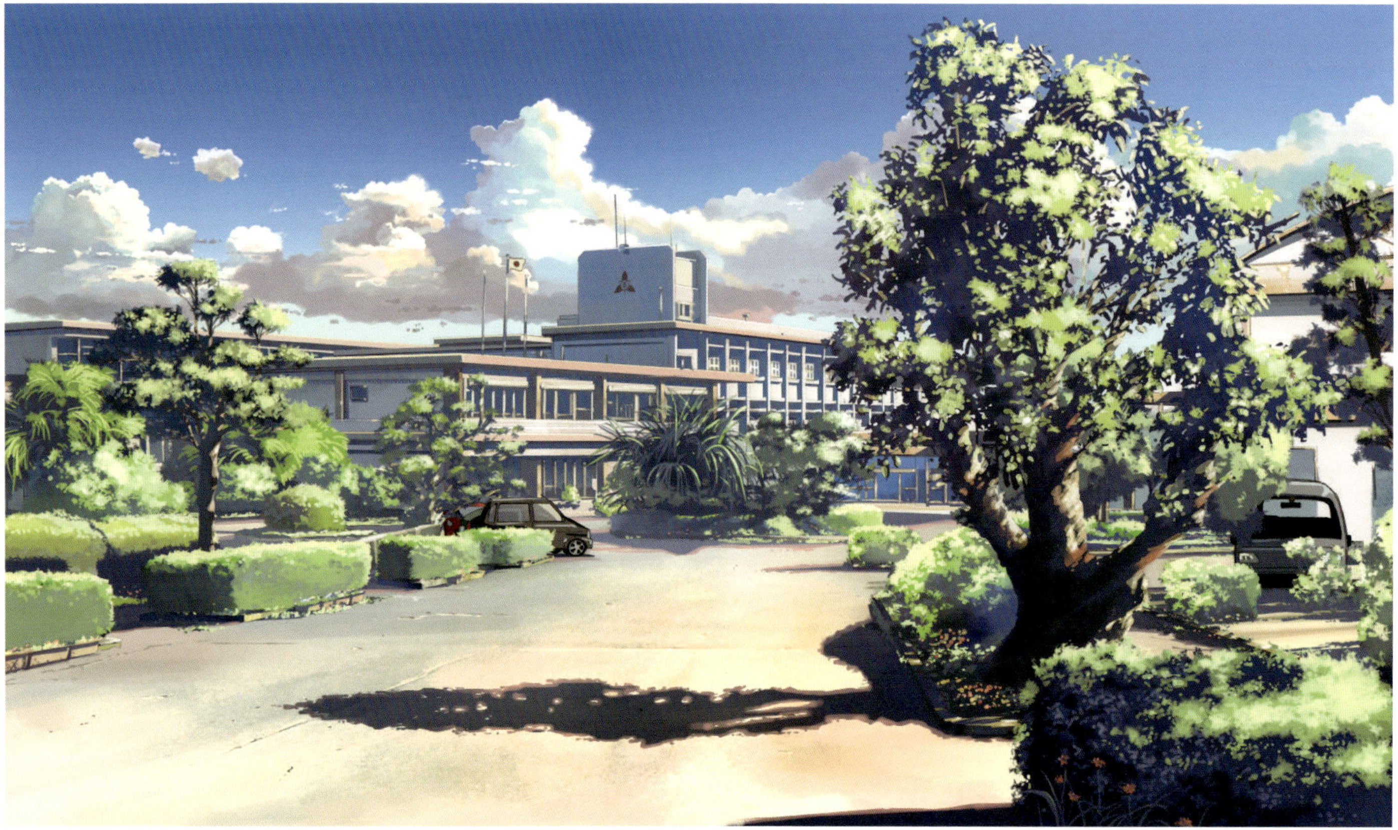

Panorama of Kanae and Takaki's school, Nakatane High. The rounded clouds give off a summery feel.

"Cosmonaut" / CUT_016 / Setting: Nakatane High School main entrance

With the school's cooperation, the whole interior of the school was photographed and put to effective use in creating the film. The photos of rockets as shown in CUT_033 were very interesting.

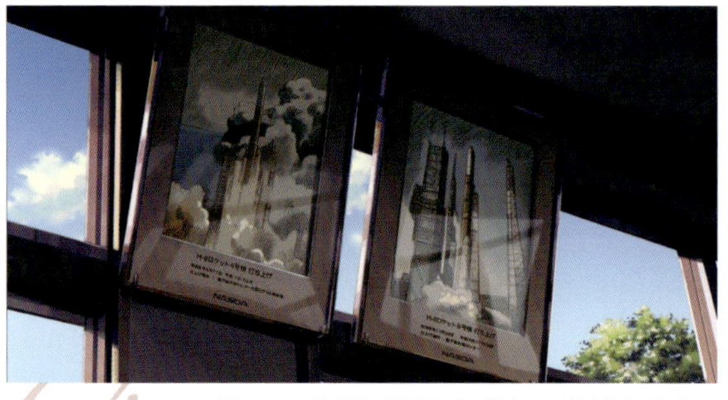

"Cosmonaut" / CUT_033 / Setting: Nakatane High School hallway

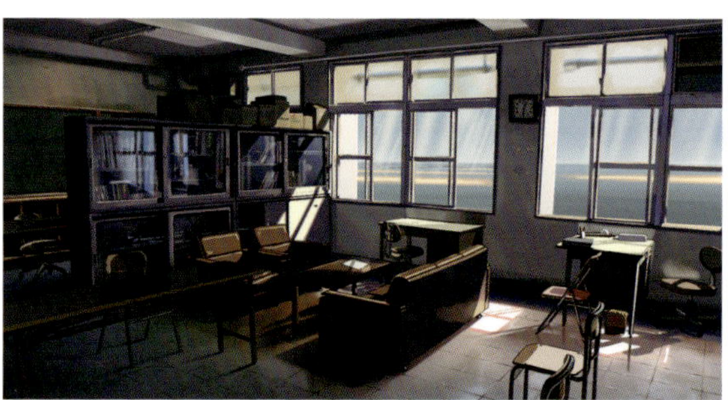

"Cosmonaut" / CUT_105 / Setting: Nakatane High School guidance counseling room.

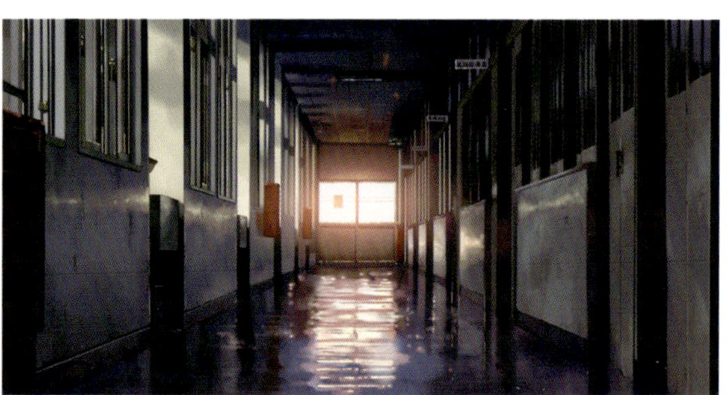

"Cosmonaut" / CUT_107 / Setting: Nakatane High School hallway

The red flowers in the flower bed in the parking lot give a hint of southern color to the scenery. The minivan that Kanae's sister drives (a Honda Stepwgn RF1/2) is a harmony cel drawn by the background artists. The minivan is based on the one driven by the coach of Nakatane High School's surfing club.

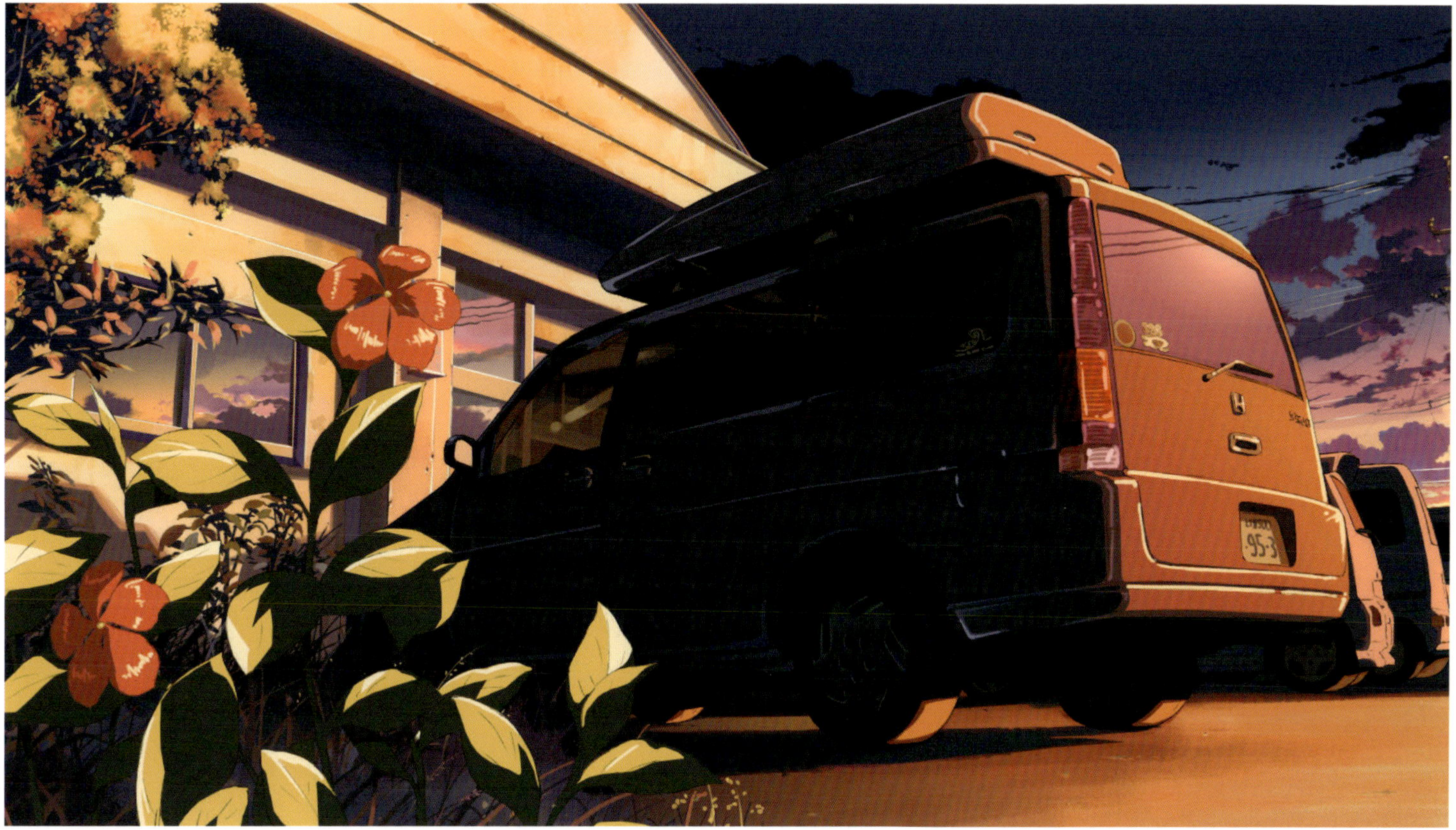

"Cosmonaut" / CUT_048 / Setting: Nakatane High School teachers' parking lot

"Cosmonaut" / CUT_076 / Setting: Nakatane High School water fountains

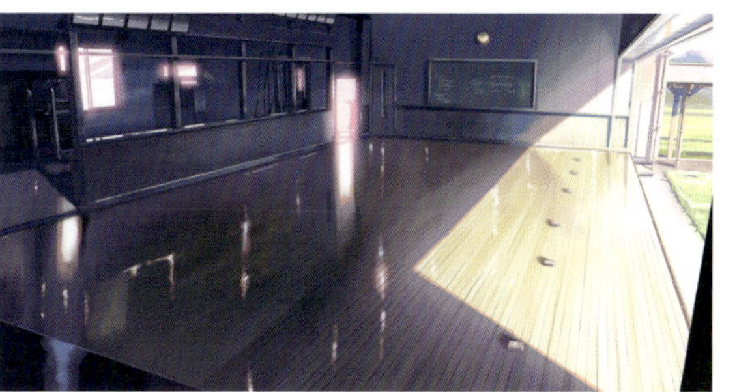

"Cosmonaut" / CUT_011 / Setting: Nakatane High School archery hall

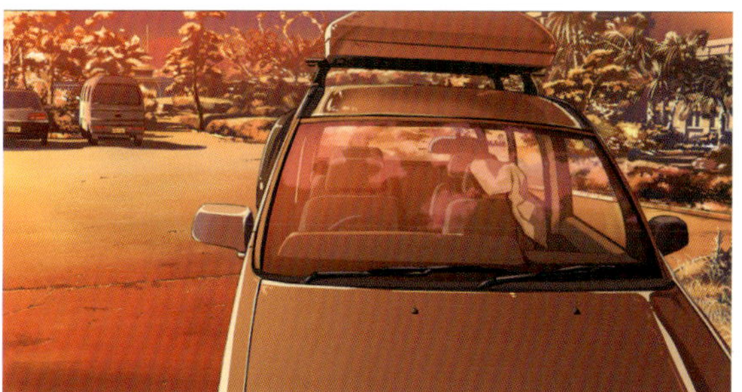

"Cosmonaut" / CUT_049 / Setting: Nakatane High School teachers' parking lot

The bicycle parking lot where Kanae always waits for Takaki. This makes frequent appearances in the film. CUT_057 and CUT_218 use the same base sketch, but when finished depict different times of day. Similarly, there are several iterations of CUT_215 showing the same angle.

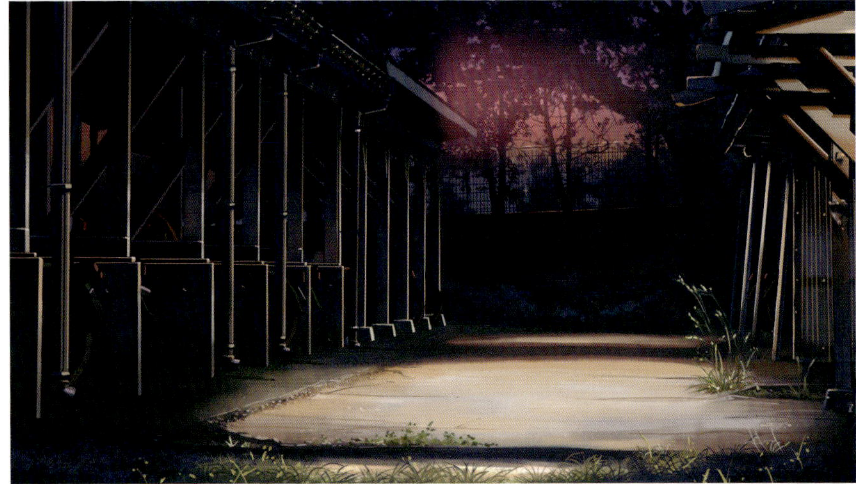

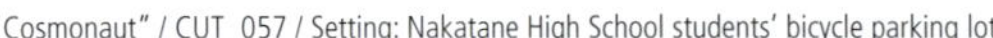

"Cosmonaut" / CUT_057 / Setting: Nakatane High School students' bicycle parking lot

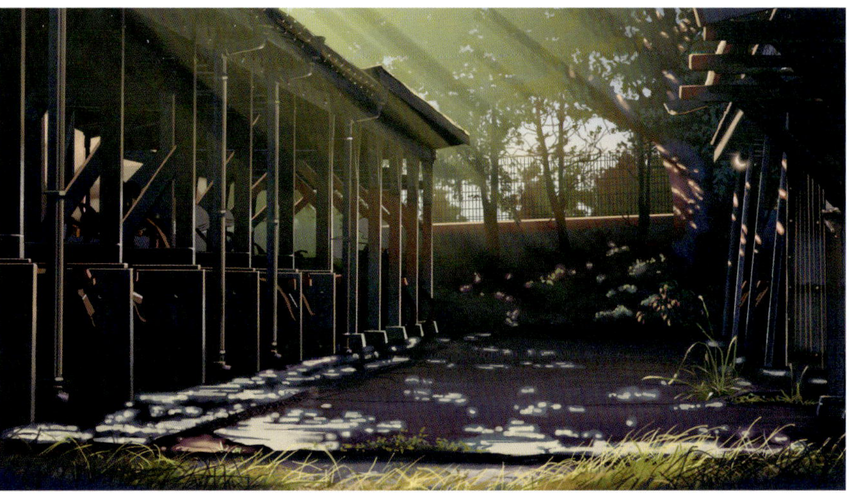

"Cosmonaut" / CUT_218 / Setting: Nakatane High School students' bicycle parking lot

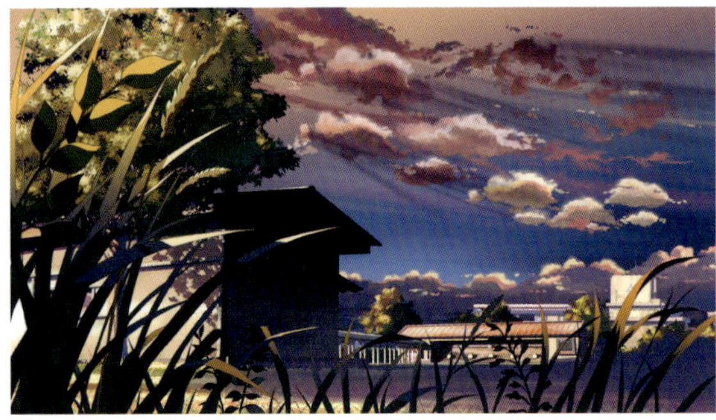

"Cosmonaut" / CUT_042 / Setting: Nakatane High School courtyard

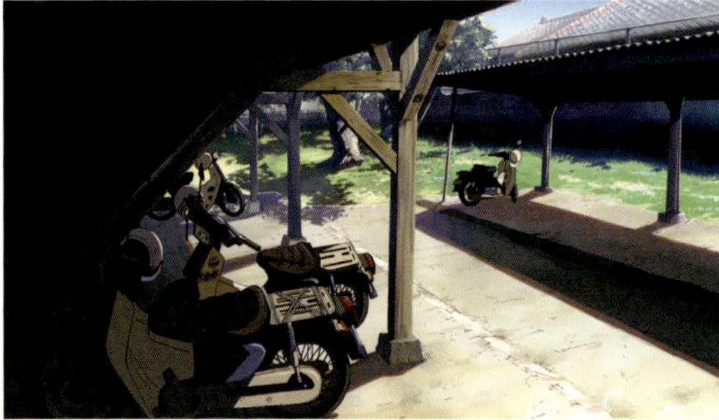

"Cosmonaut" / CUT_018 / Setting: Nakatane High School students' bicycle parking lot

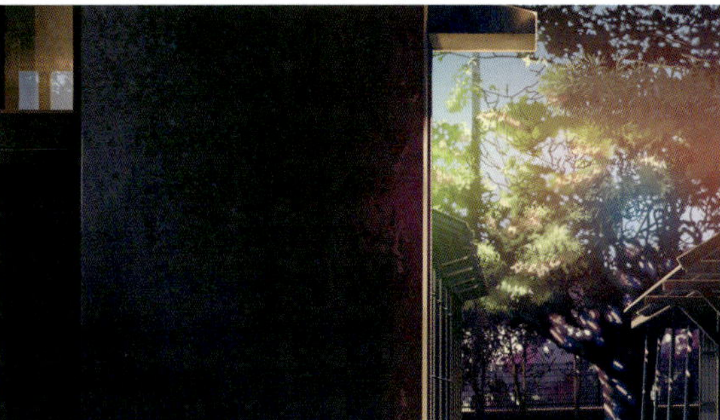

"Cosmonaut" / CUT_215 / Setting: Nakatane High School students' bicycle parking lot

The bicycle parking lot at sunset. Drawings were based on location photos. A flare effect was brushed onto CUT_051, and CUT_052 was treated with a filter.

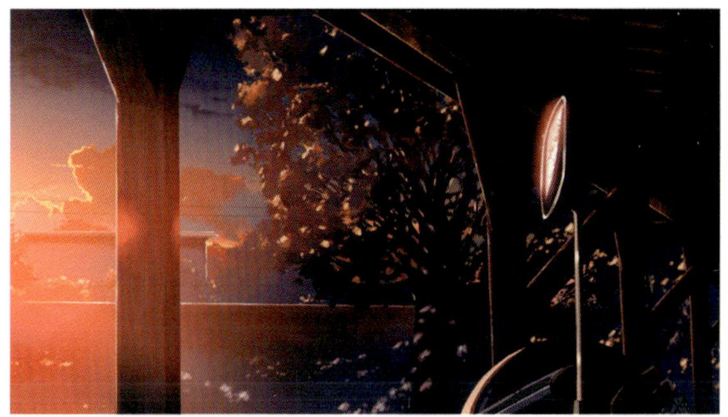

"Cosmonaut" / CUT_051 / Setting: Nakatane High School students' bicycle parking lot

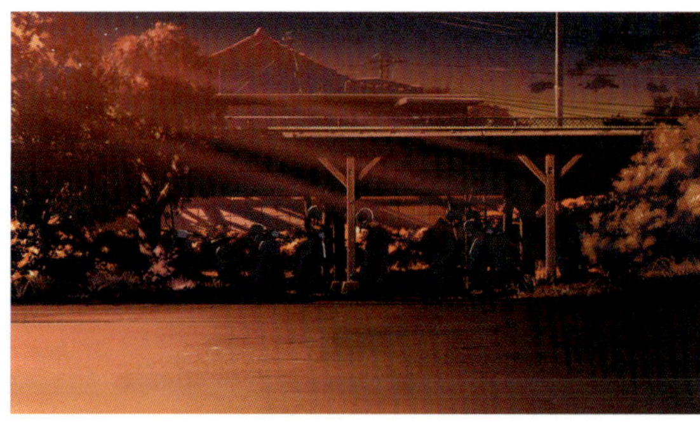

"Cosmonaut" / CUT_052 / Setting: Nakatane High School students' bicycle parking lot

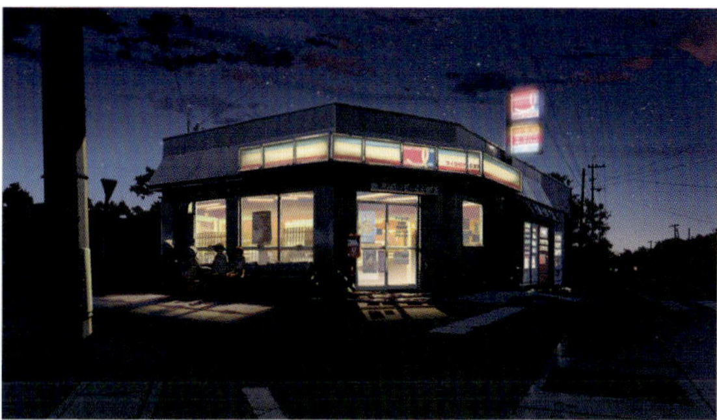

"Cosmonaut" / CUT_093 / Setting: Convenience store

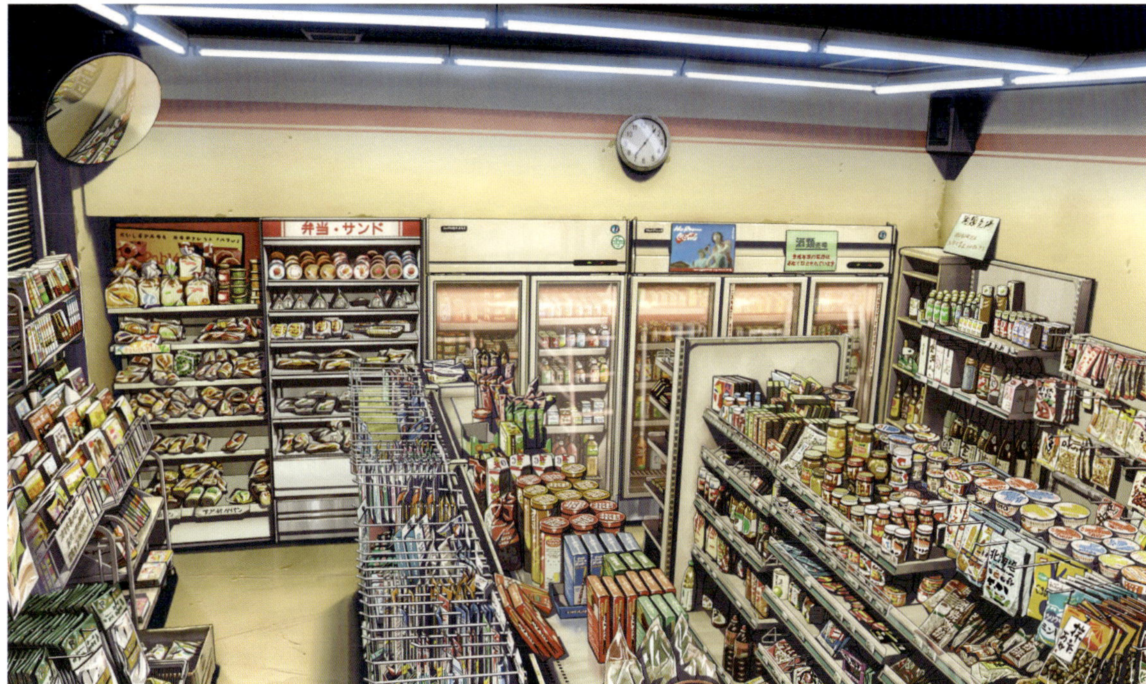

"Cosmonaut" / CUT_080 / Setting: Convenience store interior

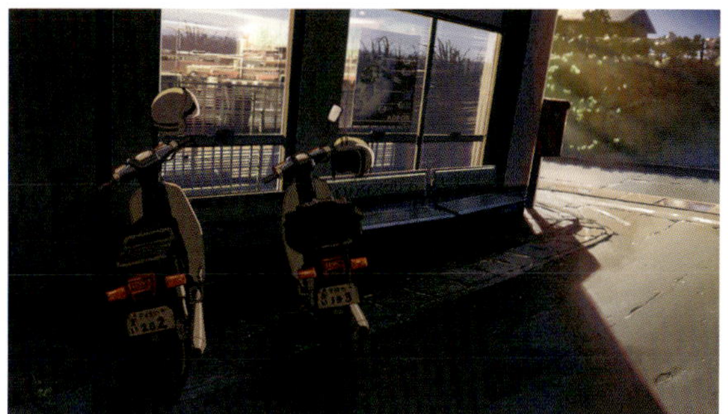

"Cosmonaut" / CUT_237 / Setting: Convenience store parking lot

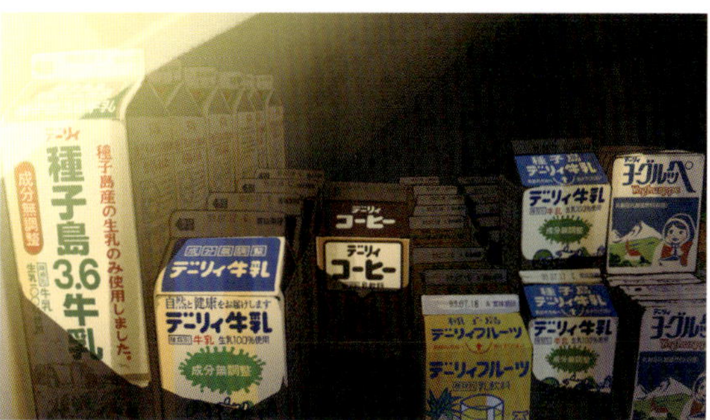

"Cosmonaut" / CUT_081 / Setting: Convenience store refrigerator

The 200 ml yogurt that Kanae always chooses and the 300 ml coffee that Takaki buys are based on actual products.
("Tanegashima Coffee" is now consolidated under the brand "Daily Coffee.")

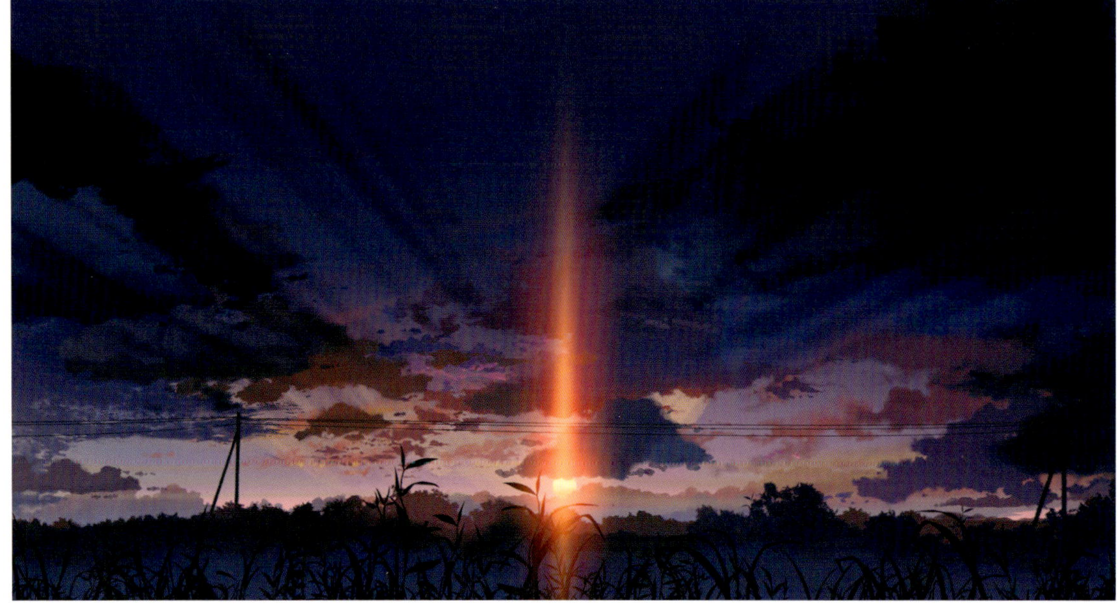

"Cosmonaut" / CUT_059 / Setting: Nakatane, near the national highway

Background artwork for the scene where Kanae and Takaki ride along the highway on their scooters after school. The sky in the far background doesn't move, the foreground elements are separated into two layers which slide at different speeds, and lighting effects were added to create the final version.

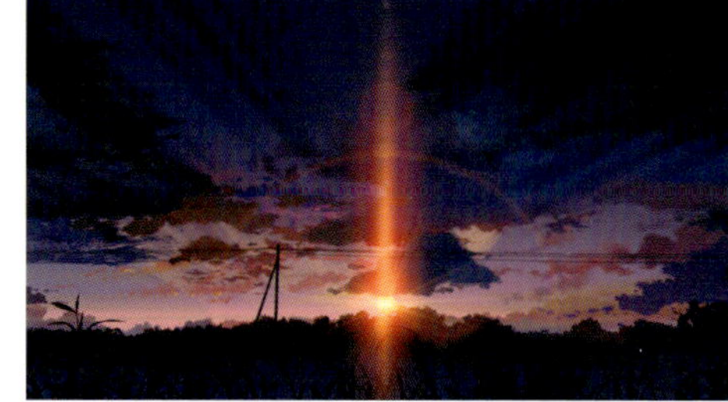

CUT_059 Final Version

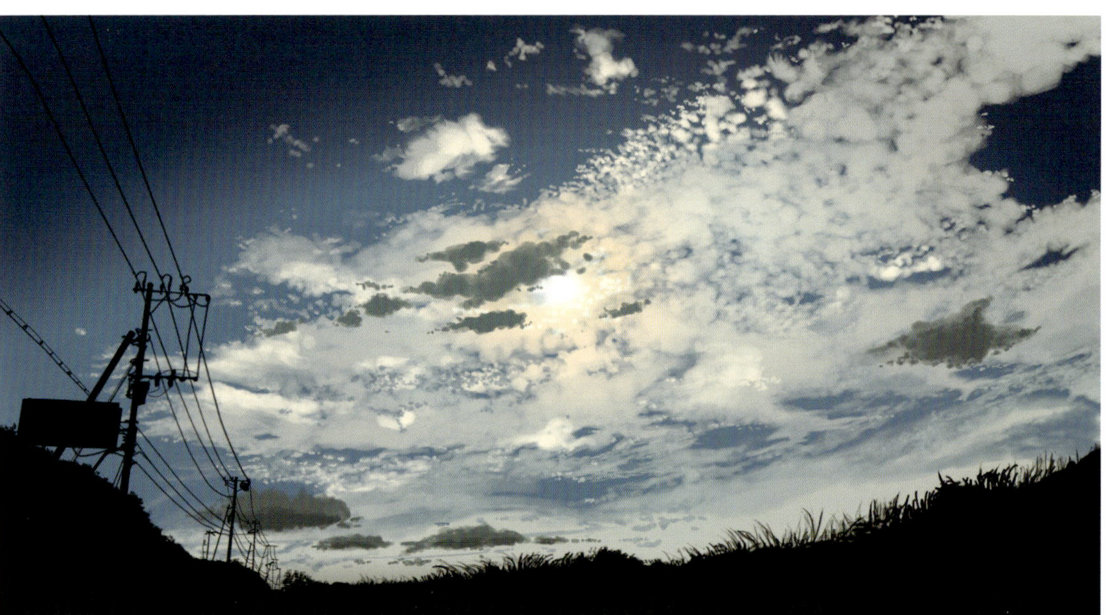

"Cosmonaut" / CUT_193 / Setting: Nakatane, near the national highway

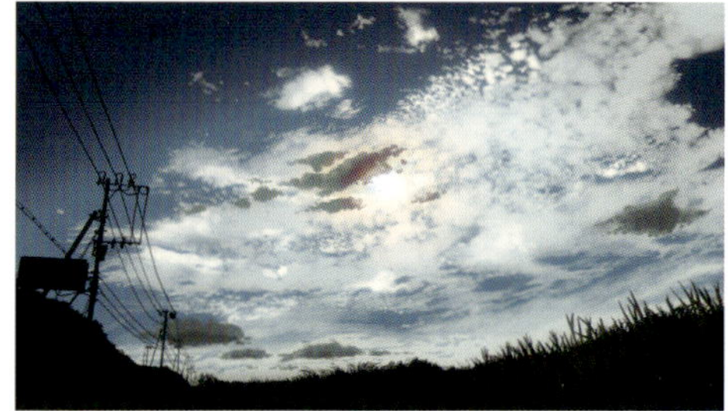

CUT_193 Final Version

This setting is the same as CUT_267, where Kanae and Takaki witness the launch of an H-IIA rocket. The shapes of the clouds suggest the approach of autumn.

Central district of Nakatane. Towering thunderclouds of midsummer lurk in the distance. Keeping in mind that it would rain in the evening, the cloudy sky was painted with grayish tones.

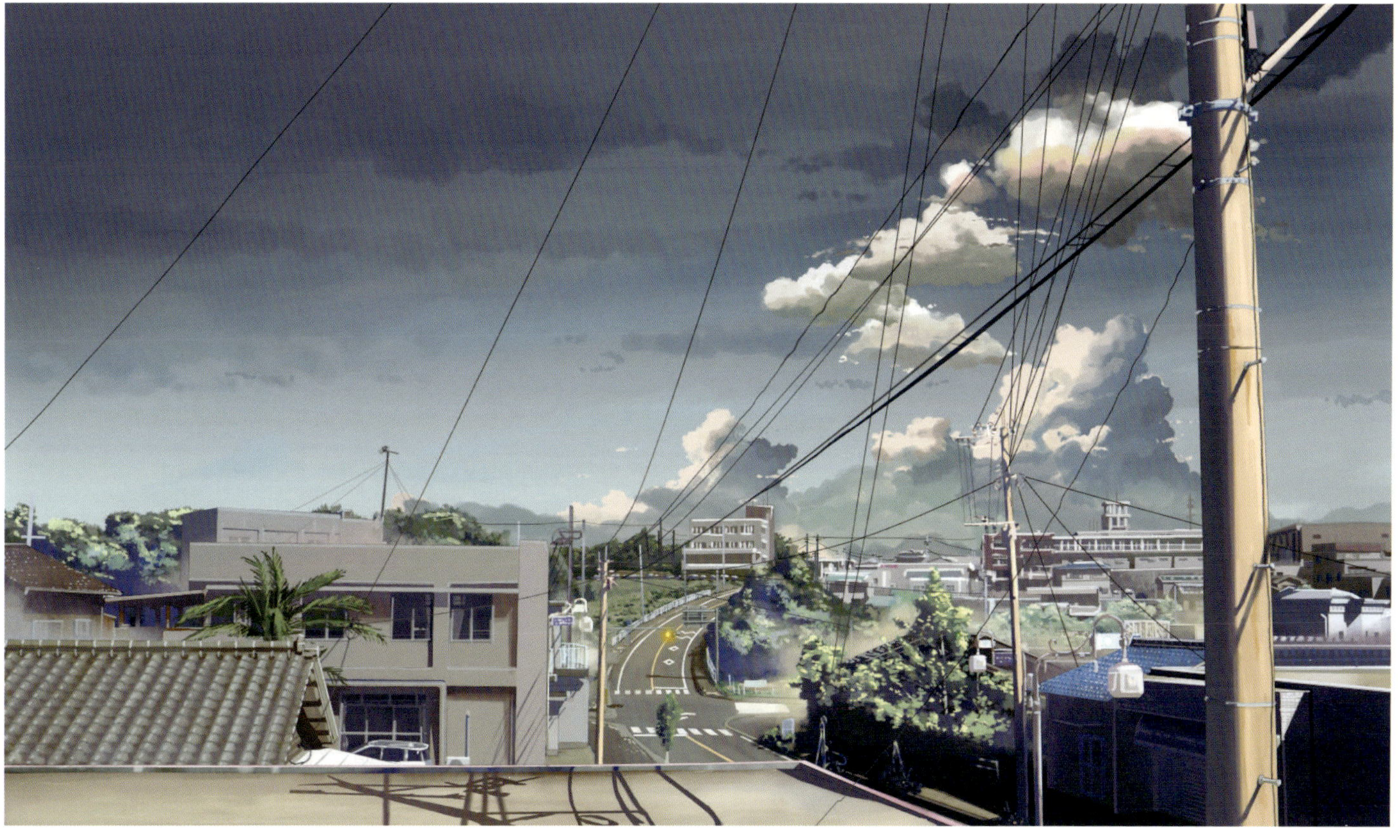

The sunset created by the staff for CUT_245 didn't appear subtropical enough, so Takumi Tanji sent Mr. Shinkai a number of revisions until the final result was achieved.

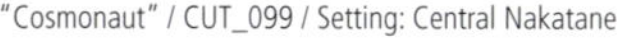

"Cosmonaut" / CUT_099 / Setting: Central Nakatane

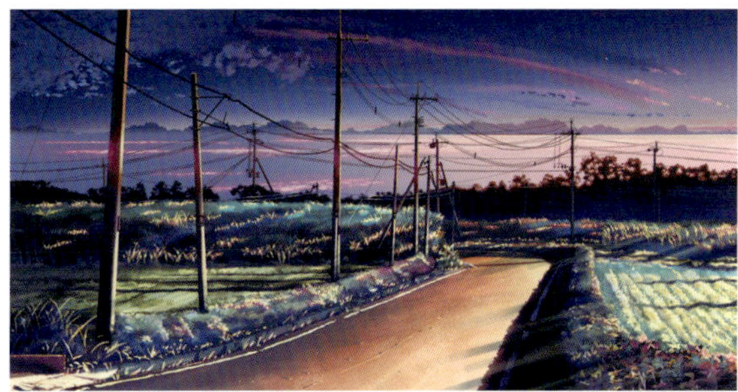

"Cosmonaut" / CUT_245 / Setting: Nakatane, near the national highway

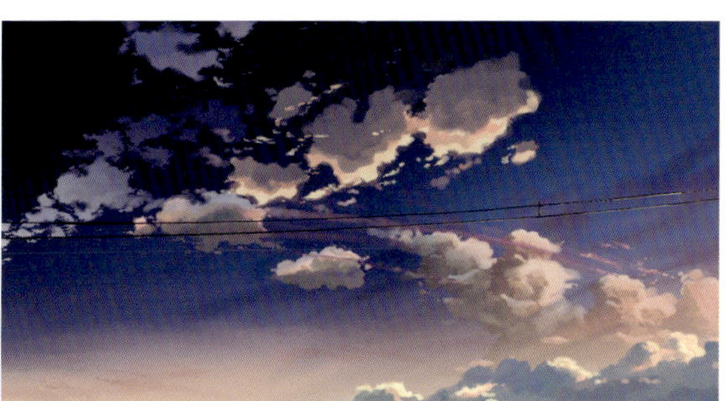

"Cosmonaut" / CUT_252 / Setting: Skies above Nakatane, near the national highway

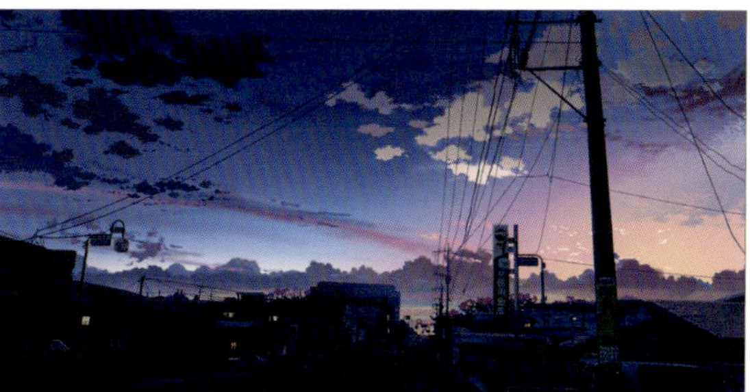

"Cosmonaut" / CUT_261 / Setting: Central Nakatane

Kanae: (*monologue*) After that day, several typhoons passed by the island, and each time they did, it became cooler.

The wind that blows across the sugarcane field got crisper.

The sky looked a little bigger, and the outlines of the clouds grew softer.

The kids in my grade who ride scooters started wearing their jackets.

Then, on a mid-October day tinged with the remains of summer, I rode a wave for the first time in six months.

(Excerpt of 5 *Centimeters per Second*, Act 2: "Cosmonaut")

Act 2 : "Cosmonaut"

A Girl's Ocean

The place where the surfing club practices in the film is mainly based on Nakayama Beach in Noma, Nakatane, which faces the Pacific Ocean. It's a popular spot among surfing enthusiasts, but as the waves there are high, regular swimming is prohibited. This is in fact one of the practice locations used by the Nakatane High School surfing club (but they don't use one particular beach; depending on the conditions of the ocean they also practice on other beaches all over the island). The contrast between Takaki burying himself in solitude as Kanae confronts a scene of abundant nature makes quite an impression. The clouds have far more dynamic movement in the skies above the vast expanse of the ocean.

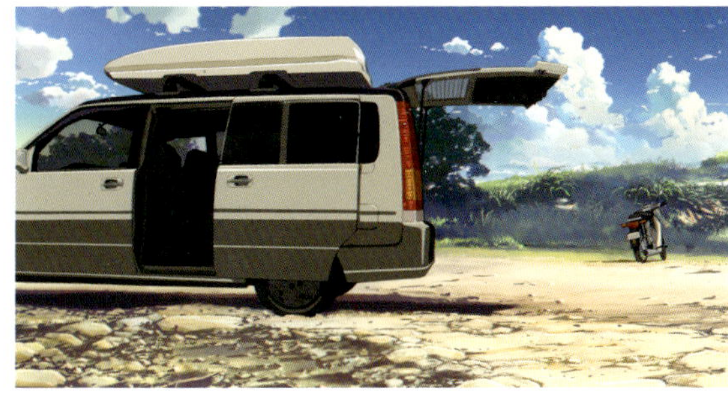

"Cosmonaut" / CUT_184 / Setting: A beach in Nakatane

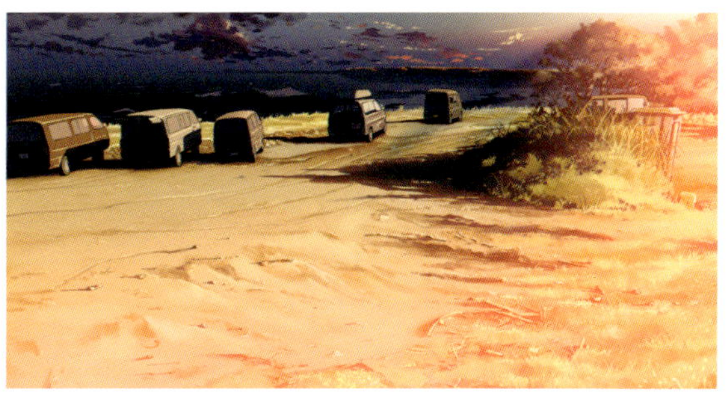

"Cosmonaut" / CUT_035 / Setting: A beach in Nakatane

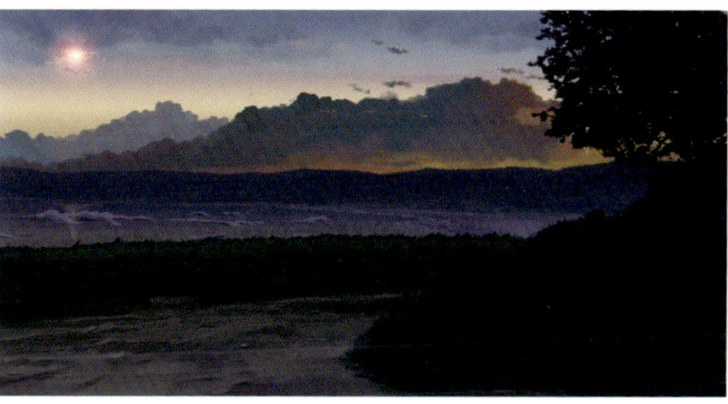

"Cosmonaut" / CUT_118 / Setting: A beach in Nakatane

Early-morning beach. Animation of moving clouds and rolling waves was added. The clouds were drawn on several layers which moved at subtly different speeds to create a sense of wide-open space.

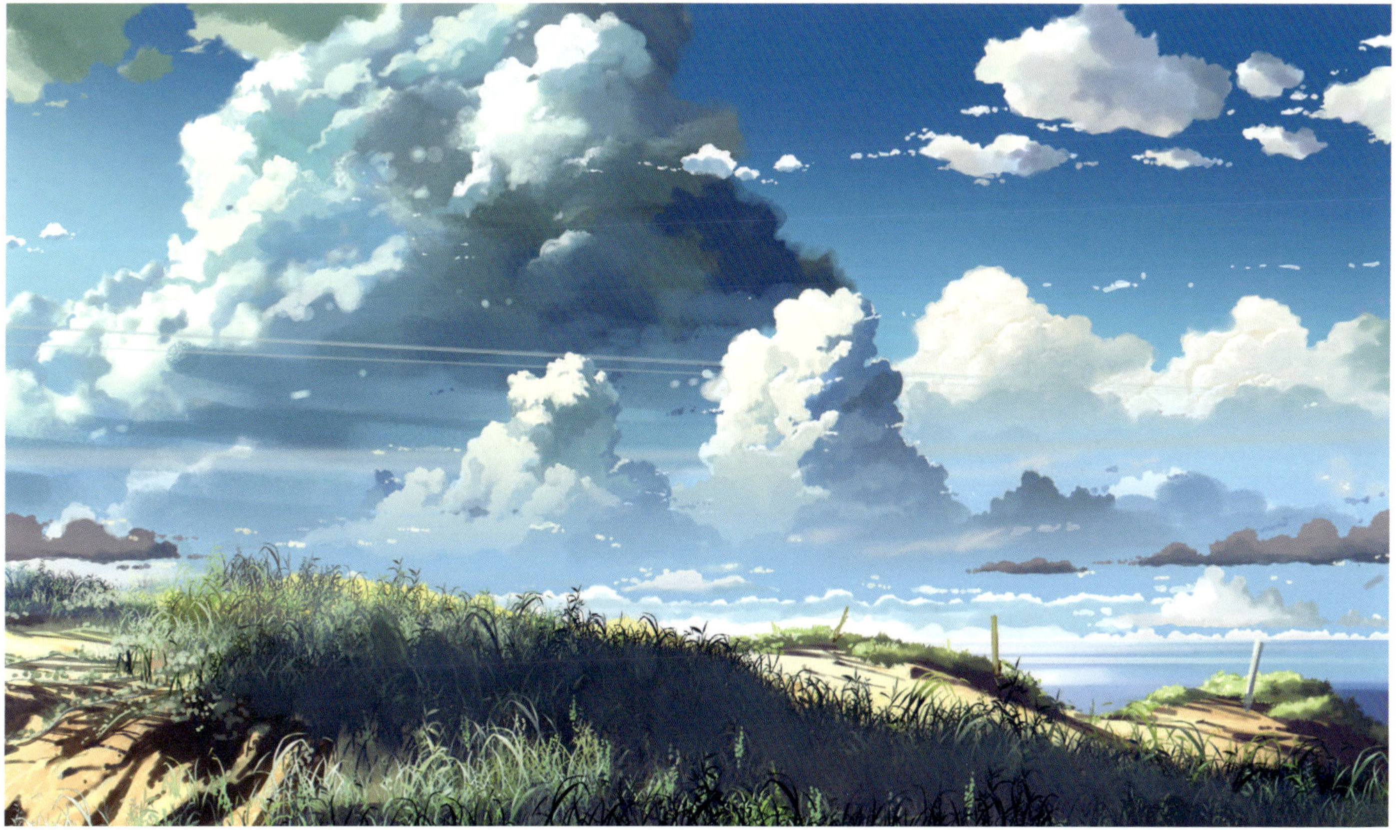

"Cosmonaut" / CUT_182 / Setting: A beach in Nakatane

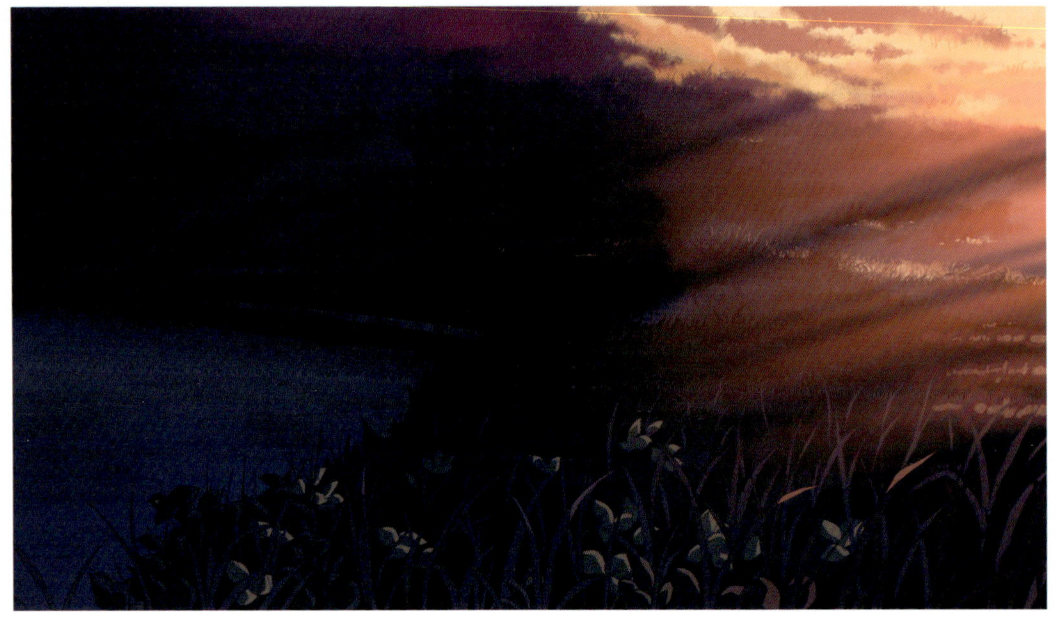

A hill by a parking lot overlooking the beach. A different angle was used for this view as well.

"Cosmonaut" / CUT_036 / Setting: A beach in Nakatane

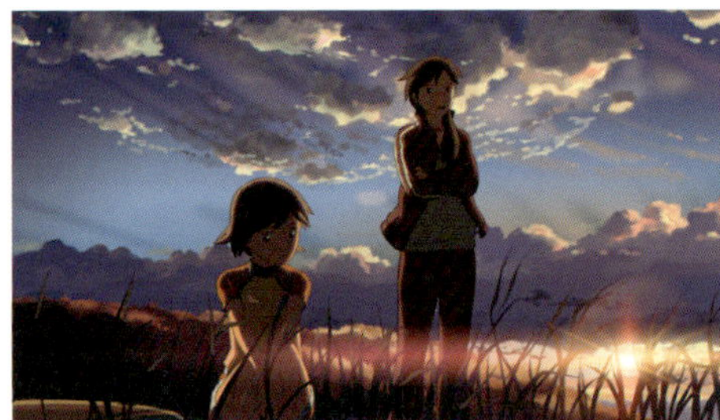

CUT_039 Final Version

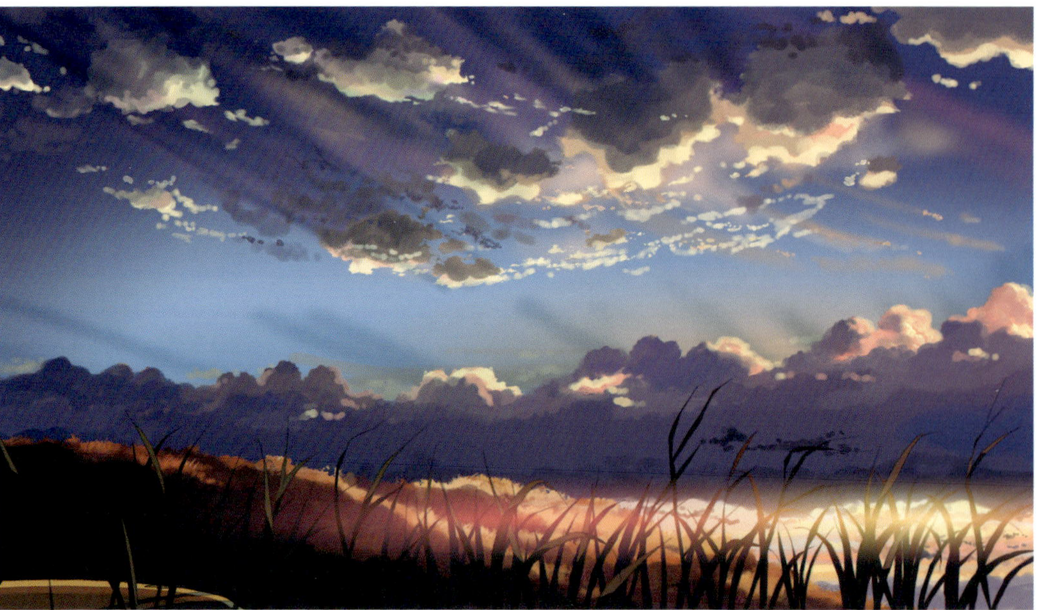

Background artwork for the cut showing Kanae talking with her older sister. The final version included animation elements of grasses in the foreground plus Kanae and her sister, and a backlit lighting effect from the setting sun was added using video software.

"Cosmonaut" / CUT_039 / Setting: A beach in Nakatane

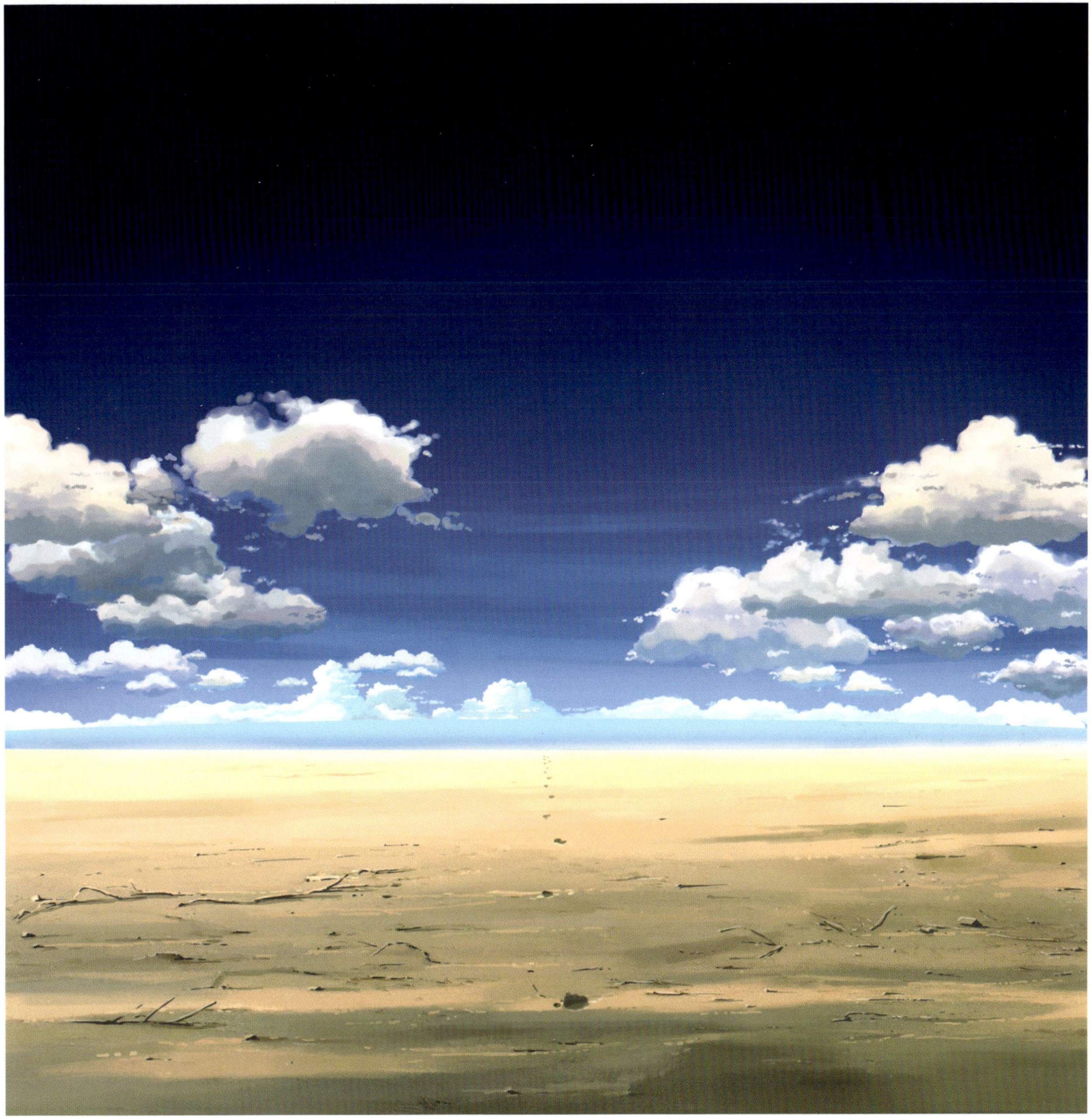

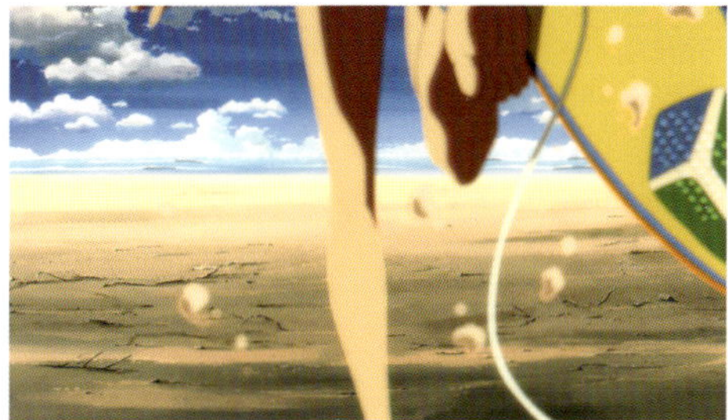

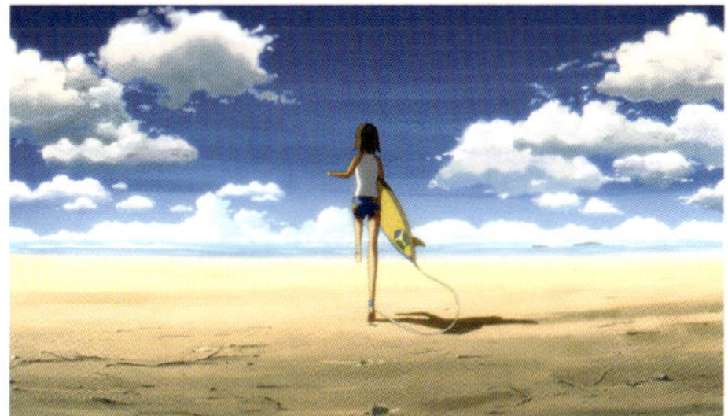

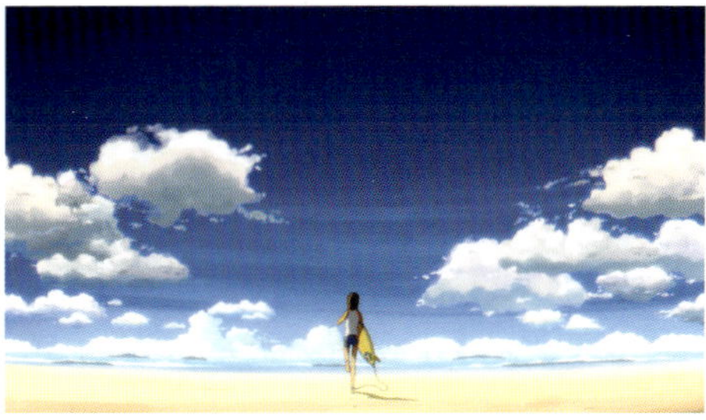

CUT_190 Final Version

This is the most memorable scene that highlights Kanae's character. In order to allow a pan upwards from Kanae's feet as she runs, the background art had to be vertically long. The visual effect of a wide-angle lens was added using video software for the final version to create a dynamic scene.

"Cosmonaut" / CUT_190 / Setting: A beach in Nakatane

Act 2 : "Cosmonaut"

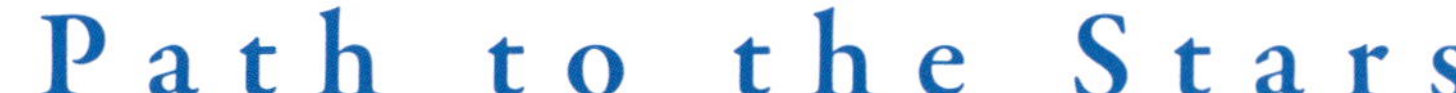

Path to the Stars

The climactic scene of Act 2, "Cosmonaut," depicts the launch of an H-IIA rocket from Tanegashima Space Center. Kanae and Takaki happen to see it on their usual route home from school. The addition of an unusual major event to what had become a familiar, everyday scene strengthens the story of Kanae's unrequited love. The rocket's stream of exhaust was drawn by the animators, and in order to represent the decay of the burst of light from the ignition, several versions of the background showing varying levels of brightness in the sky were created.

Kanae: (*monologue*) Desperately, reaching recklessly towards the sky, launching that massive object in search of something almost overwhelmingly far in the distance...

I began to understand why Tono seemed different from the others.

At the same time, I came to a very clear realization that Tono was never looking at me...

So that day I didn't say anything to Tono.

Tono is certainly nice, very nice indeed.

But, Tono's always looking past me... at something far beyond.

I guess my wishes to be with Tono will never come true.

But I still... But I still won't be able to stop loving him.

Not today, not tomorrow, not ever...

I fell asleep that night crying.

The only thoughts in my head being of Tono...

(Excerpt of *5 Centimeters per Second*, Act 2: "Cosmonaut")

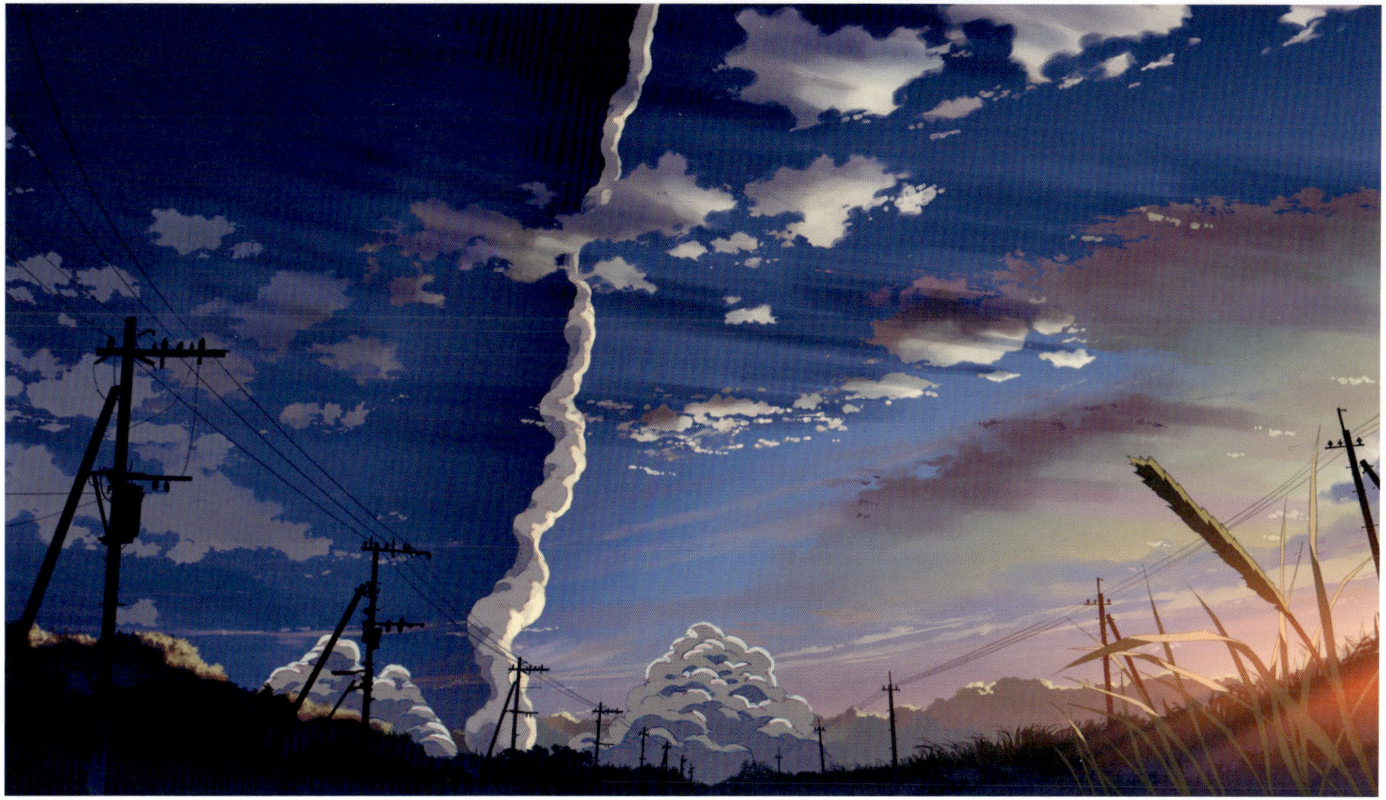

"Cosmonaut" / CUT_267 / Setting: Nakatane, near the national highway

The sky after the launch. The setting is the same as CUT_193 as shown on page 68. It's not possible to see a rocket launch from the actual location, so artistic license was used to show the launch scene. CUT_273 shows the same angle, but as several minutes have passed since CUT_267, the sun has sunk further towards the horizon.

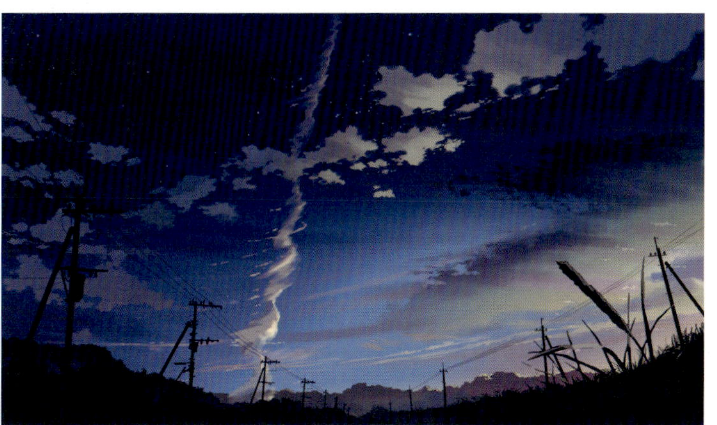

"Cosmonaut" / CUT_273 / Setting: Nakatane, near the national highway

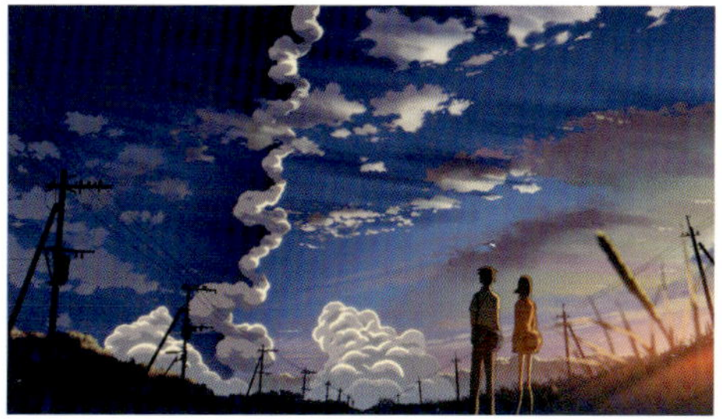

CUT_267 Final Version

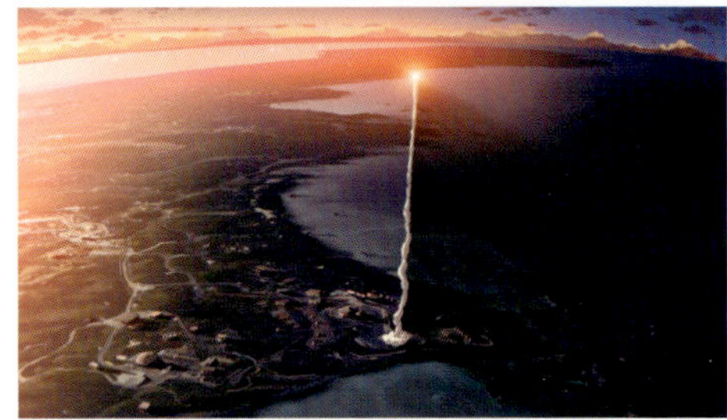

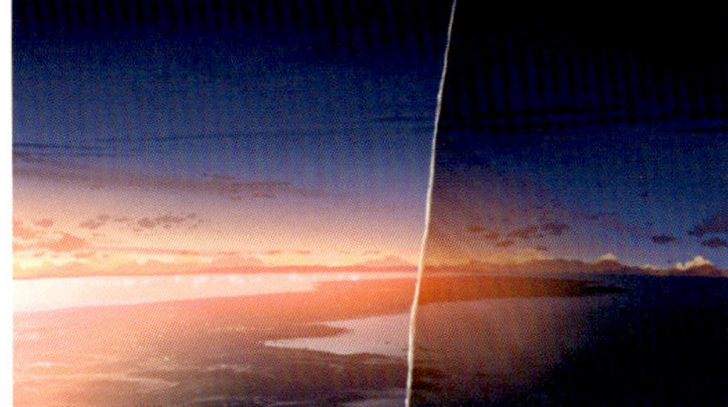

CUT_265 Final Version

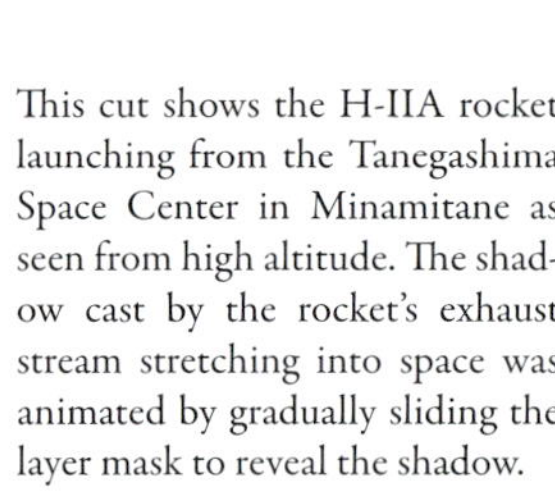

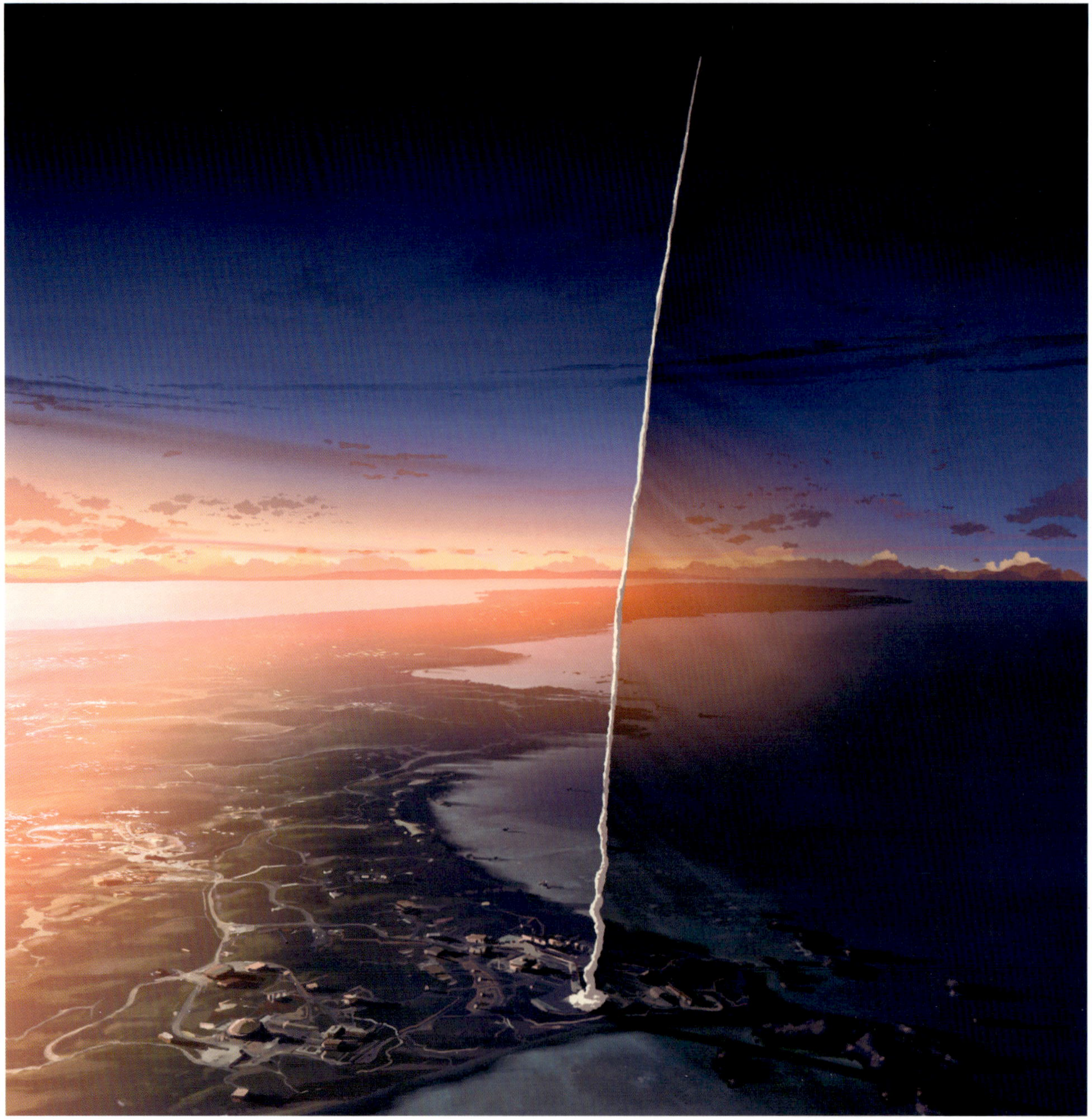

This cut shows the H-IIA rocket launching from the Tanegashima Space Center in Minamitane as seen from high altitude. The shadow cast by the rocket's exhaust stream stretching into space was animated by gradually sliding the layer mask to reveal the shadow.

"Cosmonaut" / CUT_265 / The skies above Minamitane

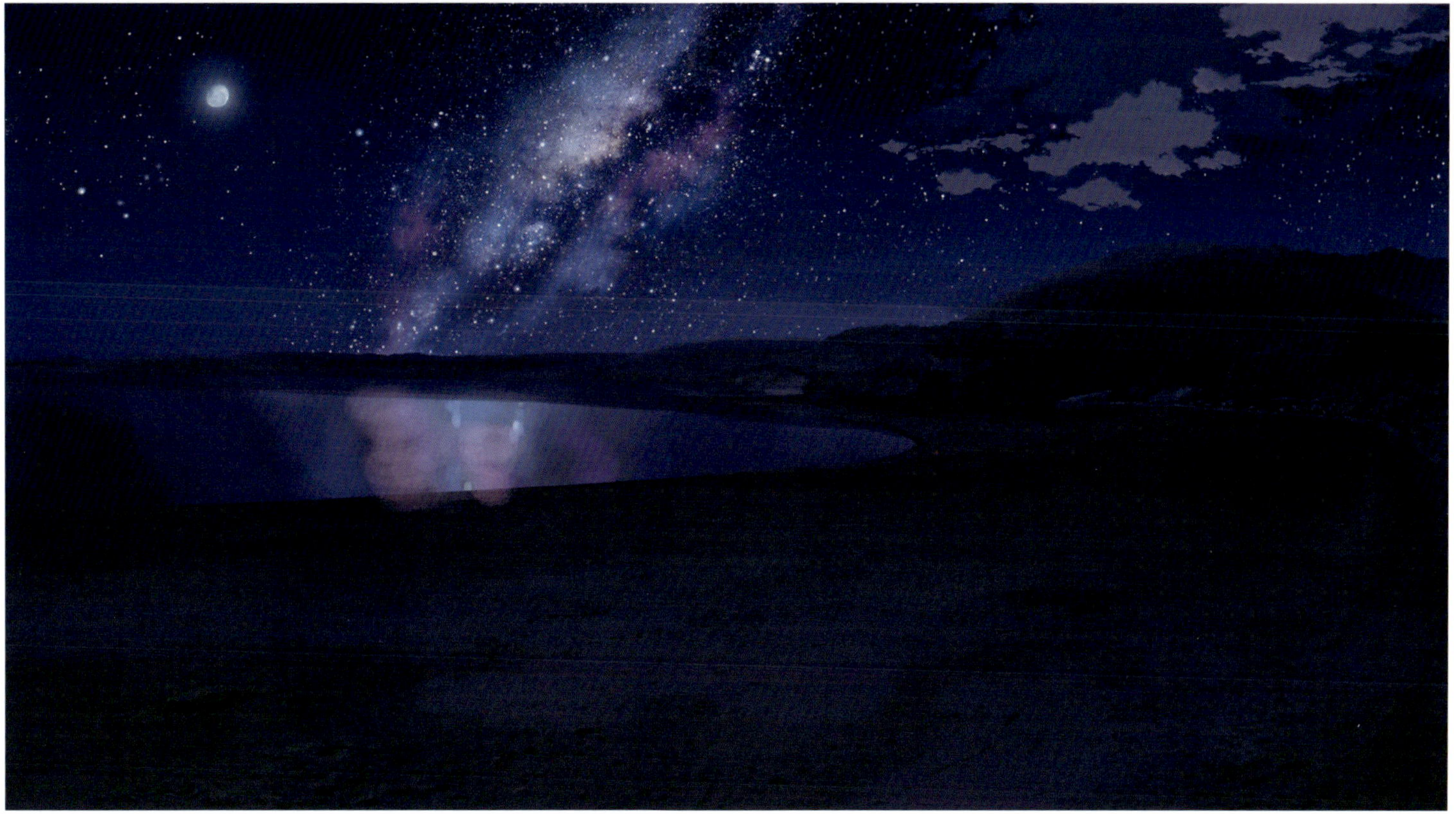

"Cosmonaut" / CUT_292 / Setting: A beach in Nakatane

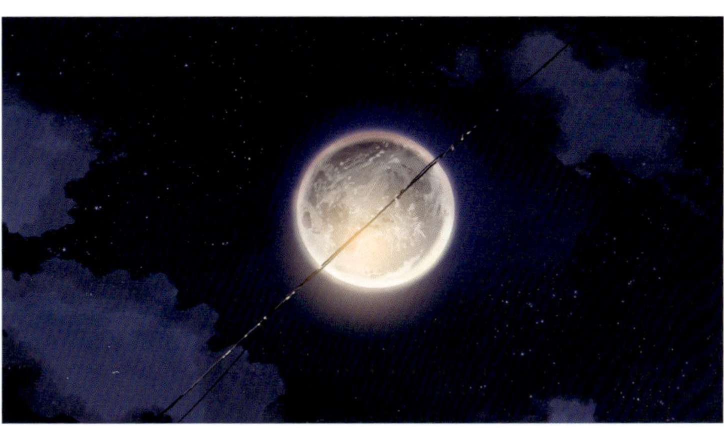

"Cosmonaut" / CUT_278 / Setting: The sky near the Sumida household in Nakatane

Takaki: (*monologue*) For the past few years, I've wanted to move on, to grasp onto something beyond my reach.

What that is, I don't even know.

All I've been able to do is go on working, not knowing where these obsessive thoughts come from.

Then one day, I realized my heart was withering, and in it there was nothing but pain.

And one morning, I realized that my beliefs, that I once held so passionately, had completely disappeared...

That was it. I couldn't take any more.

So I quit my job.

(Excerpt of 5 *Centimeters per Second*, Act 3: "5 Centimeters per Second")

Act 3 : "5 Centimeters per Second"

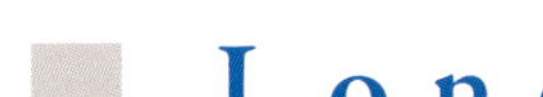

Lonely Room

The story reverts to Takaki's point of view. Takaki's apartment is set in the Tokyo neighborhood of Nakano-sakaue, and after freeing himself from his corporate job, by this time (March of 2008), Takaki has started working as a freelance programmer, as one can glean from things like "API [application programming interface] deadline" written on the whiteboard at the opening of the act. Right around the time he quits his job, we see glimpses of his slightly disorderly lifestyle, and the light from the windows is cold, but in the scenes set in spring, warm sunlight and breezes are alight on a neatly-arranged room. These changes in tone gives us insight into Takaki's changing state of mind.

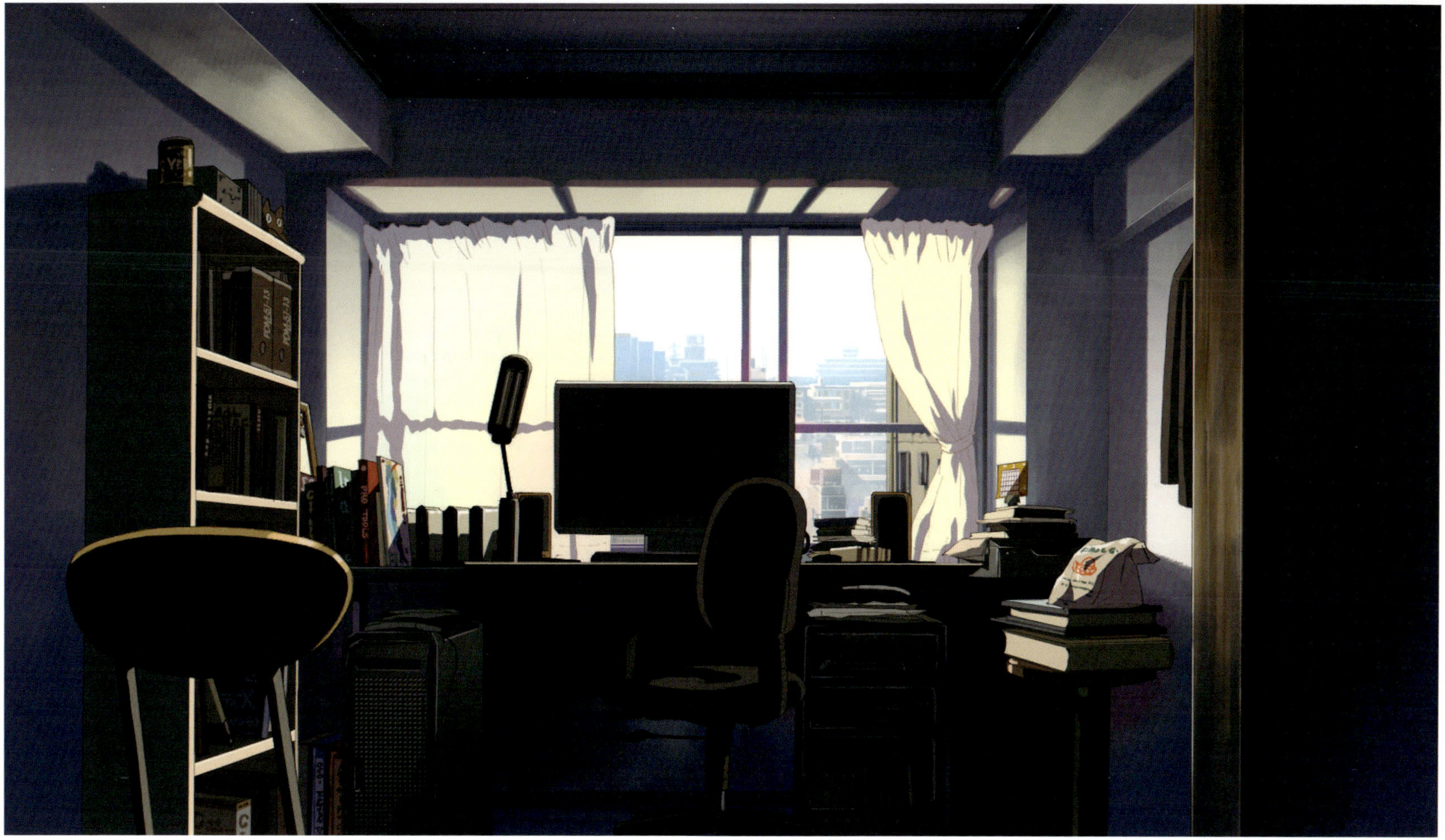

"5 Centimeters per Second" / CUT_004 / Setting: Takaki's apartment

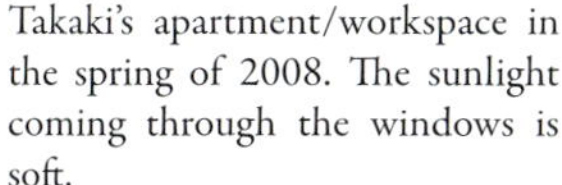

Takaki's apartment/workspace in the spring of 2008. The sunlight coming through the windows is soft.

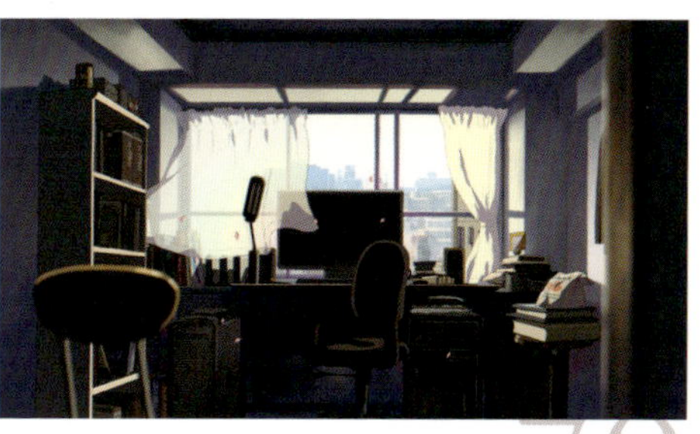

CUT_004 Final Version

Takaki's work desk. The half-eaten sandwich and sticky note with a memo scribbled on it give a lived-in feel. One can tell by the keyboard and mouse that this image is modeled on Mr. Shinkai's own desktop. Everything except the table was drawn on harmony cels.

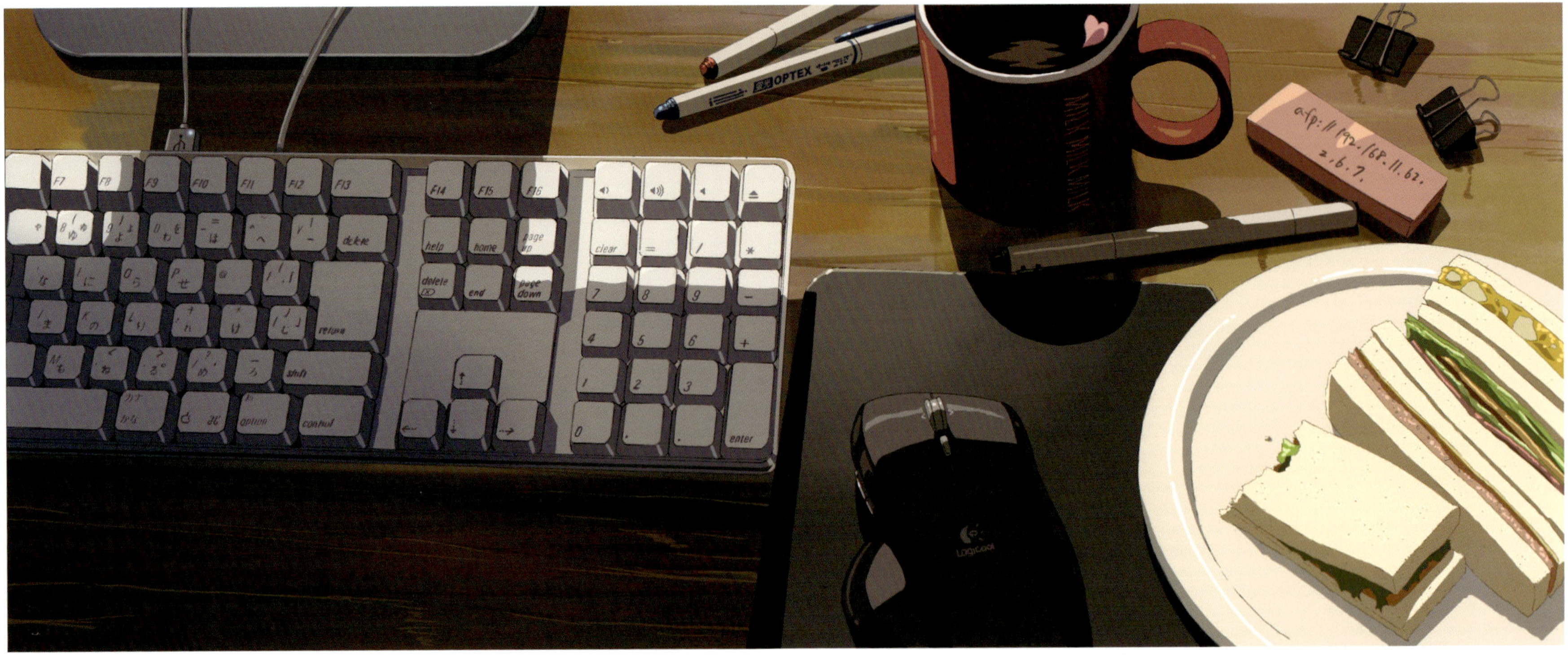

"5 Centimeters per Second" / CUT_006 / Setting: Takaki's apartment

CUT_066 and CUT_078 show Takaki's room right around the time he resigned from his job. The carelessly discarded sneakers and scattered, empty beer cans illustrate his unsettled state of mind.

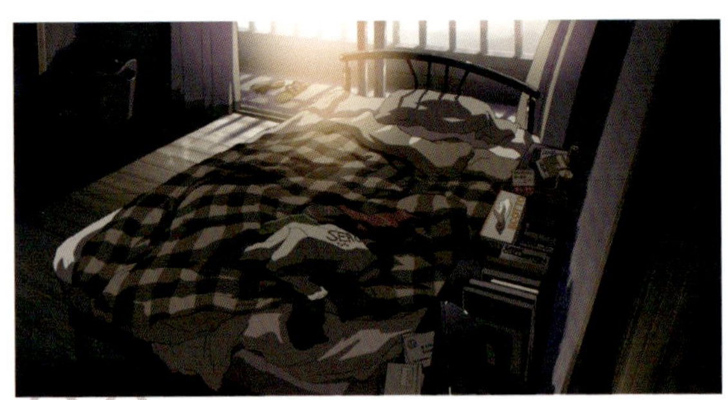

"5 Centimeters per Second" / CUT_078 / Setting: Takaki's apartment

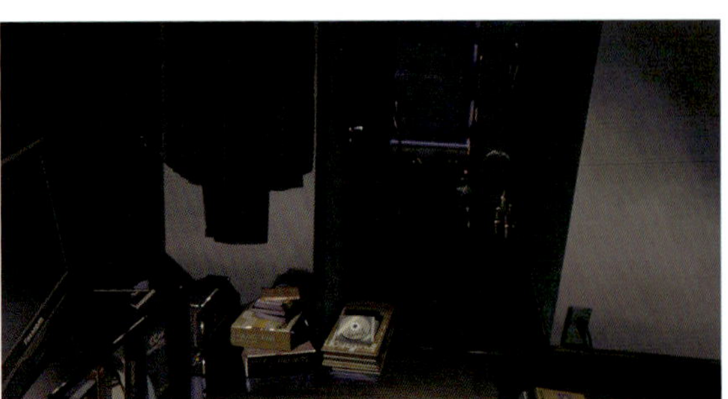

"5 Centimeters per Second" / CUT_066 / Setting: Takaki's apartment

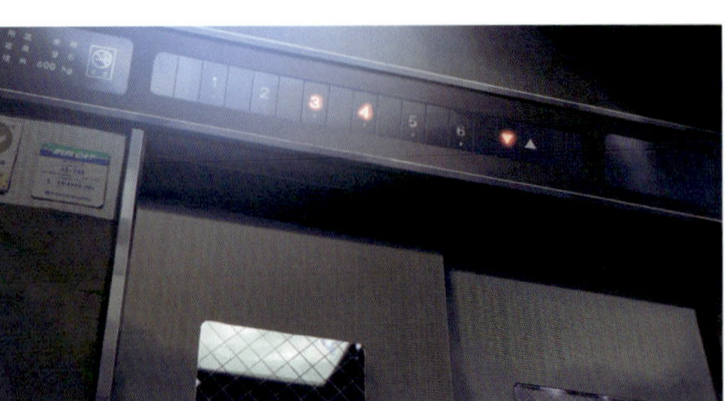

"5 Centimeters per Second" / CUT_082 / Setting: Takaki's apartment building elevator

The cell phone display was created on a separate layer from the cell phone body. A clipping mask was used to limit the visible portions of the screen, and the text was made to slide along the screen. CUT_055 shows Akari's treasure chest at her parents' home which contains the letter she wrote to Takaki when she was 14.

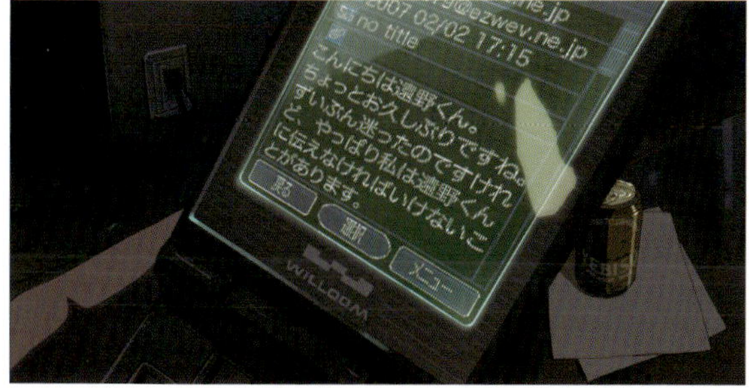

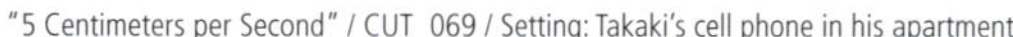
"5 Centimeters per Second" / CUT_069 / Setting: Takaki's cell phone in his apartment

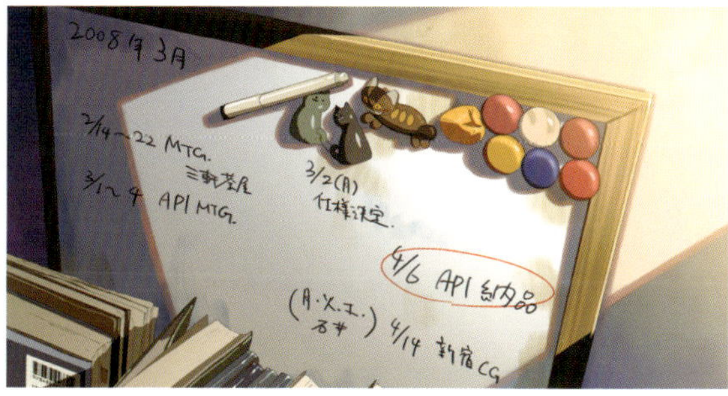

"5 Centimeters per Second" / CUT_005 / Setting: Takaki's apartment

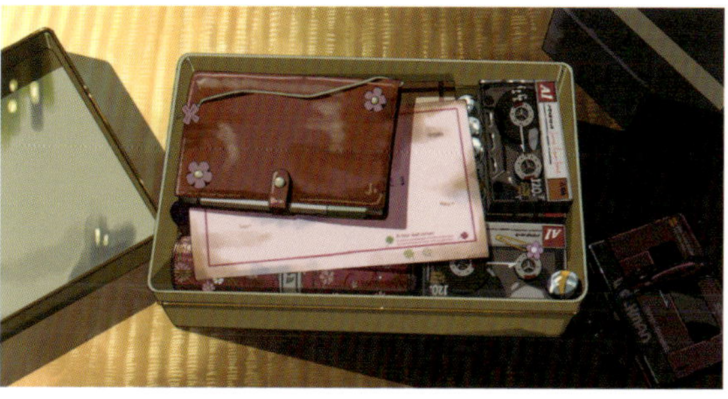

"5 Centimeters per Second" / CUT_055 / Setting: Akari's parents' home

Takaki's apartment after he quit his job. There are empty beer cans on the floor. He quit in January, and from the date on the email from his girlfriend (Mizuno), you can see that one month has passed.

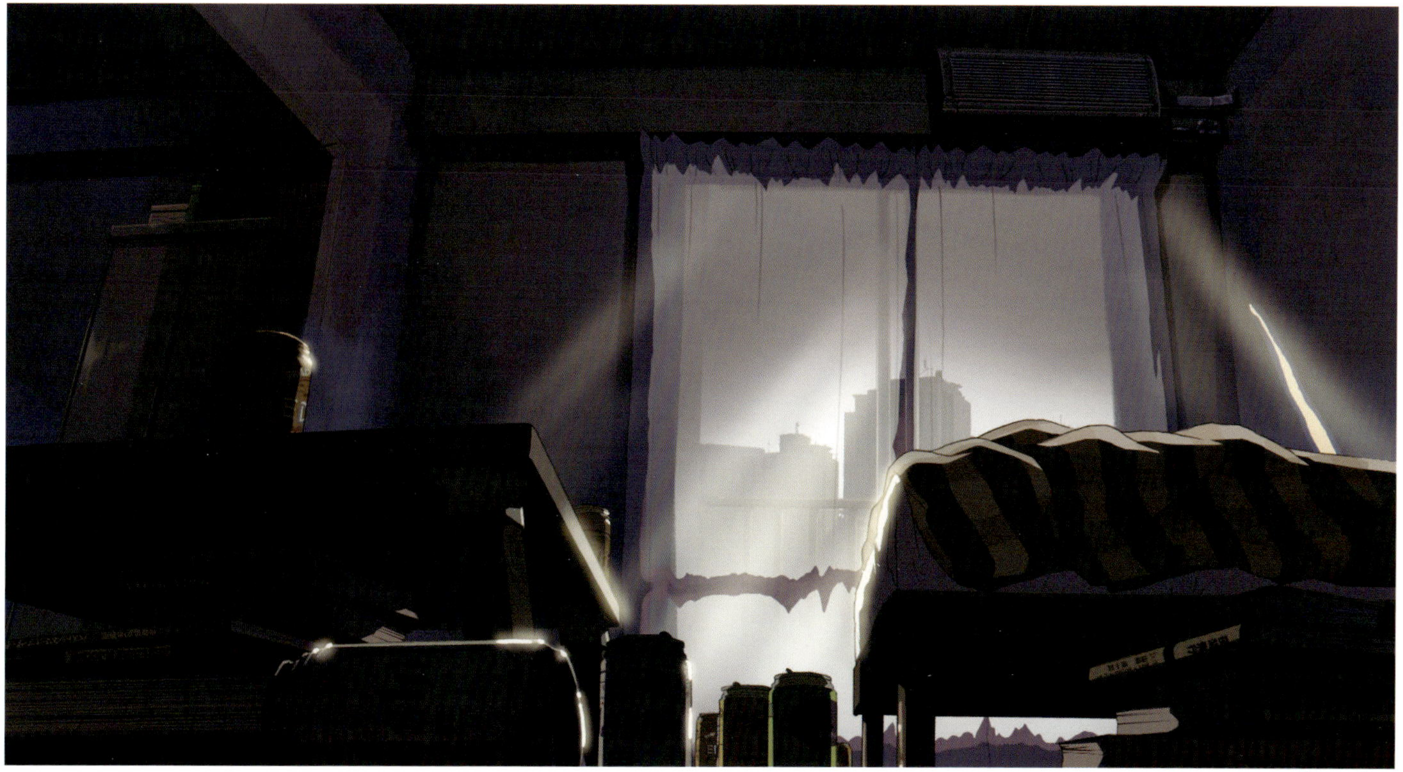

"5 Centimeters per Second" / CUT_110 / Setting: Takaki's apartment

Takaki: (*monologue*) In just living my life, it's as though sadness piles up all around me.

It's in my bed, dried in the sun; the toothbrush in my bathroom; in the memory of my cell phone...

"I still love you."

That's what the girl I'd been with for three years said in that e-mail.

She wrote, "We must've exchanged e-mails a thousand times, but I doubt our hearts got closer by even a centimeter."

(Excerpt of *5 Centimeters per Second*, Act 3: "5 Centimeters per Second")

Act 3 : "5 Centimeters per Second"

Winter Skies – Tokyo at Night

After leaving his job, Takaki wanders through Tokyo at night, from Shinjuku to Yoyogi. The route he takes from West Shinjuku to Nakano-sakaue is the way he would walk when he was a full-time employee. Shinjuku has many neon signs that light up at night, so many background artists worked very hard to recreate the details of the mixed-use buildings. Since the date is February 2nd, 2007 (as established by the email from Mizuno), the weather is snowy and the sky is covered in clouds which reflect the city lights, creating a complex palette.

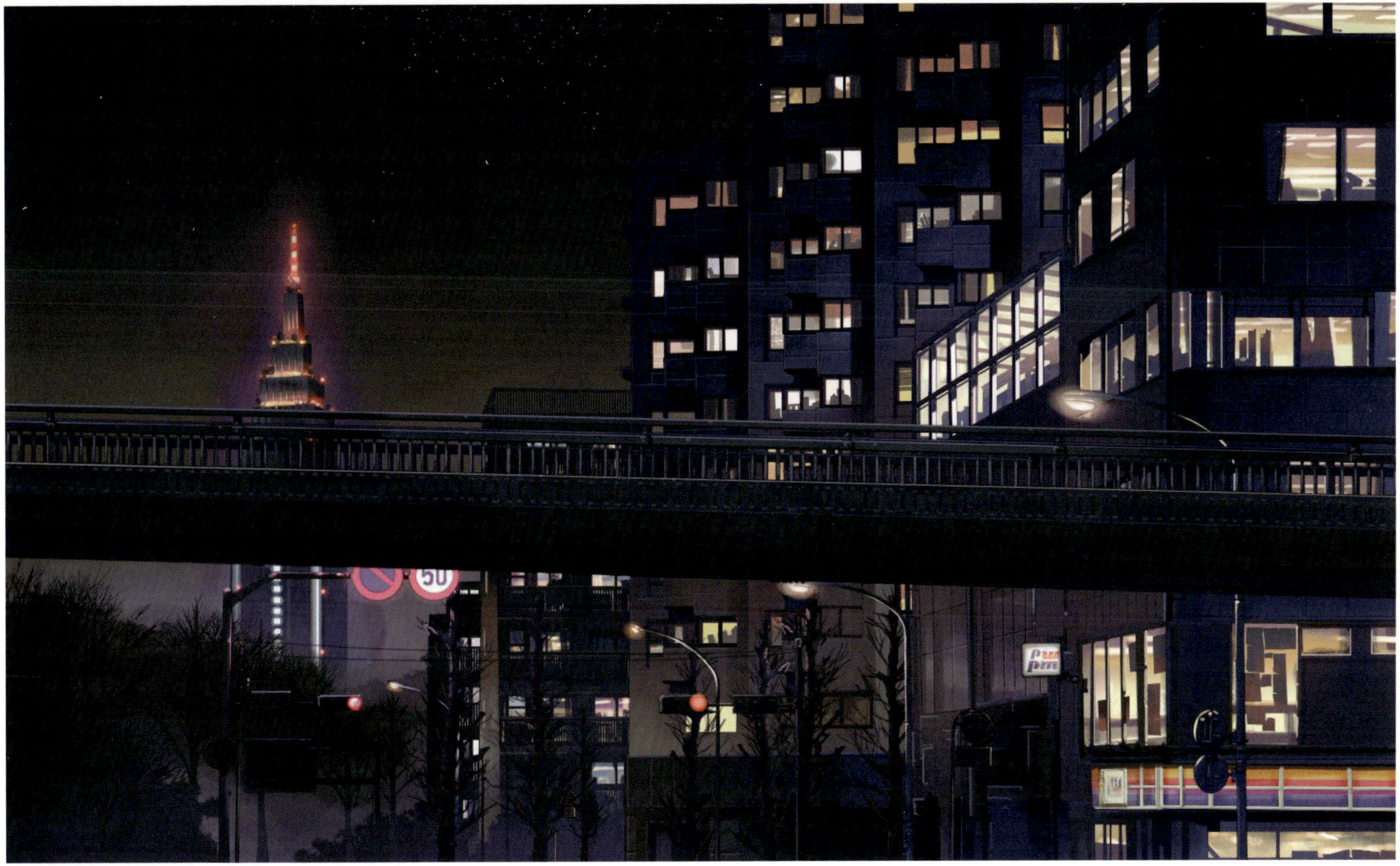

"5 Centimeters per Second" / CUT_238 / Setting: An intersection in Tokyo

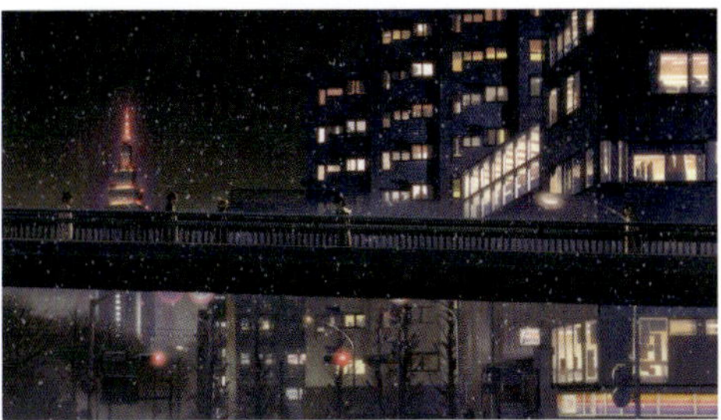

CUT_238 Final Version

Takaki walking across a pedestrian bridge over a busy intersection. The DoCoMo Tower in the distance makes for an impressive background. The pedestrian bridge and the buildings behind it are on separate layers which were used to create a multiplane effect. The final version included several animation elements of falling snow layered together.

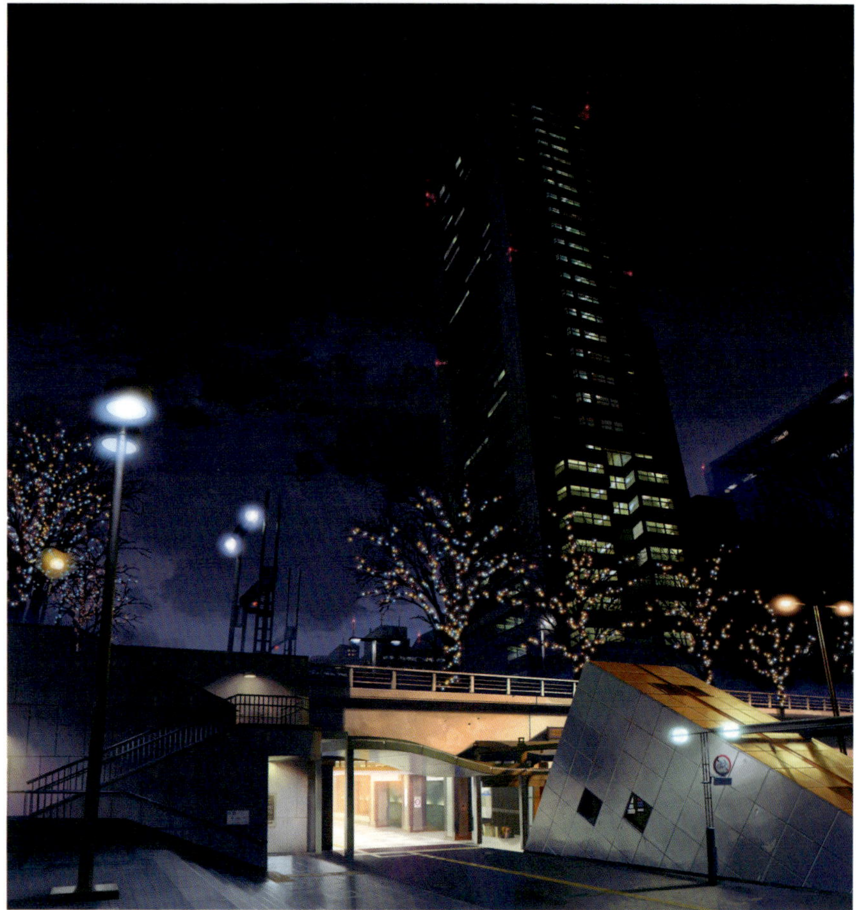

"5 Centimeters per Second" / CUT_029 / Setting: An underground passageway in Tokyo

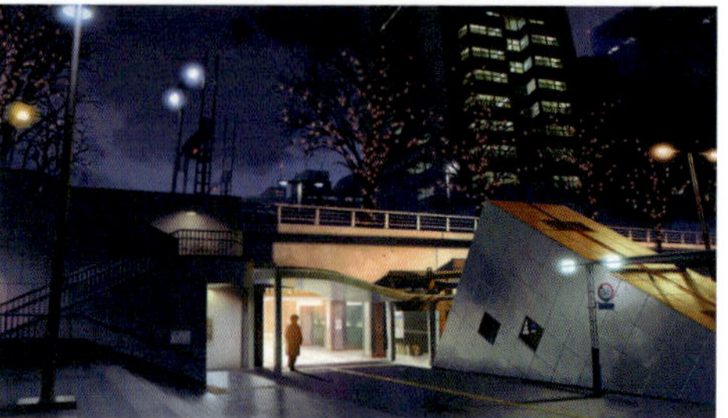

CUT_029 Final Version

A scene of snow falling in Tokyo. CUT_029 shows the exit to an underground route that one can take from Shinjuku to West Shinjuku. CUT_138 is modeled on the street in front of the Kokusai Gekijo in Kabukicho.

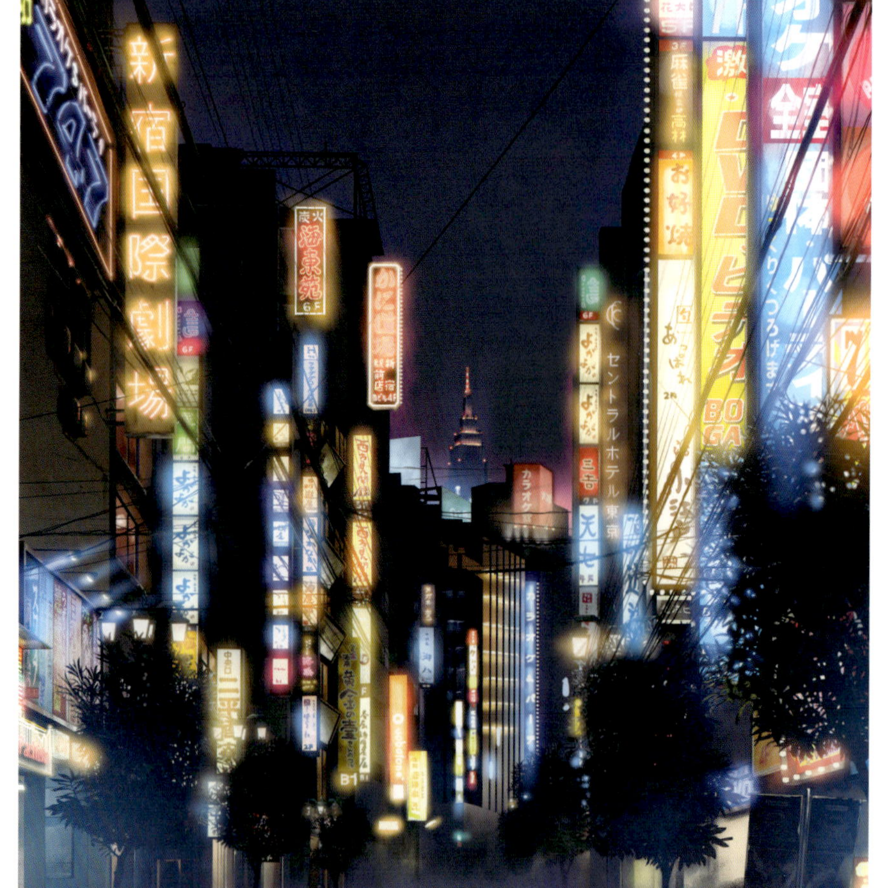

"5 Centimeters per Second" / CUT_138 / Setting: A bustling street in Tokyo

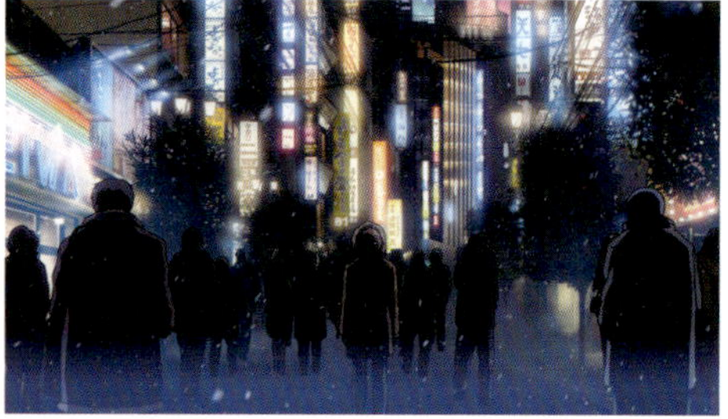

CUT_138 Final Version

A cut showing a convenience store in the city based on location photos. The names and features of the magazines are entirely fictional, and they were all drawn by hand by the background artists. There are some humorous elements placed here and there as well.

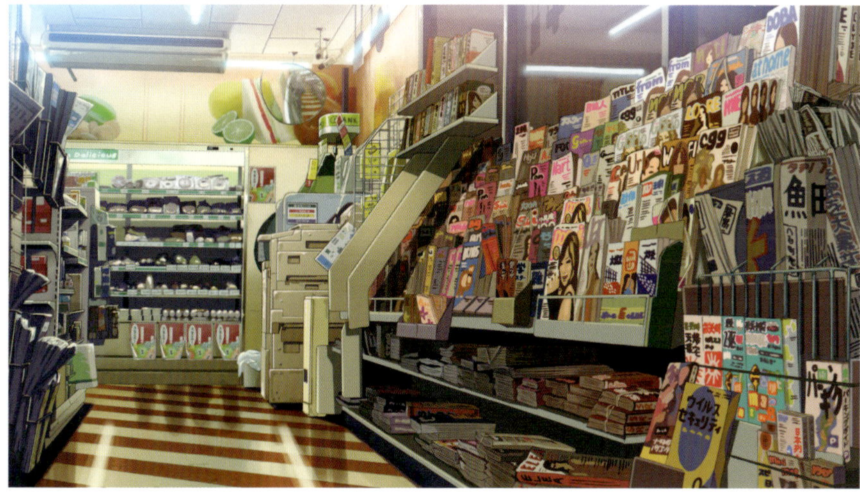

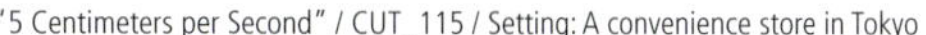

"5 Centimeters per Second" / CUT_115 / Setting: A convenience store in Tokyo

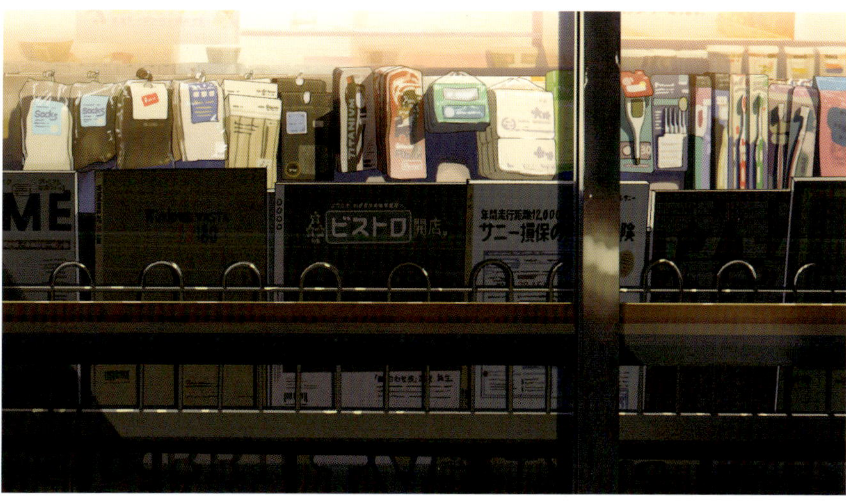

"5 Centimeters per Second" / CUT_116 / Setting: A convenience store in Tokyo

The background art for the scene where Akari returns to Tokyo from her hometown of Iwafune in Tochigi Prefecture. Please note the various angles used which are meant to remind the viewer of Takaki's train journey from Act 1. CUT_127 shows Akari's feet as she steps onto the train in sync with Takaki's feet as he walks out of the convenience store shown in the cut immediately prior. The scenery outside the window in CUT_129 was placed on multiple layers and slid sideways. Akari's reflection in the window was added with video software.

"5 Centimeters per Second" / CUT_117 / Setting: JR Oyama Station platform

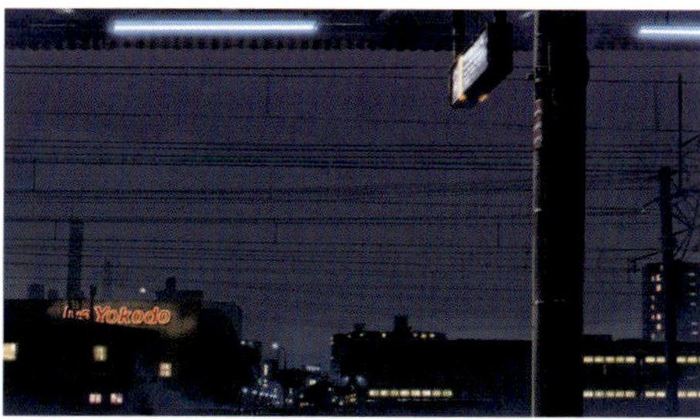

"5 Centimeters per Second" / CUT_121 / Setting: JR Oyama Station platform

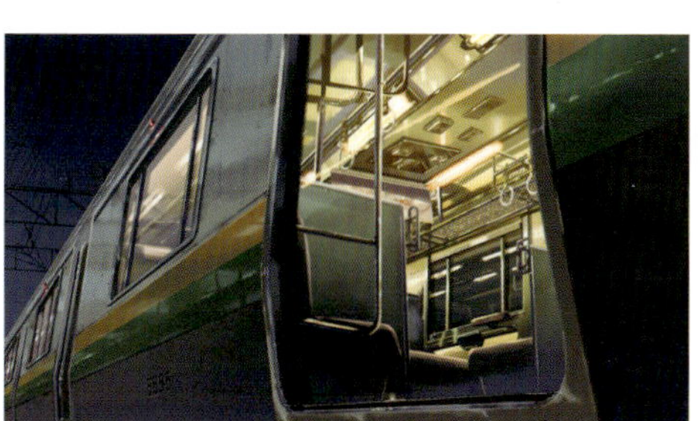

"5 Centimeters per Second" / CUT_125 / Setting: JR Oyama Station platform

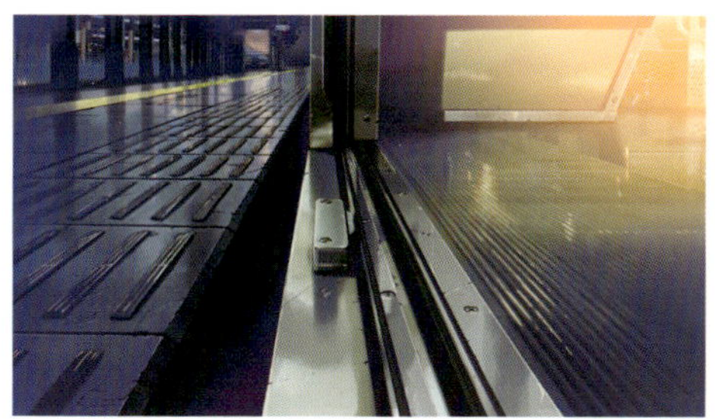

"5 Centimeters per Second" / CUT_127 / Setting: JR Oyama Station platform

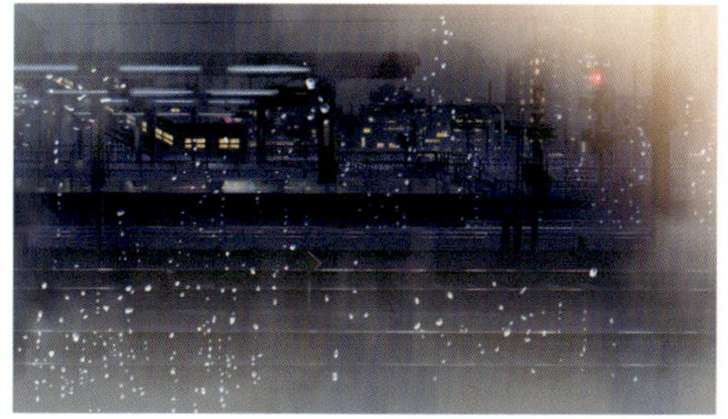

"5 Centimeters per Second" / CUT_129 / Setting: View from the window of a JR Utsunomiya Line train

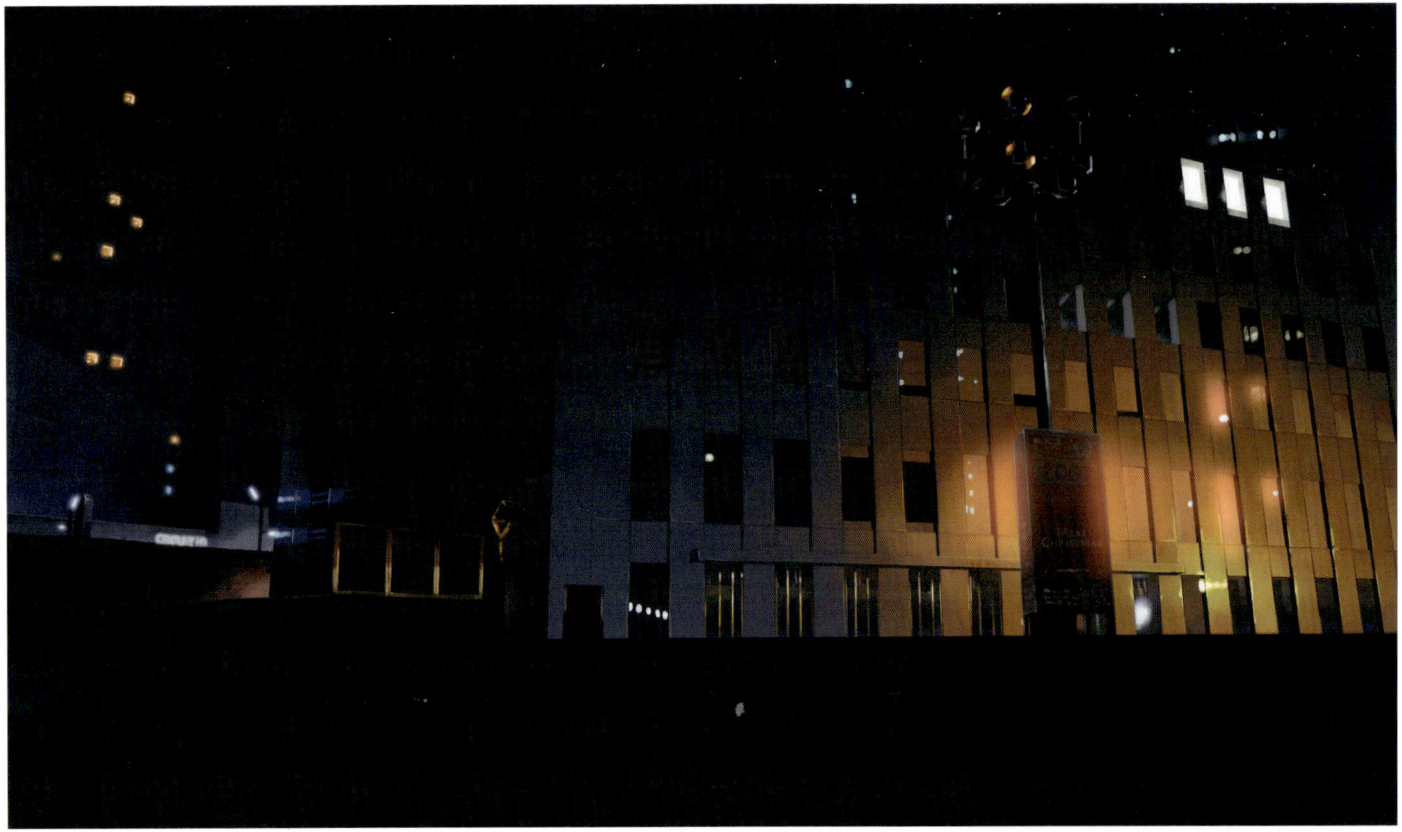

Background art for the scene where Takaki received a message on his phone from Mizuno as he walks home from Shinjuku. In order to create a late-night atmosphere, the stairs at his feet are painted over with shadows.

"5 Centimeters per Second" / CUT_031 / Setting: Office buildings in Tokyo

Scenery that changes at a dizzying pace. Each image was only shown for a second or two, and were divided into separate layers and used as animation elements.

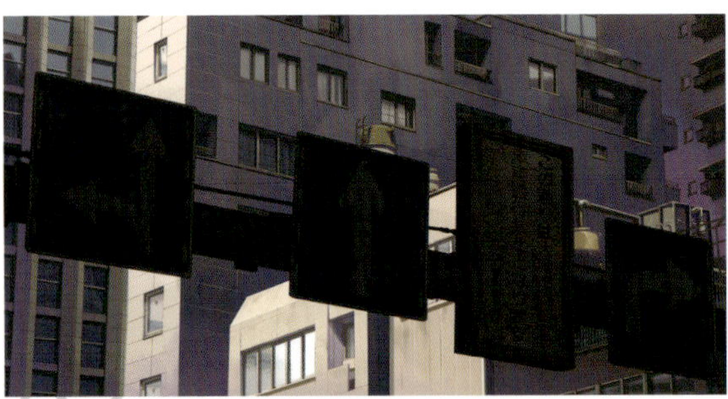

"5 Centimeters per Second" / CUT_093 / Setting: Office buildings in Tokyo

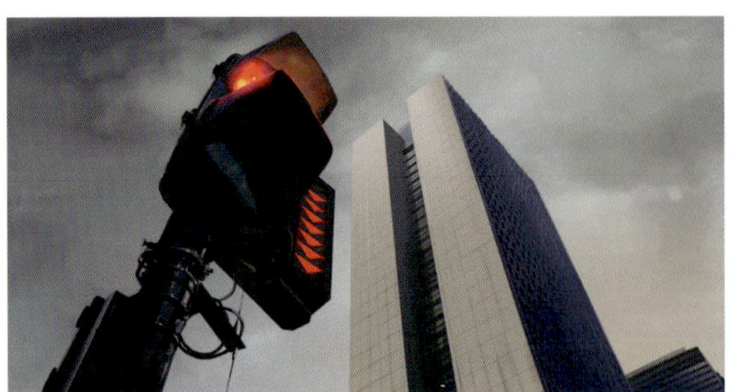

"5 Centimeters per Second" / CUT_097 / Setting: Office buildings in Tokyo

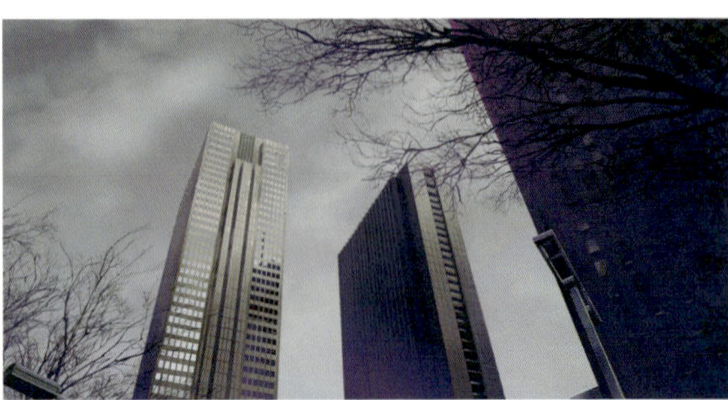

"5 Centimeters per Second" / CUT_101 / Setting: Office buildings in Tokyo

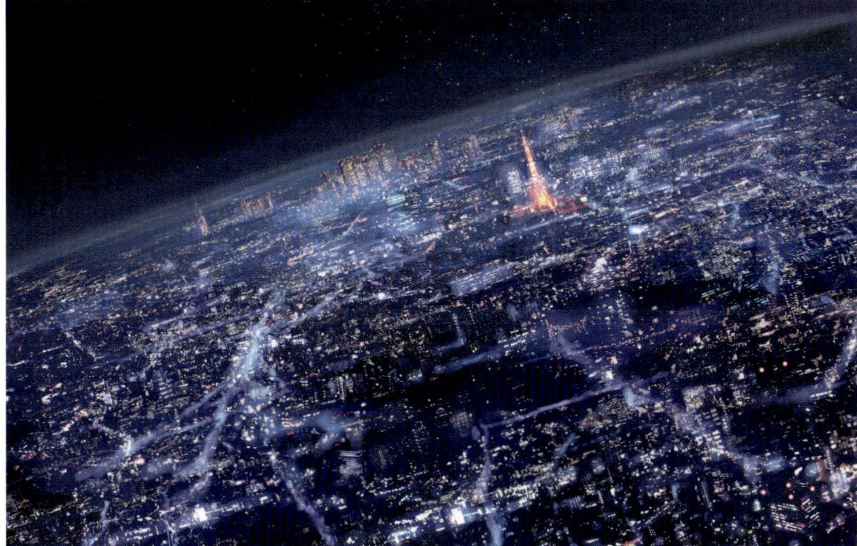

"5 Centimeters per Second" / CUT_139 / Setting: Aerial view of Tokyo

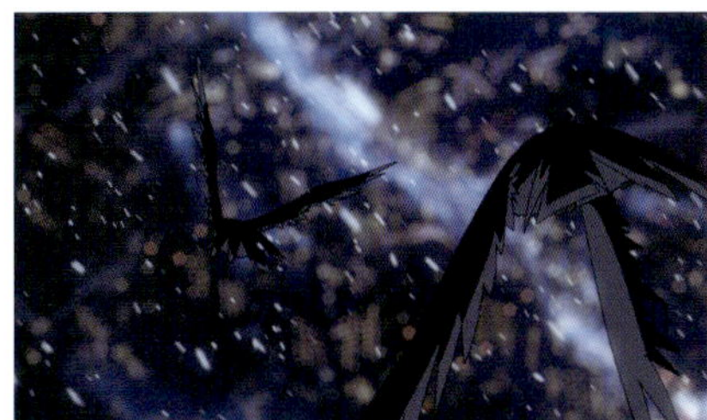

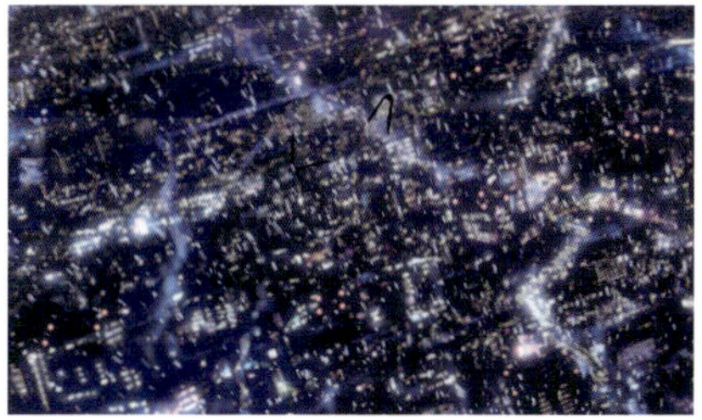

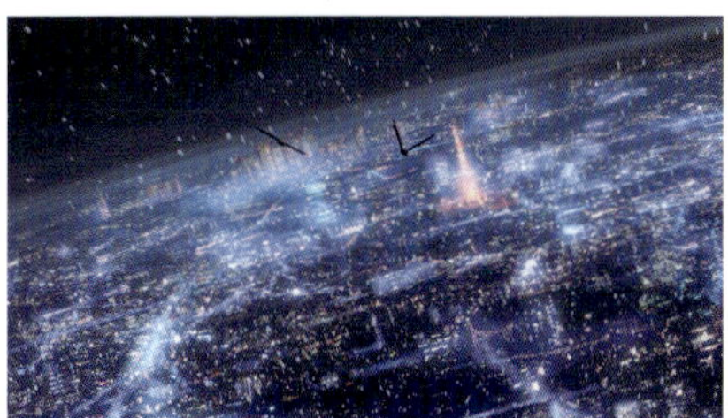

CUT_139 Final Version

Two crows flying high above Tokyo. In *5 Centimeters per Second*, birds flying above a city are included in important scenes. In Act 1 there were woodpeckers flying from Shinjuku to Tochigi, in Act 2 there was a flock of birds flying in front of the trail of exhaust left by the H-IIA rocket.

Tokyo at night, as seen from the skies above. Location photos were taken from skyscrapers in Ikebukuro, several of which were digitally combined. The location photos were taken during the day. CUT_128, CUT_139 and CUT_285 (page 103) are all based on the same location photos.

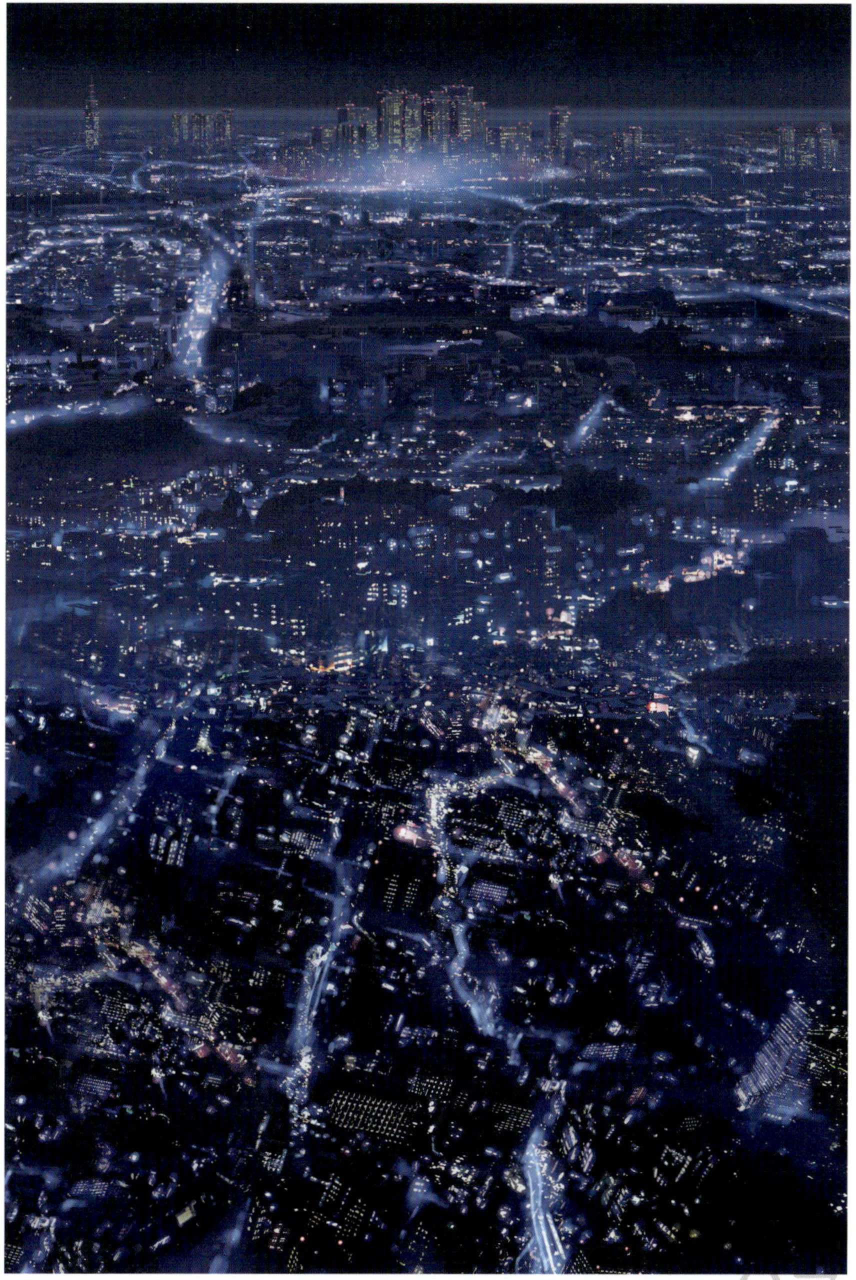

"5 Centimeters per Second" / CUT_128 / Setting: Aerial view of Tokyo

Takaki: Yesterday, I had a dream.

Akari: A dream of a long time ago.

Takaki: In the dream, we were still 14 years old.

Akari: And we were standing in a field covered with snow...

Takaki: ...where in the dim light from distant houses....

Akari: ...our footprints were all that could be seen in the new-fallen snow. And because of that...

Takaki: ...we believed we'd watch the cherry blossoms fall again someday, together.

Akari: He and I both believed it...

Takaki: ...without a shred of doubt.

(Excerpt of *5 Centimeters per Second*, Act 3: "5 Centimeters per Second")

Act 3 : "5 Centimeters per Second"

Scenes from Days Gone by

Flashbacks of places in Tokyo, over the course of 13 years, where Takaki and Akari used to walk together are shown at intervals while the song "One More Time, One More Chance" by Masayoshi Yamazaki plays. The inserted landscapes were based on snapshots but were drawn to reflect Mr. Shinkai's image of the song. When needed, the artwork was drawn on separate layers. Some pieces of artwork from Acts 1 and 2 were also used. Since the continual cascade of fast cuts were made in time with the music, it was essential to check that the right images appeared at the correct points in the song.

CUT_166 and CUT_167 are background art for the scenes where Takaki and Akari, in high school, think about one another even when far apart. While there are many differences in culture and scenery between Tochigi Prefecture and Tanegashima, the mailboxes are a common factor, and while the angle of the sun and the strength and tone of the sunlight are similar, they are depicted on opposite sides of the street, which illustrates how far apart their lives are.

"5 Centimeters per Second" / CUT_167 / Setting: The road Akari takes to high school

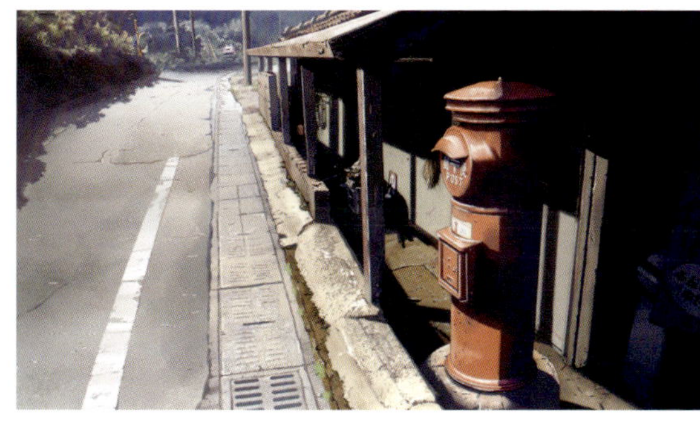

"5 Centimeters per Second" / CUT_166 / Setting: The road Takaki takes to high school

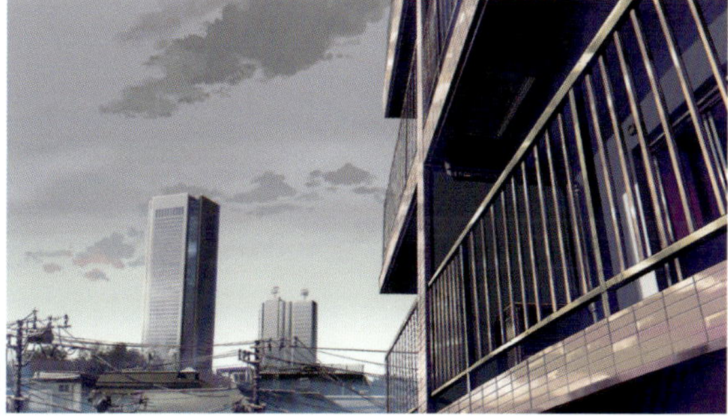

"5 Centimeters per Second" / CUT_065 / Setting: Takaki's apartment building

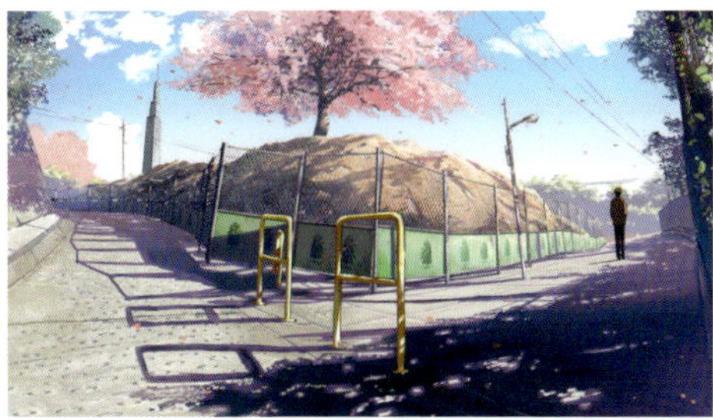

CUT_010 Final Version

This is the same place and same angle as CUT_005 (page 9) in Act 1: "Cherry Blossom." The passage of time is depicted in the stone wall that is under construction. This image is based on the same location photo as the above-mentioned cut.

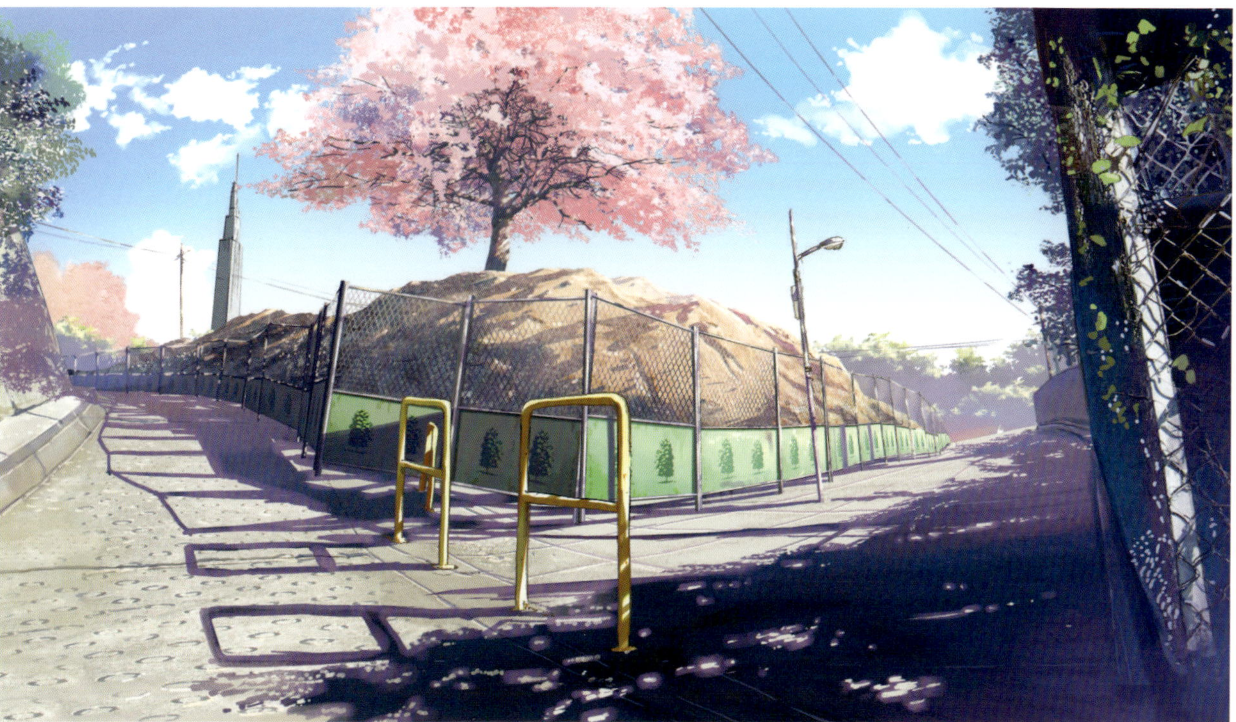

"5 Centimeters per Second" / CUT_010 / Residential area in Tokyo

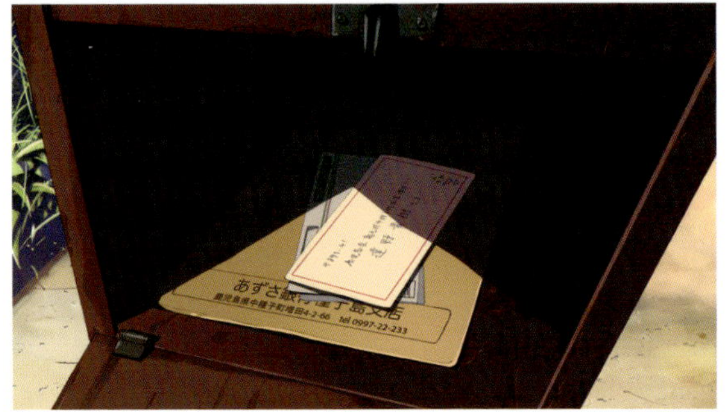

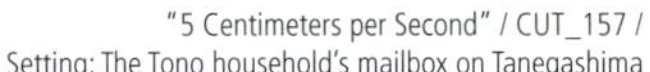

"5 Centimeters per Second" / CUT_157 /
Setting: The Tono household's mailbox on Tanegashima

"5 Centimeters per Second" / CUT_161 /
Setting: The Shinohara household's mailbox in Iwafune

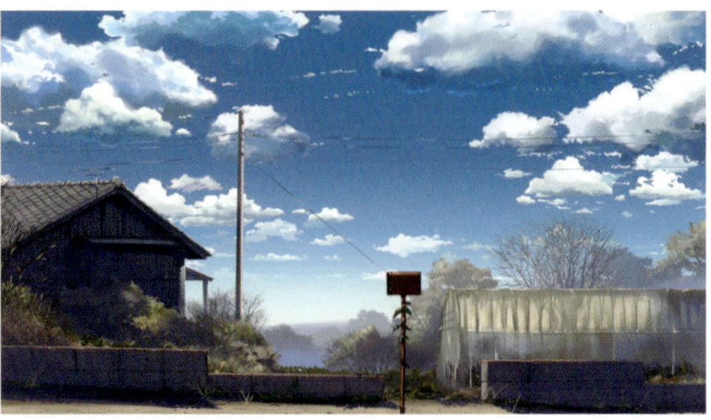

"5 Centimeters per Second" / CUT_165 /
Setting: The Tono household's mailbox on Tanegashima

Cuts that retrace Takaki's memories. CUT_157 shows his mailbox soon after he moved to Tanegashima. Here you can see that the envelope sent by Akari is of the same design as the one in CUT_055 (page 81). CUT_161 and CUT_165 show Takaki's mailbox in Tanegashima and Akari's mailbox in Iwafune from the same angle.

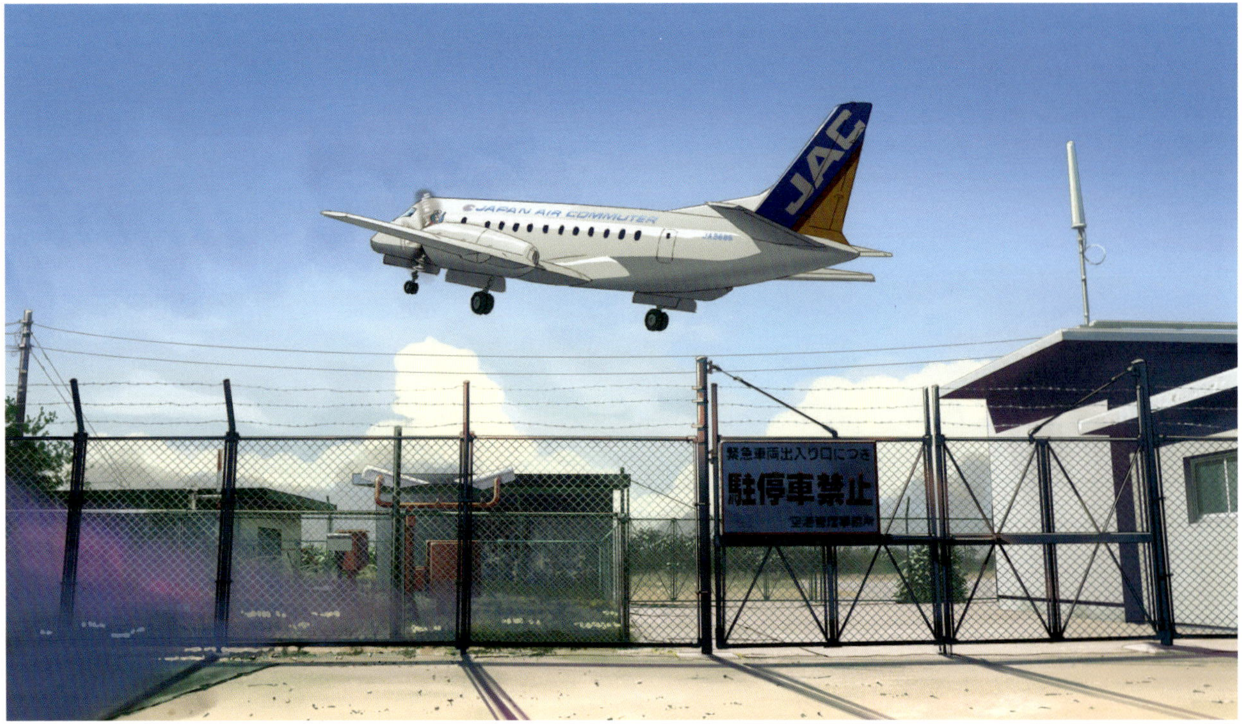

"5 Centimeters per Second" / CUT_191 / Setting: Tanegashima Airport, Nakatane

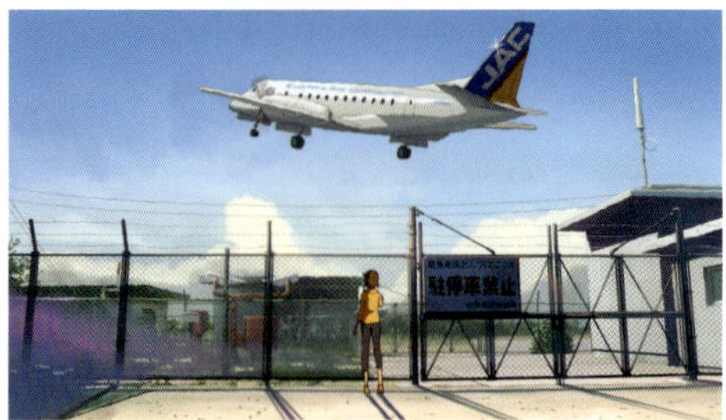

CUT_191 Final Version

Background artwork of Tanegashima Airport used in the scene where Takaki leaves the island after graduating from high school. The image of the commercial airline's YS-11 Model aircraft taking off was based on location photographs. The final version included animation of propellers on the aircraft and a cel of Kanae seeing him off.

The Iwafune Station platform where Akari waits for the train to take her to high school. This is a larger version of CUT_251 (page 47) in Act 1 "Cherry Blossom," but drawn from the same angle.

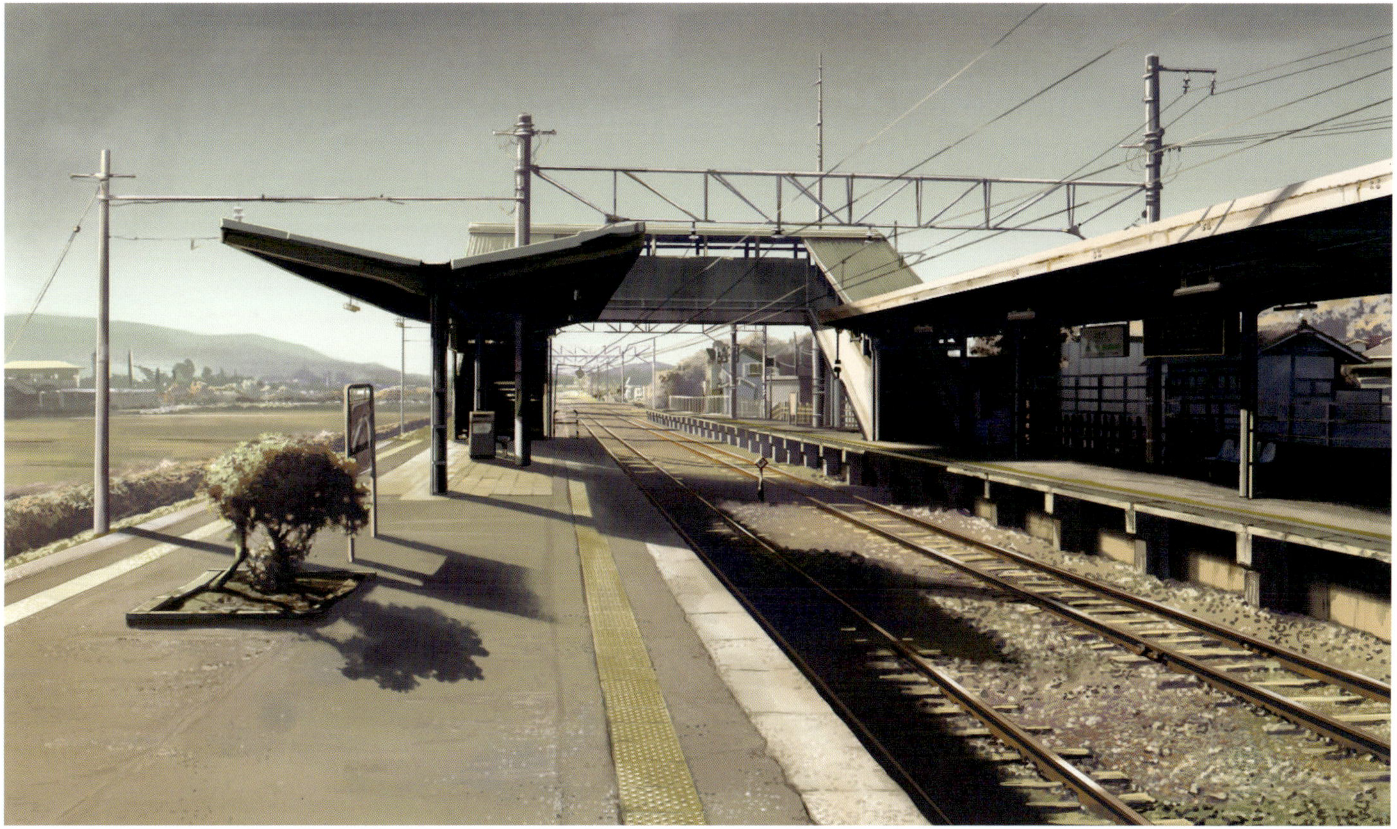

Background art for the scene where Akari's parents see her off on the train to Tokyo, where she will become a bride. CUT_043 is the same angle as CUT_249 (page 47) in Act 1: "Cherry Blossom."

"5 Centimeters per Second" / CUT_046 / Setting: JR Iwafune Station platform

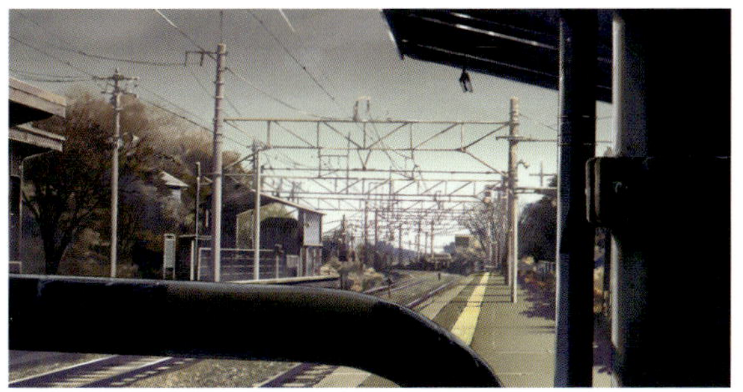

"5 Centimeters per Second" / CUT_043 / Setting: JR Iwafune Station platform

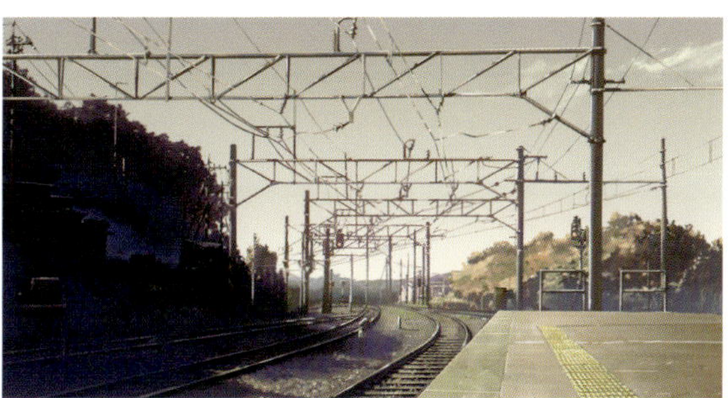

"5 Centimeters per Second" / CUT_170 / Setting: JR Iwafune Station platform

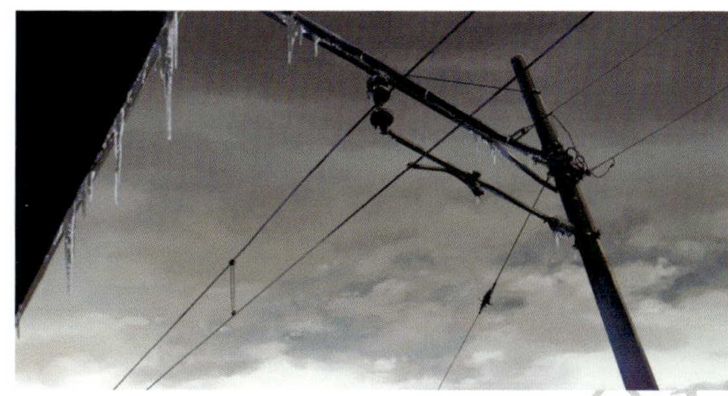

"5 Centimeters per Second" / CUT_042 / Setting: JR Iwafune Station platform

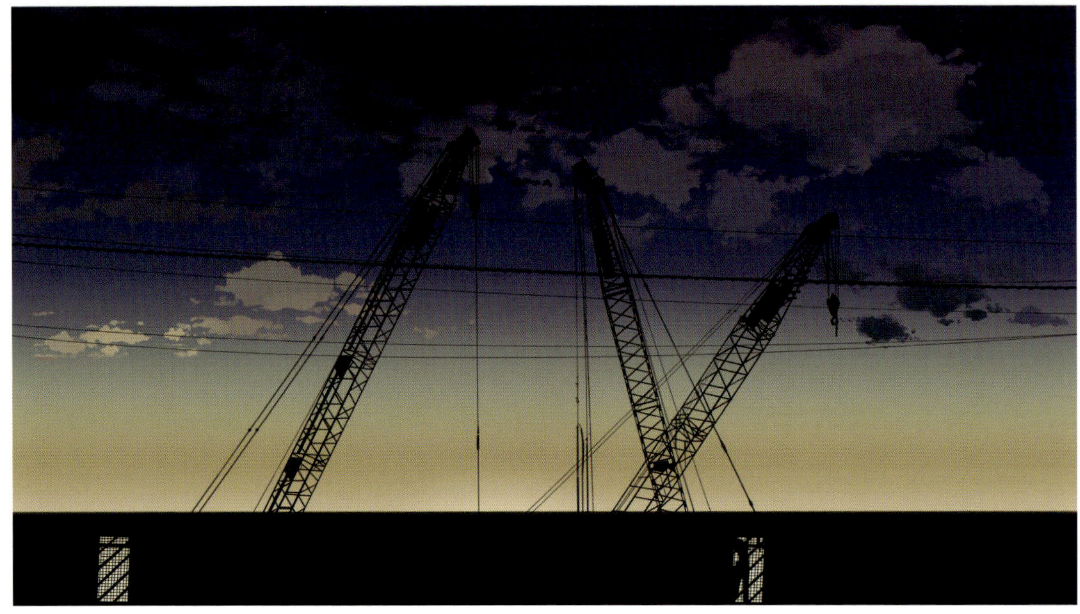

"5 Centimeters per Second" / CUT_175 / Setting: View of Tokyo

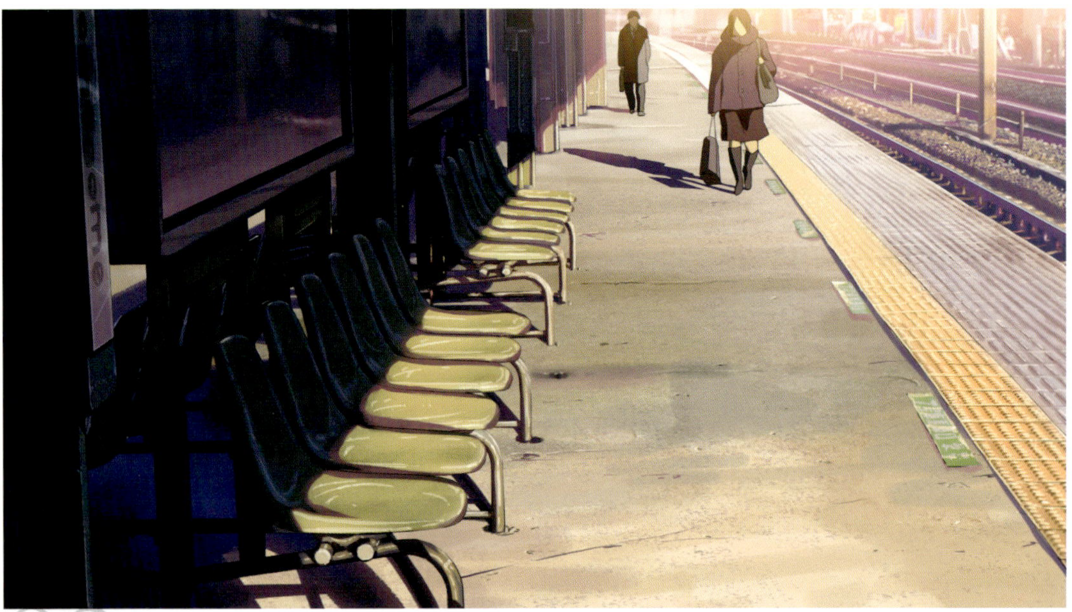

"5 Centimeters per Second" / CUT_178 / Setting: View of Tokyo

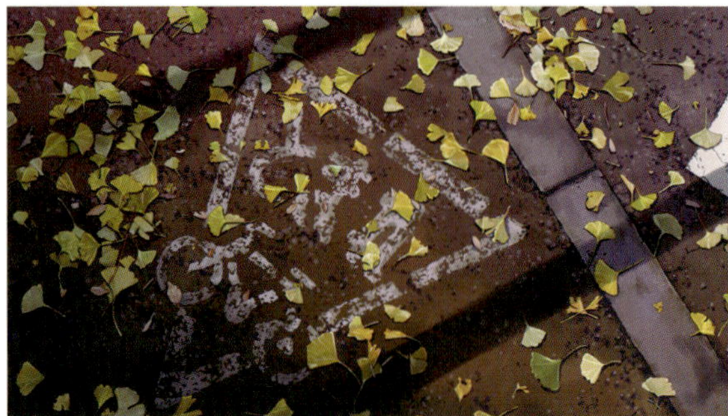

"5 Centimeters per Second" / CUT_176 / Setting: View of Tokyo

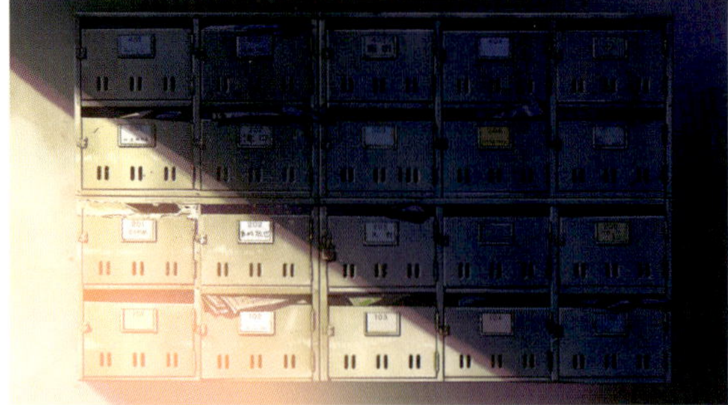

"5 Centimeters per Second" / CUT_180 / Setting: View of Tokyo

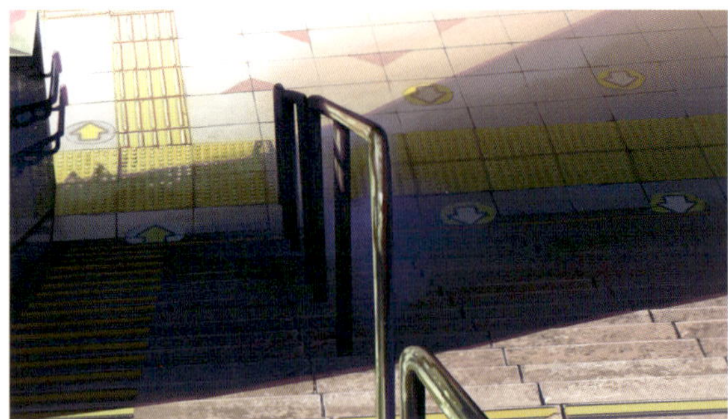

"5 Centimeters per Second" / CUT_181 / Setting: View of Tokyo

In Act 3, a great number of scenes are shown in quick succession, which memorably demonstrates the passage of time that Takaki and Akari spent apart. All of these cuts were only shown for about 0.2 seconds each, but here you can see how finely detailed each background was drawn.

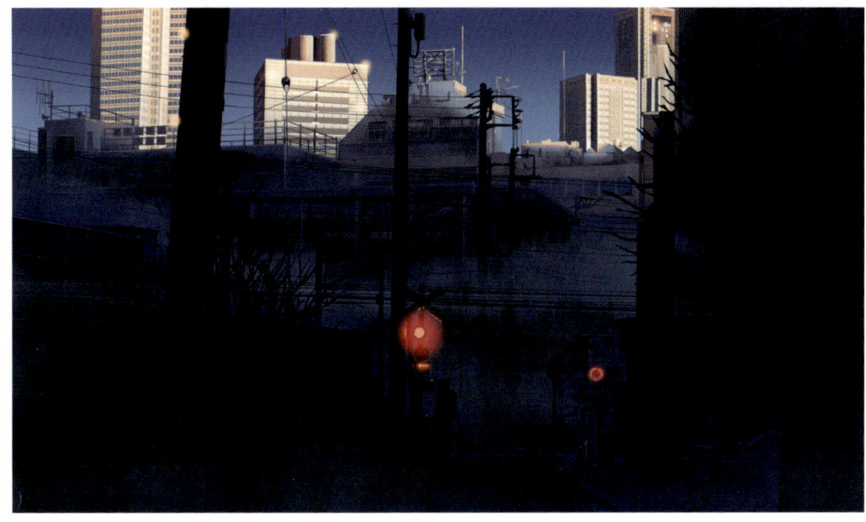

"5 Centimeters per Second" / CUT_209 / Setting: View of Tokyo

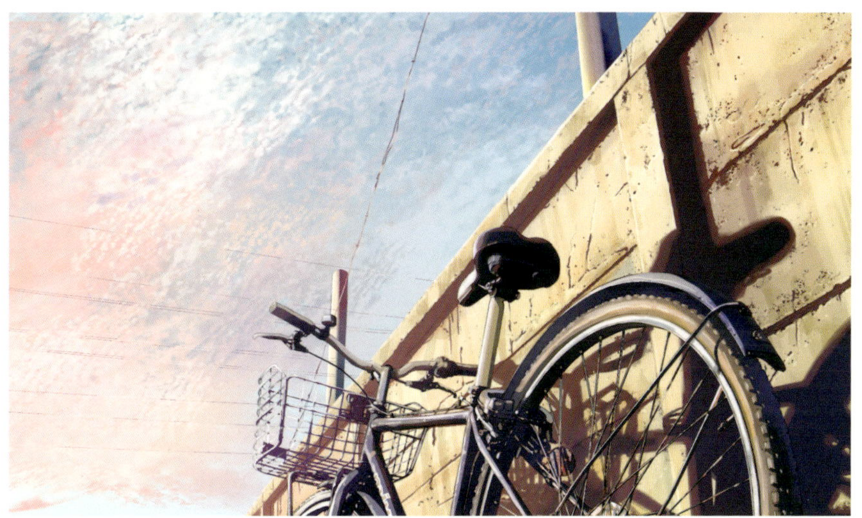

"5 Centimeters per Second" / CUT_213 / Setting: View of Tokyo

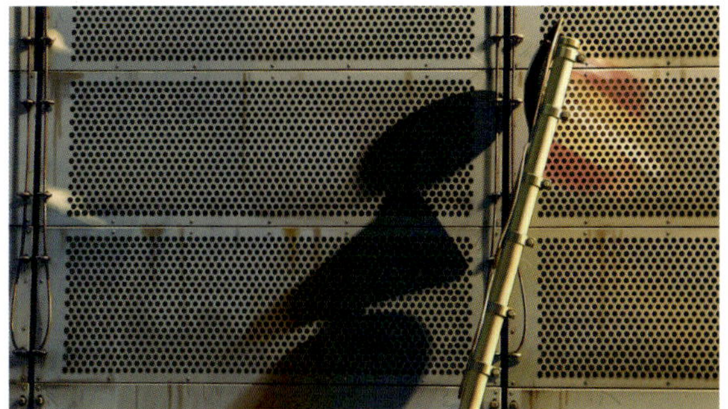

"5 Centimeters per Second" / CUT_216 / Setting: View of Tokyo

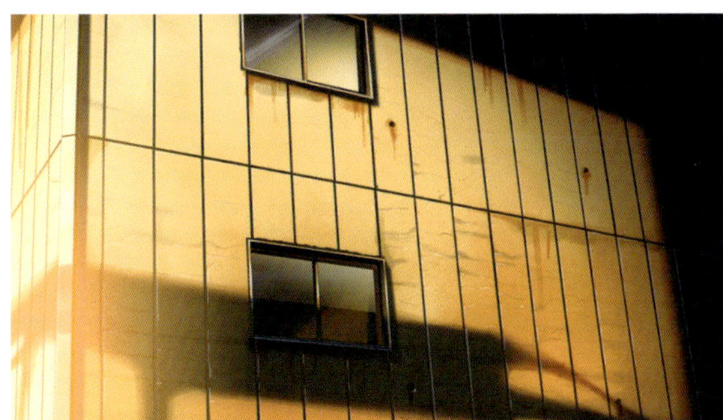

"5 Centimeters per Second" / CUT_220 / Setting: View of Tokyo

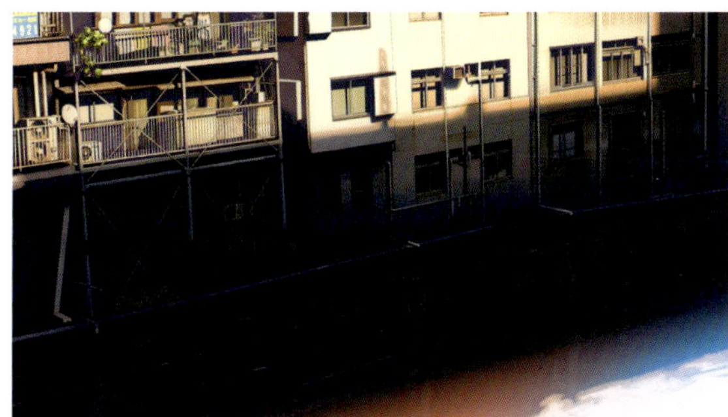

"5 Centimeters per Second" / CUT_221 / Setting: View of Tokyo

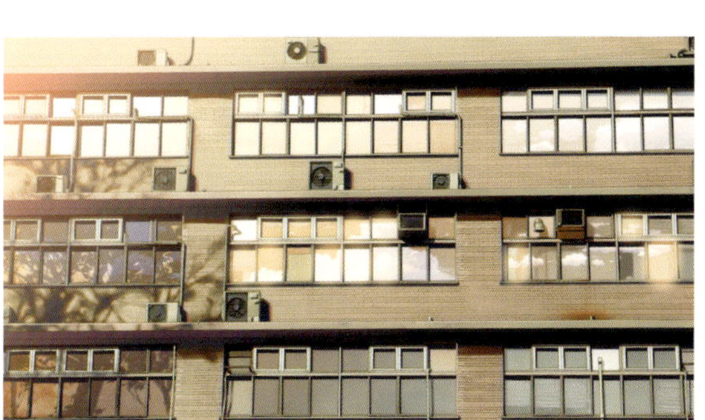

"5 Centimeters per Second" / CUT_223 / Setting: View of Tokyo

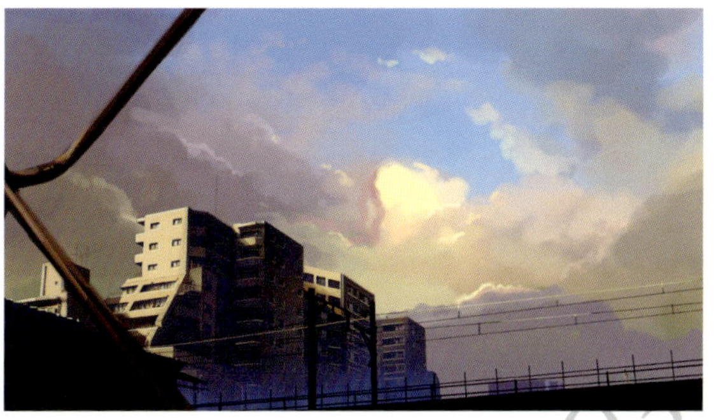

"5 Centimeters per Second" / CUT_224 / Setting: View of Tokyo

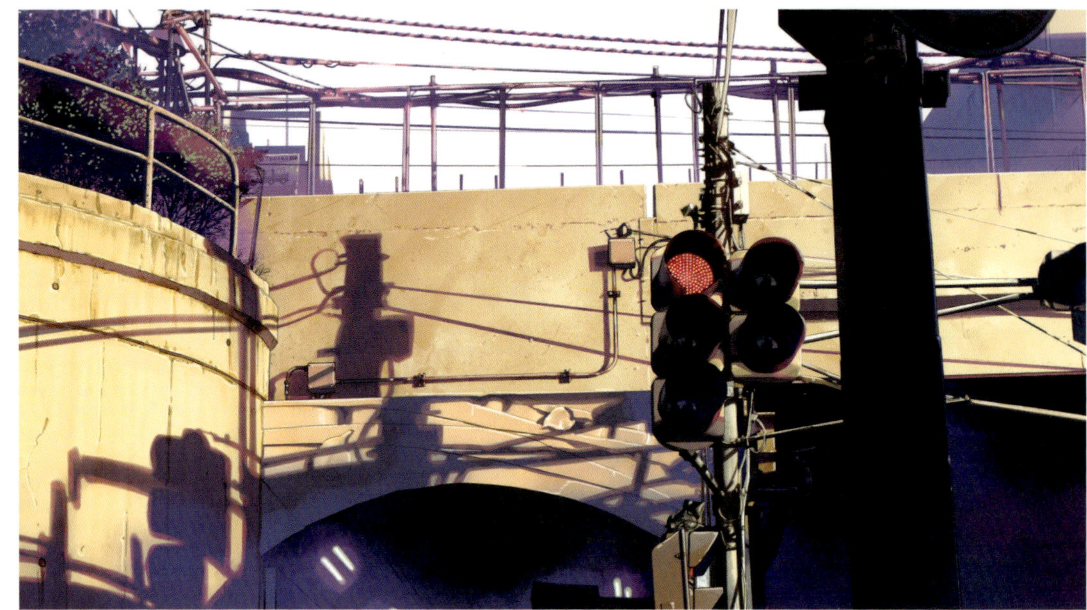

"5 Centimeters per Second" / CUT_255 / Setting: View of Tokyo

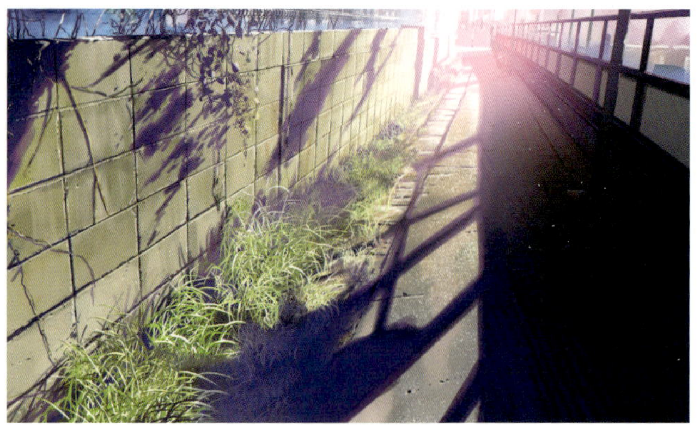

"5 Centimeters per Second" / CUT_256 / Setting: View of Tokyo

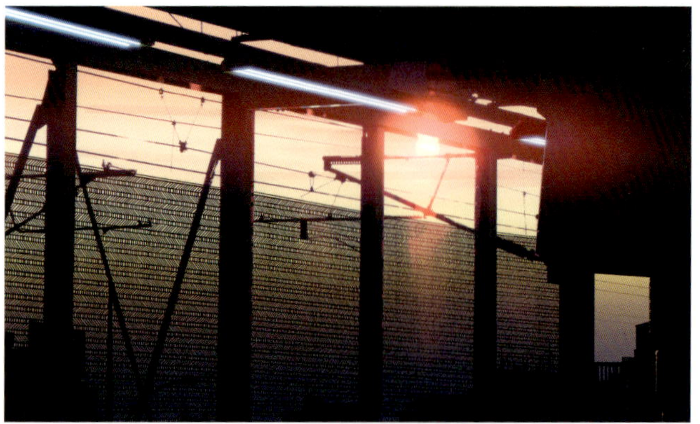

"5 Centimeters per Second" / CUT_257 / Setting: View of Tokyo

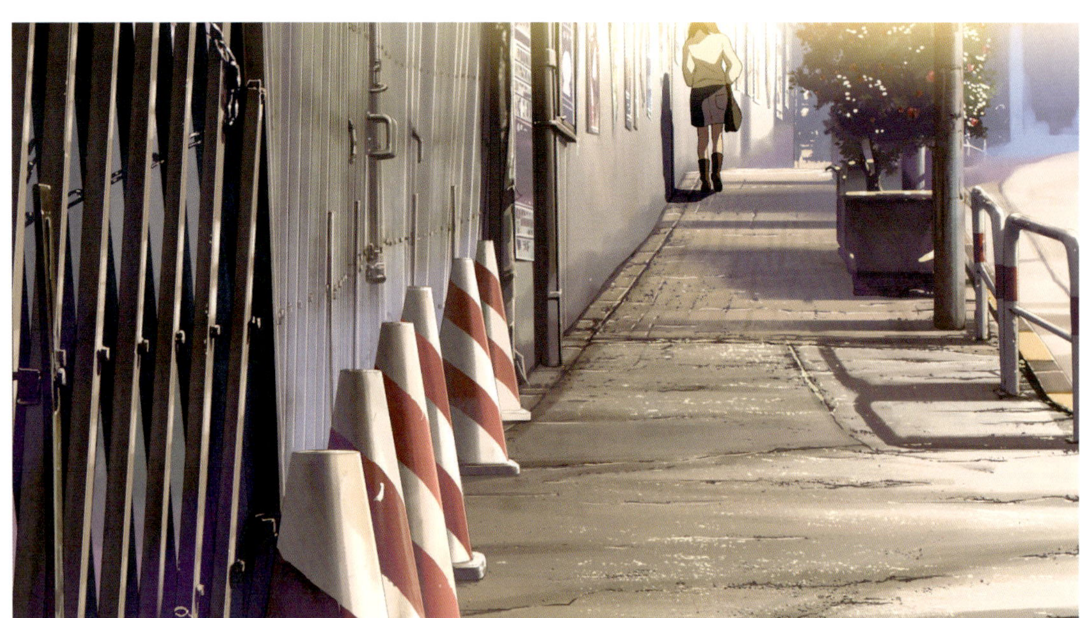

"5 Centimeters per Second" / CUT_261 / Setting: View of Tokyo

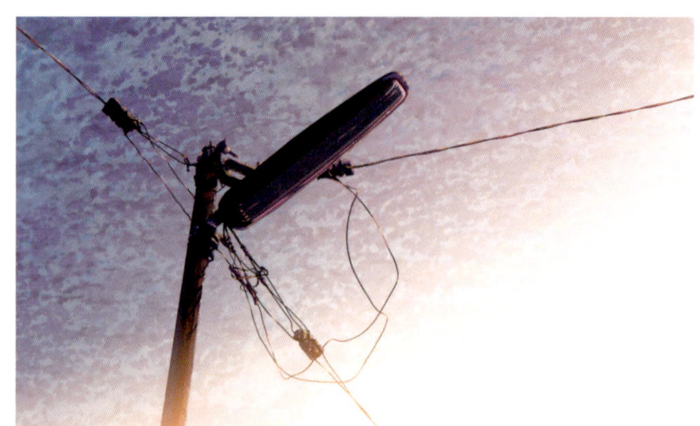

"5 Centimeters per Second" / CUT_260 / Setting: View of Tokyo

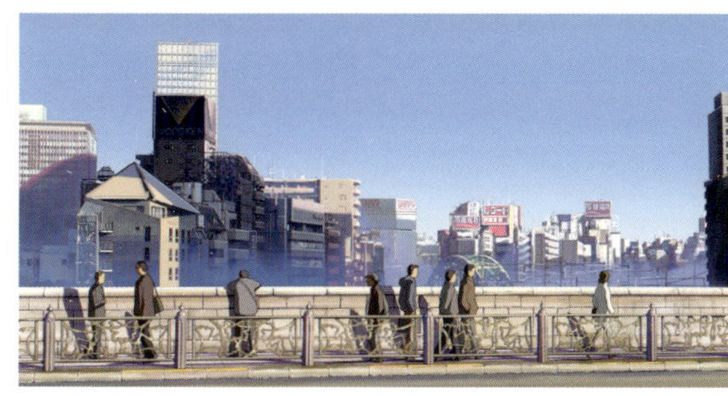

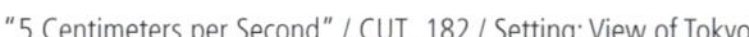

"5 Centimeters per Second" / CUT_182 / Setting: View of Tokyo

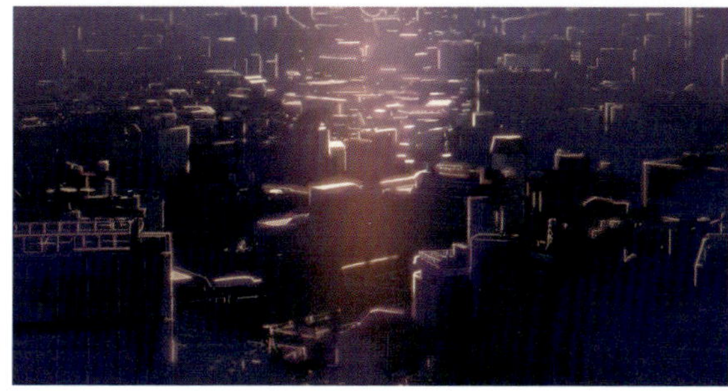

"5 Centimeters per Second" / CUT_225 / Setting: View of Tokyo

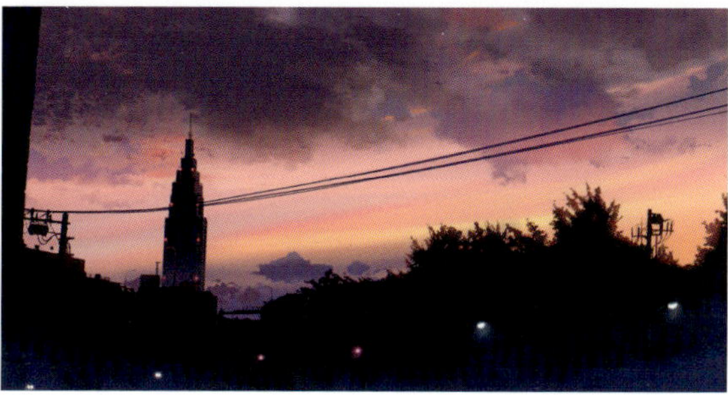

"5 Centimeters per Second" / CUT_262 / Setting: View of Tokyo

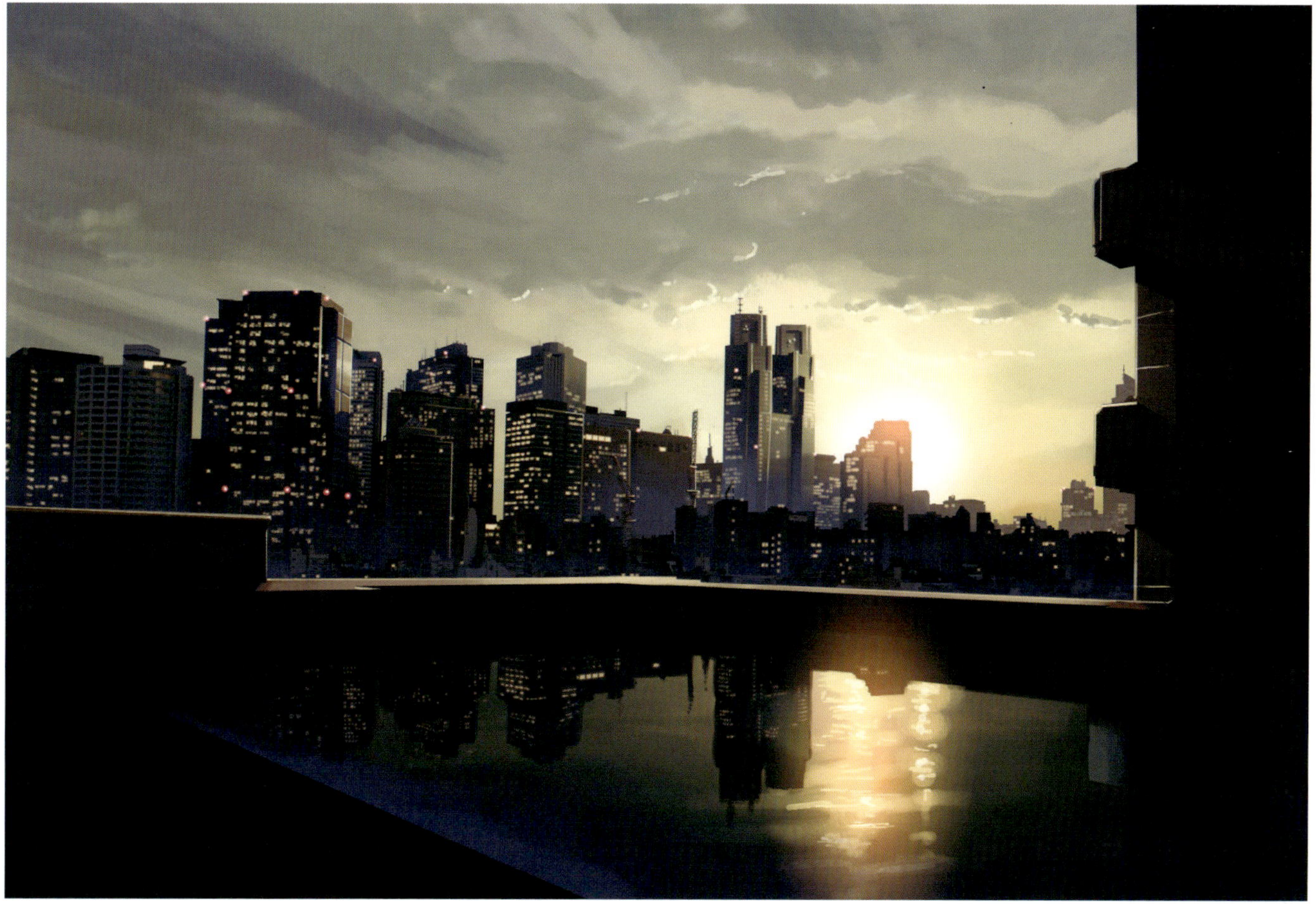

"5 Centimeters per Second" / CUT_219 / Setting: View of Tokyo

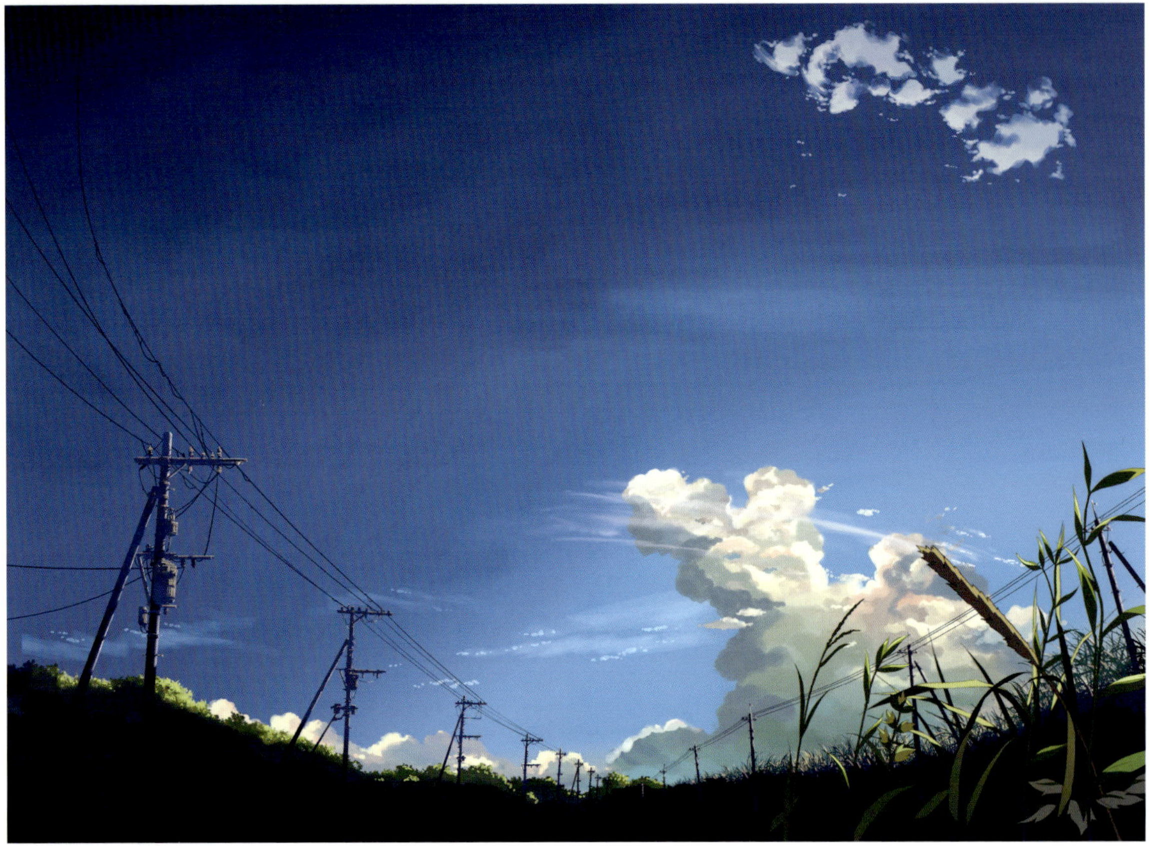

"5 Centimeters per Second" / CUT_200 / Setting: Nakatane, near the national highway

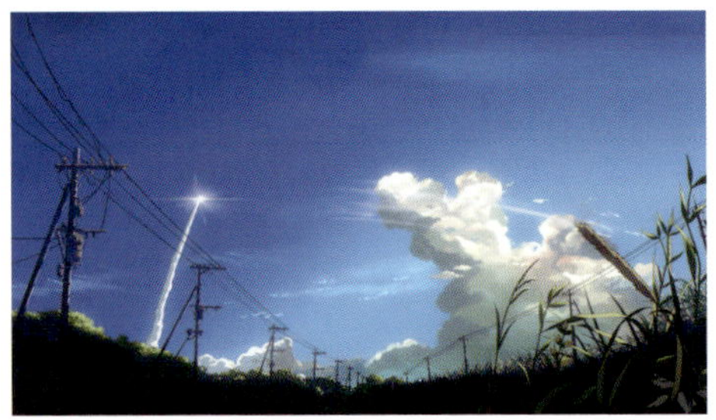

CUT_200 Final Version A

An HII-A rocket launching with nobody to see it off. This shows the same angle as CUT_267 (page 75) from Act 2.

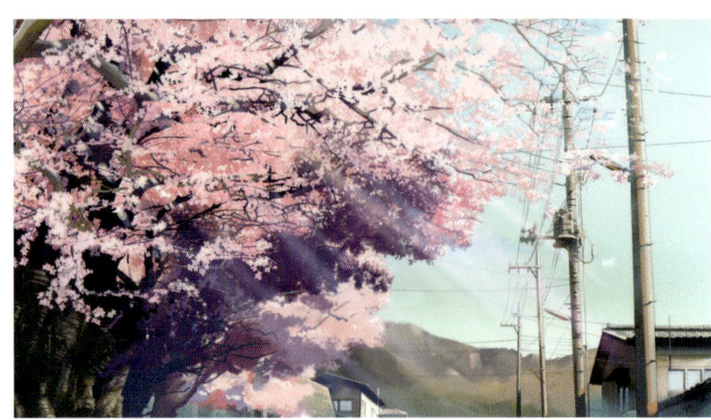

"5 Centimeters per Second" / CUT_146 / Setting: Akari's neighborhood

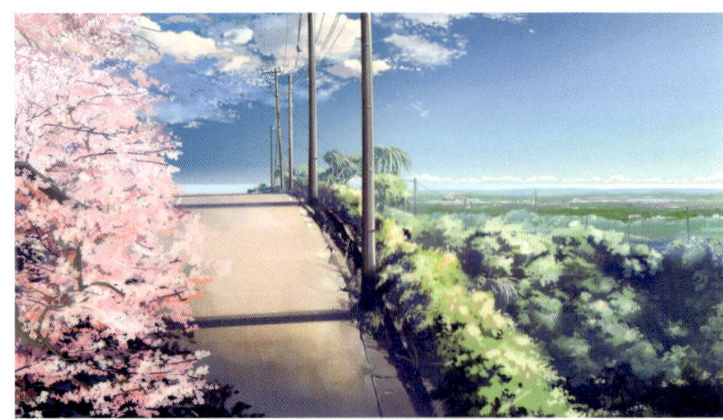

"5 Centimeters per Second" / CUT_147 / Setting: Road to school in Nakatane

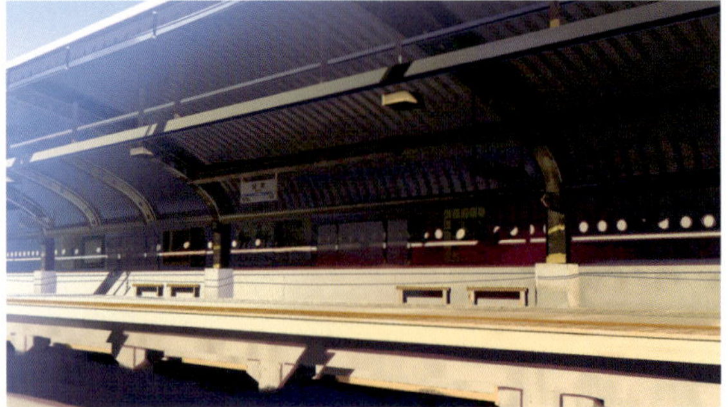

"5 Centimeters per Second" / CUT_242 / Setting: Private railway platform

Backgrounds for the scenes of Takaki and Akari's reminiscences. CUT_146 is set right after Act 1, as Akari, now in 8th grade, makes her way to school. CUT_147 shows the route Takaki and Kanae take to school on Tanegashima during the same timeframe as CUT_146. CUT_242 shows the platform where Takaki, in middle school, often spotted a girl that resembled Akari. It's never stated whether the girl was Akari herself, a doppelganger, or an illusion seen by Takaki.

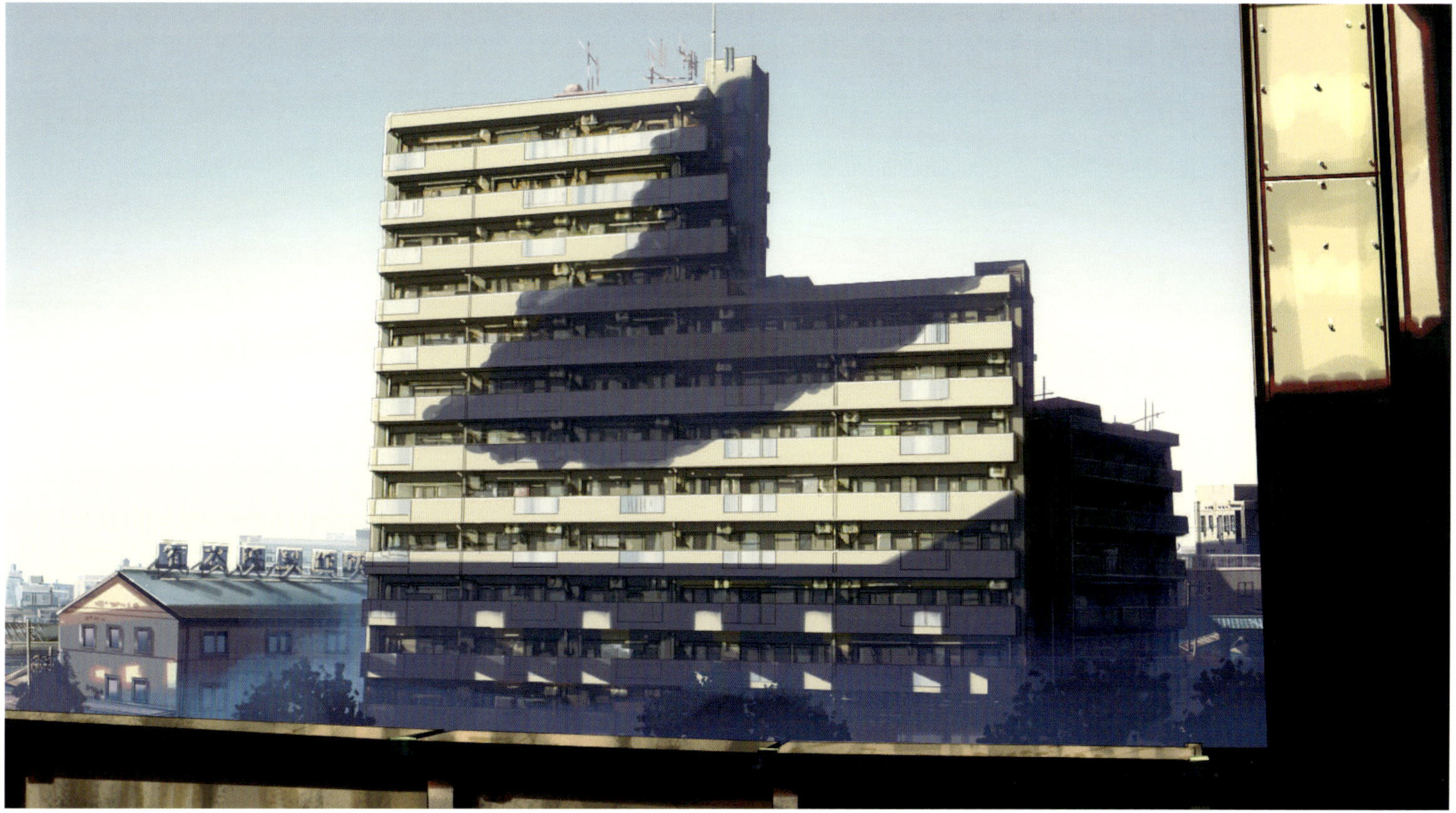

"5 Centimeters per Second" / CUT_259 / Setting: View of Tokyo

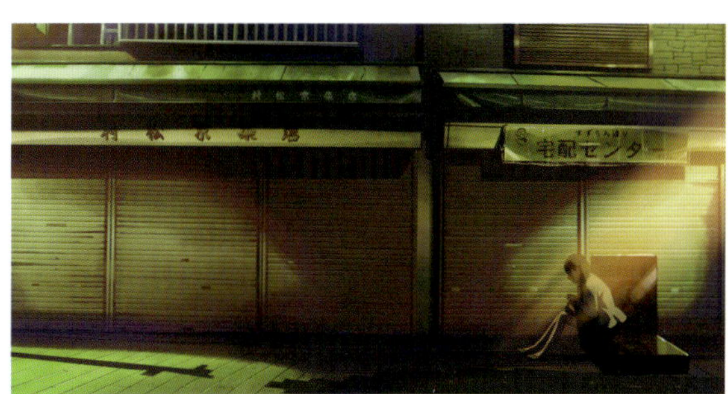

"5 Centimeters per Second" / CUT_183 / Setting: View of Tokyo

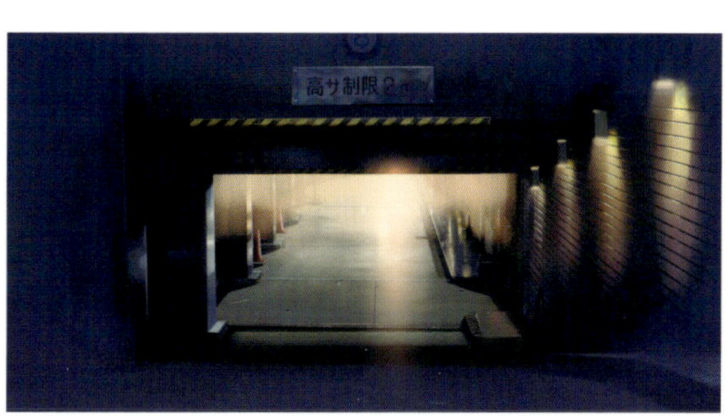
"5 Centimeters per Second" / CUT_212 / Setting: View of Tokyo

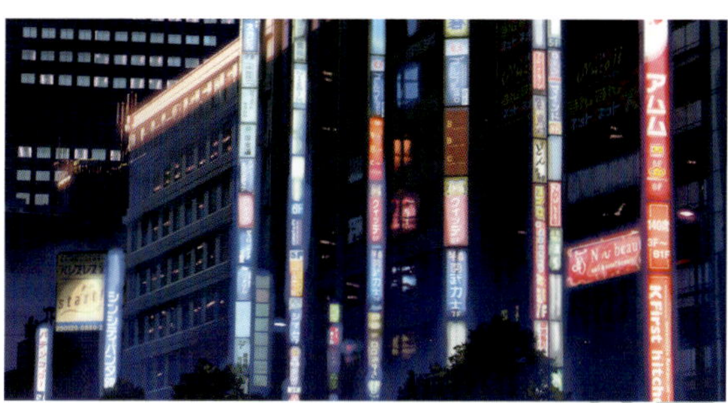
"5 Centimeters per Second" / CUT_217 / Setting: View of Tokyo

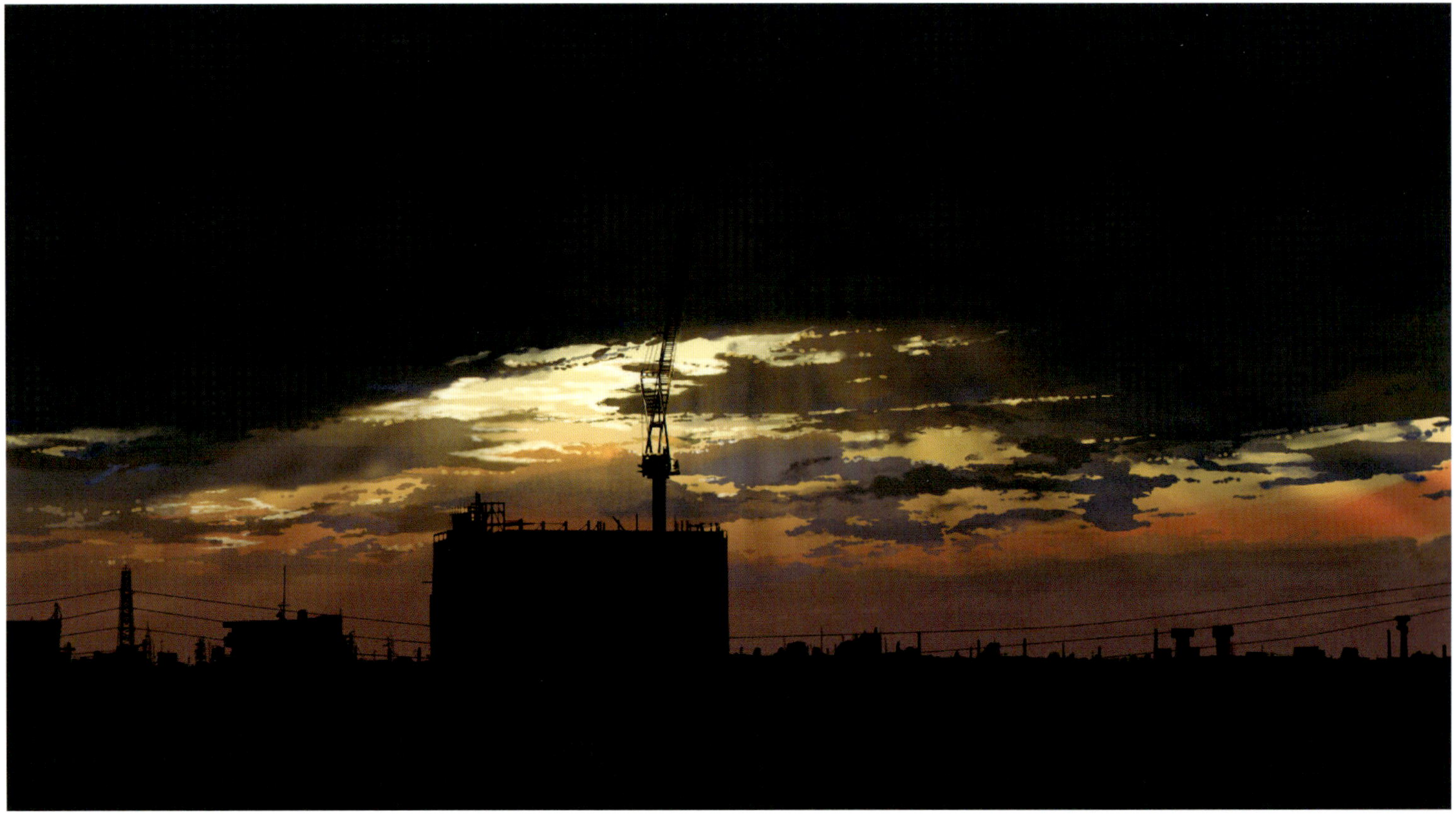

"5 Centimeters per Second" / CUT_263 / Setting: View of Tokyo

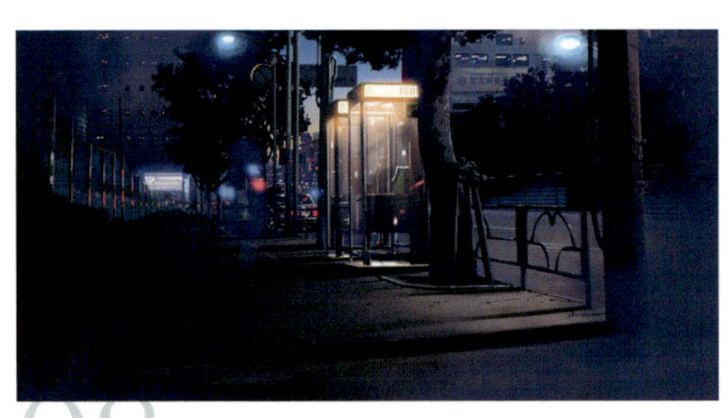

"5 Centimeters per Second" / CUT_273 / Setting: Phone booth in Tokyo

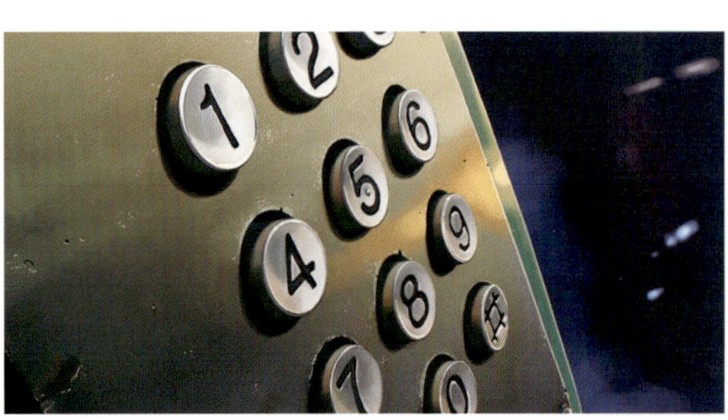

"5 Centimeters per Second" / CUT_275 / Setting: Phone booth in Tokyo

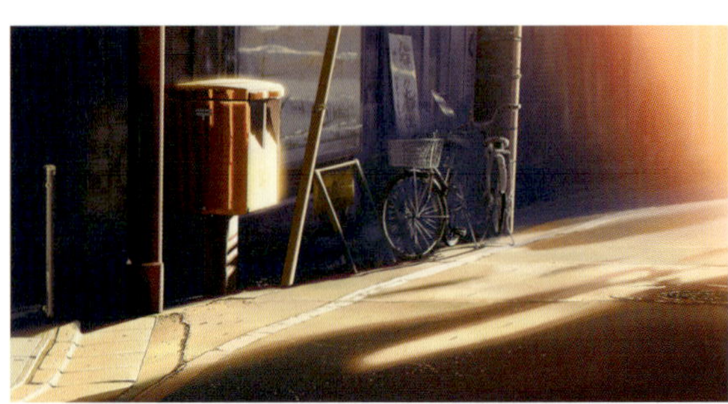

"5 Centimeters per Second" / CUT_274 / Setting: Akari's route to middle school, Iwafune

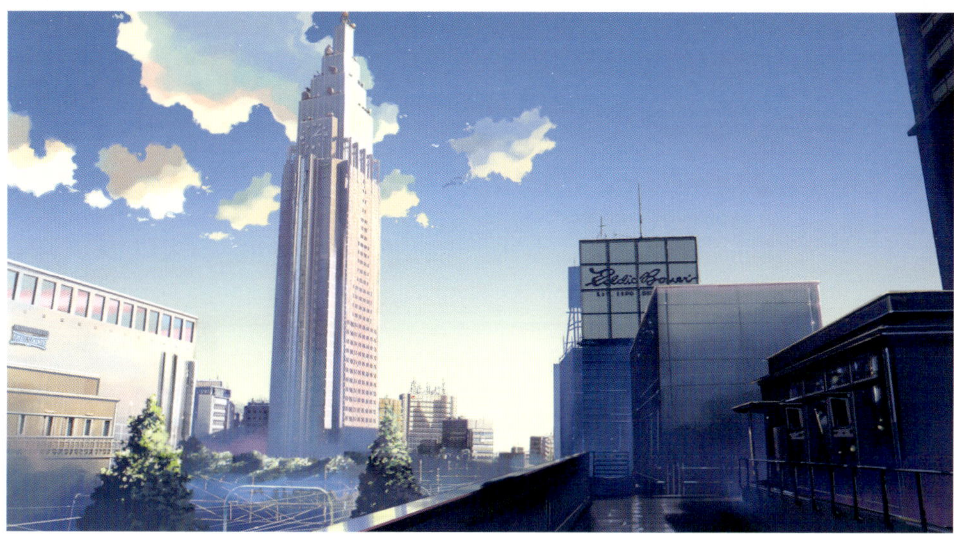

"5 Centimeters per Second" / CUT_286 / Setting: Tokyo skyscrapers

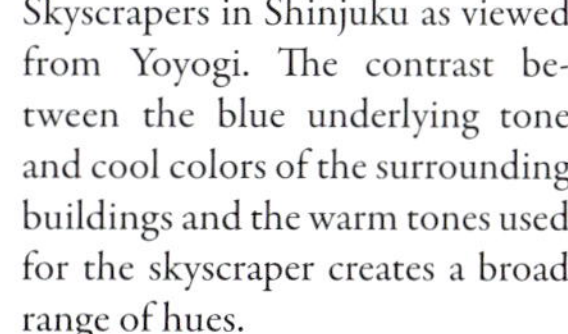

Skyscrapers in Shinjuku as viewed from Yoyogi. The contrast between the blue underlying tone and cool colors of the surrounding buildings and the warm tones used for the skyscraper creates a broad range of hues.

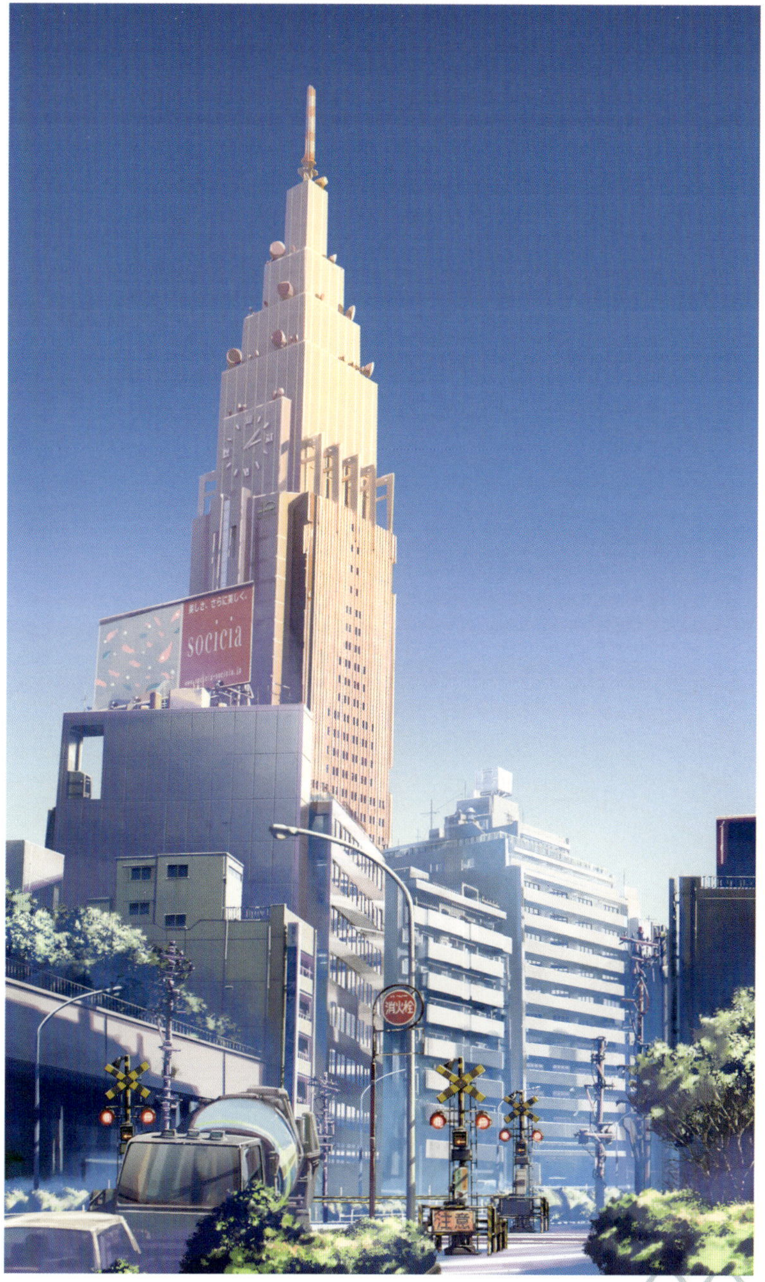

"5 Centimeters per Second" / CUT_292 / Setting: Tokyo skyscrapers

Takaki: I felt it strongly that if I turned around at that moment, she'd have turned and looked at me, too...

(Excerpt of *5 Centimeters per Second*, Act 3: "5 Centimeters per Second")

Act 3 : "5 Centimeters per Second"

Cherry Blossoms – A New Season

For the very beginning and end scenes of Act 3, the events that take place at the railroad crossings where Takaki and Akari walked together as kids become key. The train crossing is modeled on a private railway crossing in Tokyo, and is the same place depicted in Act 1. There are also many other settings aside from the rail crossing that overlap with scenes from Act 1. For the scenes that show Takaki in January and February, the overall image was very heavy and dark, while the scene where Takaki passes by the woman is drawn in refreshing, light-filled tones.

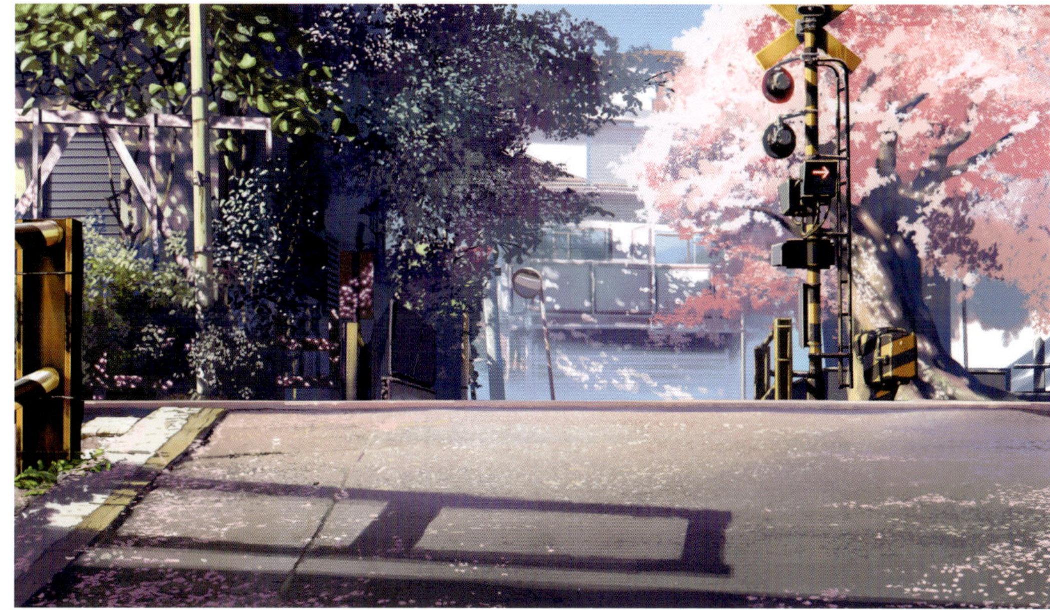

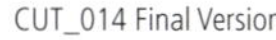

CUT_014 Final Version

"5 Centimeters per Second" / CUT_014 / Setting: Private railway crossing in Tokyo

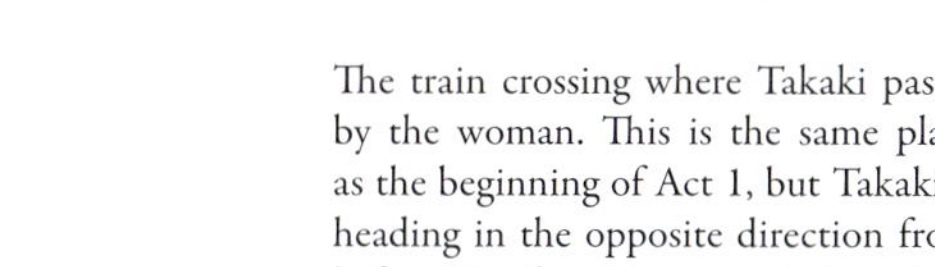

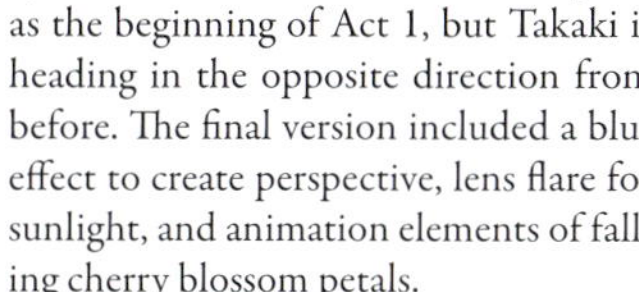

The train crossing where Takaki passes by the woman. This is the same place as the beginning of Act 1, but Takaki is heading in the opposite direction from before. The final version included a blur effect to create perspective, lens flare for sunlight, and animation elements of falling cherry blossom petals.

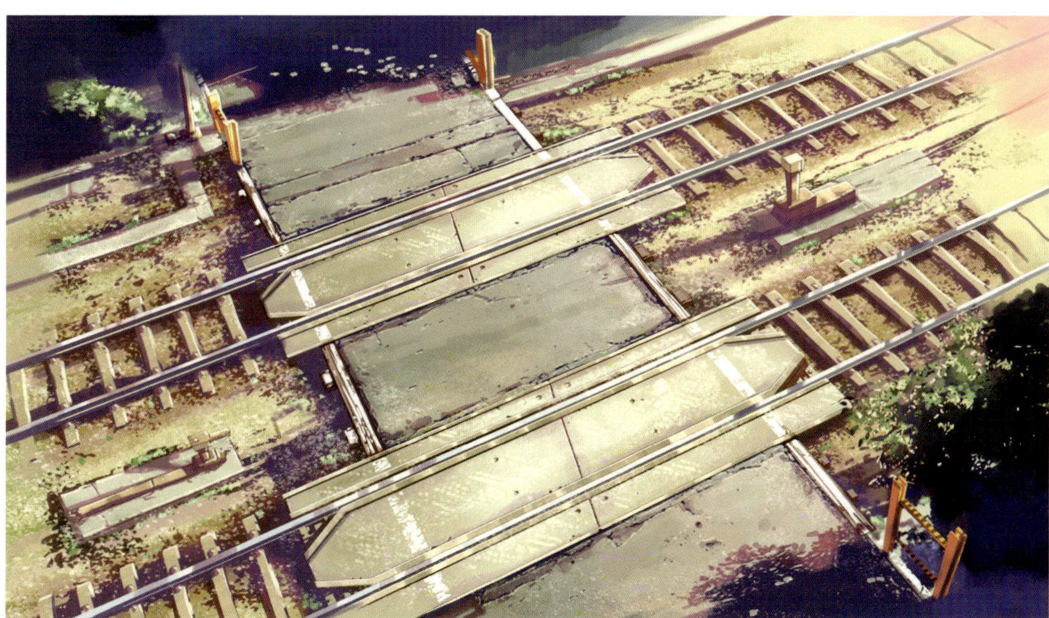

"5 Centimeters per Second" / CUT_015, CUT_019, CUT_315 / Setting: Private railway crossing in Tokyo

A cherry tree before the rail crossing. This is modeled on a cherry tree in Tokyo's Yoyogi Park, the same tree depicted in CUT_285 in Act 1 (page 51). The lamppost in the foreground is an overlay. In the final version, the skyscraper and the lamppost moved in order to portray Takaki's movement.

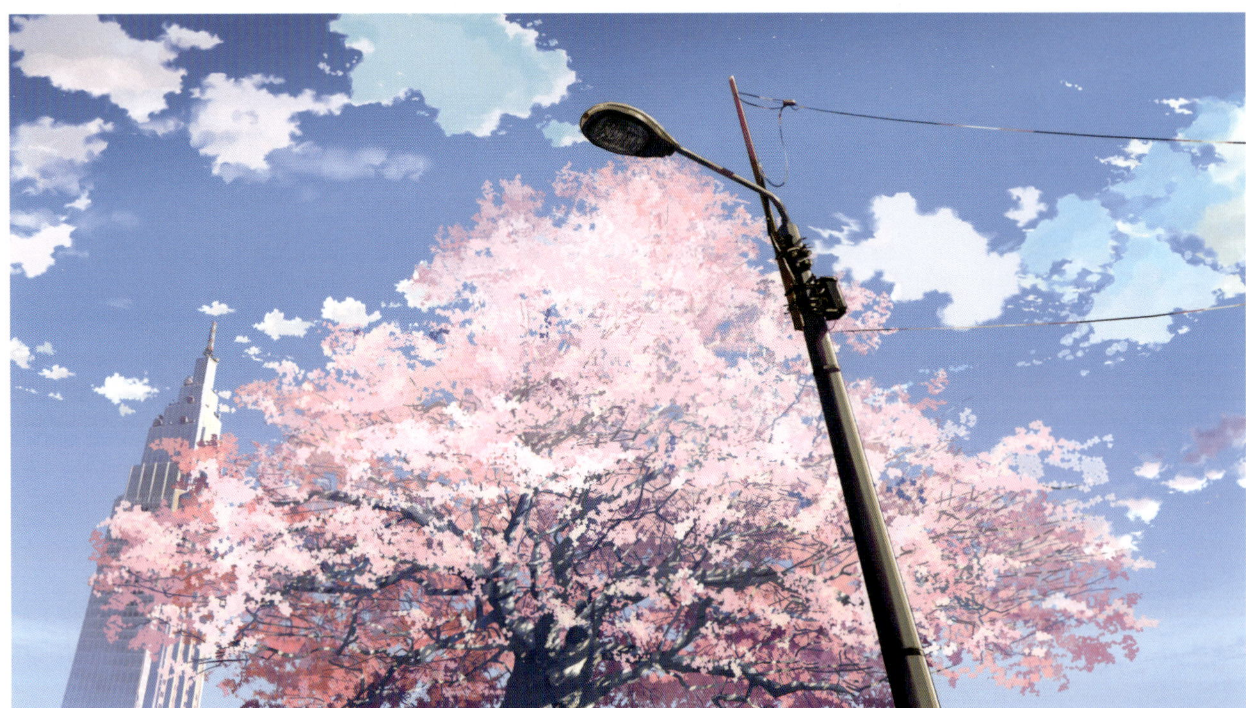

"5 Centimeters per Second" / CUT_011 / Setting: A residential district in Tokyo

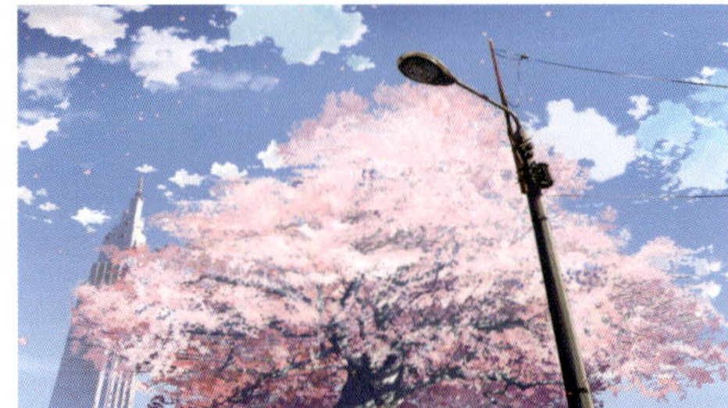

CUT_011 Final Version

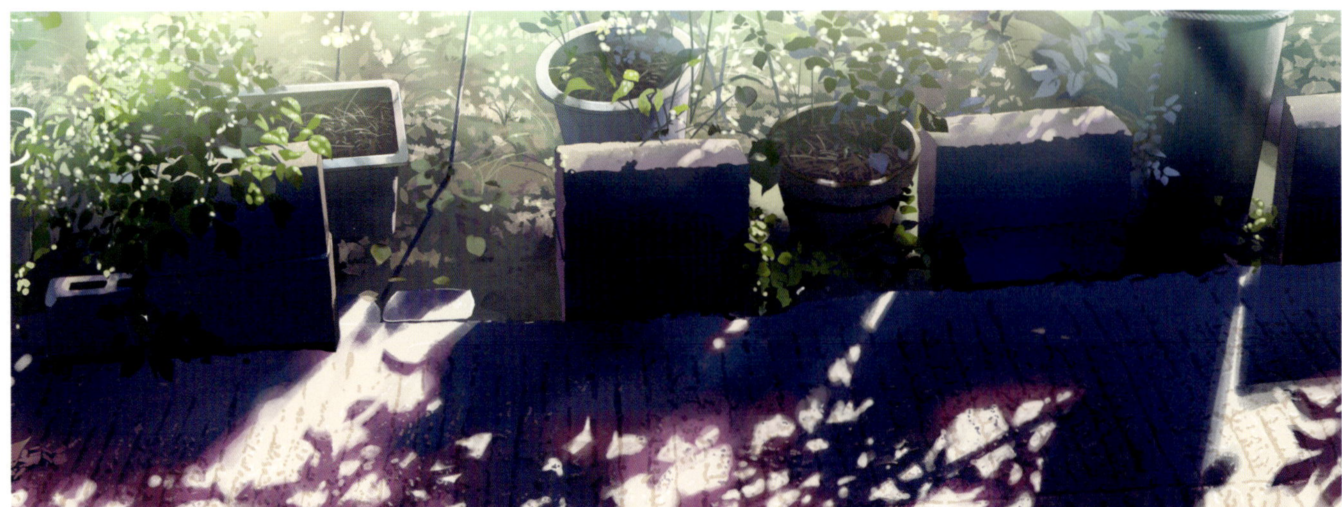

"5 Centimeters per Second" / CUT_012 / Setting: A residential district in Tokyo

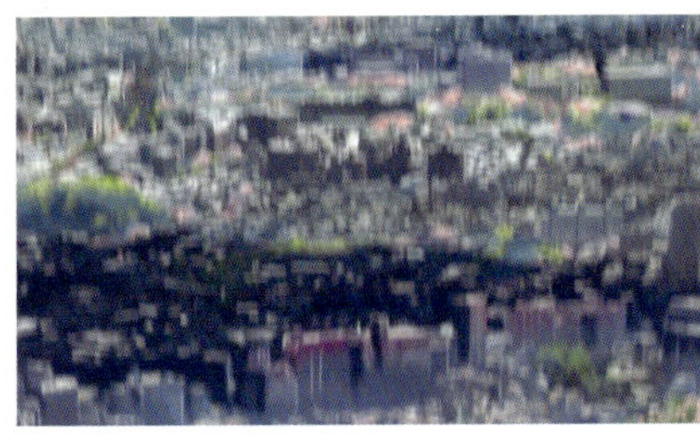

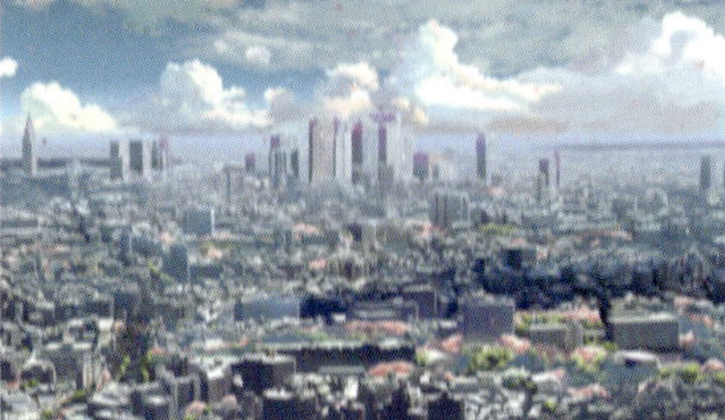

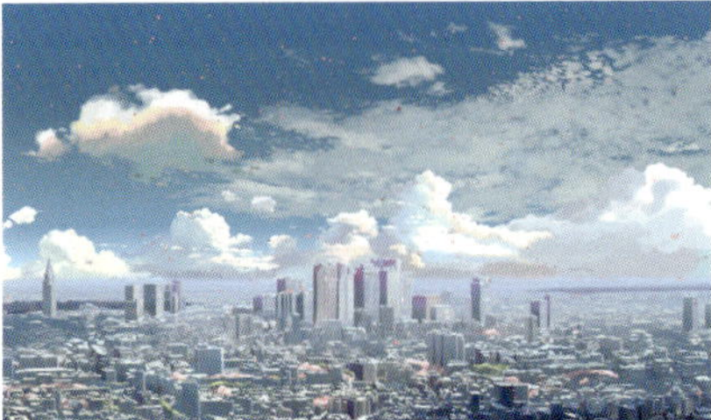

CUT_285 Final Version

CUT_285 is the background of the title card for Act 3: "5 Centimeters per Second." Since the camera pans rapidly from bottom to top, the image's perspective at the top and bottom is adjusted accordingly. The composition shows the view from skyscrapers in Ikebukuro looking towards Shinjuku, but as it wasn't possible to capture all the elements in a single photo, the rough sketch was based on a combination of several photographs.

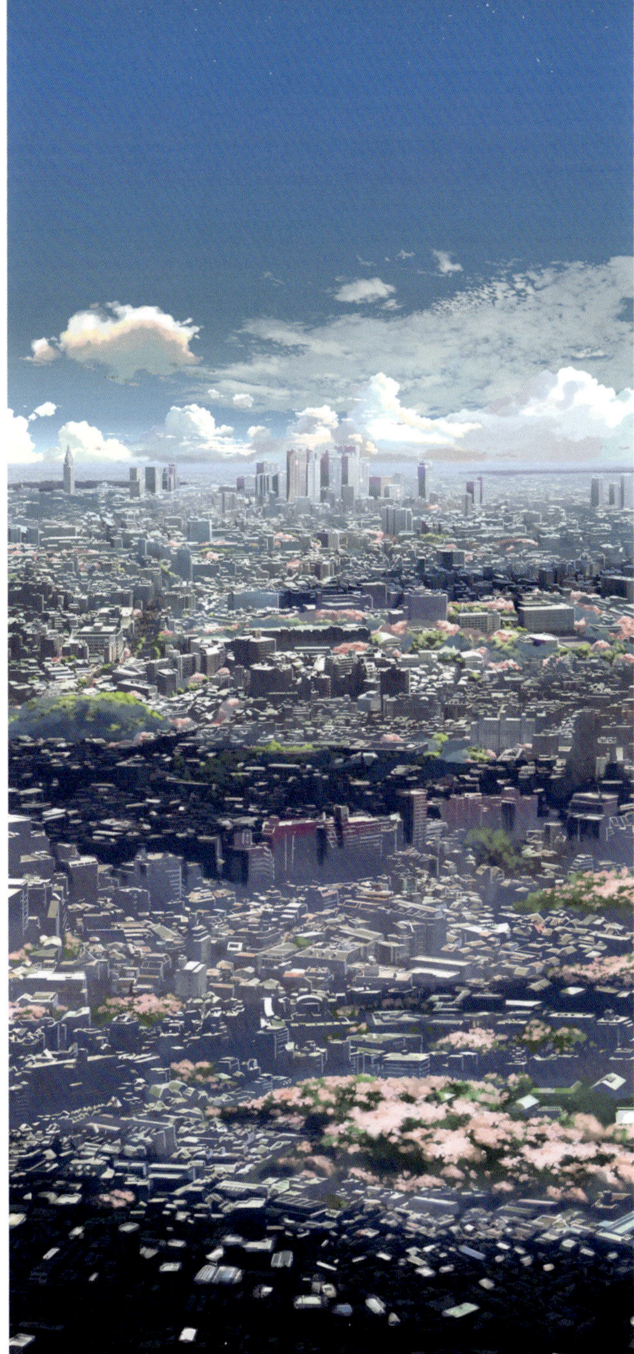

"5 Centimeters per Second" / CUT_285 / Setting: Panorama of Tokyo

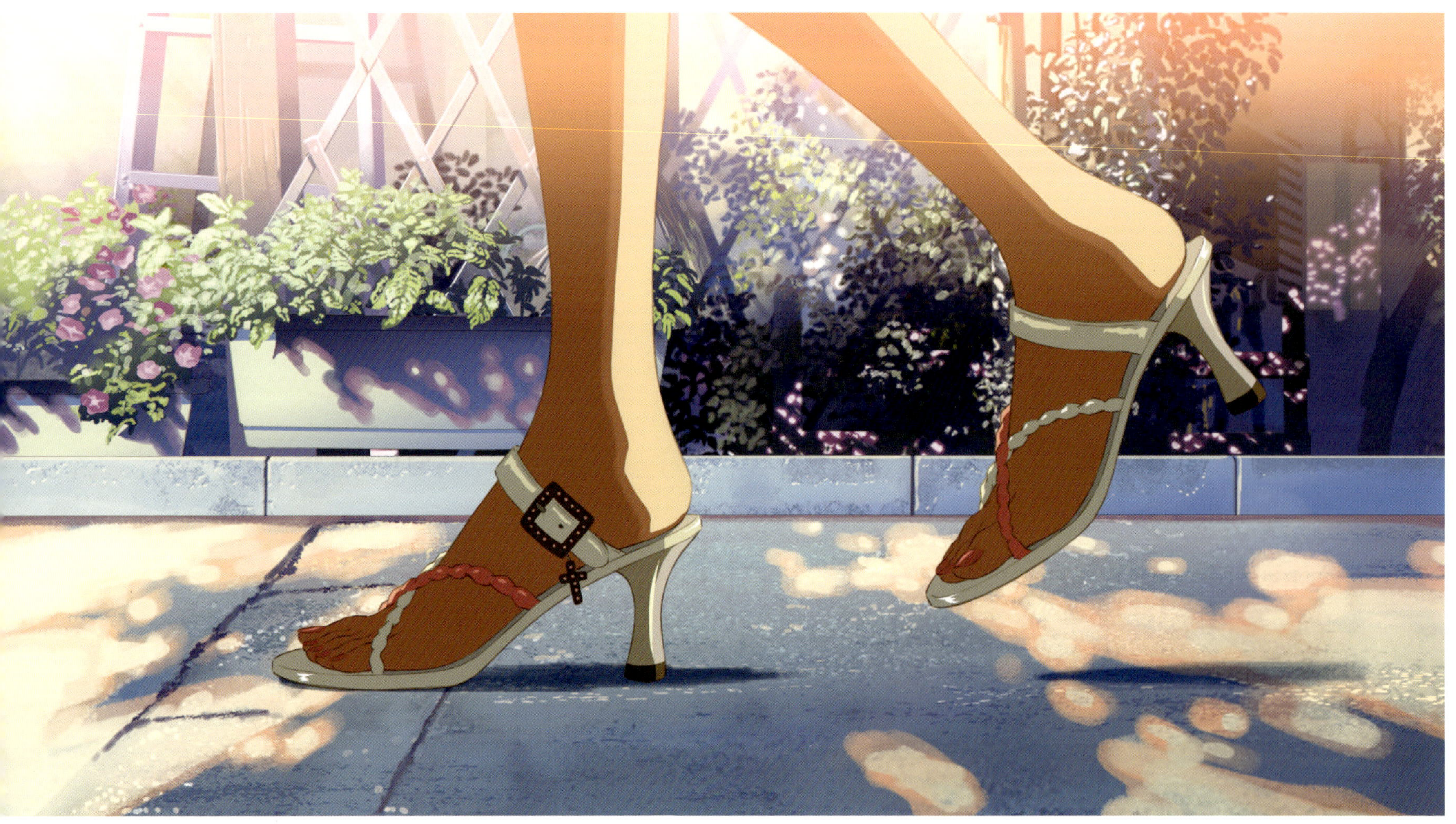

"5 Centimeters per Second" / CUT_310 / Setting: A residential district in Tokyo

This cut shows the great contrast in the density of detail in the background art. The colors of the plants change in gradations, which brings forth a depth that isn't intrusive. In the film *5 Centimeters per Second*, in order for the character cels to balance with the background art across all acts, mid-tones were brushed on between the normally colored areas and the shadow colored areas. Cels were drawn using pencil, and as such there are bold and thin areas of the lines. Therefore artists could not use the "fill" tool in their software program to automatically color in areas, so each color was individually applied by hand. The characters' coloring specifications take the background art's color palette into consideration each and every cut.

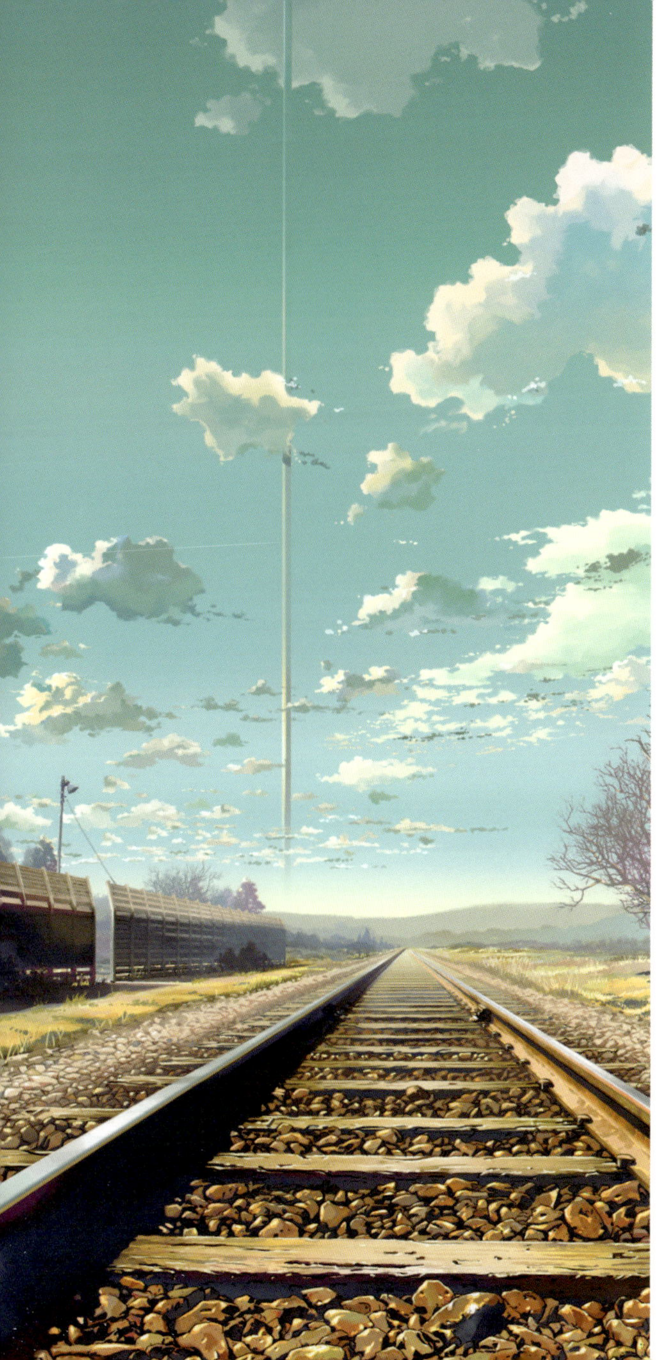

The Place Promised in Our Early Days

Japanese theatrical release: November 20, 2004
DVD release: February 17, 2005 (JP); July 12, 2005 (US)
HD DVD, Blu-Ray Disc release: April 18, 2008 (JP)

Best Animated Film, 59th Mainichi Film Awards, 2004
Award for Art in the 36th Seiun Award Division, 2005 Japan Sci-Fi Convention
Silver Prize in Best Animated Film Division, Canada Fantasia Film Festival
Special Distinction, Feature Film Division, 9th Seoul Comics and Animation Festival
Jury Recommended Feature-Length Animation, Animation Division, 9th Japan Media Arts Festival, 2005

Running time: 91 minutes

Staff:
Original Creator, Screenwriter, Director: Makoto Shinkai
Character Design/Chief Animation Director: Ushio Tazawa
Art Director: Takumi Tanji, Makoto Shinkai
Music: Tenmon
Producer: Makoto Shinkai/CoMix Wave Films

Background Art: Takumi Tanji, Akira Hirosawa, Akiko Majima, Yasushi Ebihara, Kiyoshi Ochiai, Arata Toma, Tasuku Watanabe, Hong Ju Heun, Makoto Shinkai

Background Art Assistants: Yuko Tanaka, Kaoru Akiya, Sanae Miura, Chang Sung Hee, Kim Seong Sik

The Place Promised in Our Early Days

Distant Time

At first, production began on *The Place Promised in Our Early Days* with Mr. Shinkai slated to handle all of the background artwork himself, as he had done with *Voices of a Distant Star*. In light of a realistic production schedule, however, the main members of the current background art team of Shinkai Productions were gathered for the film. Mr. Shinkai himself had no hands-on experience with commercial animation, and considering that all of the background art would be created using CG, he chose artists who were not stereotypical animation production workers, since there were no existing animation background artwork companies which they could hire for the job. This resulted in a group mainly consisting of art school graduates, starting with Takumi Tanji, who were highly skilled in the fundamentals of painting. This decision resulted in art that best supports the particular aesthetic of Shinkai's works.

Sayuri: (*happily*) Huh? Hiroki!

Hiroki: Sayuri... You're going home late.

Sayuri: Yeah, I was late because I was practicing.

Takuya: Violin?

Sayuri: Yeah. You're not with Takuya?

Hiroki: Yeah, I was also doing club activities.

Sayuri: I notice you sometimes practice your archery by yourself.

Hiroki: Yeah well, I'm... I'm not really that good yet. My mind wanders a lot.

SFX: *preeet (train whistle)*

SFX: *ktun... ktun...*

Sayuri: Do you have any plans during spring break?

Hiroki: Yeah. I'm gonna be working with Takuya.

Sayuri: Work? I'm jealous! Where?

Hiroki: At a military factory in Hamana, working on guided missiles 'n stuff.

Sayuri: Hmm. It's great you've got a job. I've only got my club activities.

Hiroki: Really?

Sayuri: Yeah...

Train Station Announcement: (*off-screen*) The next station is Naka-Oguni, Naka-Oguni. After Naka-Oguni, we'll stop at Odaira.

Sayuri: Oh, this is my stop. You know, yesterday, I had a dream I would go home with you like this.

(Excerpt of *The Place Promised in Our Early Days*)

The school lives of Hiroki, Takuya and Sayuri during their middle school days were strongly influenced by Mr. Shinkai's own school-era experiences. The setting in the film is Aomori Prefecture, but from time to time you can see images of Mr. Shinkai's home prefecture of Nakano in the school scenes.

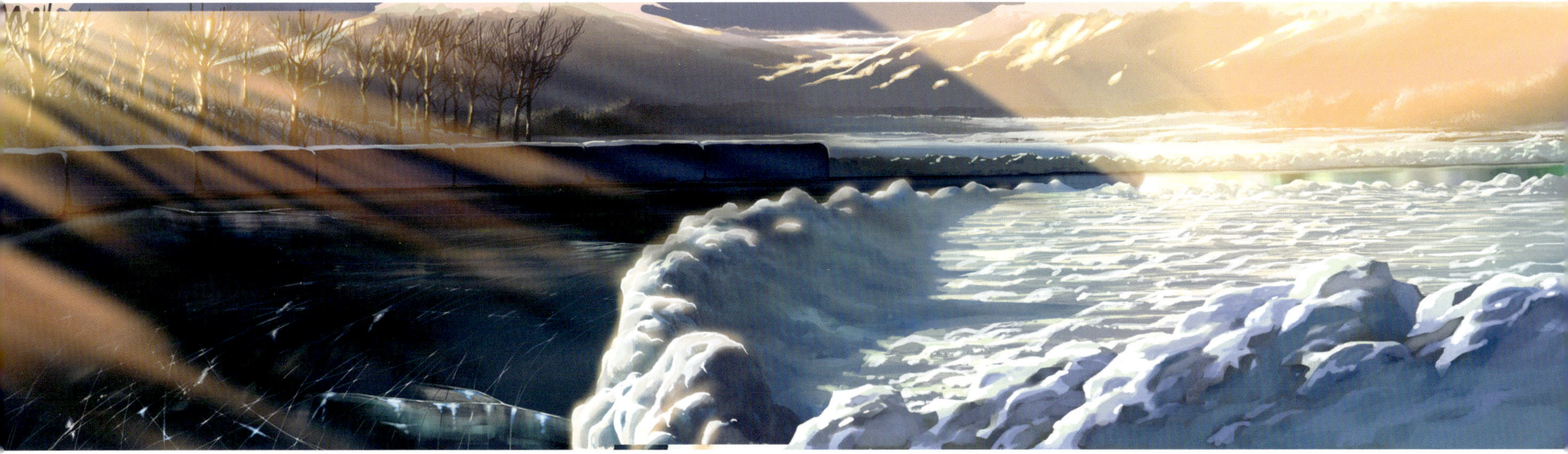

The Place Promised in Our Early Days / CUT_1-033 / Setting: Tsugaru, Aomori Prefecture

The middle school that the three kids attend is based on location photos of the former Nishienden Elementary School in Ueda City, Nagano Prefecture. CUT_1-042 was the first background artwork handled by Takumi Tanji as a test.

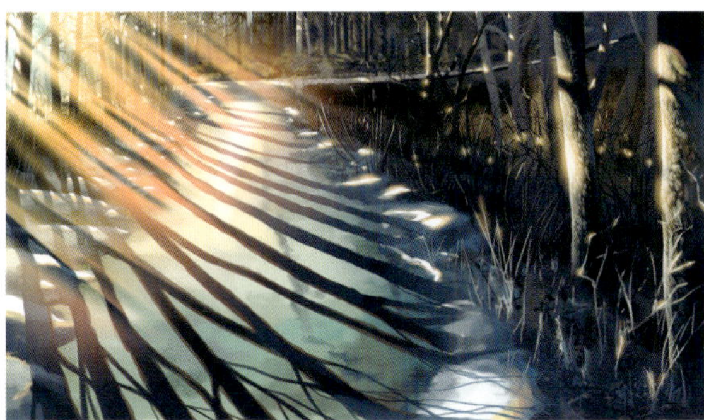

The Place Promised in Our Early Days / CUT_1-042 / Setting: Tsugaru, Aomori Prefecture

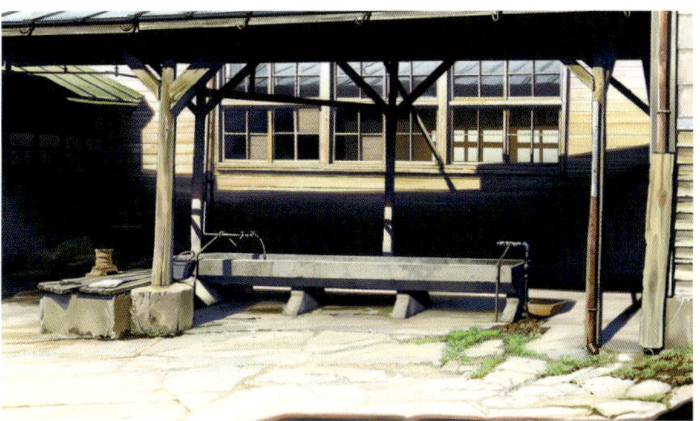

The Place Promised in Our Early Days / CUT_1-047 / Setting: High school drinking fountain, Tsugaru, Aomori Prefecture

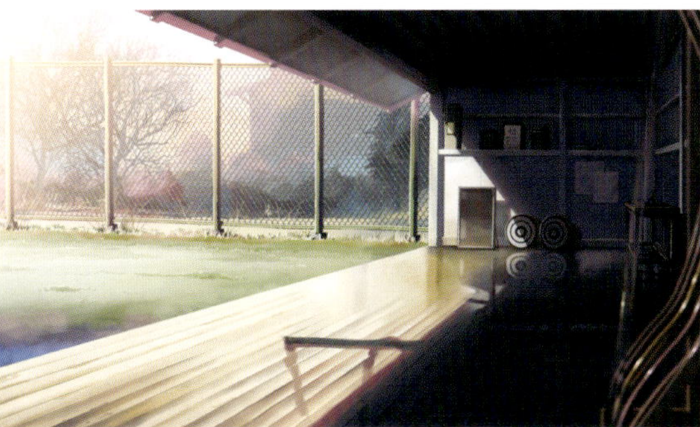

The Place Promised in Our Early Days / CUT_1-056 / Setting: High school archery practice hall, Tsugaru, Aomori Prefecture

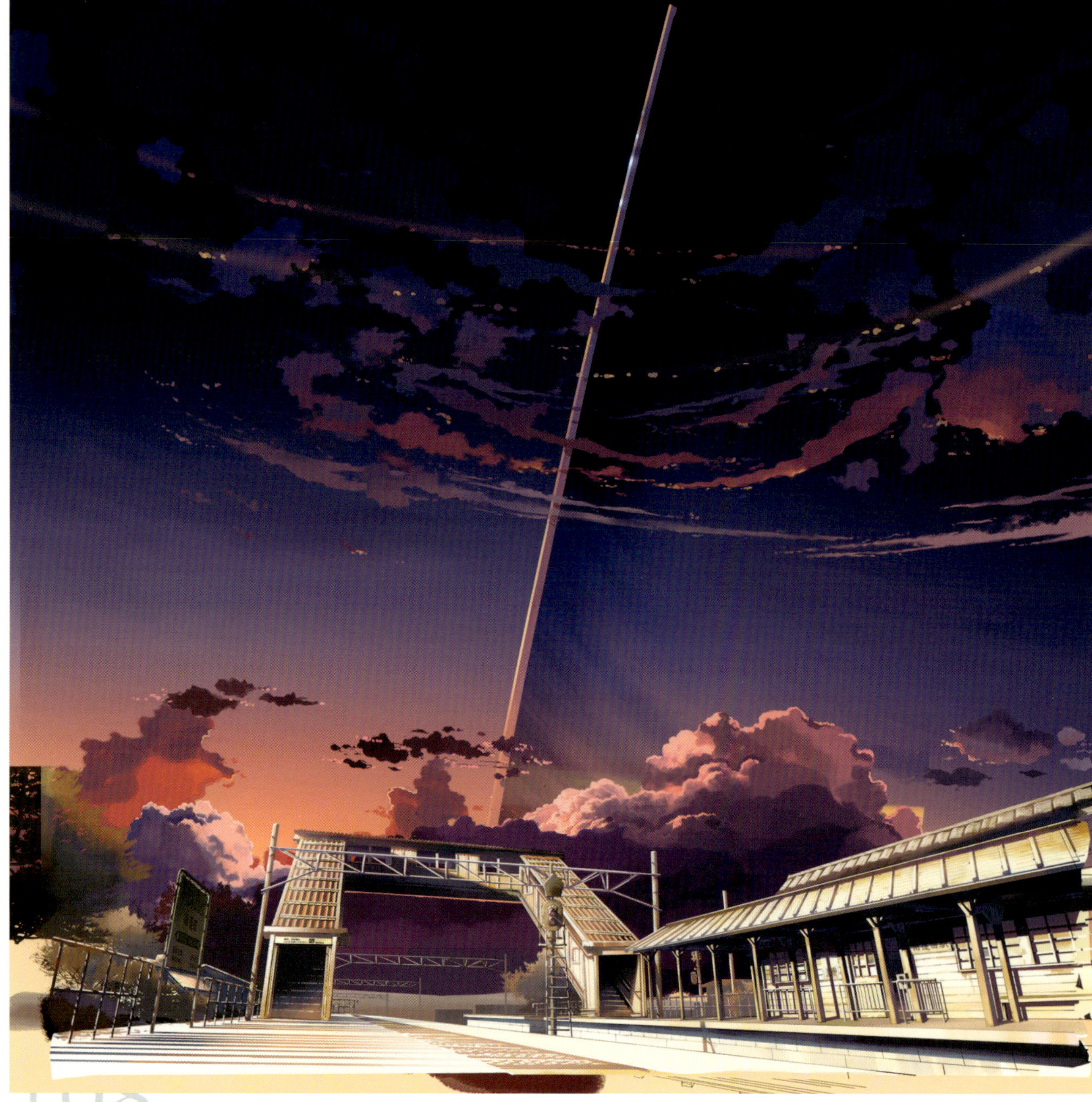

South Yomogita Station is modeled on the JR Kanita Station in Aomori Prefecture. This angle, with the Tower visible in the distance beyond the far-off clouds, creates a greater sense of enormousness and vast distance. You can see the extreme perspective used in creating the artwork when the camera angle shifts.

The Place Promised in Our Early Days / CUT_1-020 /
Setting: South Yomogita Station, Tsugaru, Aomori Prefecture

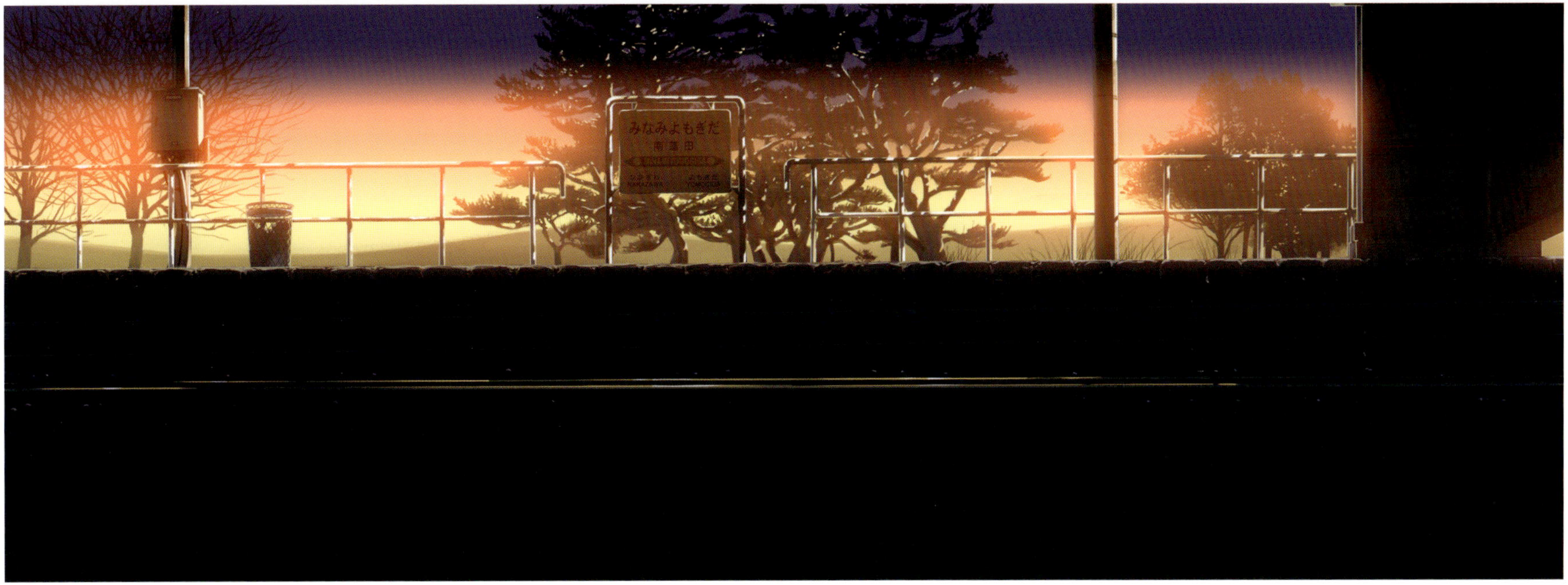

The train station near the middle school that Hiroki and his friends attend. This cut is a good example of the contrast used in creating the artwork. Lighting effects were later added to control the variance of detail and draw in the viewer's eye.

The Place Promised in Our Early Days / CUT_1-014 /
Setting: South Yomogita Station, Tsugaru, Aomori Prefecture

CUT_1-012 and CUT_1-064 depict the same location during different seasons. In the places where a multi-plane effect was added, the artwork was prepared on separate layers.
CUT_1-078 is Naka-Oguni Station where Sayuri disembarks the train (but is modeled after a different station).

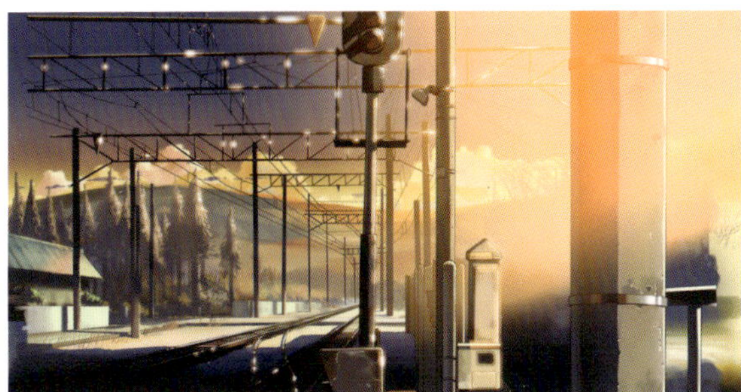

The Place Promised in Our Early Days / CUT_1-012 /
Setting: South Yomogita Station, Tsugaru, Aomori Prefecture

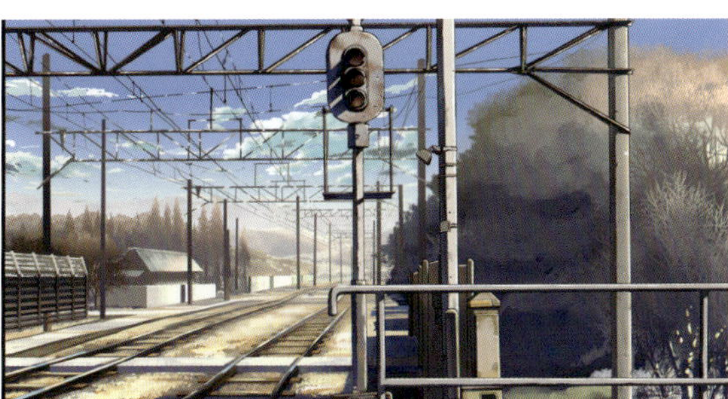

The Place Promised in Our Early Days / CUT_1-064 /
Setting: South Yomogita Station, Tsugaru, Aomori Prefecture

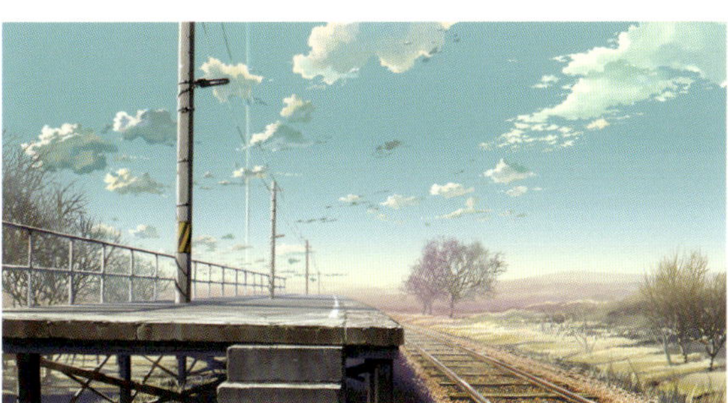

The Place Promised in Our Early Days / CUT_1-078 /
Setting: Naka-Oguni Station, Tsugaru, Aomori Prefecture

The Place Promised in Our Early Days

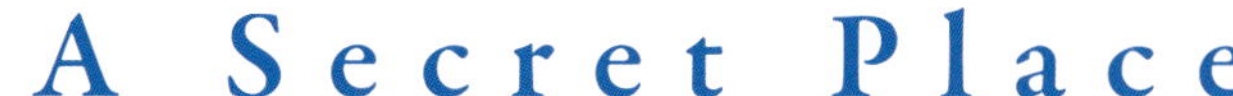

A Secret Place

Hiroki and Takuya rebuild a plane, named Bella Ciela, in an old station building on an abandoned rail line and a car repair garage out in a meadow. The location appears to be near Tappizaki Cape on the northern end of the Tsugaru Peninsula. As this location does not actually exist, 3DCG was used to create the base sketch, and the angles were adjusted as needed before it was handed over to the animation and background art staff. The lake in which the abandoned rail line has sunk is deftly used as an element to depict the passage of time and the psychological states of the characters.

Hiroki: (*monologue*) In those days I felt that time and place would continue on like that for the rest of my life.

The Tower that was beyond clouds that I admired became an important promised place to me.

I think there was nothing for us to fear at that moment.

The world and history were moving right nearby, but in those days, I thought that the night fragrance floating through the train, my faith in my friends, and Sayuri's presence that made the air tremble were the only things in the world.

However, even then, the premonition that such times would not last very long lurked in the depths of my heart...

(Excerpt of *The Place Promised in Our Early Days*)

In the background of the repair garage where Hiroki and Takuya fix up Bella Ciela, distant clouds were drawn on a separate layer so they could slide across the sky.
In CUT_1-276, you can see the sidetrack next to the sunken station which the boys used to launch Bella Ciela.

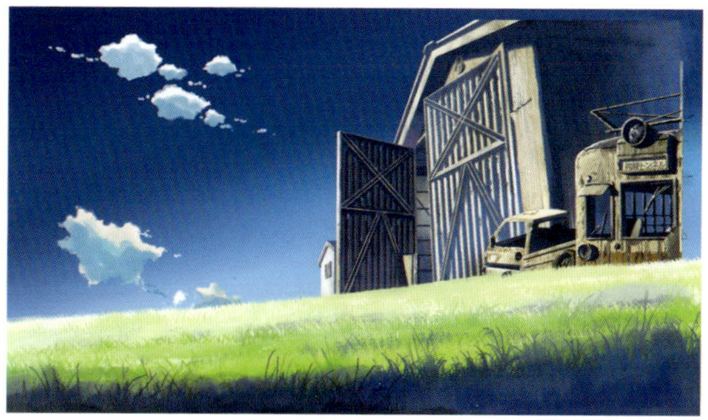

The Place Promised in Our Early Days / CUT_1-275 /
Setting: Abandoned Station, Tsugaru, Aomori Prefecture

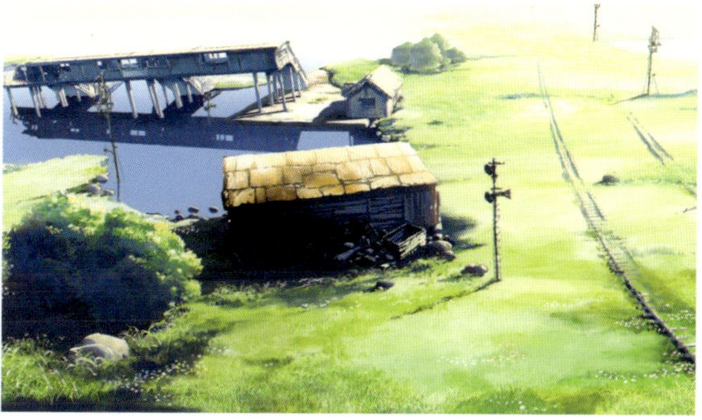

The Place Promised in Our Early Days / CUT_1-276 /
Setting: Abandoned Station, Tsugaru, Aomori Prefecture

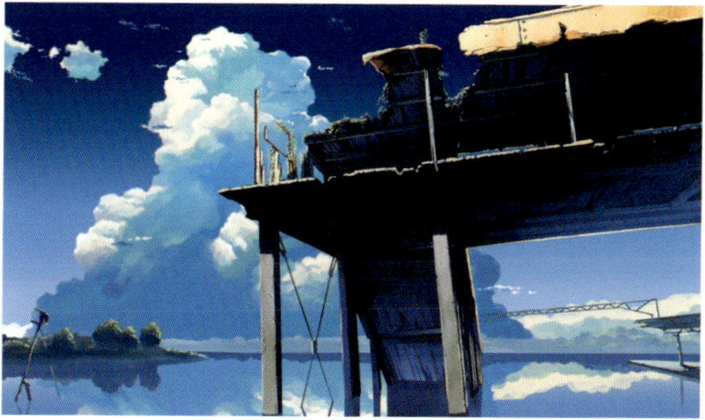

The Place Promised in Our Early Days / CUT_1-282 /
Setting: Abandoned Station, Tsugaru, Aomori Prefecture

A panorama cut filled from end to end with artwork. A large amount of data had to be created to allow a pan from left to right.
The clouds were drawn on separate layers. In the far distance, you can see the Tower on Hokkaido.

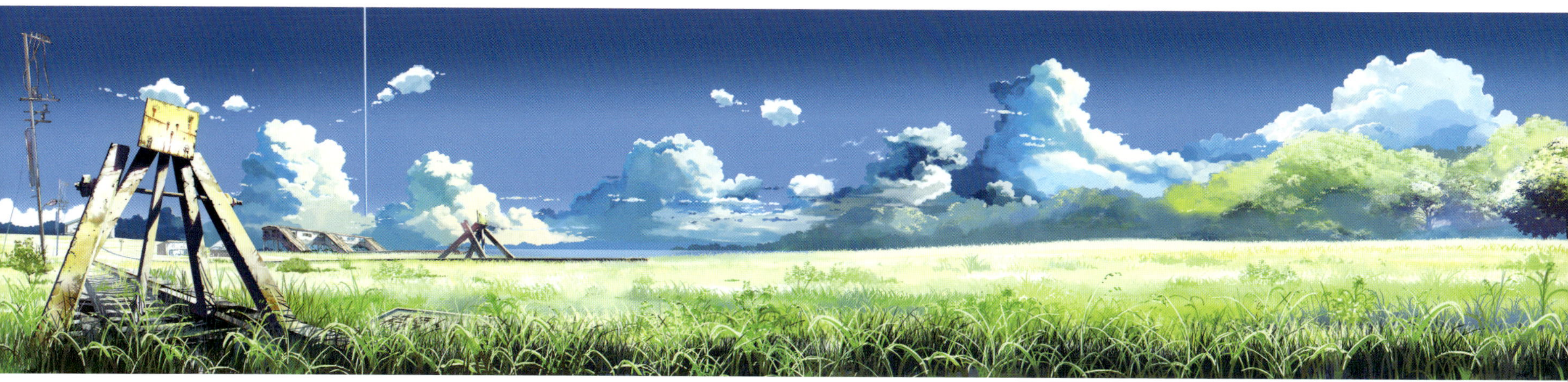

The Place Promised in Our Early Days / CUT_1-185 / Setting: Abandoned Station, Tsugaru, Aomori Prefecture

A sunset during summer vacation. The string of small clouds stretching across the sky hints at the approaching autumn. The sunlight was added at the compositing stage (where the artwork data is recorded using video software in order to prepare it for broadcast, etc.). In the darkest shadows, the level of detail on the grass was curtailed.

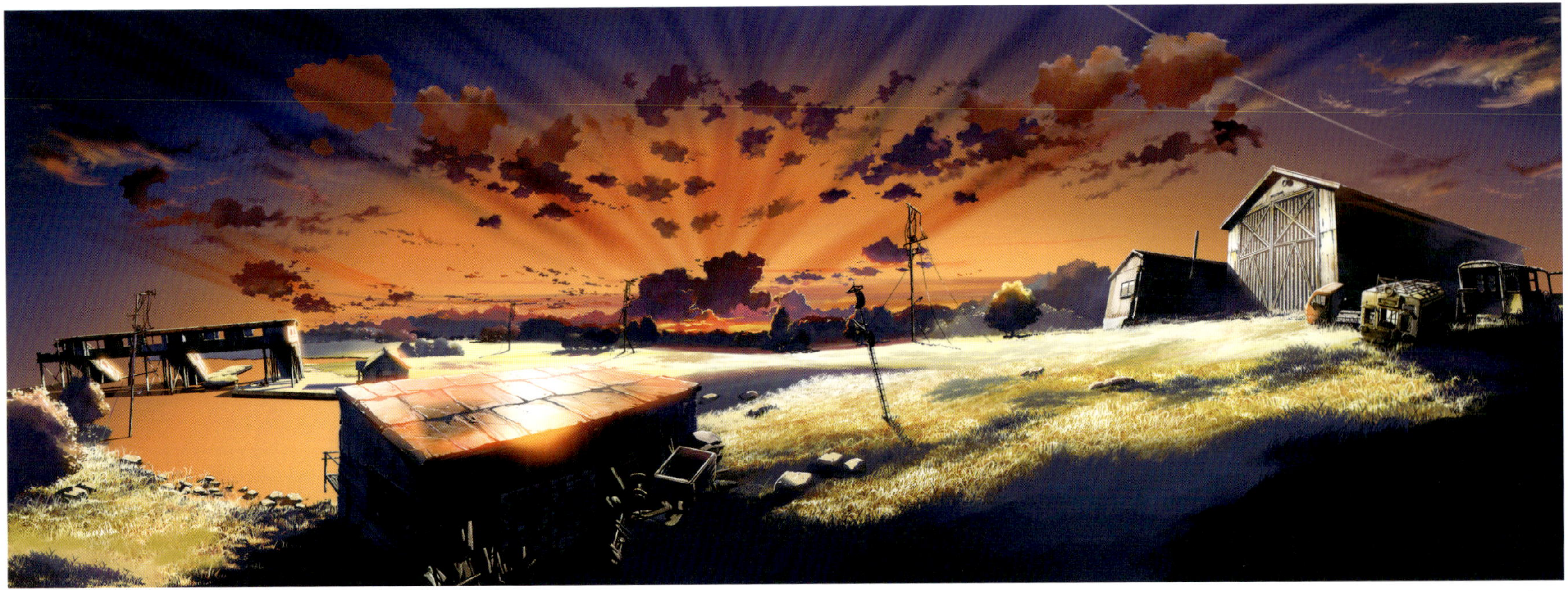

The Place Promised in Our Early Days / CUT_1-198 / Setting: Abandoned Station, Tsugaru, Aomori Prefecture

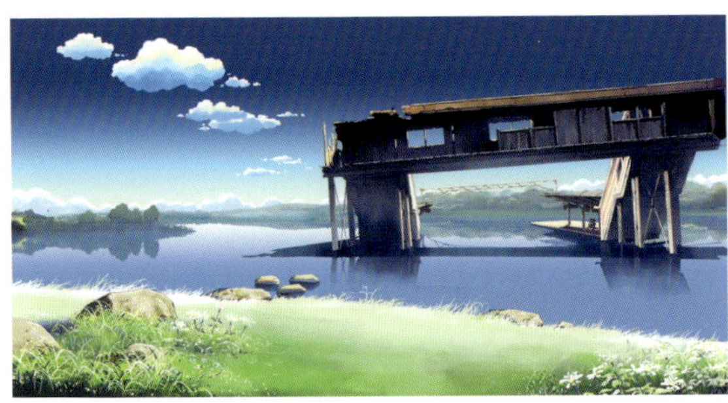

The Place Promised in Our Early Days / CUT_1-309 / Setting: Abandoned Station, Tsugaru, Aomori Prefecture

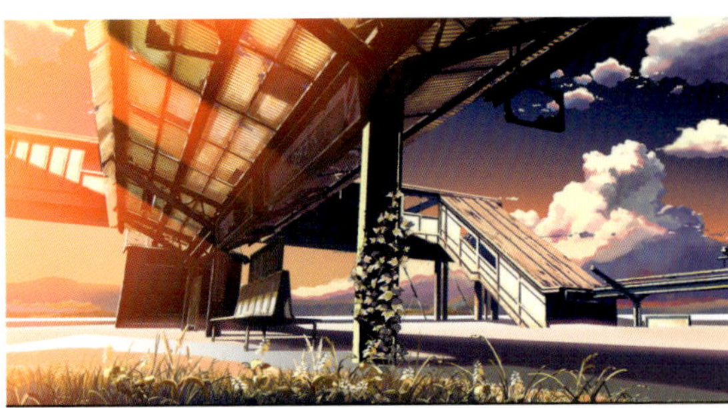

The Place Promised in Our Early Days / CUT_1-323 / Setting: Abandoned Station, Tsugaru, Aomori Prefecture

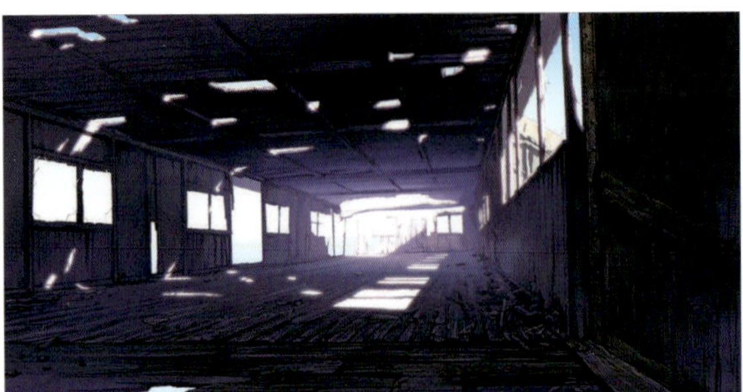

The Place Promised in Our Early Days / CUT_1-280 / Setting: Abandoned Station, Tsugaru, Aomori Prefecture

The old car repair garage where the boys fix up and store Bella Ciela. All the elements except the building in the scenes set here were drawn on harmony cels.

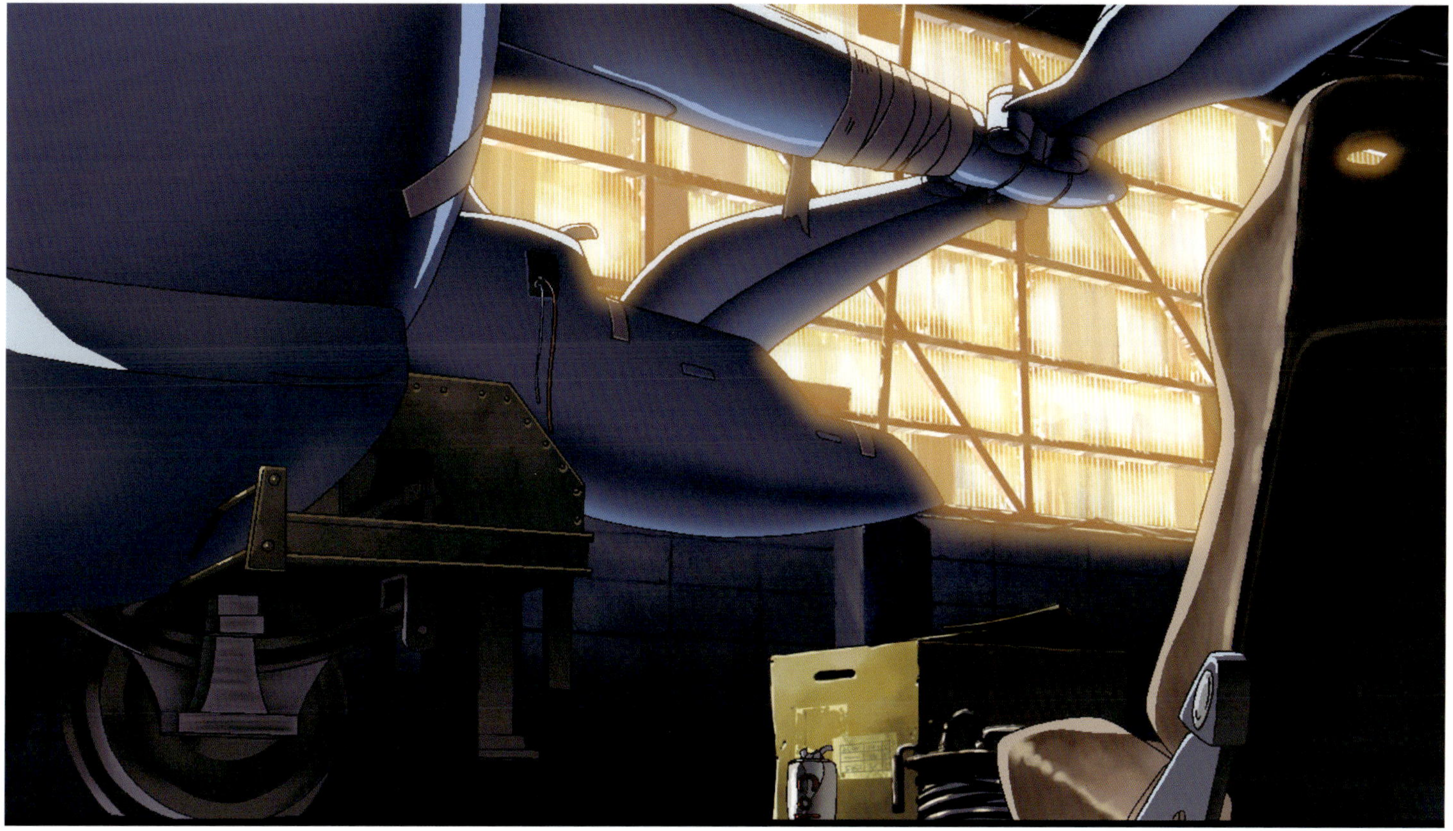

The Place Promised in Our Early Days / CUT_1-296 / Setting: Abandoned Station, Tsugaru, Aomori Prefecture

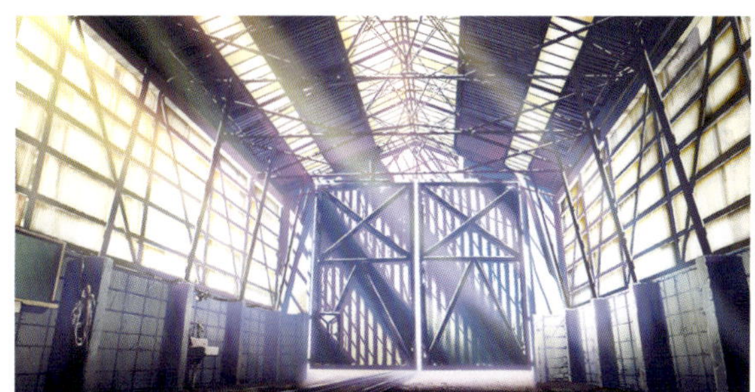

The Place Promised in Our Early Days / CUT_1-189 / Setting: Abandoned Station, Tsugaru, Aomori Prefecture

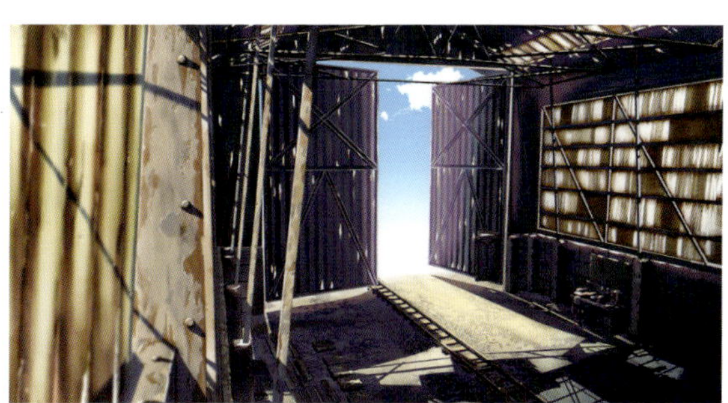

The Place Promised in Our Early Days / CUT_1-274 / Setting: Abandoned Station, Tsugaru, Aomori Prefecture

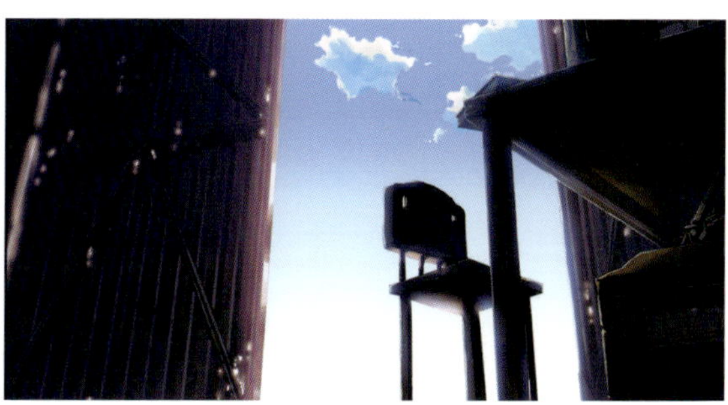

The Place Promised in Our Early Days / CUT_1-293 / Setting: Abandoned Station, Tsugaru, Aomori Prefecture

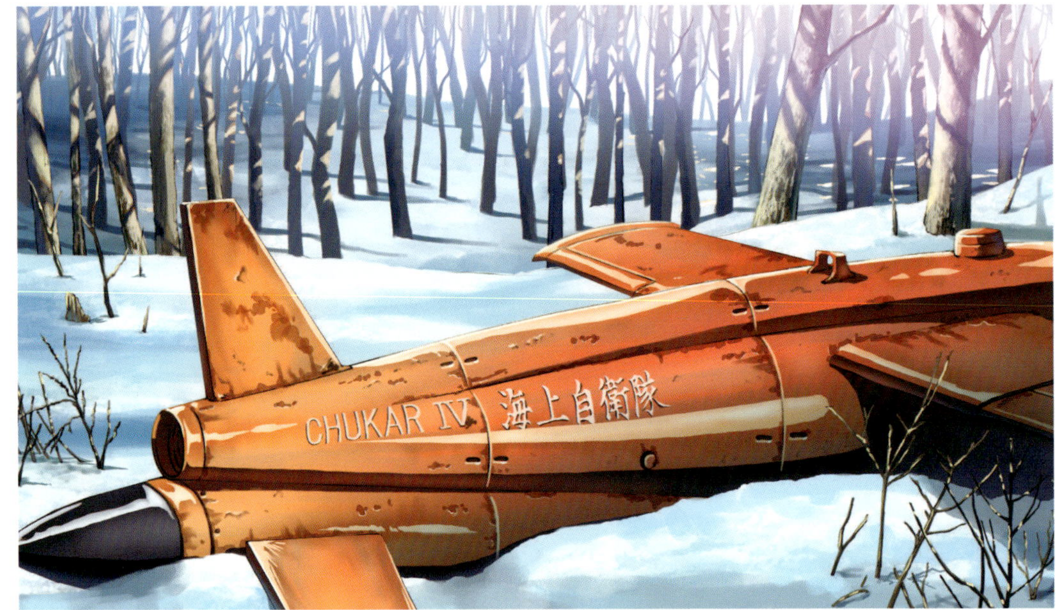

The Place Promised in Our Early Days / CUT_1-091 / Setting: Tsugaru, Aomori Prefecture

The Maritime Self-Defense Force unmanned high-speed target drone (CHUKAR IV) was modeled on an actual CHUKAR III drone.

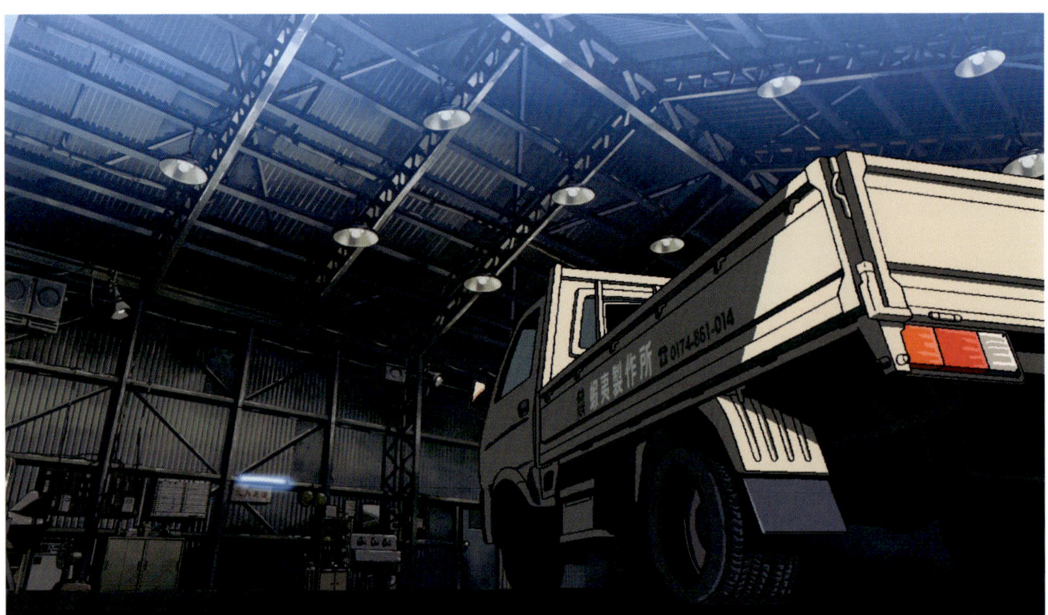

The Place Promised in Our Early Days / CUT_1-096 / Setting: Emishi Plant, Tsugaru, Aomori Prefecture

The truck parked in the Emishi Plant was created on a cel by the animators.

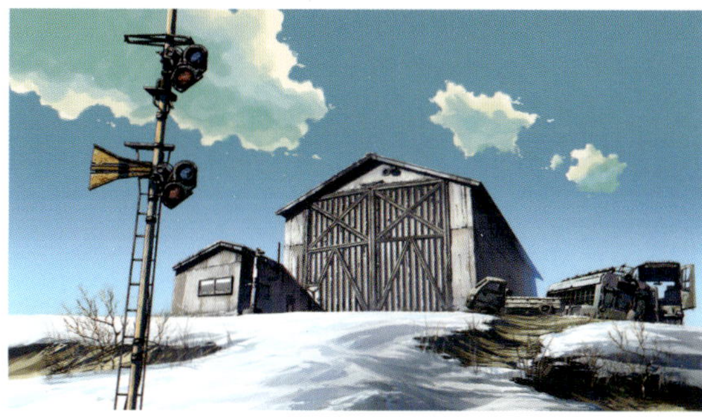

The Place Promised in Our Early Days / CUT_1-109 /
Setting: Abandoned Station, Tsugaru, Aomori Prefecture

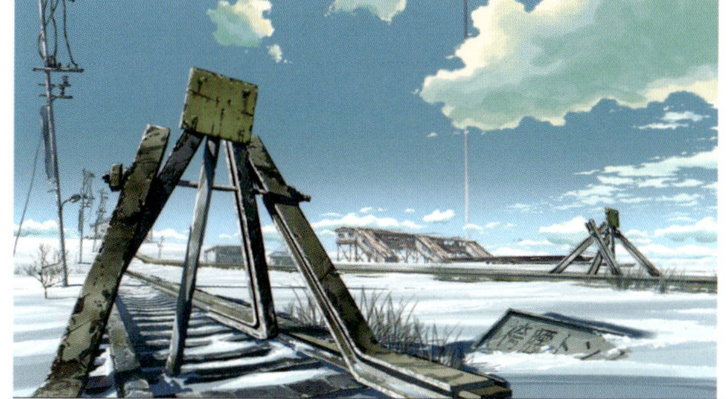

The Place Promised in Our Early Days / CUT_1-107 /
Setting: Abandoned Station, Tsugaru, Aomori Prefecture

The abandoned train station in the snow. Beyond the car repair garage lies the Tsugaru Strait, Hokkaido, and the Tower. Here you can see where Hiroki and Takuya moved Bella Ciela from the garage to the very end of the sidetrack and launched it towards Hokkaido.

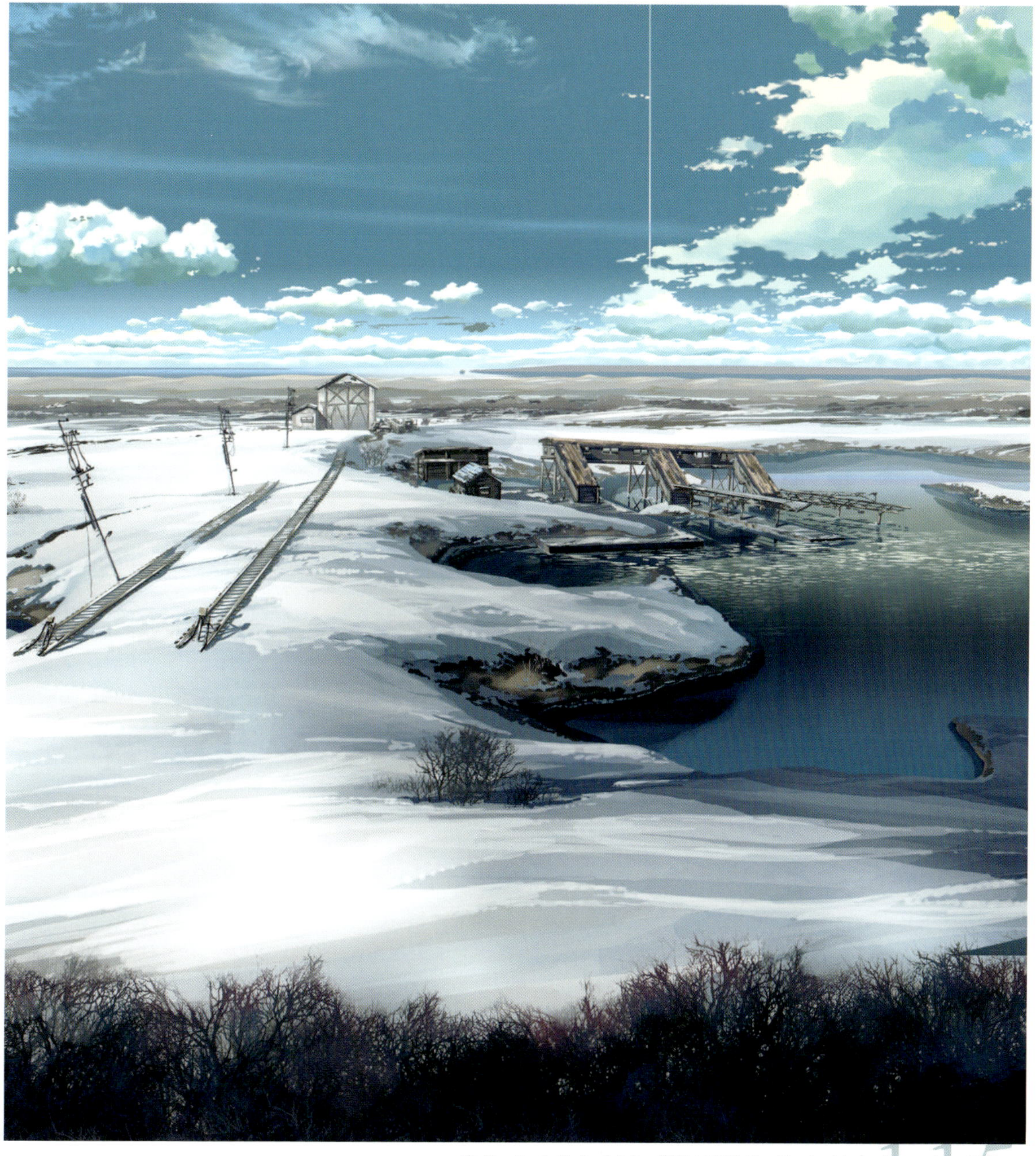

The Place Promised in Our Early Days / CUT_1-106 / Setting: Abandoned Station, Tsugaru, Aomori Prefecture

The Place Promised in Our Early Days

Lost Time – Tokyo

After Sayuri's disappearance, Hiroki loses his passion for the Tower and decides to leave his hometown and live alone in Tokyo. The middle act of the film takes place 3 years after the end of the first, and depicts the lives of Hiroki and Takuya, both now 17 years old, and the unstable condition of a world on the brink of war. The skies of Tokyo, compared with those shown in Aomori in the first act, are drawn using darker, heavier shades, with less contrast to the clouds. Actual Tokyo locations were used for the backgrounds; Hiroki's neighborhood is modeled on West Shinjuku, and the route he takes to school is based on the neighborhoods between Itabashi and Ikebukuro. The venue of the conference attended by Professor Tomizawa is modeled on Yasuda Auditorium at Tokyo University.

Hiroki: (*monologue*) Living alone, the nights felt long.

When I couldn't whittle away the time very well, I walked to the nearby station and killed time pretending that I was waiting for someone.

When I grew tired of that, I walked all the way back to my room as slow as I could.

I had friends in high school, but other than the times I'm wearing the school uniform, I somehow couldn't bring myself to wanna be around them that much.

In a city where more than 30 million people live, come to think of it, there was no one whom I wanted to see or whom I wanted to talk to.

In the midst of those days, I sometimes dreamt of Sayuri.

In that dream, I would look for her, frantic.

But she was at some cold place all by herself.

And in the end I would always fail to find her.

But Sayuri's aura, one that made my heart tremble, remained within my body even after waking up.

(Excerpt of *The Place Promised in Our Early Days*)

A back street near Hiroki's apartment. The skyscrapers of West Shinjuku are visible across the vacant lot. This is modeled on a street near the production studio used for *The Place Promised in Our Early Days*. The wide-angle lens effect is visible on the edges of the image.

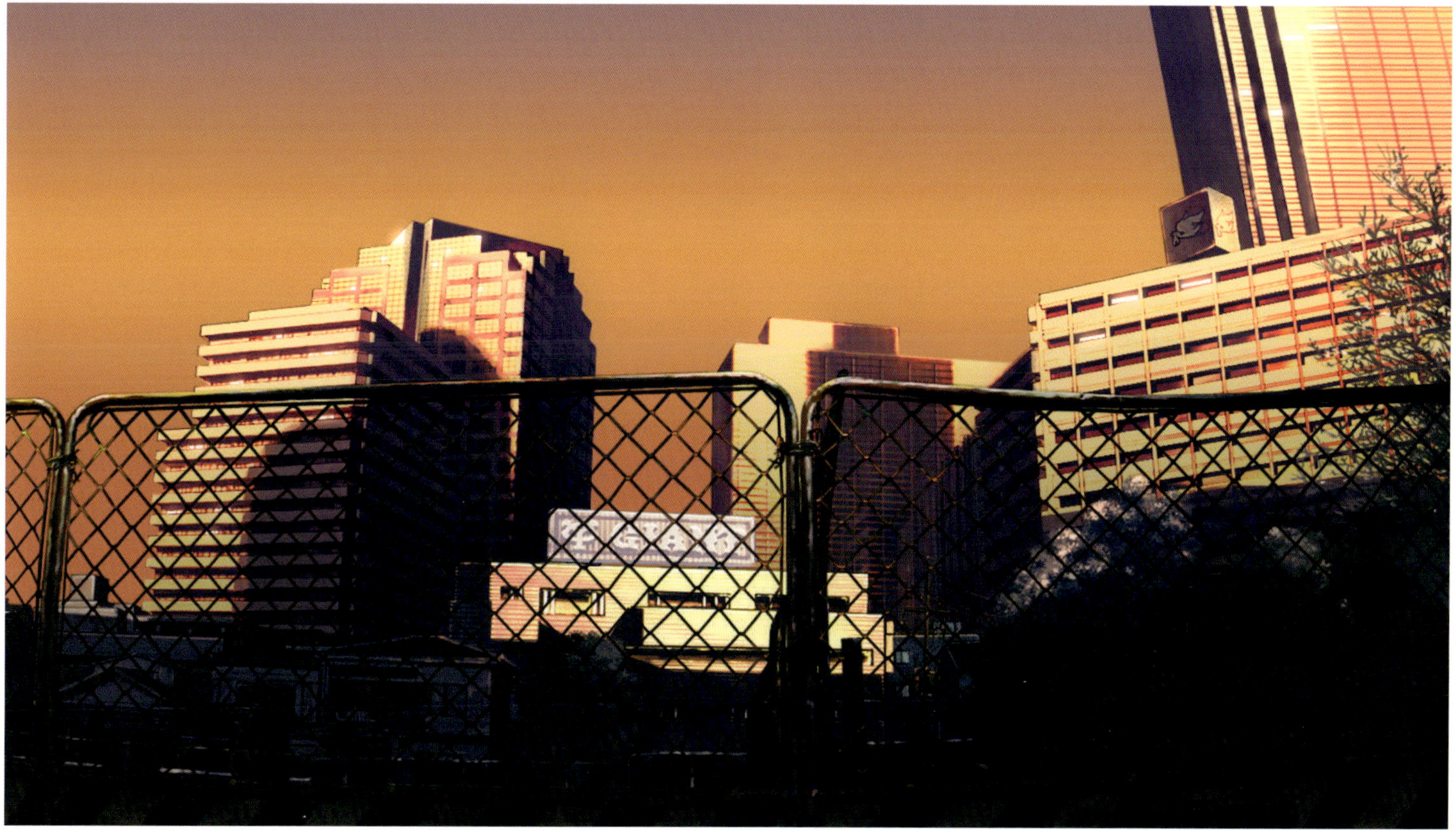

The Place Promised in Our Early Days / CUT_2-515 / Setting: West Shinjuku, Tokyo

In CUT_2-429, the Tower is faintly drawn in the distance, visible even from Tokyo when looking north. This is intended to allow the audience to feel the massive scale of the Tower.

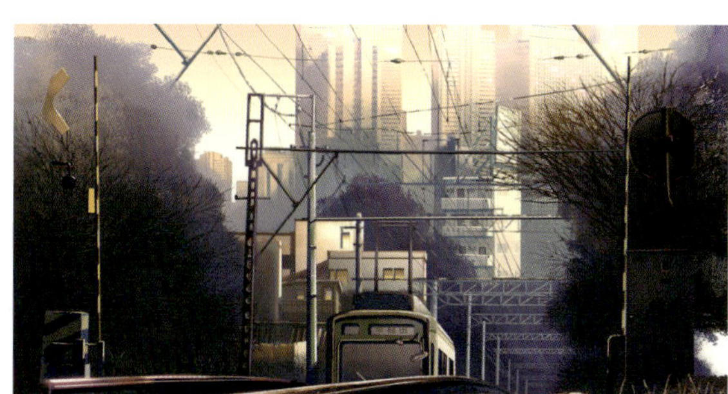

The Place Promised in Our Early Days / CUT_2-505 / Setting: Near Otsuka Station, Tokyo

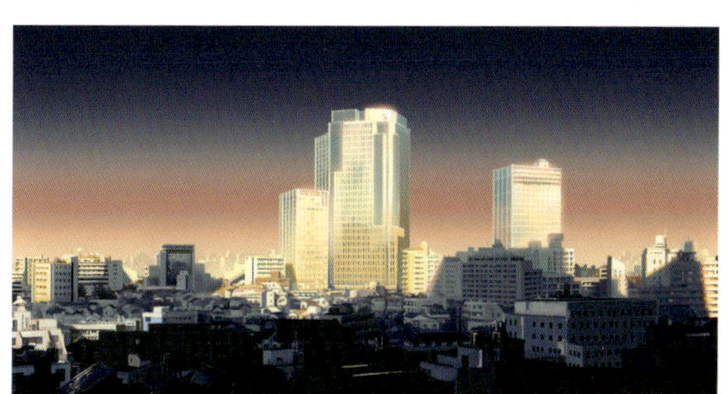

The Place Promised in Our Early Days / CUT_2-526 / Setting: West Shinjuku, Tokyo

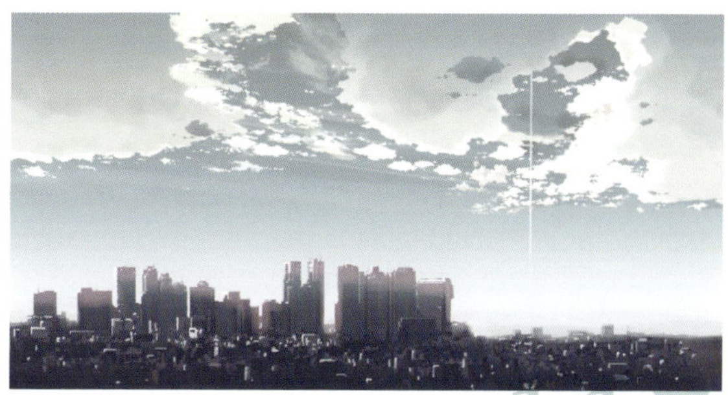

The Place Promised in Our Early Days / CUT_2-429 / Setting: Panorama of Tokyo

A cut showing the view of Shinjuku from Ikebukuro. The Tower, shining endlessly in the setting sunlight, makes an impression. In real life, from this angle one wouldn't be able to see a tower on Hokkaido, but artistic license was exercised in depicting the Tower.

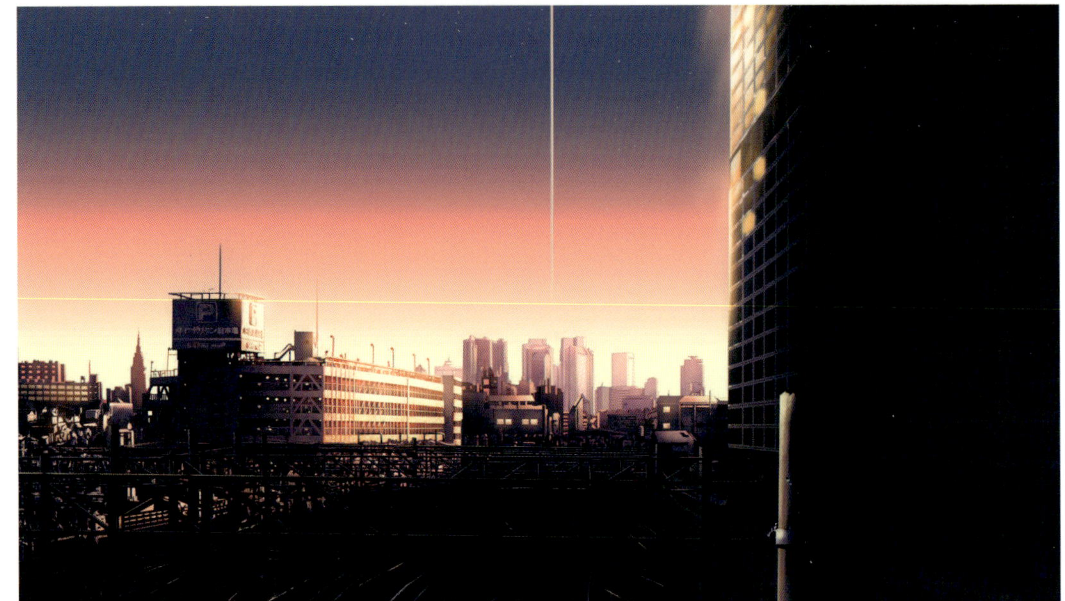

The Place Promised in Our Early Days / CUT_2-509 / Setting: Near Ikebukuro Station, Tokyo

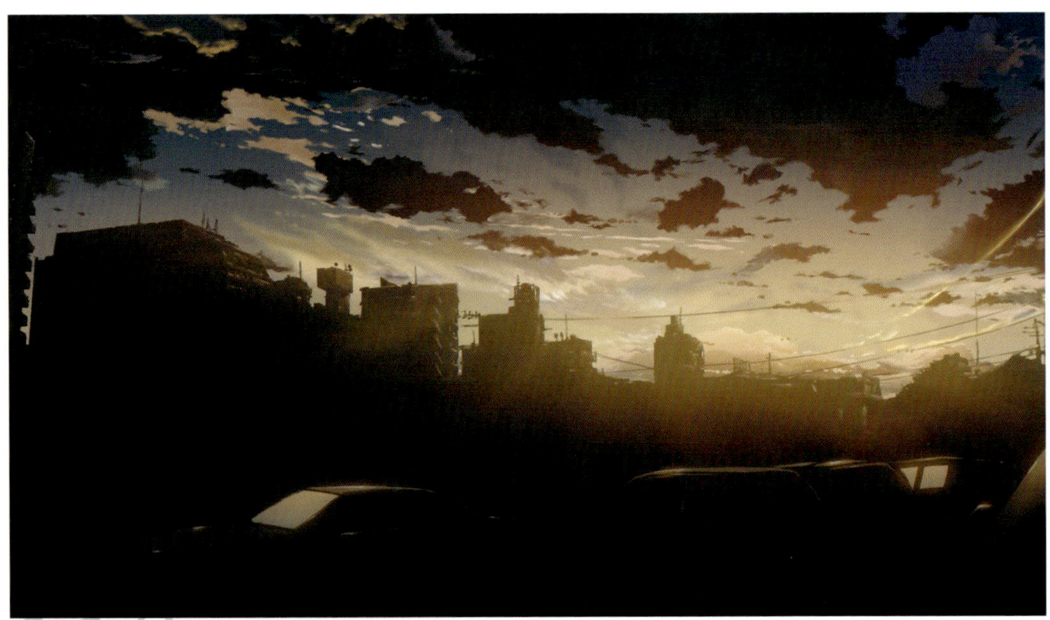

The Place Promised in Our Early Days / CUT_2-622 / Setting: Near Ikebukuro Station, Tokyo

The auditorium, based on Yasuda Auditorium in Tokyo University, where the Japanese military's research results were announced. Various buildings of Tokyo University are based on the Aomori Army College. The Engineering Building No. 2, finished in 2005, was still incomplete at this point.

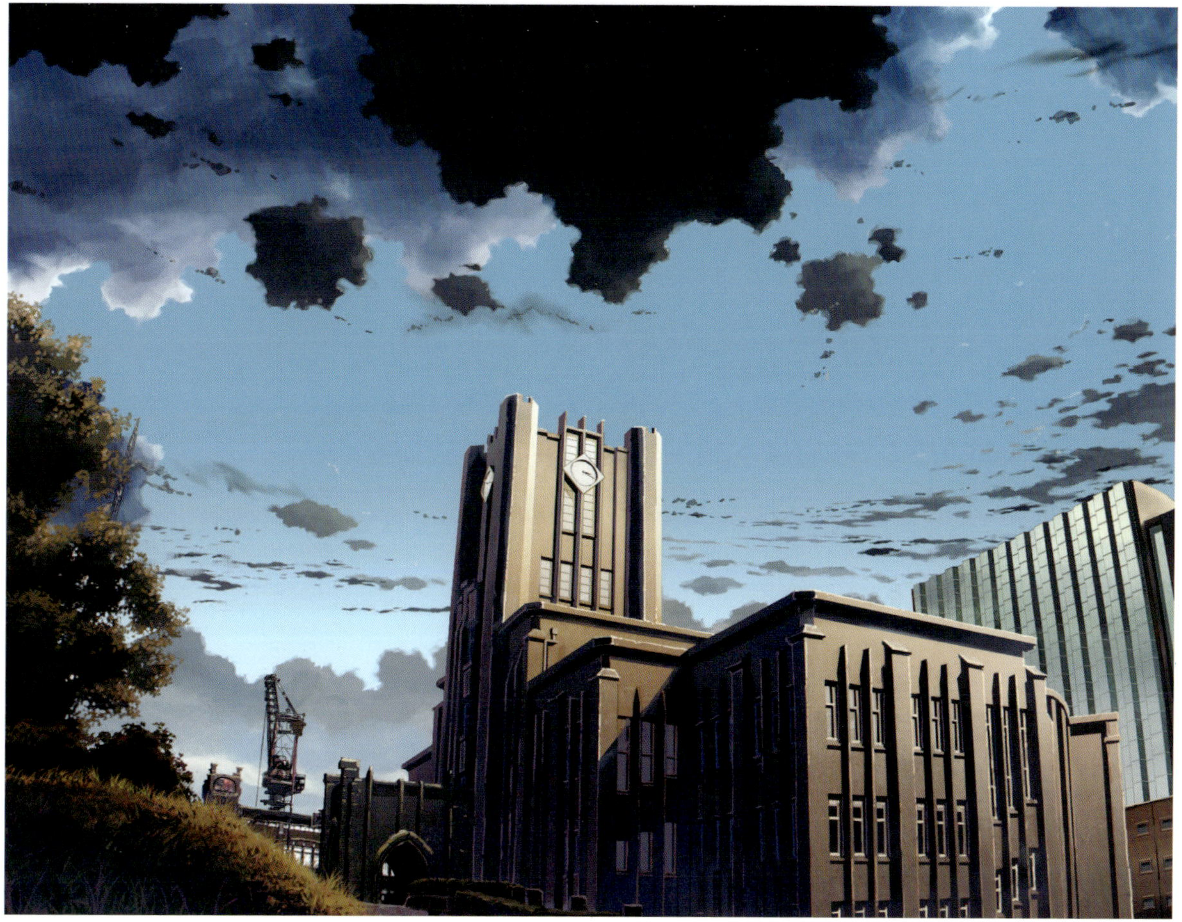

The Place Promised in Our Early Days / CUT_2-443 / Setting: Campus of a national university, Tokyo

CUT_2-455 depicts the accessway of the Law & Letters Building No. 2. CUT_2-444 is a hallway in Yasuda Auditorium.

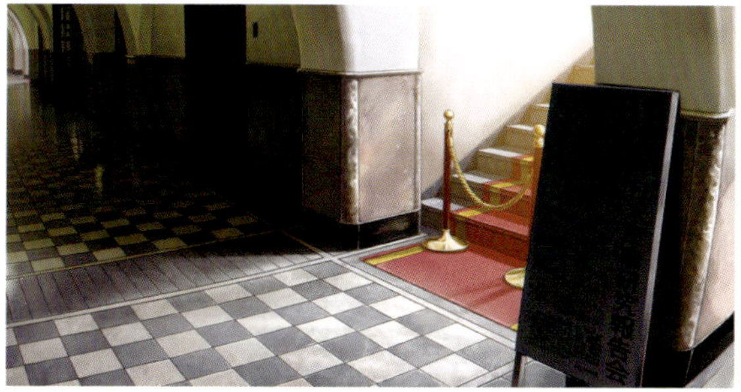

The Place Promised in Our Early Days / CUT_2-444 / Setting: Campus of a national university, Tokyo

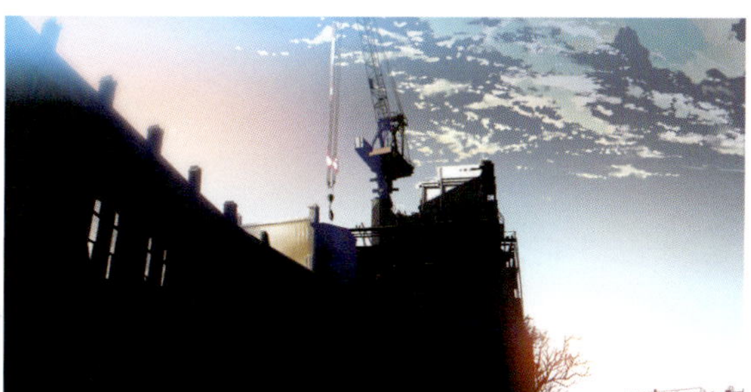

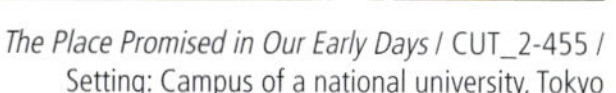

The Place Promised in Our Early Days / CUT_2-455 / Setting: Campus of a national university, Tokyo

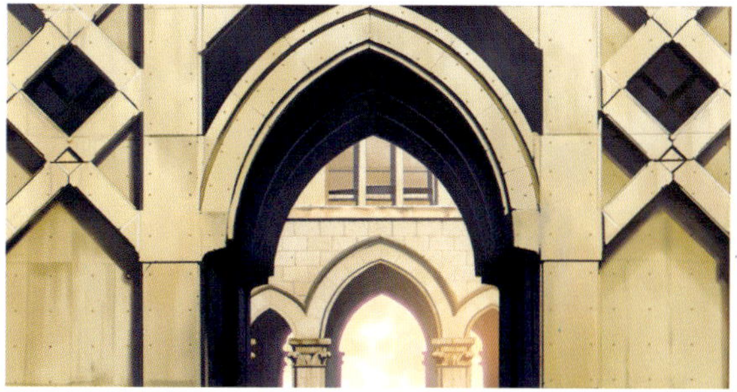

The Place Promised in Our Early Days / CUT_2-453 / Setting: Campus of a national university, Tokyo

Hiroki's apartment. CUT_2-516 is the entryway. Please note the differences in the rays of light between outdoor and indoor settings. This was modeled on an actual apartment in West Shinjuku.

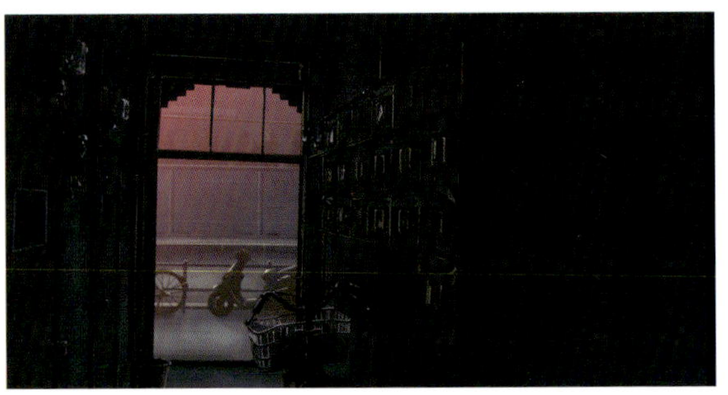

The Place Promised in Our Early Days / CUT_2-516 / Setting: Hiroki's apartment entryway, Tokyo

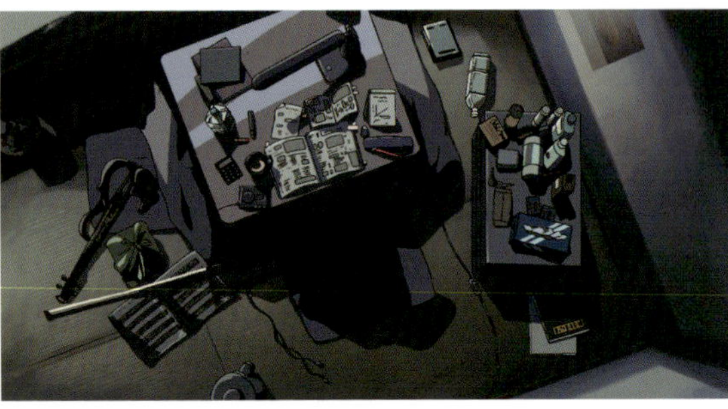

The Place Promised in Our Early Days / CUT_2-589 / Setting: Inside Hiroki's apartment, Tokyo

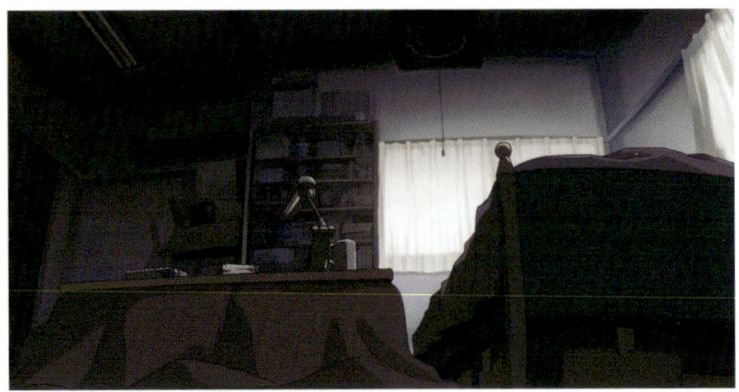

The Place Promised in Our Early Days / CUT_2-593 / Setting: Inside Hiroki's apartment, Tokyo

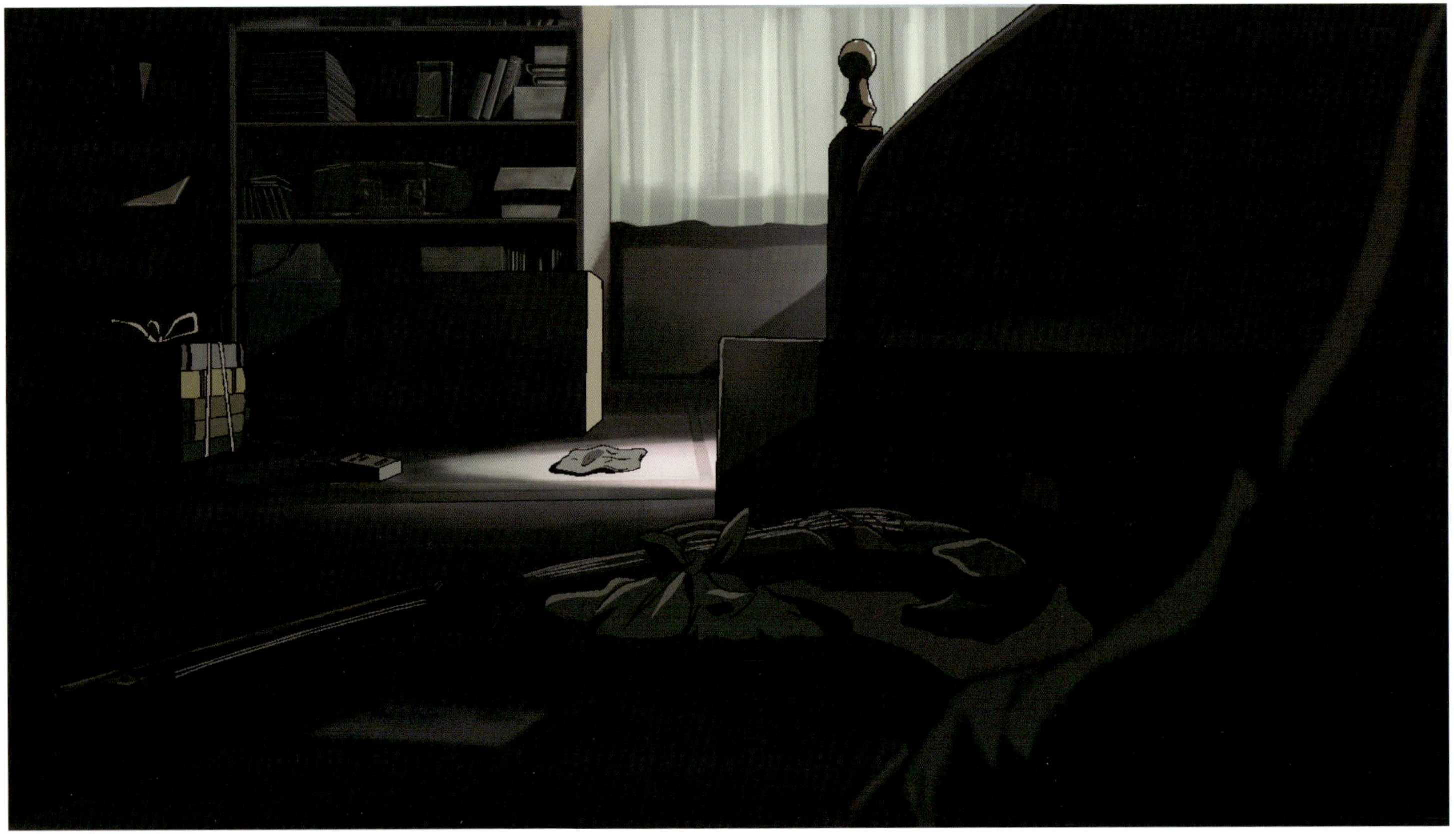

The Place Promised in Our Early Days / CUT_2-590 / Setting: Inside Hiroki's apartment, Tokyo

The drinking and dining district where Okabe and Tomizawa secretly meet. This is modeled on Memory Lane in Shinjuku, and the pub they go to is based on an actual pub. In CUT_2-476, the movie posters above the rotary outside Shinjuku Station's East Entrance make it clear when the location photos were taken.

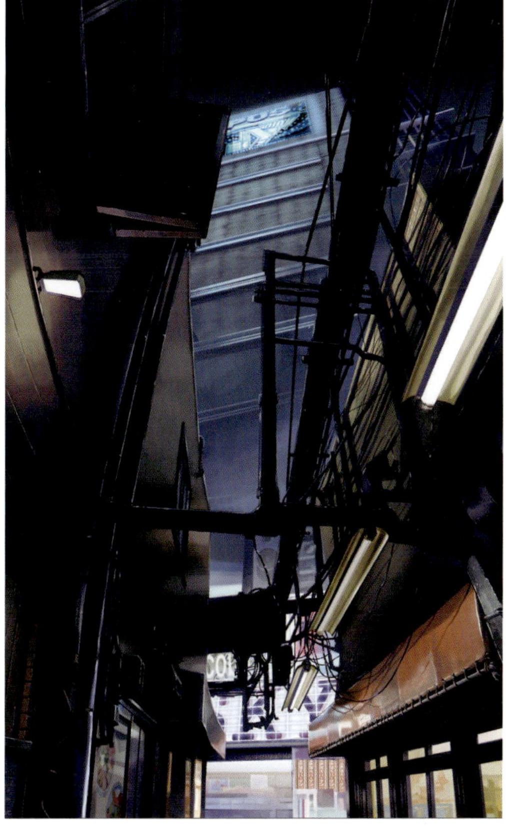

The Place Promised in Our Early Days / CUT_2-458 / Setting: Drinking and dining district, Tokyo

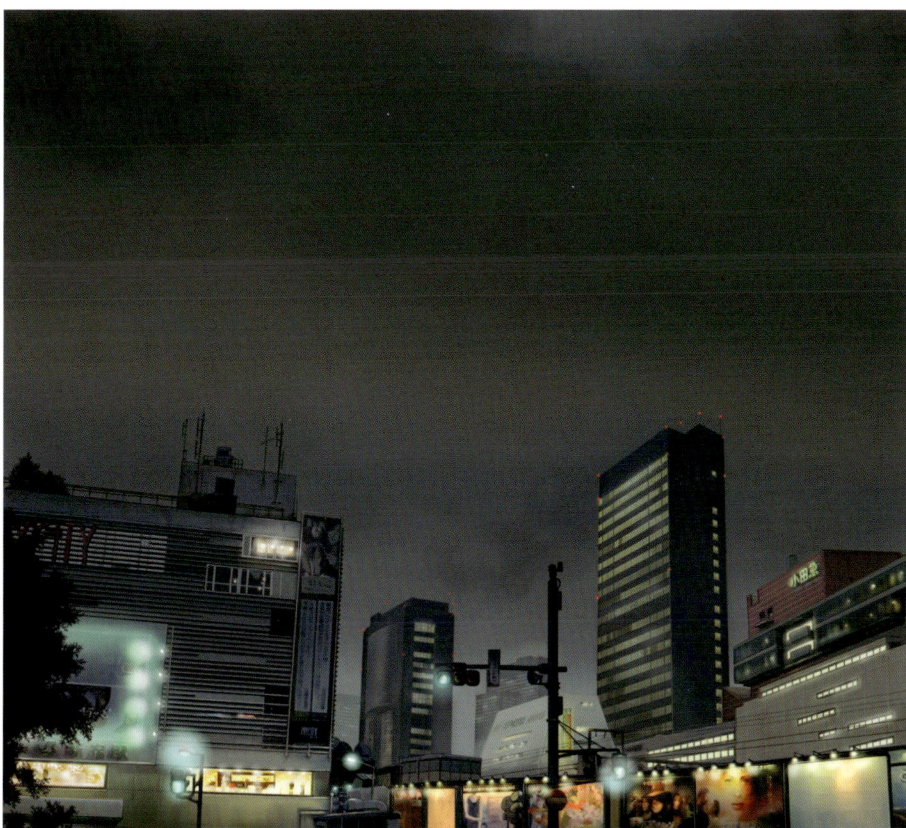

The Place Promised in Our Early Days / CUT_2-476 / Setting: Near Shinjuku Station's East Entrance, Tokyo

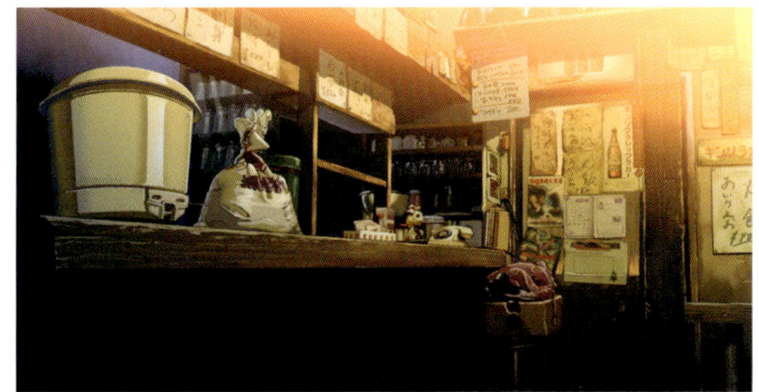

The Place Promised in Our Early Days / CUT_2-460 / Setting: Interior of a pub, Tokyo

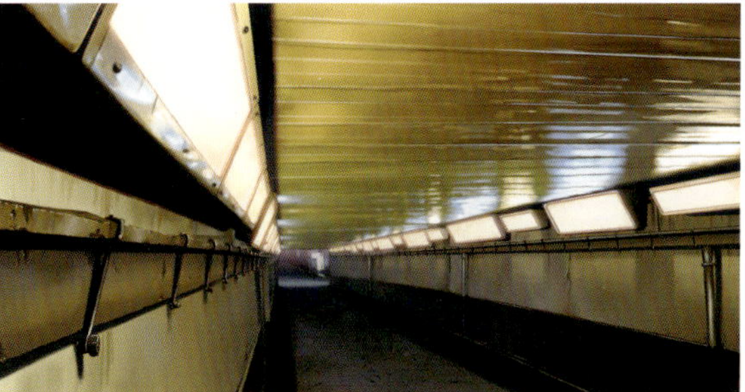

The Place Promised in Our Early Days / CUT_2-475 / Setting: Tunnel, Tokyo

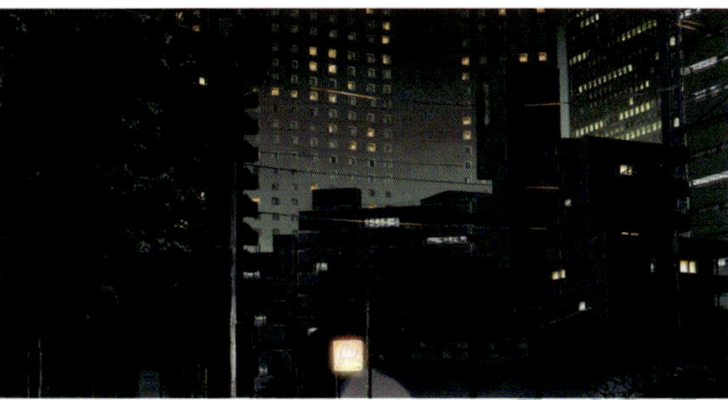

The Place Promised in Our Early Days / CUT_2-525 / Setting: A park in Ikebukuro, Tokyo

The Place Promised in Our Early Days

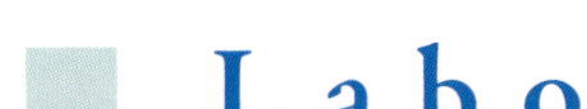

Laboratory

The ever-sleeping Sayuri is transferred from a hospital in Tokyo to the Aomori Army College, where Tomizawa's research facility is located. The main scenes set in the Army College campus, in Tomizawa's laboratory, and the special hospital ward are the scenes that evoke the science-fiction nature of this film. The story's progression is based mainly on the characters' conversations and the lab experiment scenes. For this reason, multiple scenes are set against the same backdrops (yet with altered details). There are many backgrounds that are similar to those seen in more conventional animated works.

Tomizawa: The onset was in the summer of her third-year in middle school. The cause is unknown. The hours of sleep gradually got longer. And she was able to stay awake for only limited periods of time only during the first two months. This girl has been asleep for three years. And you're telling me she's having some sort of dream?

Doctor: That's what the recorded brain waves show.

Tomizawa: Hmm. The DNA test?

Doctor: On page six.

Tomizawa: Yes, I see. She's from a divided family. Fine.

Uh, this is the request document from the Ministry of Health, Labor and Welfare. As soon as the transfer date is decided you'll receive the official documents.

What's this letter?

Doctor: Something that the patient was writing at the beginning of hospitalization.

Tomizawa: Did you read it?

Doctor: No.

Tomizawa: (*off-screen*) Emishi Plant...

(Excerpt of *The Place Promised in Our Early Days*)

Sayuri, the bed and the machinery are all drawn on cels. At first glance it appears complicated, but the background art is drawn using a very simple structure. Also, the parts hidden underneath the cels were not drawn in.

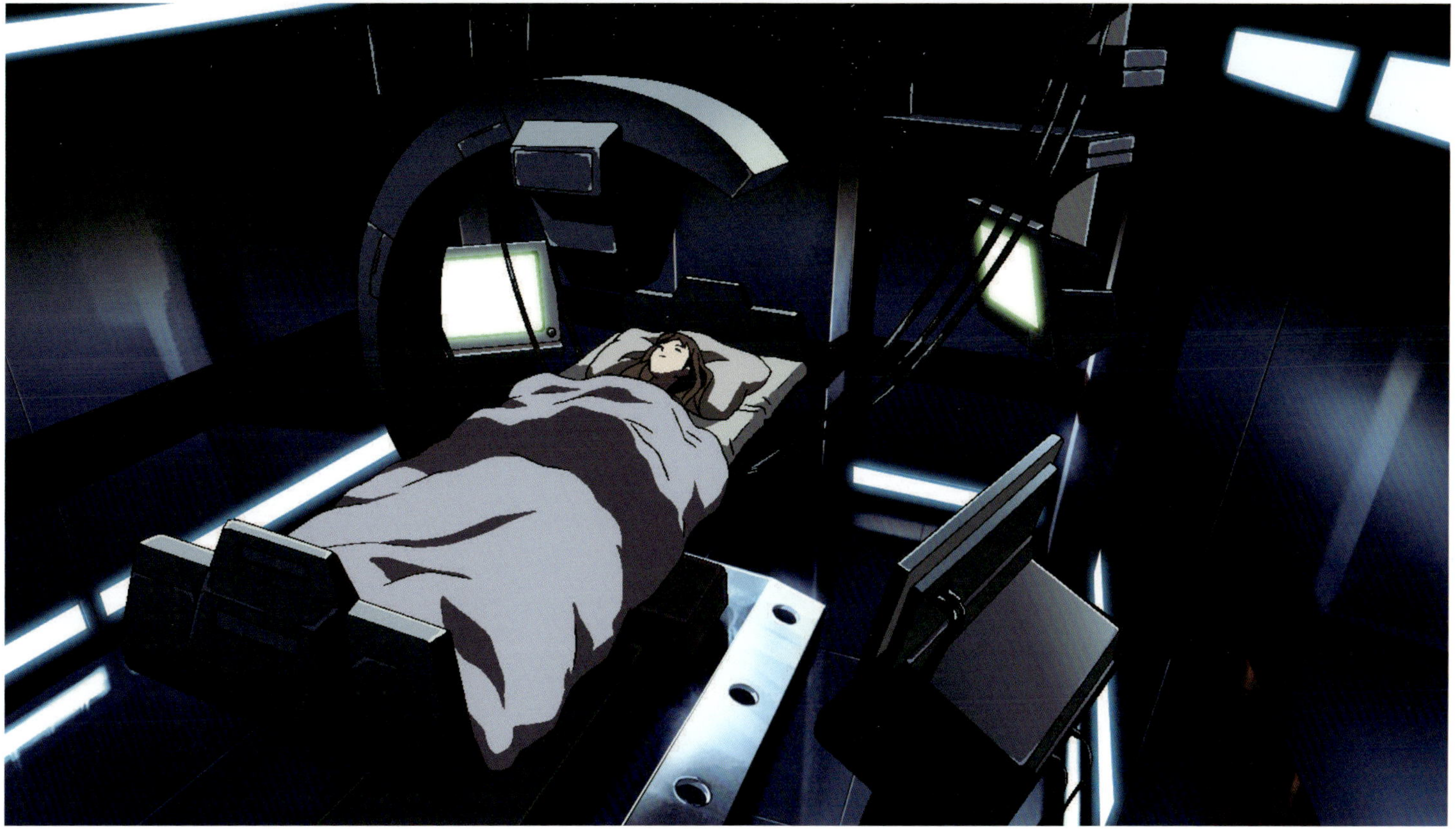

The Place Promised in Our Early Days / CUT_2-656 / Setting: Special hospital ward, Aomori Army College

For CUT_2-336 and CUT_2-352, which show experiments in progress, character cels and special effects for the experiments were added, so the background art was kept very simple.

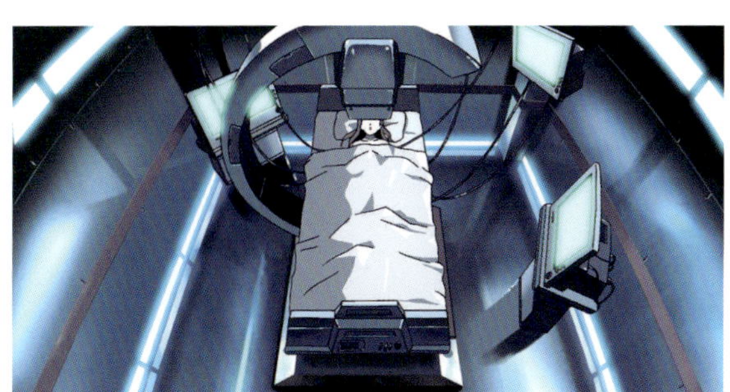

The Place Promised in Our Early Days / CUT_3-026 / Setting: Special hospital ward, Aomori Army College

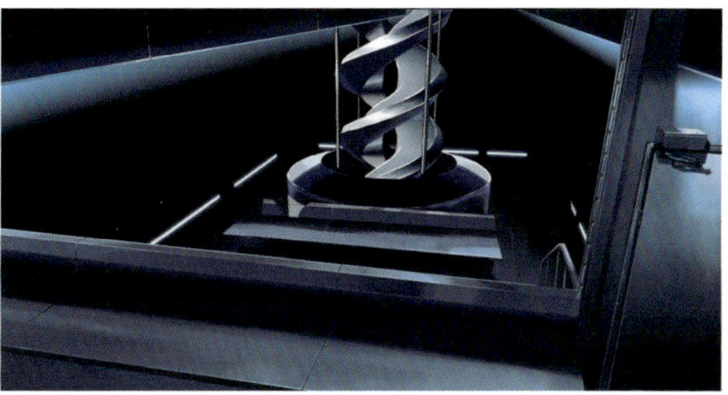

The Place Promised in Our Early Days / CUT_2-336, CUT_2-352 / Setting: Tomizawa's lab, Aomori Army College

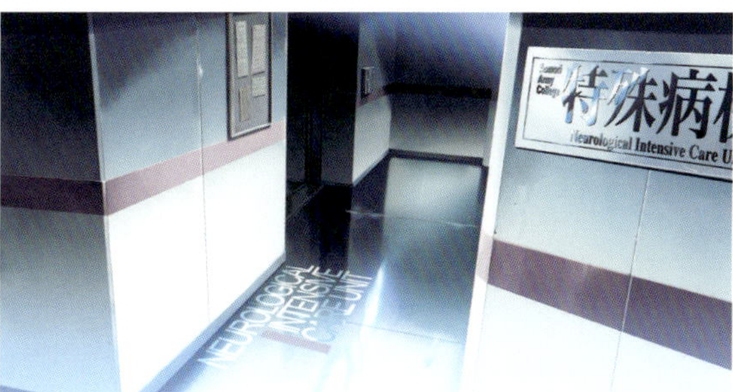

The Place Promised in Our Early Days / CUT_3-168 / Setting: Special hospital ward, Aomori Army College

Sayuri: A cold, deep wind blew there, a wind that seemed as if it had come from a far-away universe. And the air had the smell of the different universe.

SFX: (*sounds of wind*)

SFX: *keeee* (*sounds of Bella Ciela's engines, far in the distance*)

Sayuri: (*off-screen*) Sky, clouds, and a collapsed town, no matter how far I walk there's no one.

I feel cold.

Why am I in a place like this?

Somebody... Hey, somebody... Hiroki...

(Excerpt of *The Place Promised in Our Early Days*)

The Place Promised in Our Early Days

Parallel Universe – Sayuri's Loneliness

This is the world that appears in the dreams of the ever-sleeping Sayuri. Sayuri wanders endlessly through a desolate, empty landscape. At the beginning, the scenery is similar to what exists in reality (except everything has been turned into ruins), but the moment she encounters Hiroki and the Tower's activity intensifies, the scenery changes to one where there's nothing but a succession of oddly-shaped Towers. These backgrounds become major supporting factors in the film. The overall intensity of the colors is low, and images are modulated in monotones. In the images showing clusters of strange Towers, you can see finely-detailed cave paintings.

This is the image of the decayed world that Sayuri sees initially. A video of a large explosion was prepared, and special effects were added to the station building and surface of the water in time with the explosion.

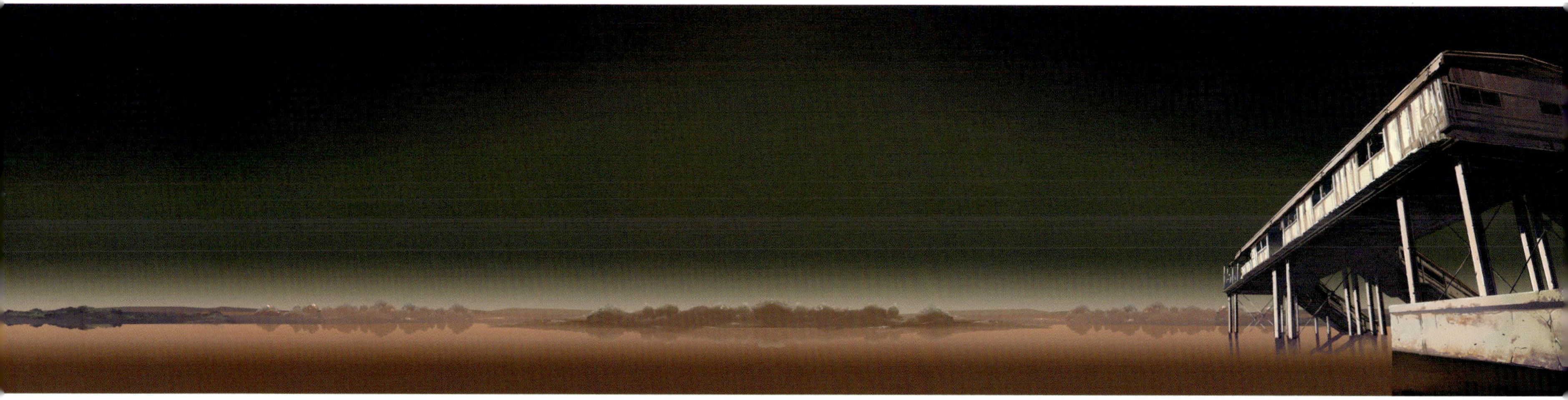

The Place Promised in Our Early Days / CUT_1-288 / Setting: Abandoned Station, Tsugaru, Aomori Prefecture (Sayuri's imagination)

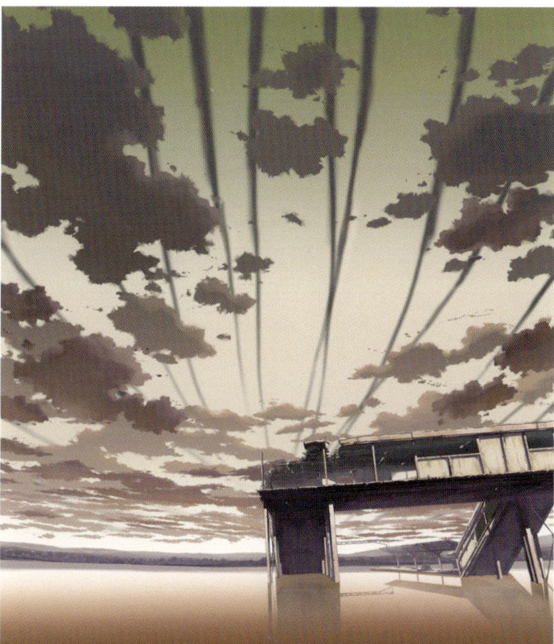

The Place Promised in Our Early Days / CUT_1-284 /
Setting: Abandoned Station, Tsugaru, Aomori Prefecture (Sayuri's imagination)

The formation of military jets flying towards the Tower leaves contrails in the sky. The abundance of greenery that had been used in the scenery of the abandoned station changed completely into an oppressive image, creating a sense of unease and tension.

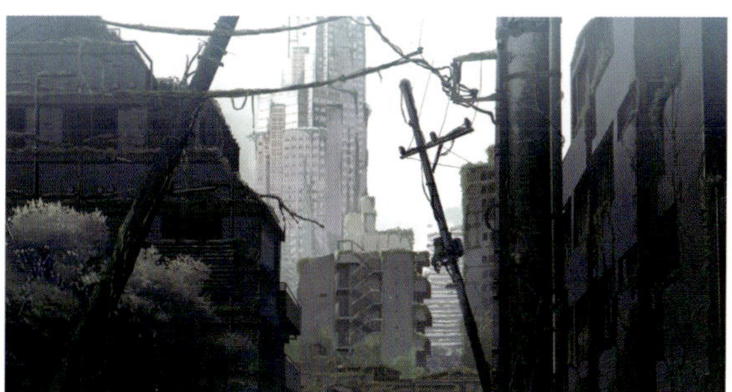

The Place Promised in Our Early Days / CUT_2-598 /
Setting: Buildings in Tokyo (Sayuri's imagination)

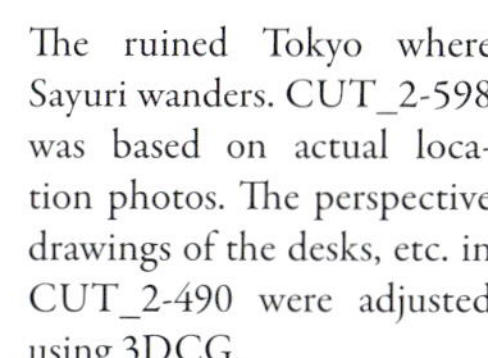

The ruined Tokyo where Sayuri wanders. CUT_2-598 was based on actual location photos. The perspective drawings of the desks, etc. in CUT_2-490 were adjusted using 3DCG.

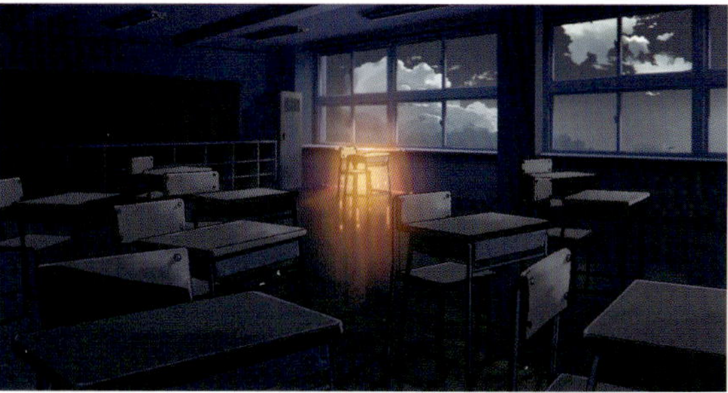

The Place Promised in Our Early Days / CUT_2-490 /
Setting: Hiroki's school in Tokyo (Sayuri's imagination)

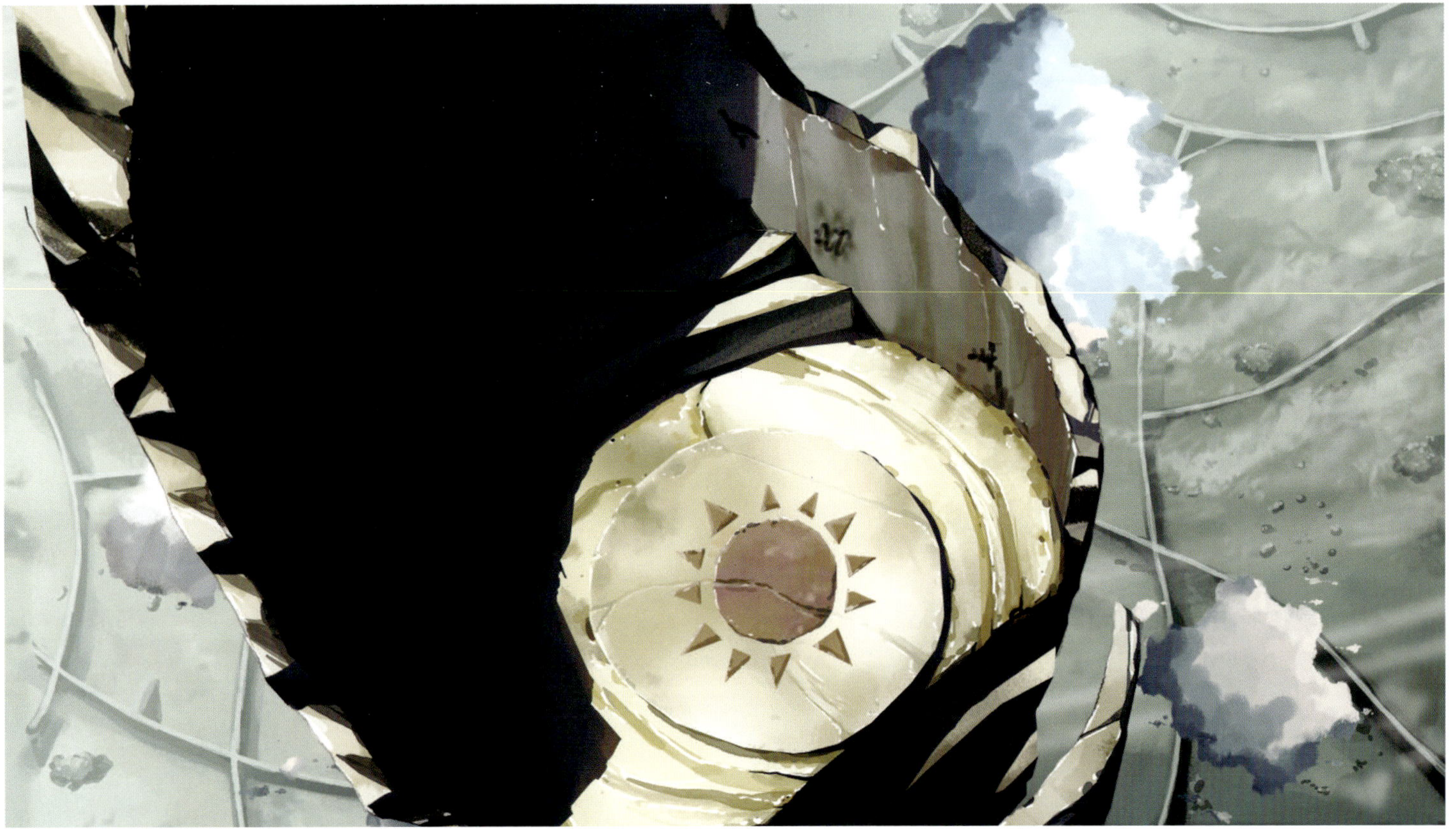

A scene showing the strange Towers that appear in the parallel dimension. There are patterns that look like cave paintings on the walls and floors of the Towers, giving the impression that these are relics of an old civilization. Within the group of oddly-shaped Towers is one that rises straight up, resembling the Tower in the real world.

The Place Promised in Our Early Days / CUT_2-583 / Setting: Parallel universe (Sayuri's imagination)

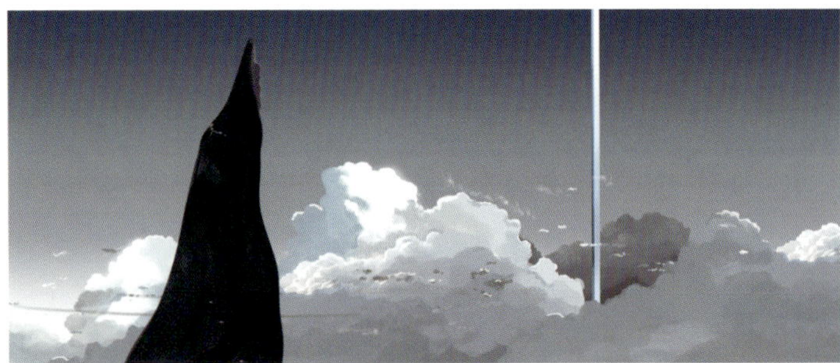

The Place Promised in Our Early Days / CUT_2-497 / Setting: Parallel universe (Sayuri's imagination)

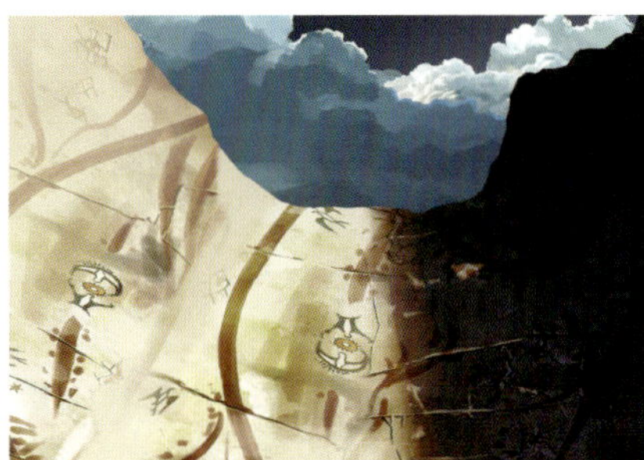

The Place Promised in Our Early Days / CUT_2-582 / Setting: Parallel universe (Sayuri's imagination)

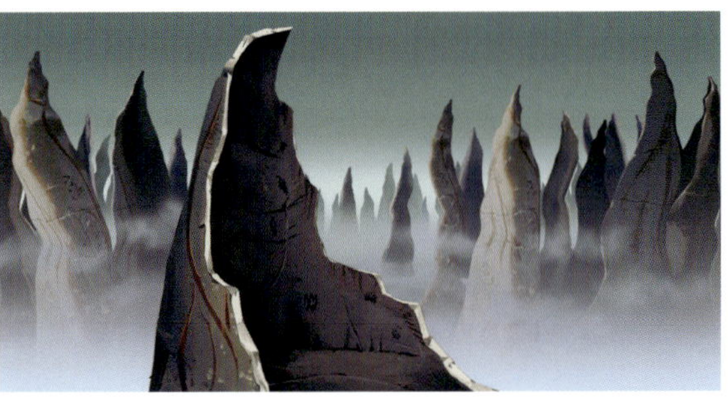

The Place Promised in Our Early Days / CUT_3-006 / Setting: Parallel universe (Sayuri's imagination)

Background art for the scene towards the end of the act where Sayuri has "a premonition of awakening." The portion of the Tower visible in the foreground is the same in both CUT_2-477 and CUT_3-235.

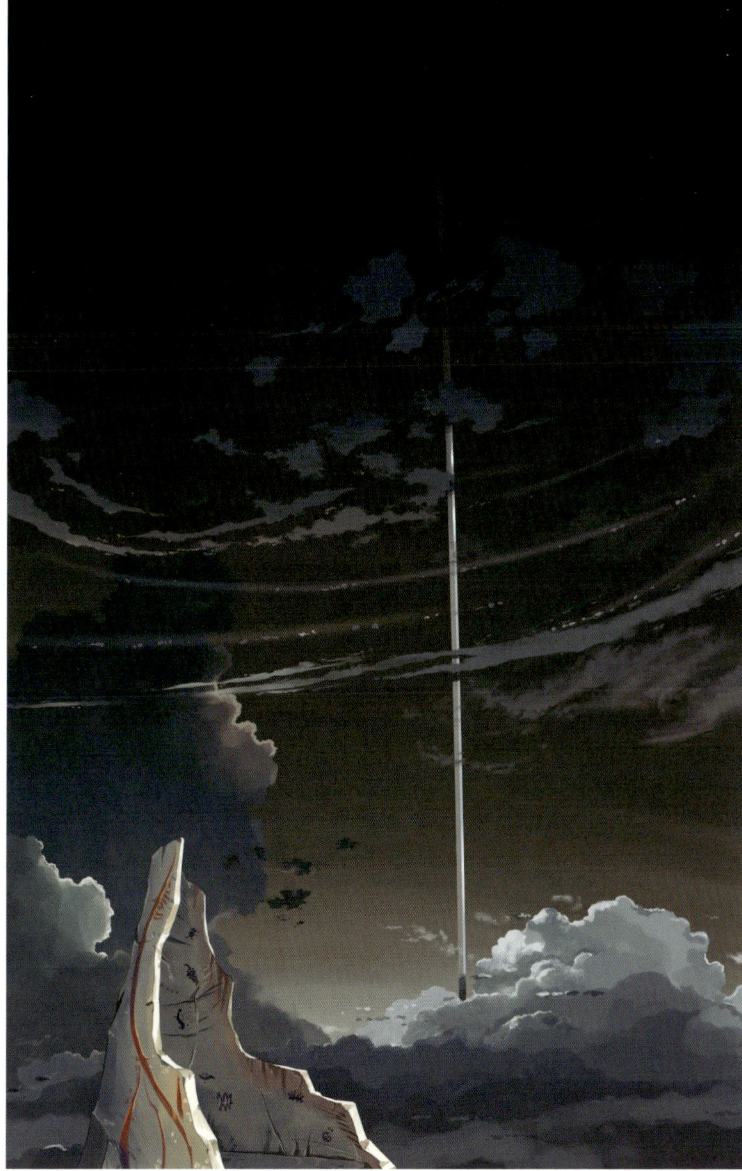

The Place Promised in Our Early Days / CUT_2-477 / Setting: Parallel universe (Sayuri's imagination)

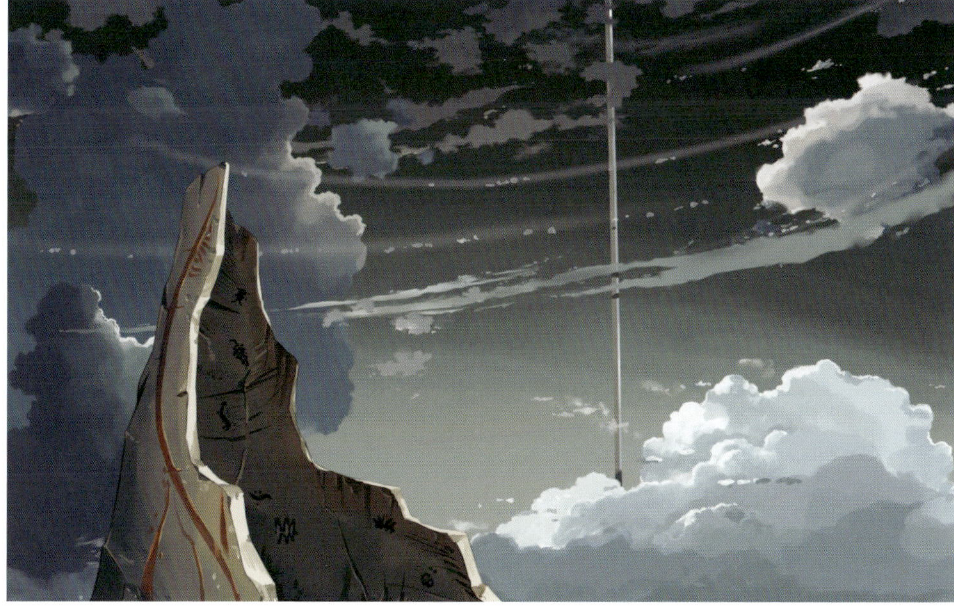

The Place Promised in Our Early Days / CUT_3-235 / Setting: Parallel universe (Sayuri's imagination)

Strange clouds swirl around the Tower in the parallel universe. Please note the sky, which was rendered using both warm and cool grays to create a complex sense of depth.

The Place Promised in Our Early Days

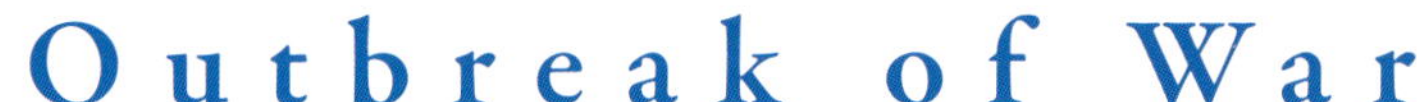

Outbreak of War

The Tower's state of operation is close to activation as Sayuri changes, and the long-lasting deadlock between the Alliance and the Union is about to give way to hostilities. The climax of *The Place Promised in Our Early Days* has a series of dynamic animated battle scenes. In the scenes where Hiroki and Takuya continue to restore Bella Ciela, many of the same angles and backgrounds are reused from similar scenes at the beginning, but several were redrawn to depict the passage of time and change of seasons.

Hiroki: (*slightly irritably*) Takuya! Which version of BIOS do you think I should use? You changed the rudder, didn't you? I don't have the one after that.

Takuya: It's in this. It also has one for the seeker missile. What else do you have to do?

Hiroki: I still have to do a little bit of wiring on the superconducting motor, I think. And then just some fine-tuning of the software.

Takuya: Five more hours 'til war declaration. Flying is gonna take you right in the middle of the fighting. I'll do the software, so you can finish up the wiring.

Hiroki: Yeah. Takuya, what's up with that error message?

Takuya: What?

Hiroki: The one with the Version Check.

Takuya: Version Check? Uh, isn't that the part you put together three years ago?

Hiroki: Oh, really?

Takuya: You haven't changed...idiot.

(Excerpt of *The Place Promised in Our Early Days*)

In order to contact a Union agent, Okabe takes Takuya and a subordinate to infiltrate Union-territory waters.

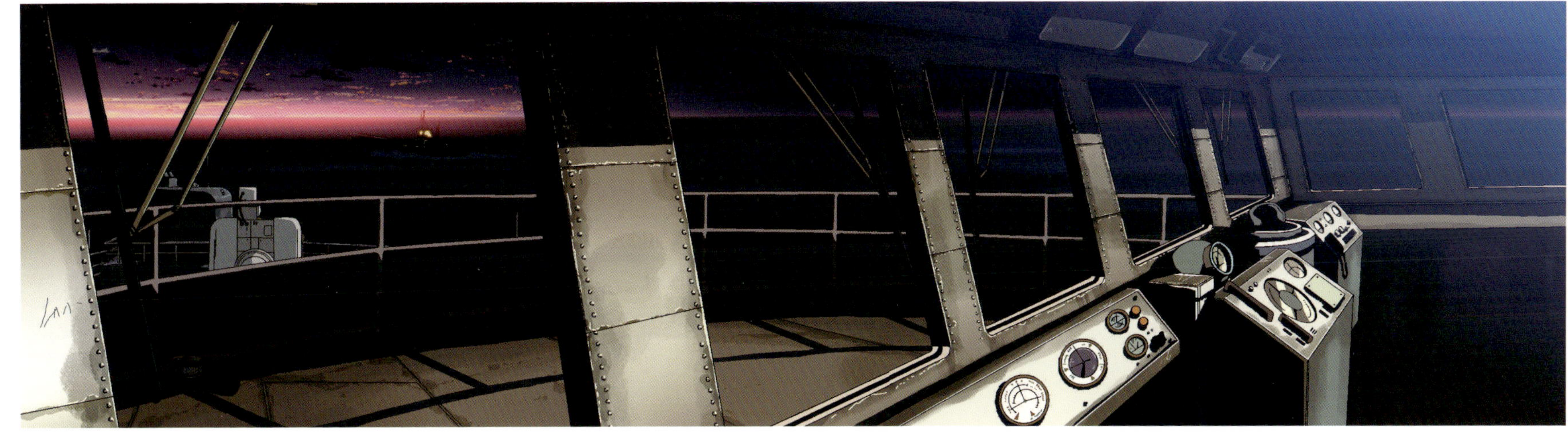

The Place Promised in Our Early Days / CUT_2-571 / Setting: Fishing boat, Tsugaru Strait, Aomori

The waves in CUT_2-569 were animation. In the firefight scene, animation of bullet impacts was added to the harmony cels of the boat parts.

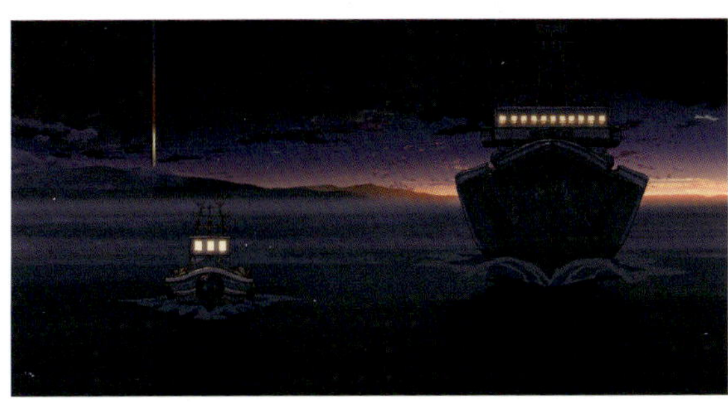

The Place Promised in Our Early Days / CUT_2-569 / Setting: On Tsugaru Strait, Aomori

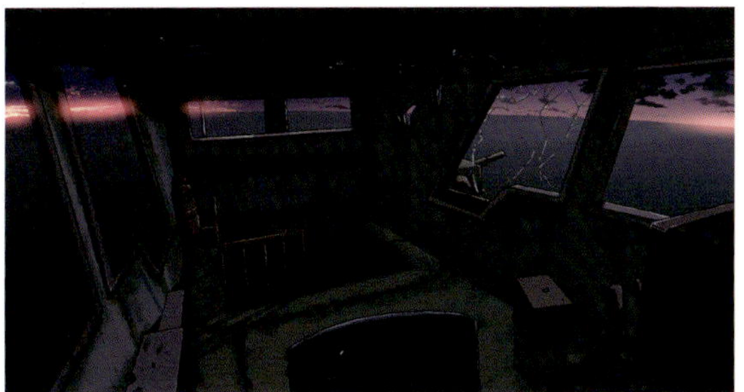

The Place Promised in Our Early Days / CUT_2-576 / Setting: Fishing boat, Tsugaru Strait, Aomori

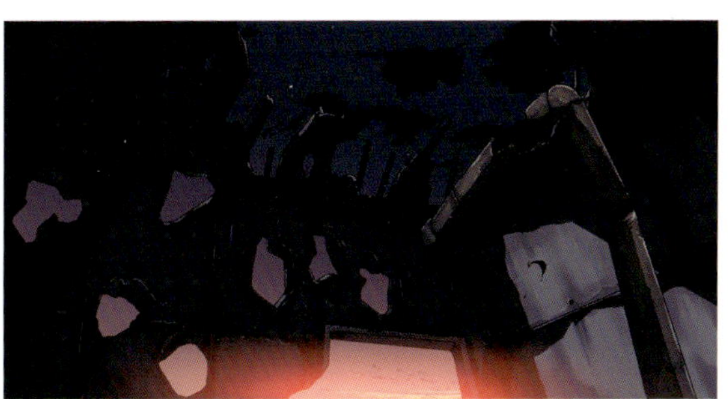

The Place Promised in Our Early Days / CUT_2-578 / Setting: Fishing boat, Tsugaru Strait, Aomori

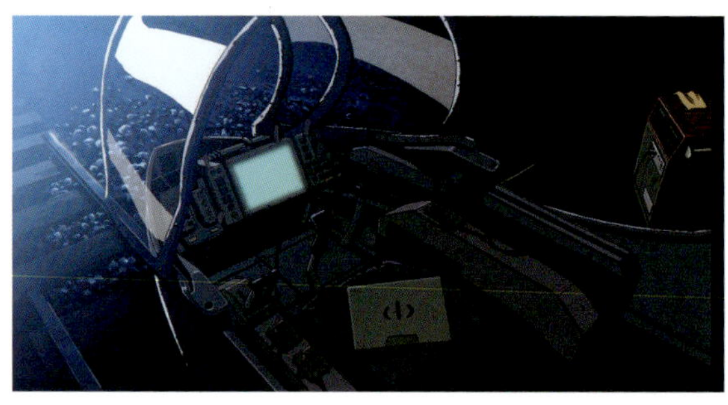

The Place Promised in Our Early Days / CUT_3-070 / Setting: Abandoned station, Tsugaru, Aomori

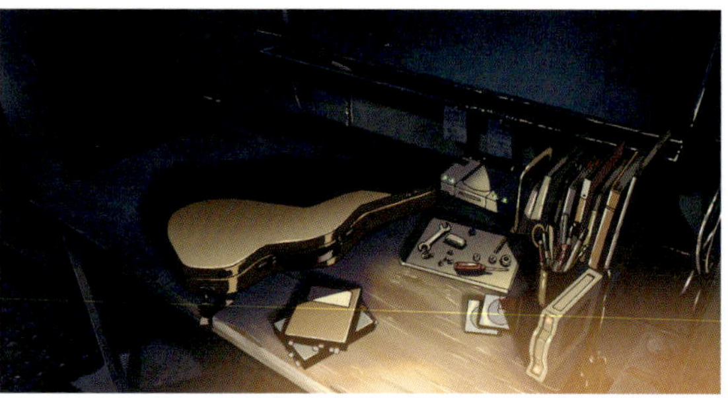

The Place Promised in Our Early Days / CUT_3-074 / Setting: Abandoned station, Tsugaru, Aomori

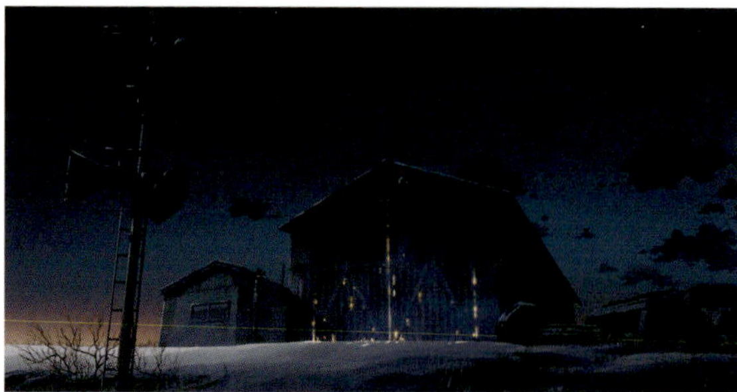

The Place Promised in Our Early Days / CUT_3-207 / Setting: Abandoned station, Tsugaru, Aomori

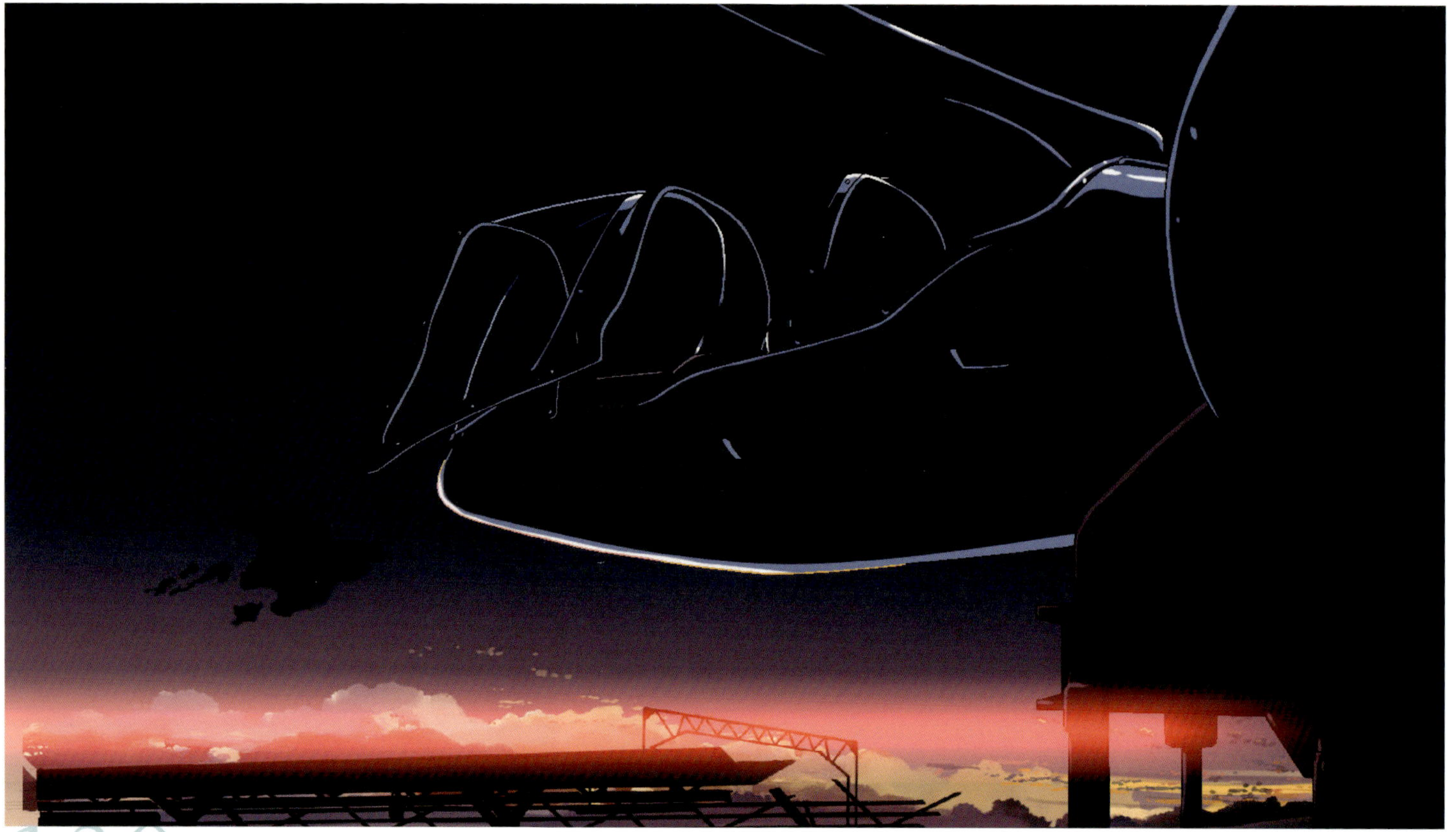

CUT_3-207 uses the same base sketch as CUT_1-109 (page 115).

The Place Promised in Our Early Days / CUT_3-250, CUT_3-253 / Setting: Abandoned station, Tsugaru, Aomori

The gunfire used in CUT_3-270 was reproduced by creating two versions of the background art in two separate frames, which were then alternated back and forth. In CUT_3-246, a lens effect was added to the jet nozzle of the helicopter to create fluctuating air movements caused by the backfire.

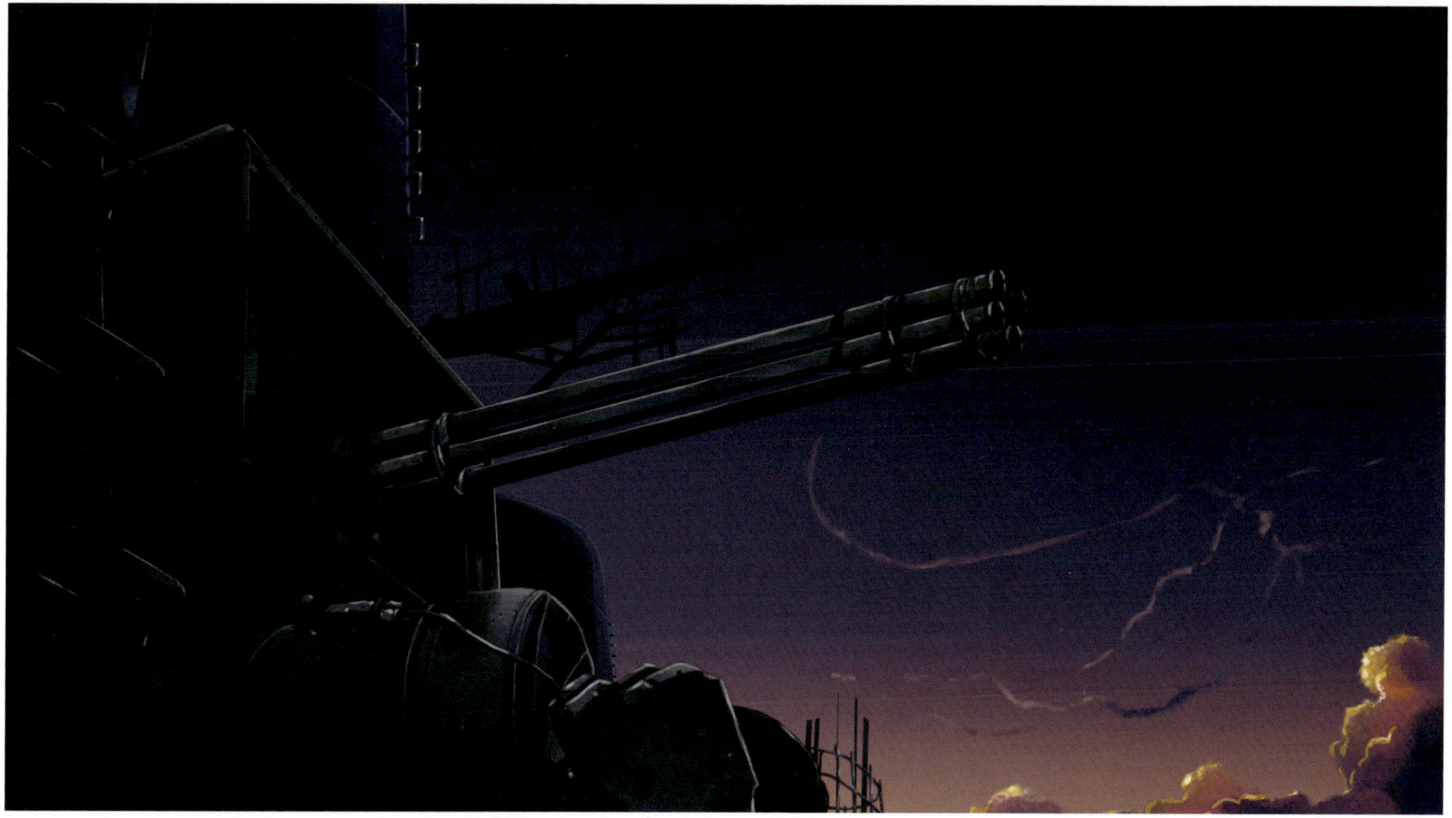

The Place Promised in Our Early Days / CUT_3-270 / Setting: Alliance battleship, Tsugaru Strait, Aomori

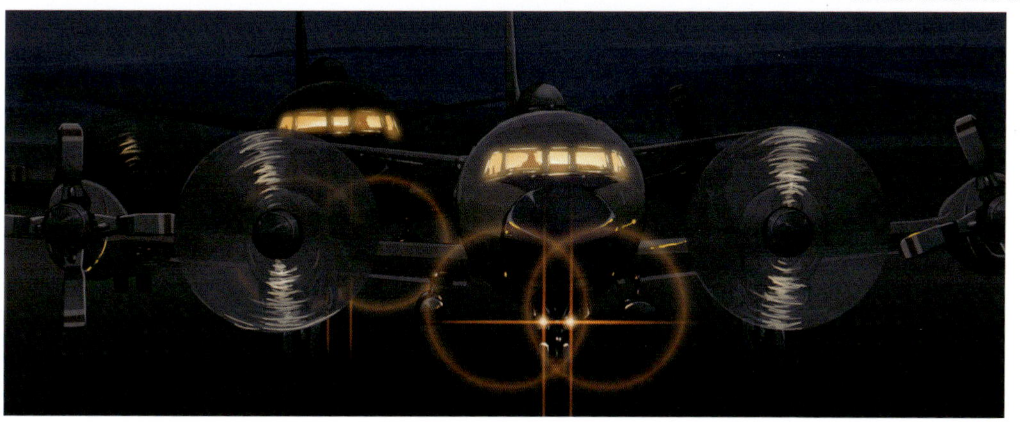

The Place Promised in Our Early Days / CUT_3-245 / Setting: Above Tsugaru Strait, Aomori

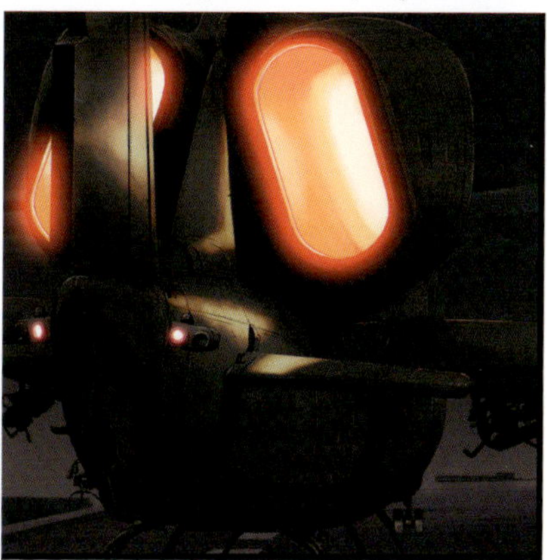

The Place Promised in Our Early Days / CUT_3-246 / Setting: Alliance aircraft carrier, Tsugaru Strait, Aomori

CUT_3-273 shows aerial combat between Alliance and Union fighter jets as seen from Bella Ciela as she flies close to the water's surface.

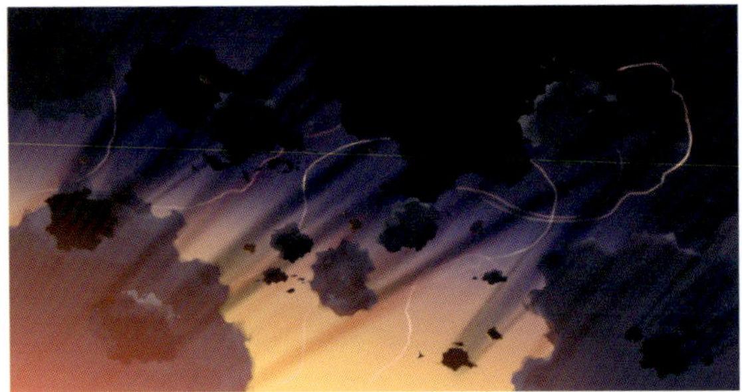

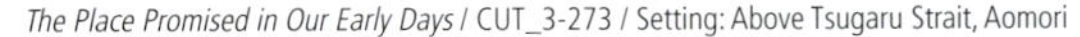
The Place Promised in Our Early Days / CUT_3-273 / Setting: Above Tsugaru Strait, Aomori

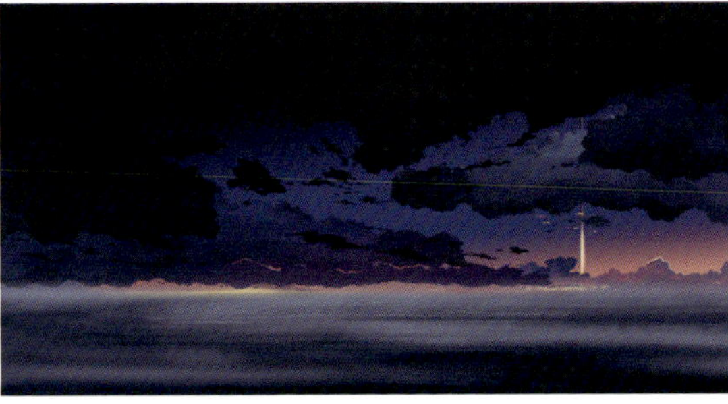
The Place Promised in Our Early Days / CUT_3-279 / Setting: Above Tsugaru Strait, Aomori

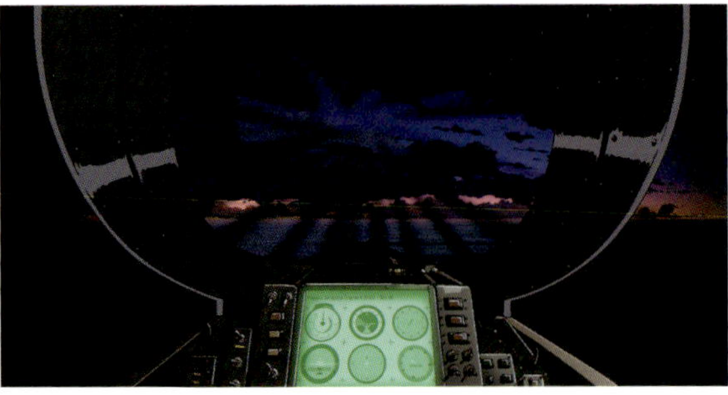
The Place Promised in Our Early Days / CUT_3-267 / Setting: Above Tsugaru Strait, Aomori

CUT_3-281 has a very wide panoramic background as it is used in the scene showing Bella Ciela's precarious flight.

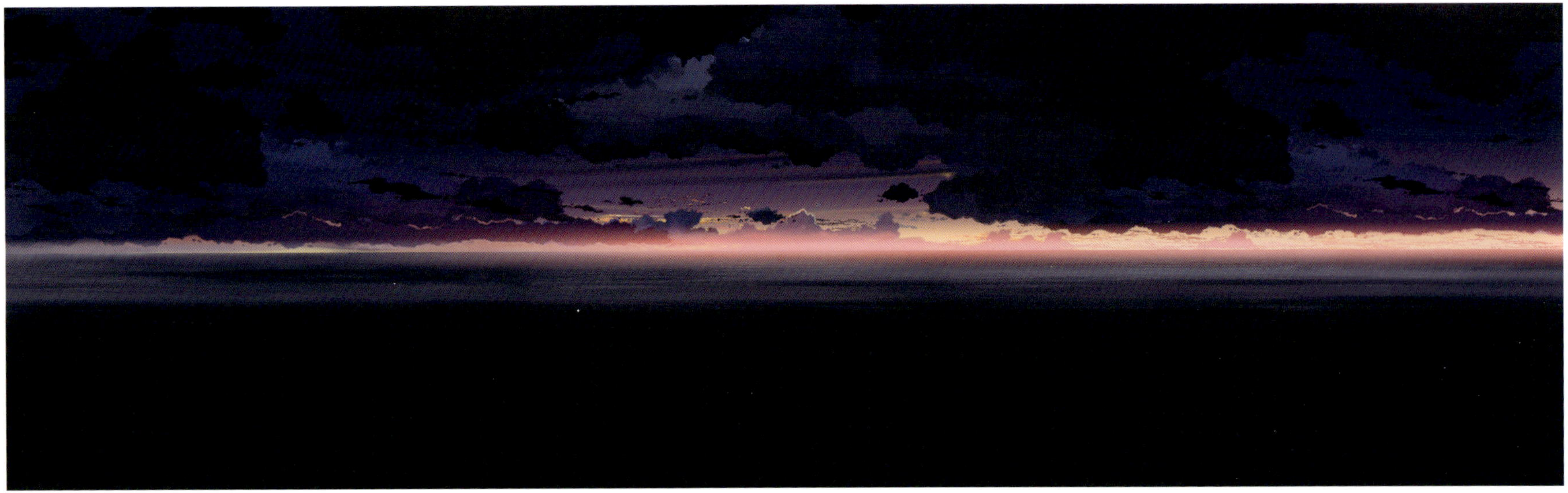

The Place Promised in Our Early Days / CUT_3-281 / Setting: Above Tsugaru Strait, Aomori

CUT_3-290 is the background artwork for the scene where Bella Ciela, after slipping through the air battle, reaches Hokkaido and then climbs to a stable altitude.

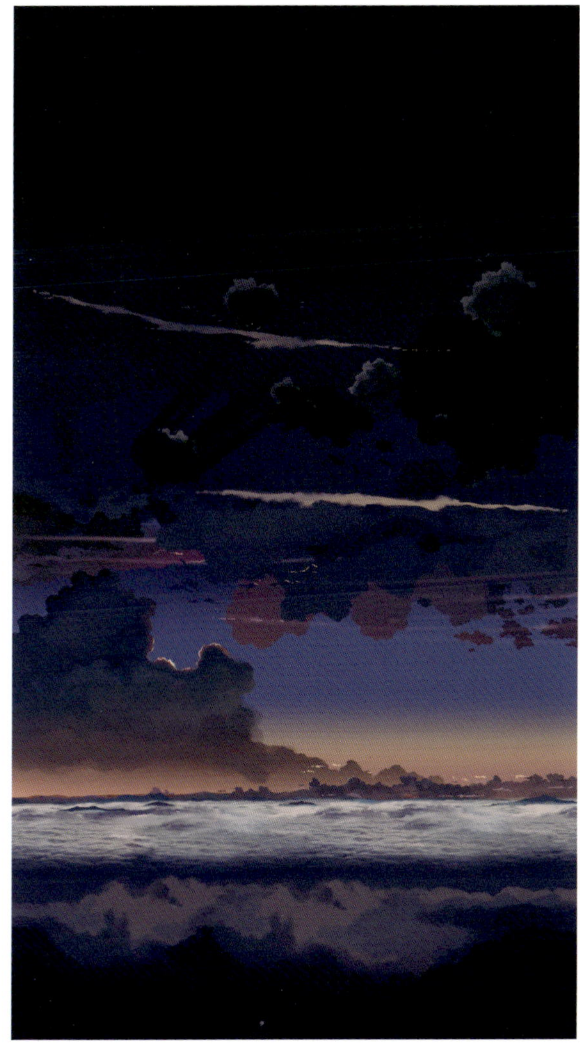

The Place Promised in Our Early Days / CUT_3-290 / Setting: Above Tsugaru Strait, Aomori

The Place Promised in Our Early Days / CUT_3-285 / Setting: Above Tsugaru Strait, Aomori

Hiroki:	Sayuri...
Sayuri:	I have... I have to tell you something very important...
	(*weeping*) But it's gone!
Hiroki:	Everything will be all right because you are awake now. Now we can do everything over again.
Hiroki:	Welcome back, Sayuri.

(Excerpt of *The Place Promised in Our Early Days*)

The Place Promised in Our Early Days

Reunion at the End of the World

The highlights of the final scene of *The Place Promised in Our Early Days* are when Sayuri awakens and the Tower is destroyed. From the heavy, cold atmosphere during the air battle, Bella Ciela flies high, close to the stratosphere, where blue skies can be seen (in order to save fuel and because the air is so thin at that altitude, the propulsion was switched from the jets to the superconductor motor-powered propellers). This gives the viewers a sense of spaciousness and exhilaration. The blue skies here show a very high-altitude perspective, close to outer space, so they were drawn with the most intense blues used in the entire film. Please note the visuals from within the Tower that are similar to the visuals used in the parallel dimension.

Background artwork for the scenes of Bella Ciela's flight. In order to give a sense of space, the sky, Tower, and clouds were all drawn on separate layers, and were combined with a 3DCG rendering of Bella Ciela using video software.

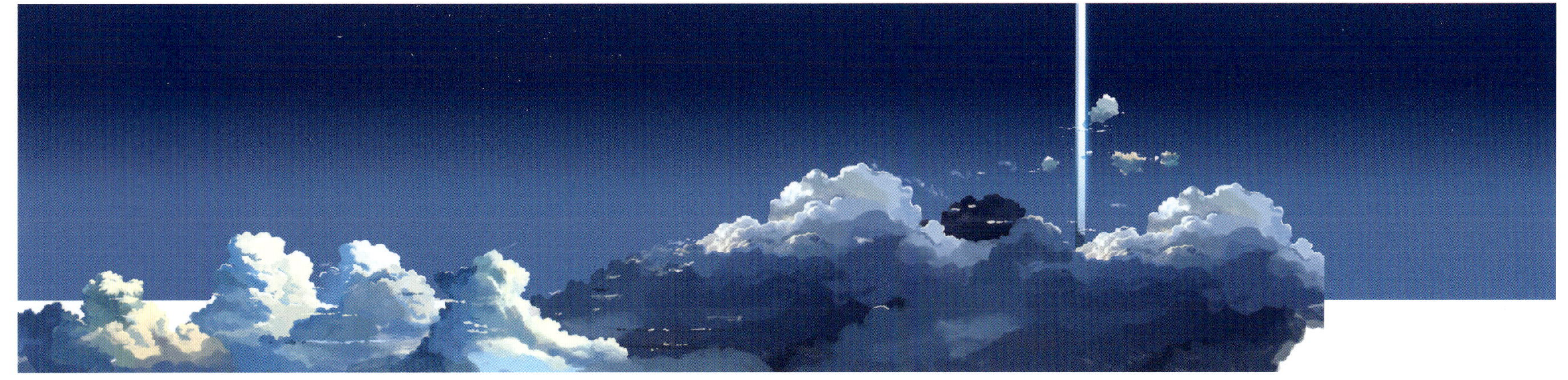

The Place Promised in Our Early Days / CUT_3-300 / Setting: In the skies above Hokkaido, heading towards Hakodate

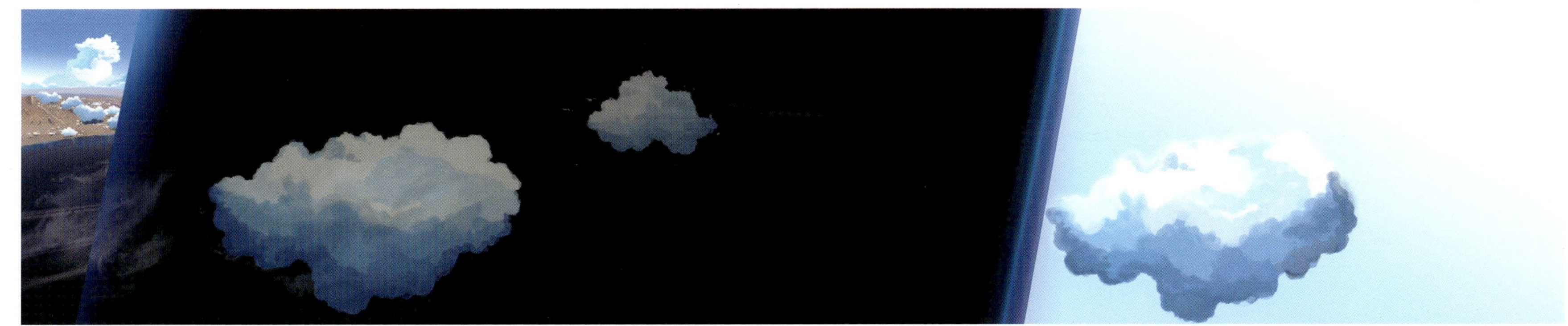

The Place Promised in Our Early Days / CUT_3-304 / Setting: Hokkaido, in the skies above the Tower

The Place Promised in Our Early Days / CUT_3-318 / Setting: In the skies above Hokkaido, heading towards Hakodate

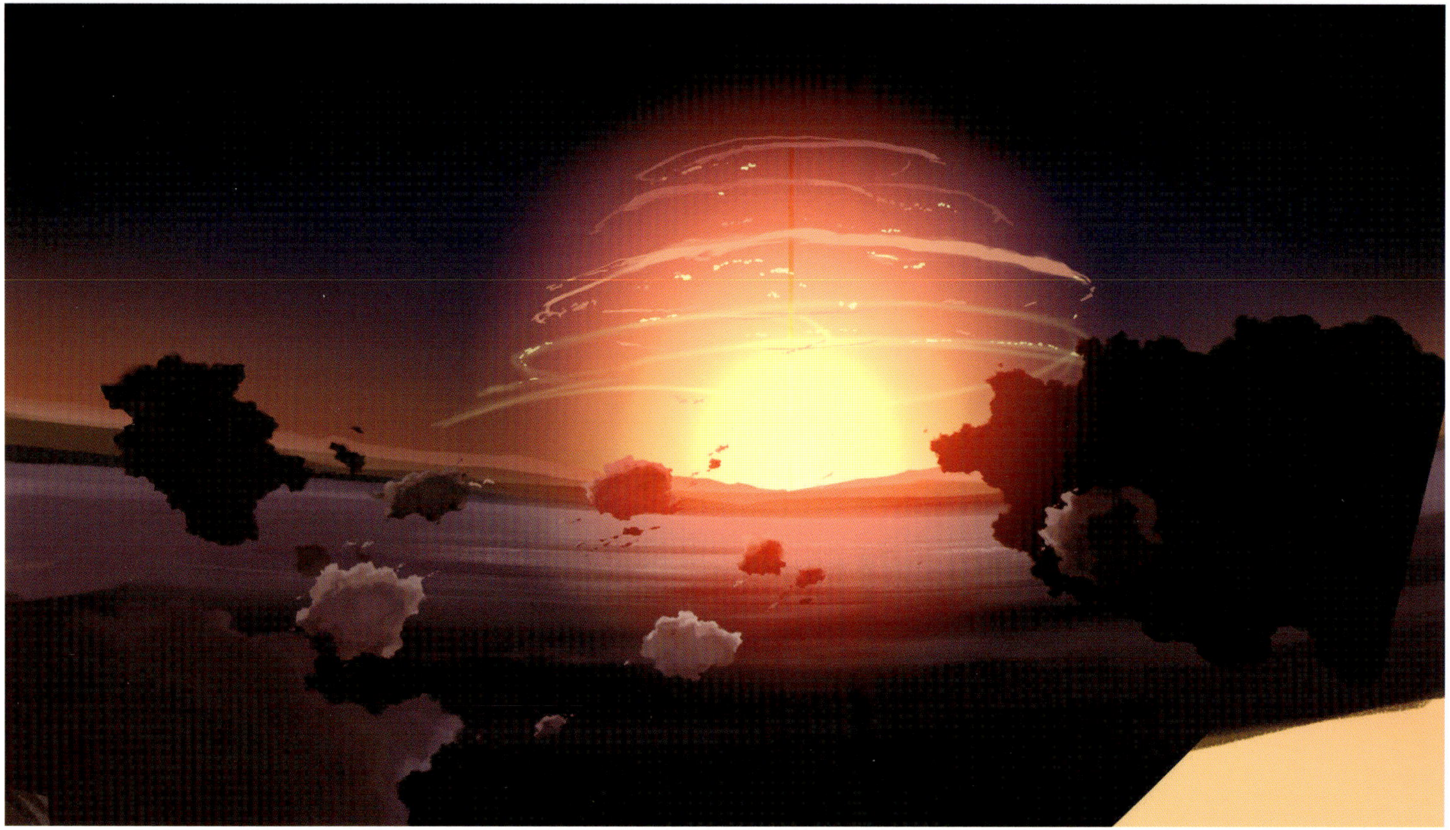

The Tower being destroyed by a seeker missile launched by Bella Ciela. The burst of light from the explosion was created with CG.

The Place Promised in Our Early Days / CUT_3-348 / Setting: Hokkaido as seen from Tsugaru Strait

CUT_3-323 shows the inside of the Tower from a high vantage point. From this angle, you can see the complex patterns drawn on the inside of the tower. CUT_3-324 and CUT_3-327 show the world being eaten up by the Tower's activity. Also note the spiral clouds rising up.

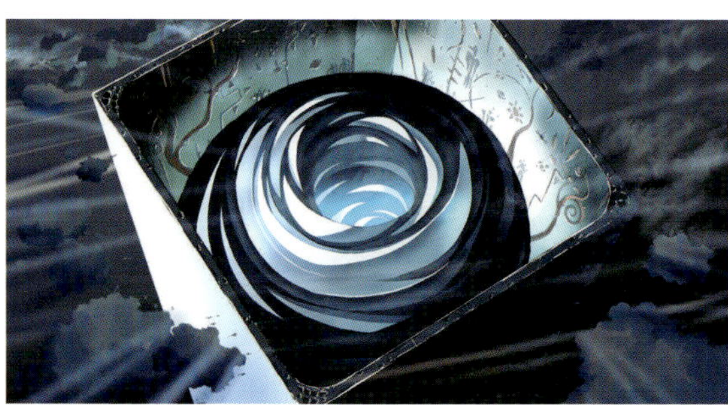

The Place Promised in Our Early Days / CUT_3-323 / Setting: Hokkaido, in the skies above the Tower

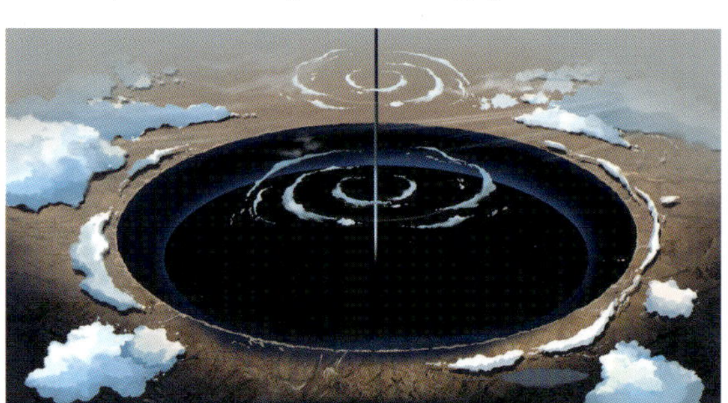

The Place Promised in Our Early Days / CUT_3-324 / Setting: Hokkaido, in the skies above the Tower

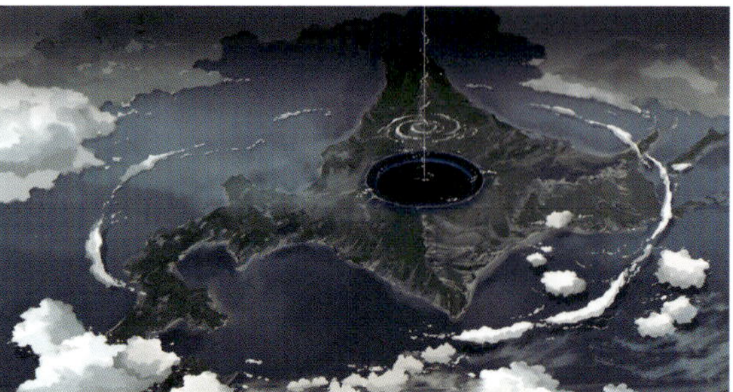

The Place Promised in Our Early Days / CUT_3-327 / Setting: Above Hokkaido

Hiroki and the recently-awakened Sayuri in Bella Ciela, flying away from the place where the Tower stood. Bella Ciela's propellers were animated 3DCG elements. A halation effect was brushed onto Bella Ciela's fuselage.

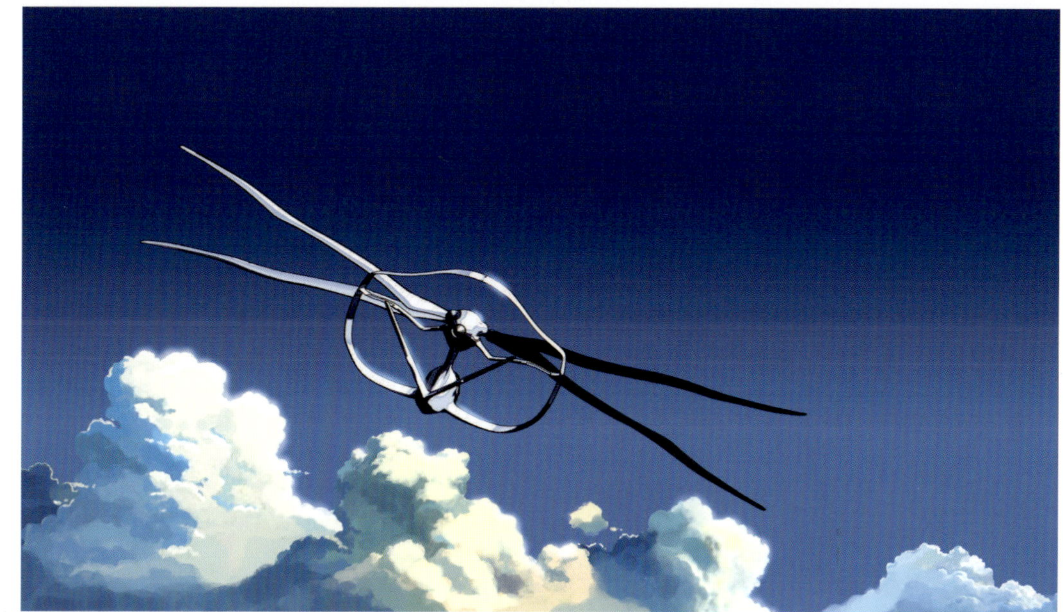

The Place Promised in Our Early Days / CUT_3-360 / Setting: Above Hokkaido

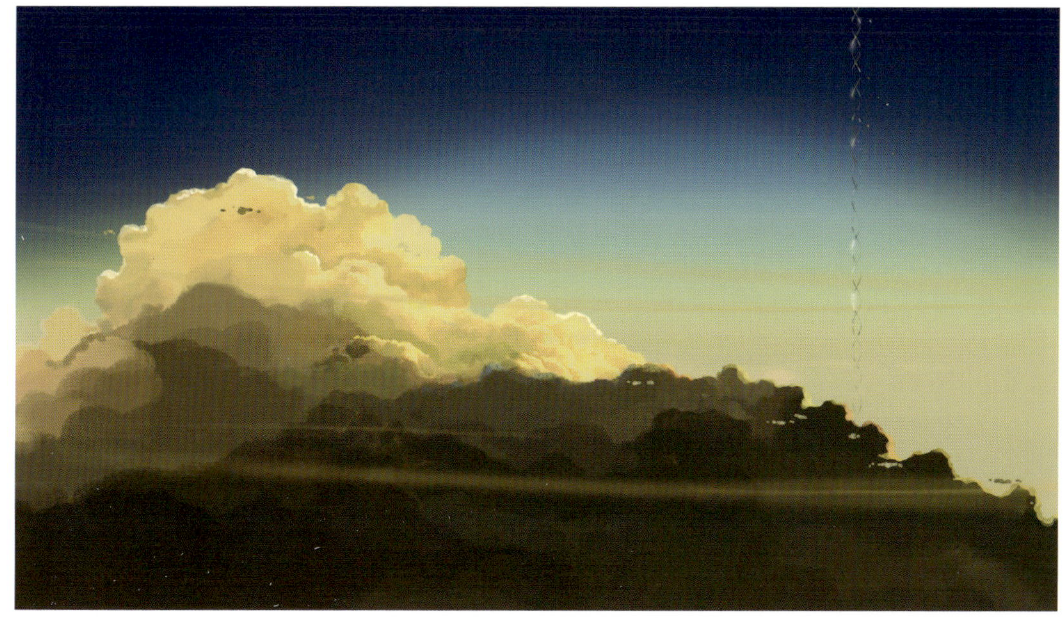

The Place Promised in Our Early Days / CUT_3-355 / Setting: Above Hokkaido

The smoke rising high into the sky give a sense of the massive scale of the explosion. The animation of the collapse of the Tower, as the cladding falls away leaving the spiral insides exposed, was created using CG.

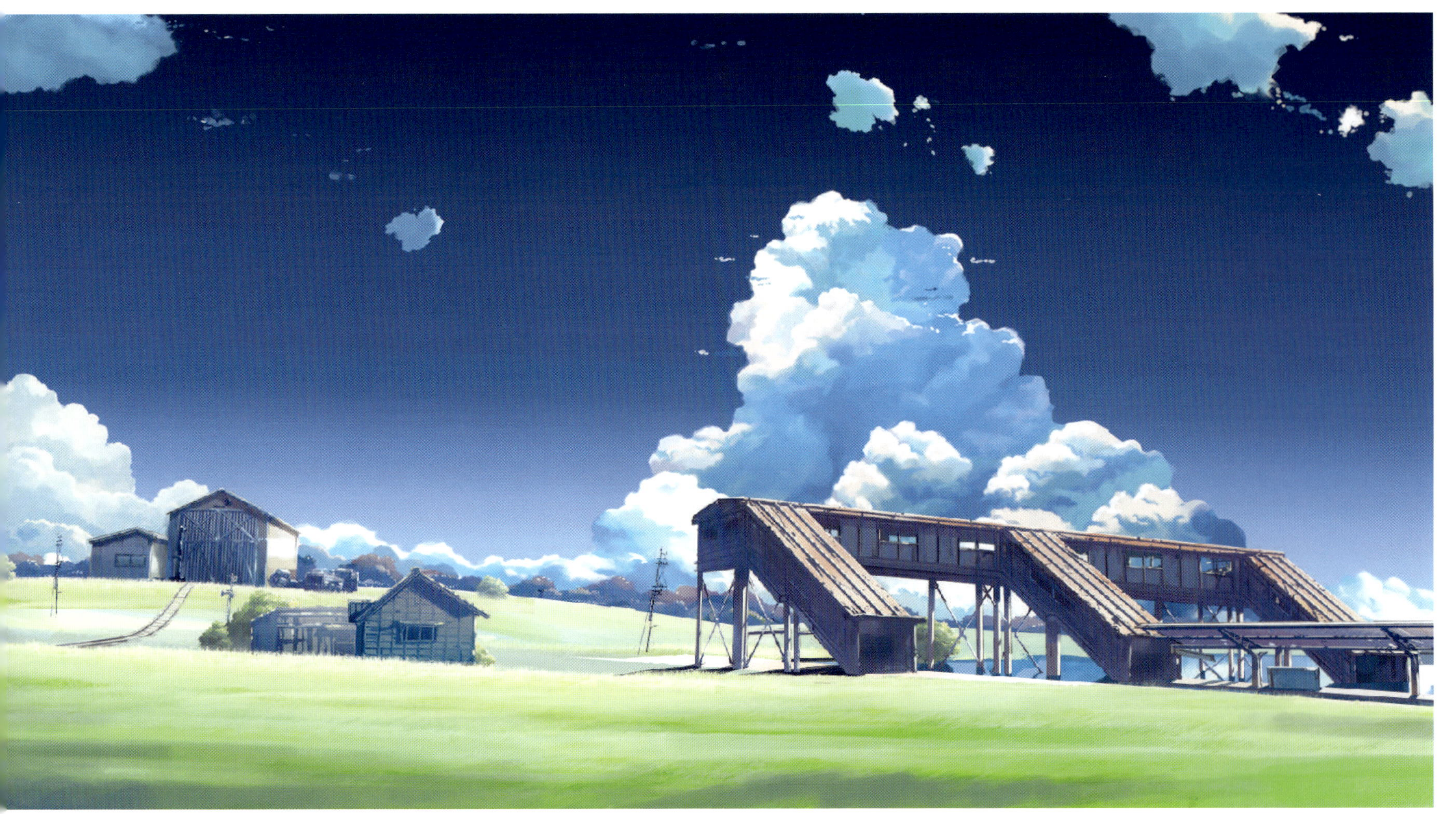

The abandoned train station, several years later. This final cut gives the sense that an era had ended, as the Tower no longer looms in the distance to the north. From the shape of the clouds and the angle of the sunlight, you can tell that this is a summer morning.

The Place Promised in Our Early Days / CUT_3-361 / Setting: Abandoned Station, Tsugaru, Aomori

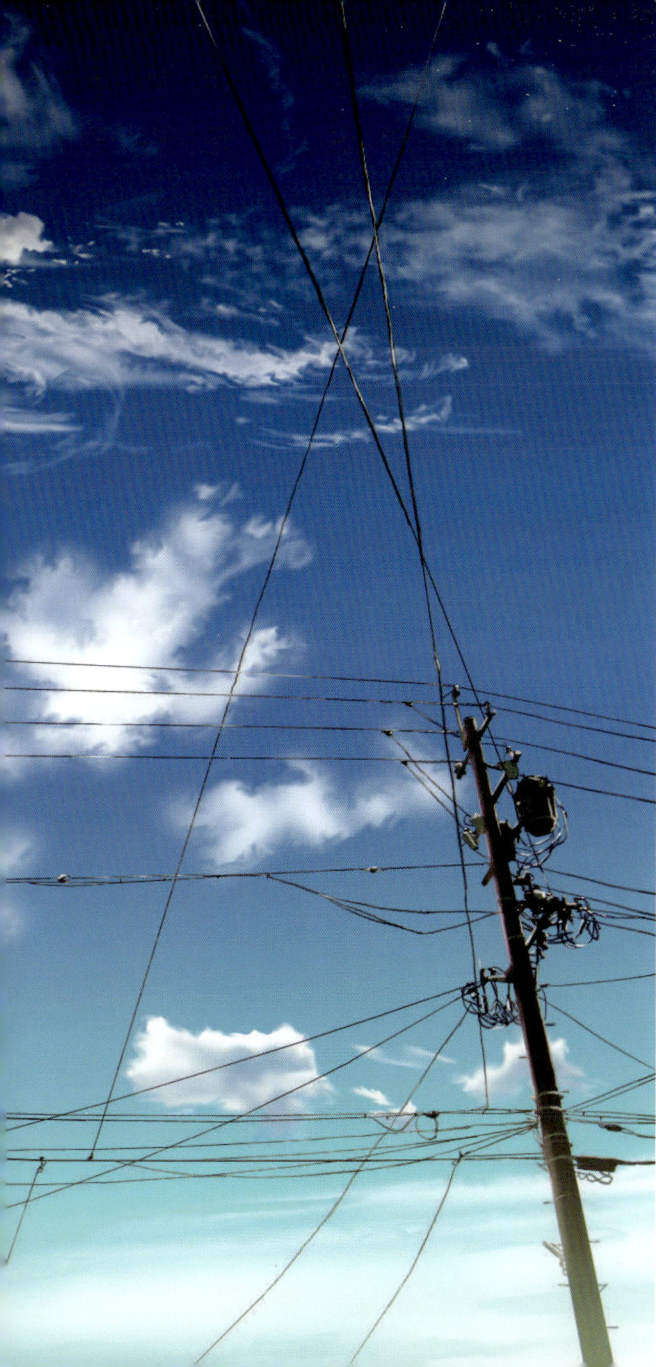

Voices of a Distant Star

Premiere: Tollywood Short Film Theatre, Tokyo, Japan, February 2, 2002
DVD release: April 19, 2002 (JP); June 10, 2003 (USA)
Award of Excellence, Public Offering Division, 1st Tokyo International Animation Fair 21, 2002
Image Design Award, Digital Content Grand Prix 2002
Packaged Work Award, 7th Animation Kobe
Digital Art Special Prize, 6th Japan Media Arts Festival
Seiun Award, Media Division, 34th Japan Sci-Fi Convention, 2003
Best Director, 8th AMD Award Festival

Running time: 25 minutes

Staff:
Original Creator, Director, Screenwriter, Animator, Producer: Makoto Shinkai
Music: Tenmon

Cast:
Mikako Nagamine: Sumi Muto (Original: Mika Shinohara)
Noboru Terao: Chihiro Suzuki (Original: Makoto Shinkai)

Mikako: Until about the time I was in middle school, I had a vague idea that the word "world" meant the area where the signals from my cell phone could reach...

But why is it my cell phone never reaches anyone...?

Hello? Hey, is anyone there? How far should I go?

I'm lonely... Noboru...?

I'm going home.

Hey... Where am I?

Oh... That's right... I'm not in that world anymore...

(Excerpt of *Voices of a Distant Star*)

Voices of a Distant Star

From Here to Eternity – Endless Summer

This was Makoto Shinkai's maiden work, the anime that put him on the map as a filmmaker. After winning the top prize in the Public Offering category at the 1st Tokyo International Animation Fair 21, the film went on to win several more awards. It was then released theatrically and on DVD in several foreign markets, and garnered praise from overseas reviewers. It was notable that Mr. Shinkai himself handled nearly every aspect of production, except for music, starting with the original concept and direction, and including artwork production, 3DCG and editing. He is credited with immediately expanding the possibilities of the use of digital tools in film production. After this, animated video production became another option for individuals. As this film was created using NTSC standard, the resolution is lower than Shinkai's later works.

View from a high-rise apartment. The apartment was created using 3DCG. In CUT_A-10, the line art for the stairs was rendered using 3DCG, then colorized. The sketches of the cityscapes were based on location photos.

Voices of a Distant Star / CUT_A-10 / Setting: Apartment building emergency stairwell, Saitama

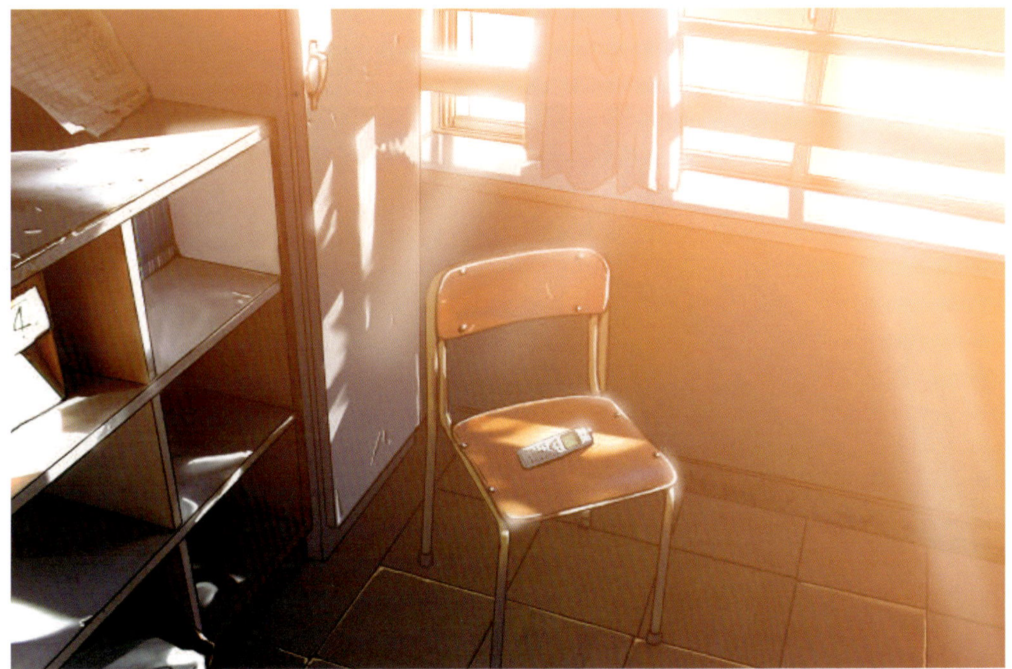

Voices of a Distant Star / CUT_A-18 / Setting: A classroom in Mikako and Noboru's middle school

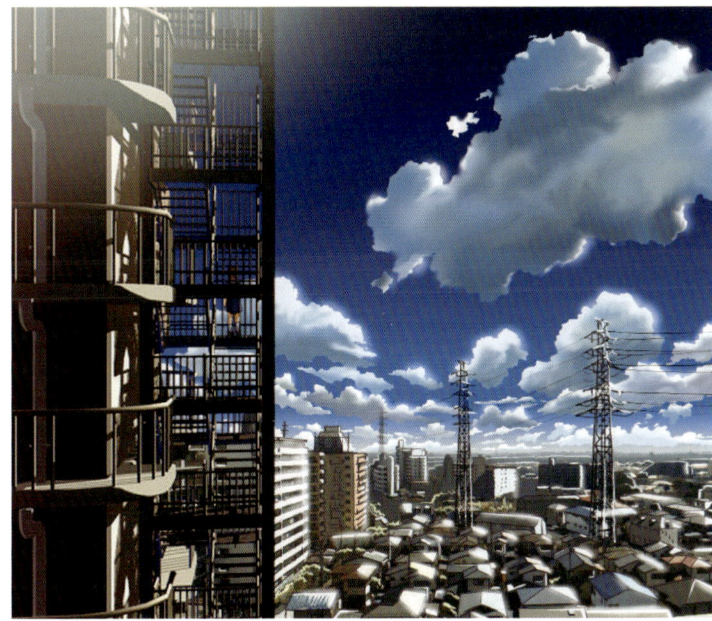

Voices of a Distant Star / CUT_A-07 / Setting: Apartment building emergency stairwell, Saitama

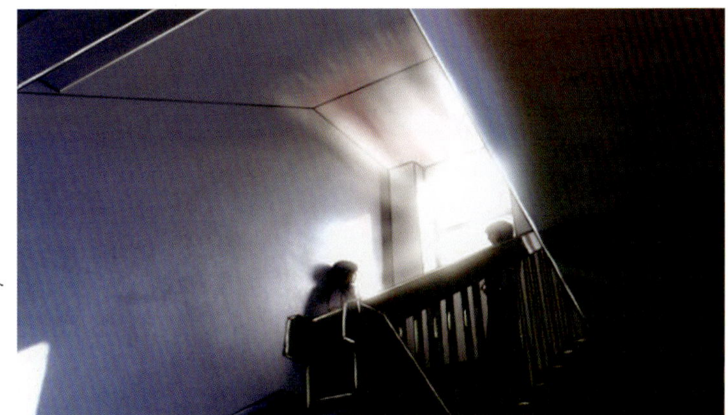

Voices of a Distant Star / CUT_B-03 / Setting: A stairwell in Mikako and Noboru's middle school

The base sketch of CUT_B-03 was based on location photos. CUT_A-18, which shows a chair in a classroom, is a still image that was used in the title card.

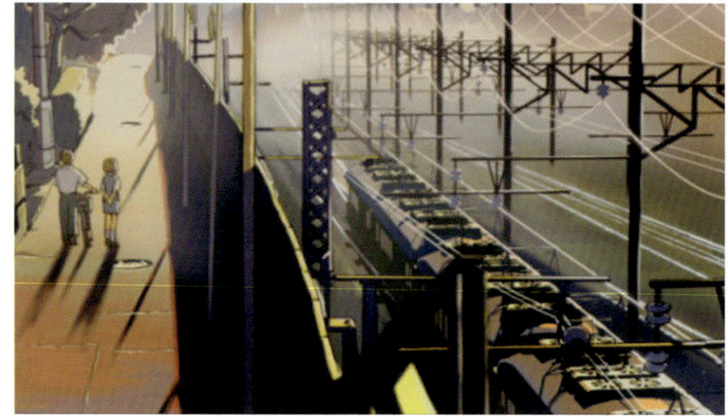

Voices of a Distant Star / CUT_B-12 / Setting: The road Mikako and Noboru take to school in Saitama

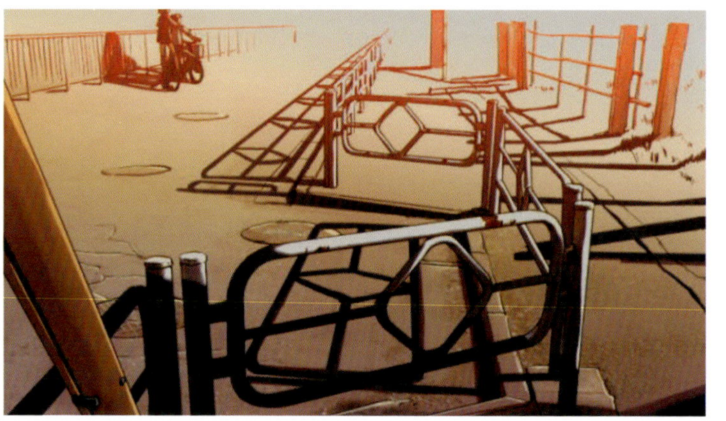

Voices of a Distant Star / CUT_B-29 / Setting: The road Mikako and Noboru take to school in Saitama

The train in CUT_B-12 is a 3DCG animation element. The utility poles were drawn using elements based on 3DCG sketches. The images of Mikako and Noboru as they walk up the hilly road were drawn on cels.

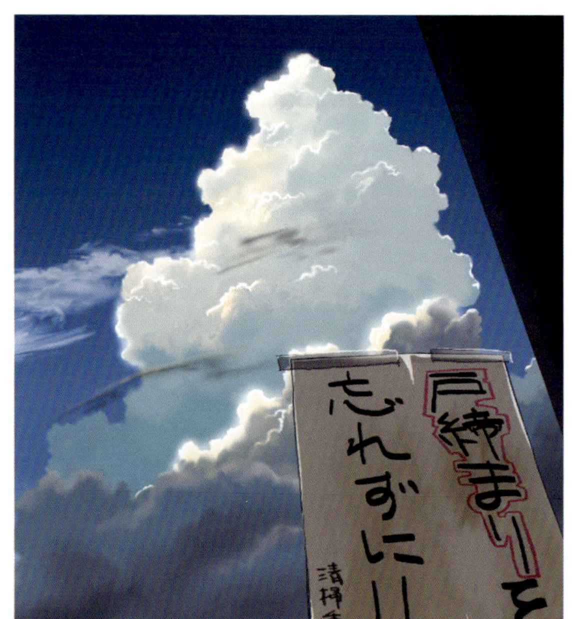

Voices of a Distant Star / CUT_B-06 /
Setting: The road Mikako and Noboru take to school in Saitama

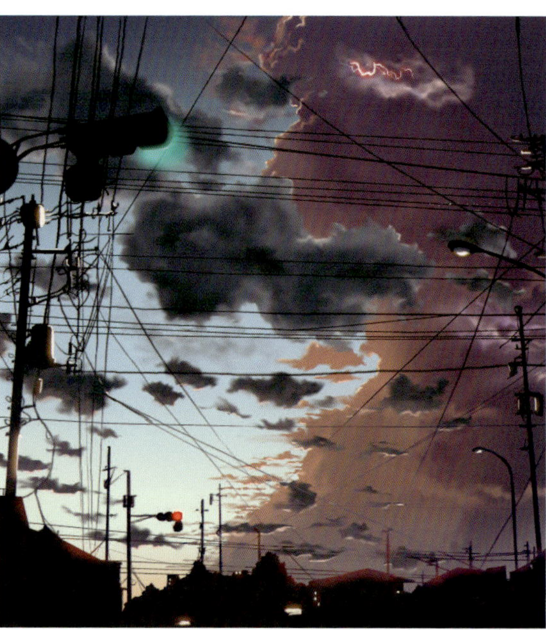

Voices of a Distant Star / CUT_B-21 /
Setting: Scenery along the road Mikako and Noboru take to school in Saitama

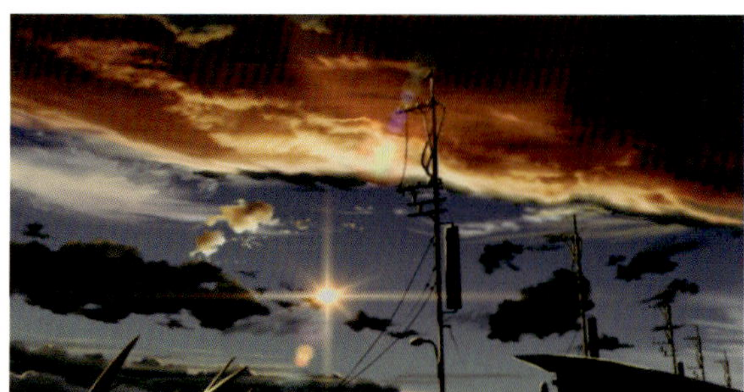

Voices of a Distant Star / CUT_B-26 /
Setting: Scenery along the road Mikako and Noboru take to school in Saitama

CUT_B-22, CUT_F-03 and CUT_I-24 all show the same location but at different seasons, times, and weather conditions. They all use the same base sketch, yet each cut shows a different expression. For the final version of each cut, sunlight flare effects and animated elements of rain and snow were added.

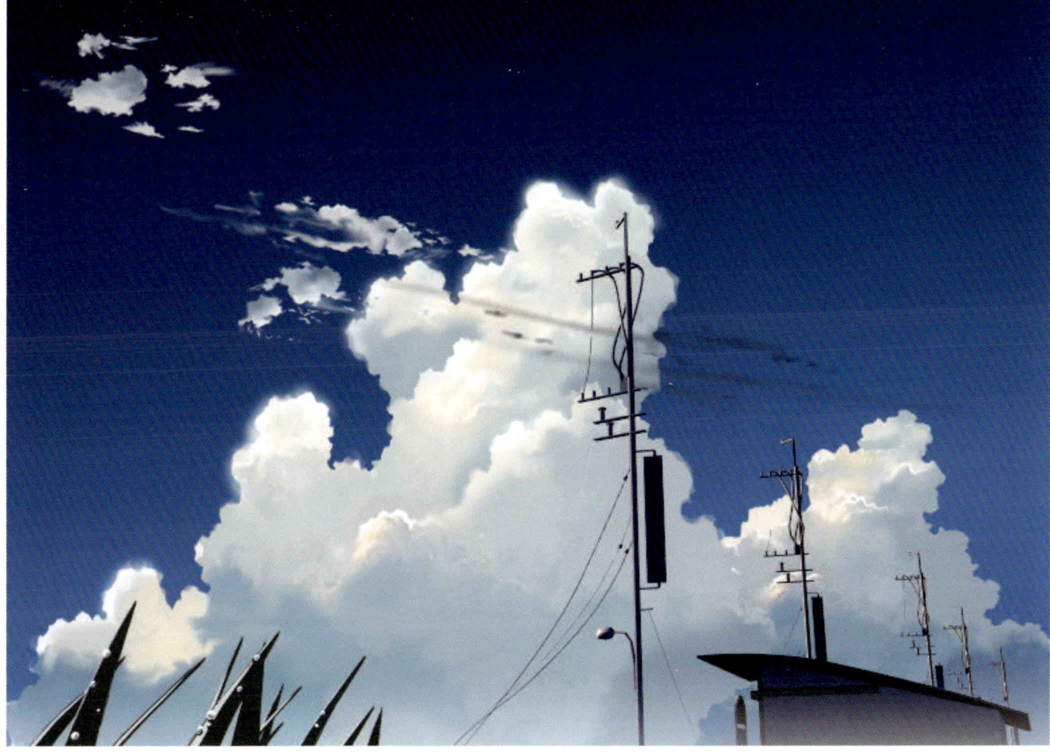

Voices of a Distant Star / CUT_F-28 / Setting: Bus stop at the top of a staircase, Saitama

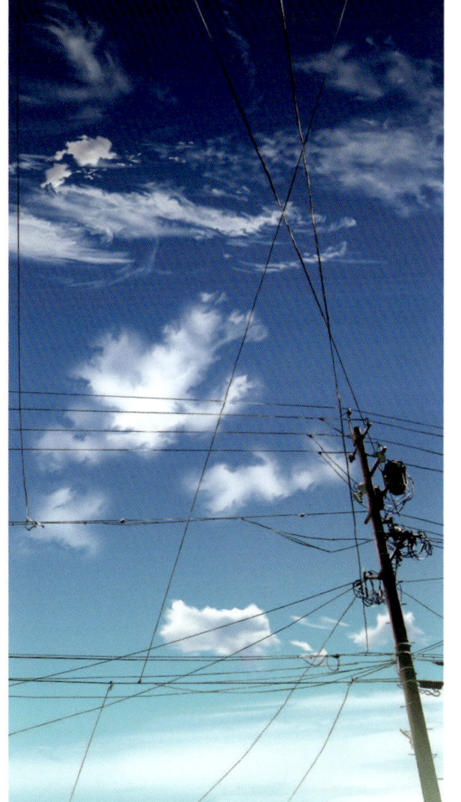

Voices of a Distant Star / CUT_D-01 / Setting: Along the road Mikako and Noboru take to school in Saitama

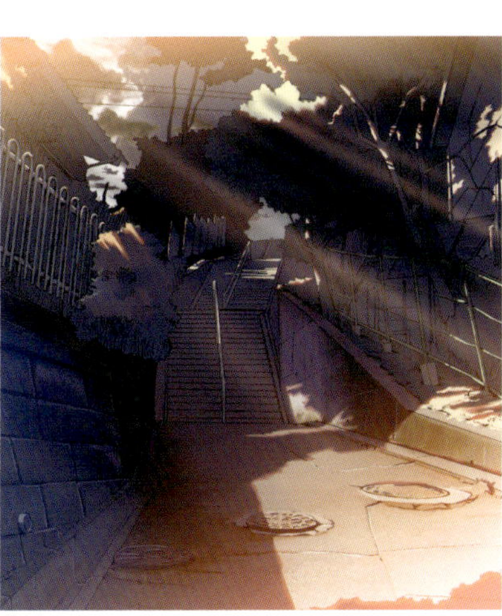

Voices of a Distant Star / CUT_B-22 / Setting: Along the road Mikako and Noboru take to school in Saitama

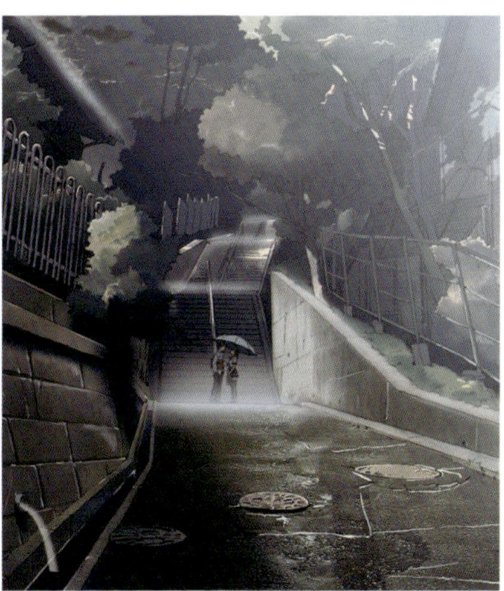

Voices of a Distant Star / CUT_F-03 / Setting: Along the road Mikako and Noboru take to school in Saitama

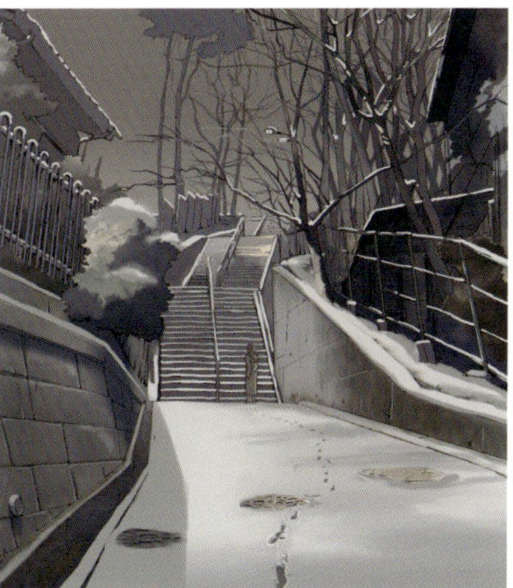

Voices of a Distant Star / CUT_I-24 / Setting: Along the road Mikako and Noboru take to school in Saitama

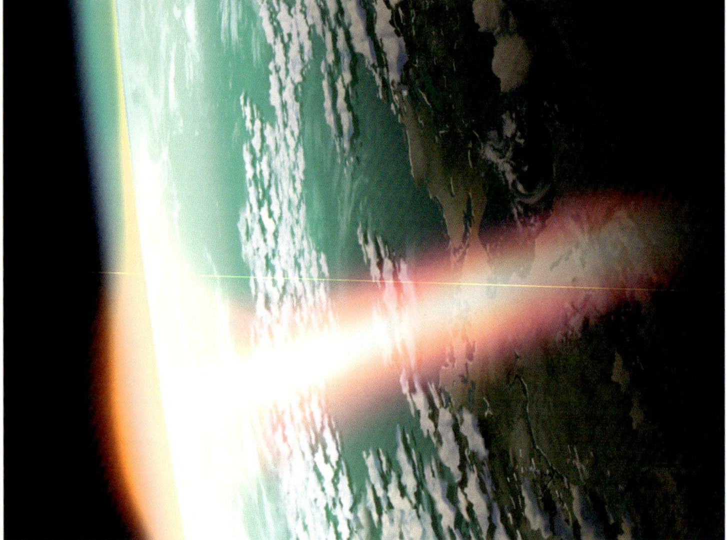

Voices of a Distant Star / CUT_A-16 / Setting: Above the planet Agartha

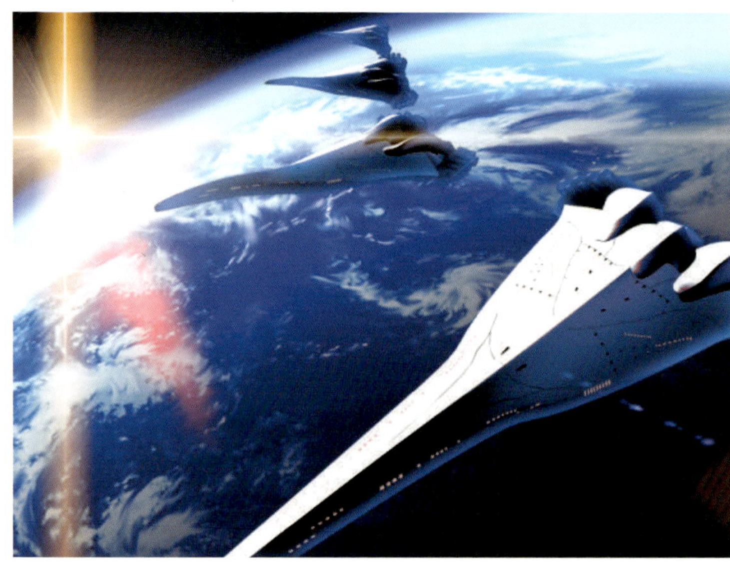

Voices of a Distant Star / CUT_D-10 / Setting: In satellite orbit above Earth

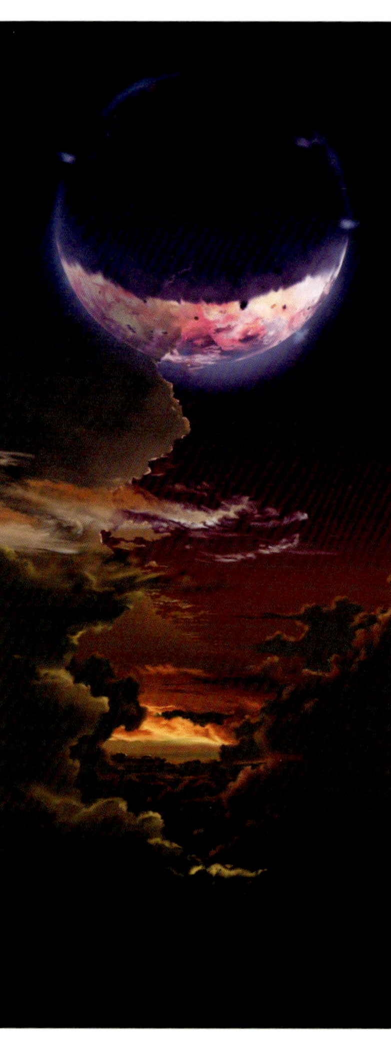

Voices of a Distant Star / CUT_C-26 / Setting: View of Io from Jupiter

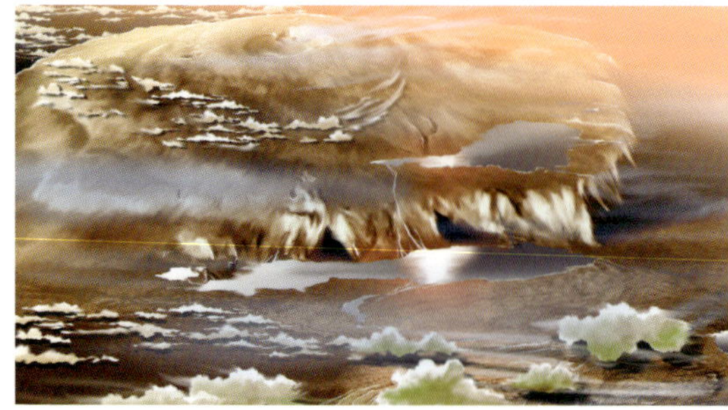

Voices of a Distant Star / CUT_C-14 / Setting: Above Olympus Mons on Mars

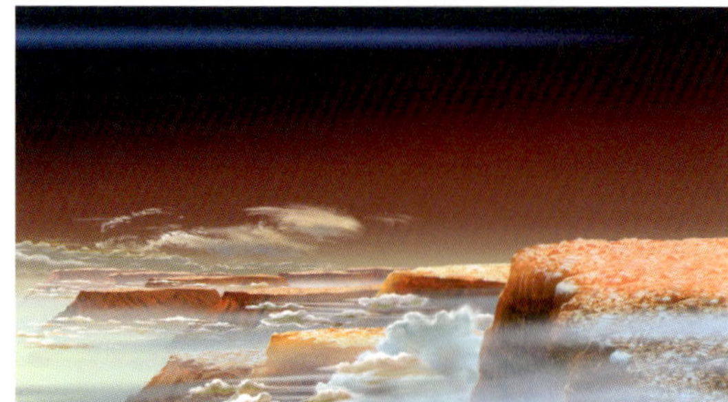

Voices of a Distant Star / CUT_C-21 / Setting: Surface of Mars

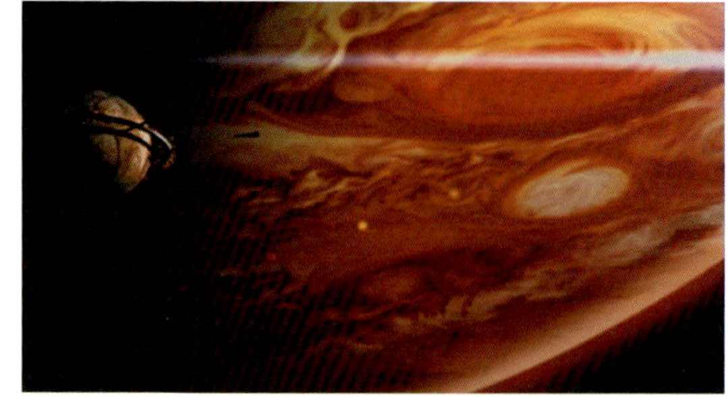

Voices of a Distant Star / CUT_C-23 / Setting: In satellite orbit above Jupiter

The spacecraft carrier Lysithea in CUT_D-10 is a 3DCG element. It was combined with the background art and the sunlight using video software. In CUT_C-23, Jupiter and its moon, Io, were drawn on separate layers, which were combined with animation of a flux tube.

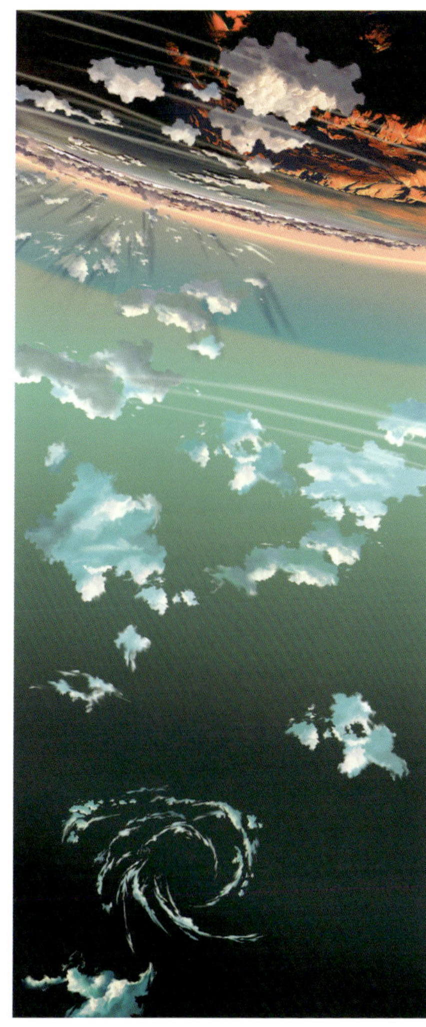

Voices of a Distant Star / CUT_I-01 / Setting: Above the planet Agartha

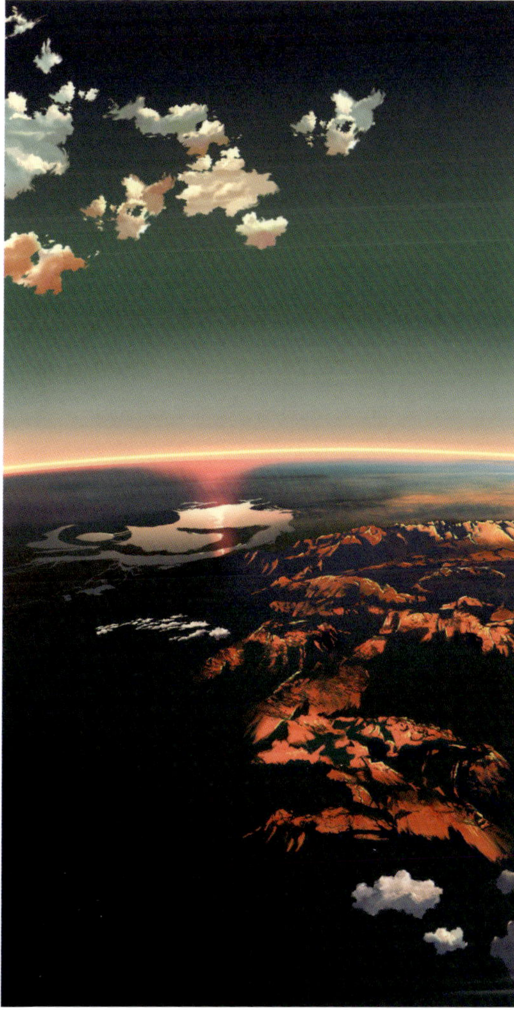

Voices of a Distant Star / CUT_I-02 / Setting: Above the planet Agartha

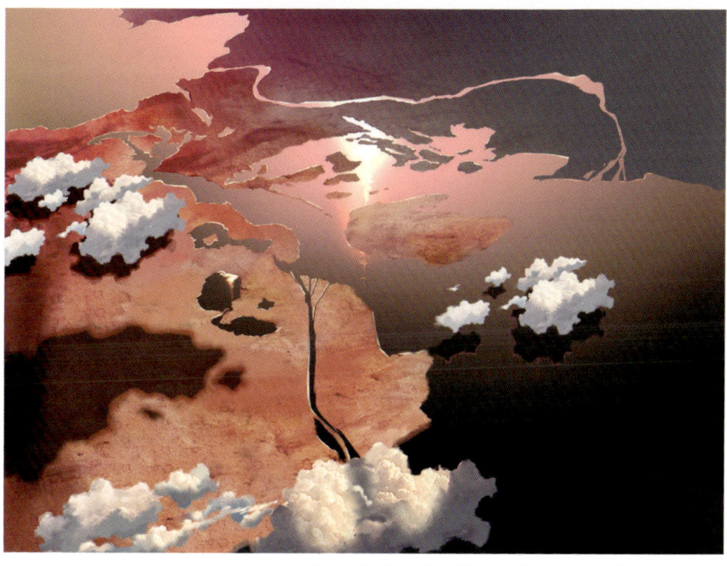

Voices of a Distant Star / CUT_I-03 / Setting: Above the planet Agartha

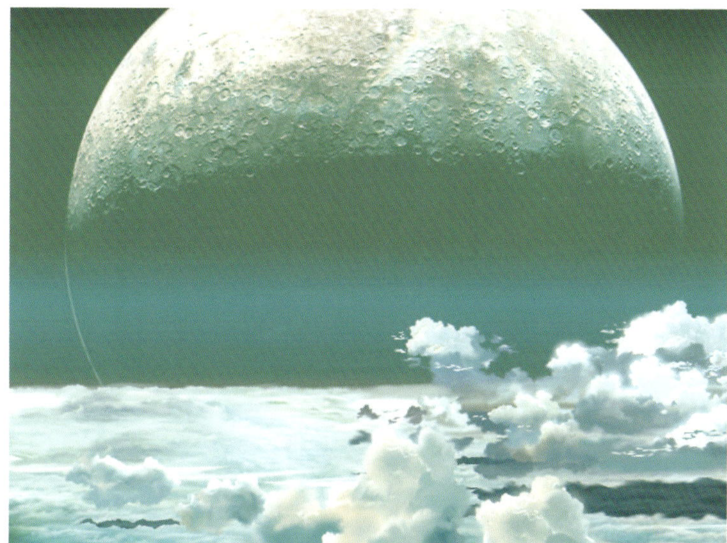

Voices of a Distant Star / CUT_I-11 / Setting: Above the planet Agartha

For the high-altitude shots of planets such as CUT_I-02 and CUT_I-03, 3DCG-rendered perspective lines were used as a base, then drawings were created using aerial shots as reference.
In CUT_I-11, the moon and clouds were drawn on separate layers, which were combined with the 3DCG Tracer (robot).

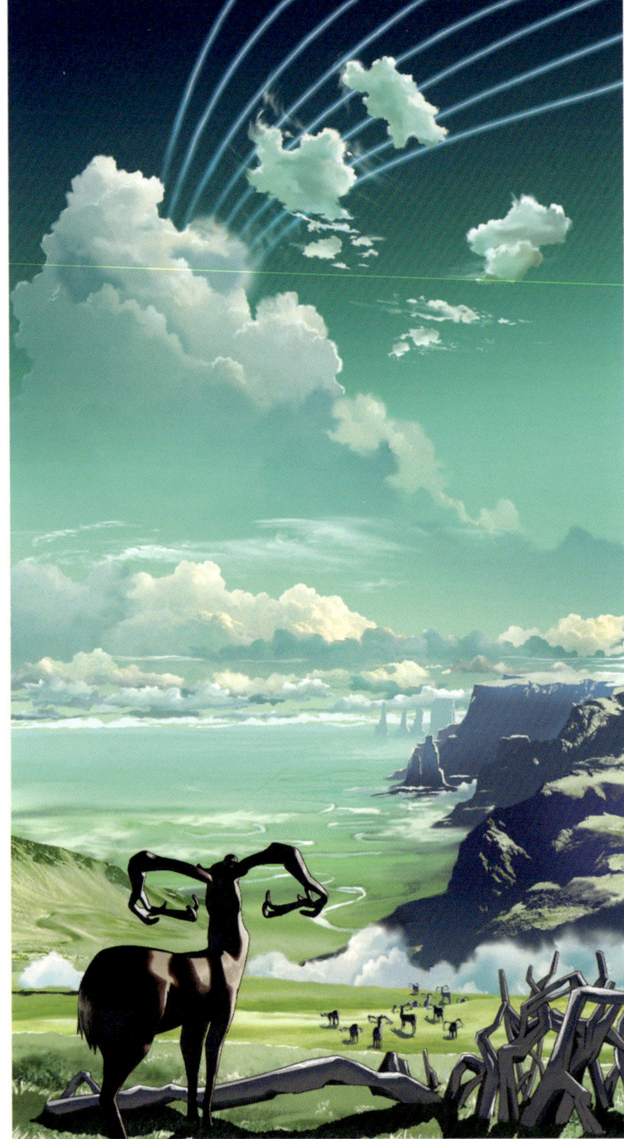

Voices of a Distant Star / CUT_G-05 / Setting: Surface of the planet Agartha

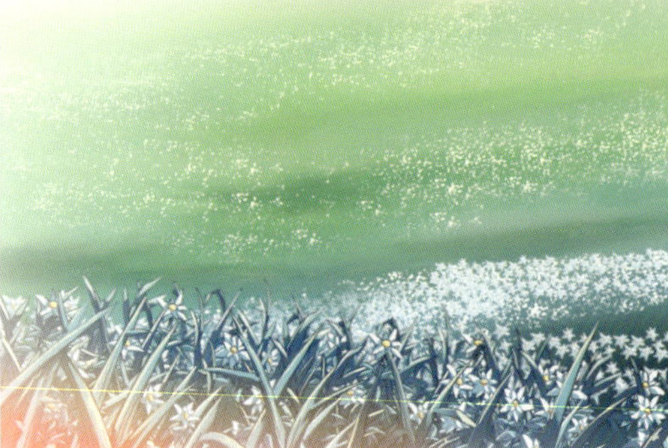

Voices of a Distant Star / CUT_G-11 / Setting: Surface of the planet Agartha

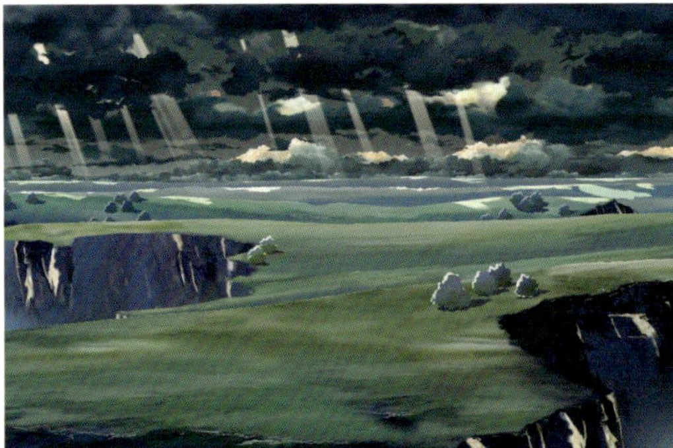

Voices of a Distant Star / CUT_G-18 / Setting: Surface of the planet Agartha

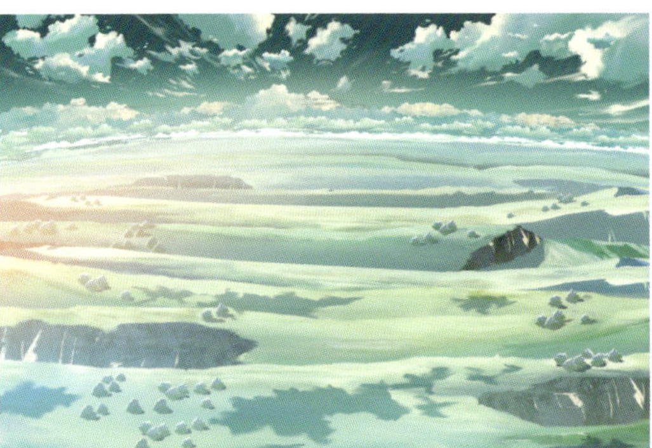

Voices of a Distant Star / CUT_G-40 / Setting: Surface of the planet Agartha

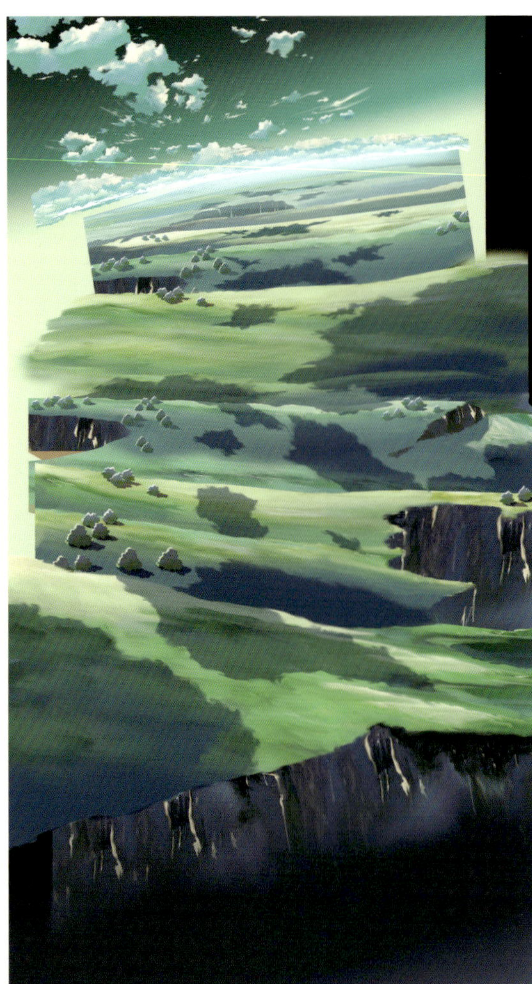

Voices of a Distant Star / CUT_G-41 / Setting: Surface of the planet Agartha

The surface of Agartha, the fourth planet in the Sirius System. CUT_G-41 places CUT_G-40 in the distance, with foreground added in. The final version of CUT_G-18 included the 3DCG Tracer and sunlight, as well as animation of falling rain.

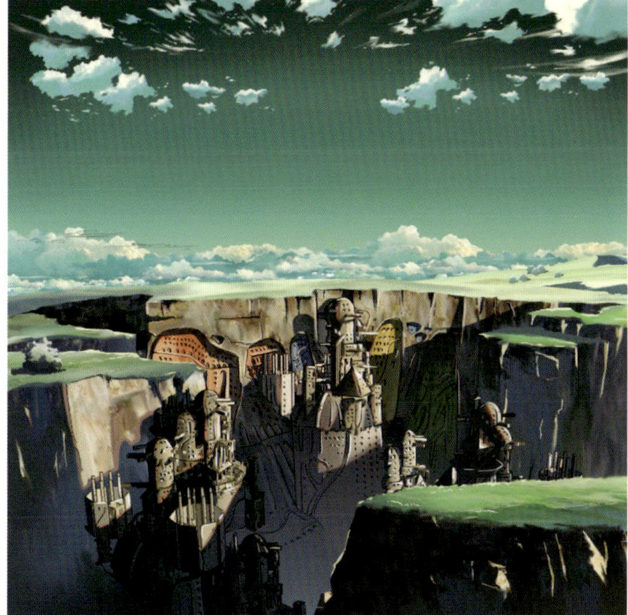

Voices of a Distant Star / CUT_G-42 / Setting: Surface of the planet Agartha

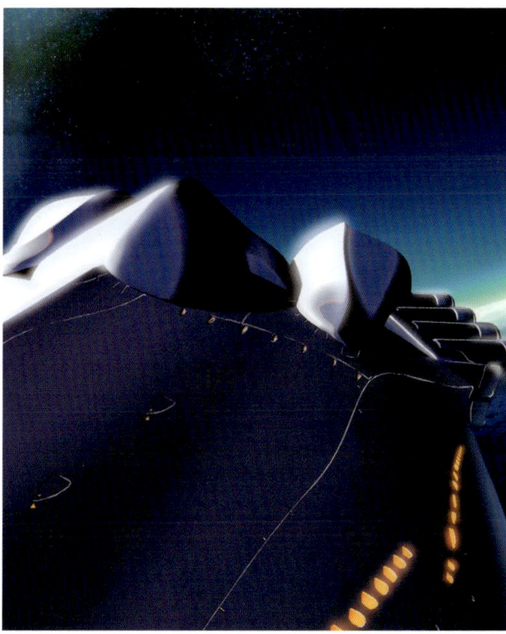

Voices of a Distant Star / CUT_I-35 / Setting: Spacecraft carrier Lysithea orbiting Agartha

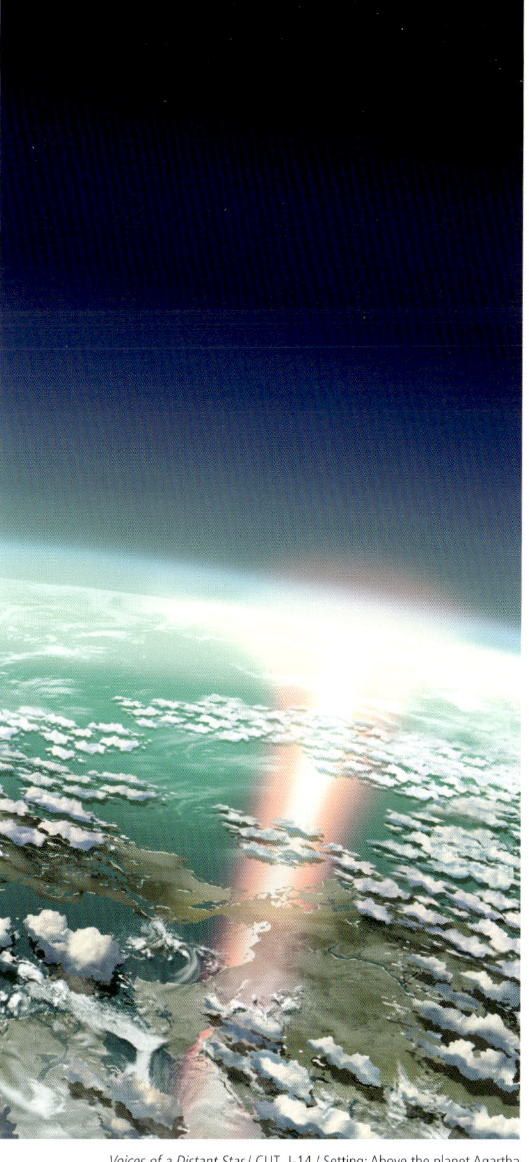

Voices of a Distant Star / CUT_I-14 / Setting: Above the planet Agartha

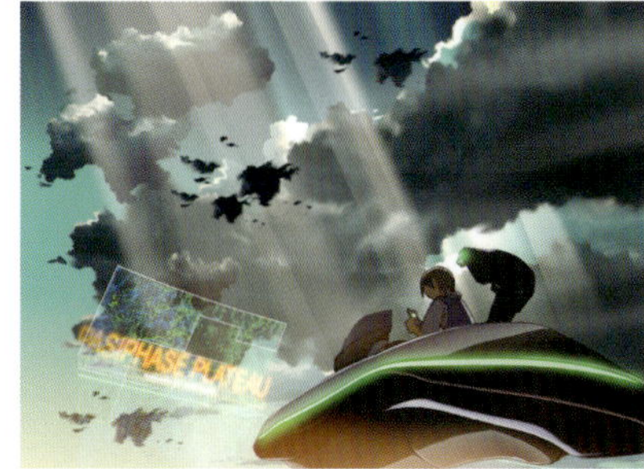

Voices of a Distant Star / CUT_G-27 / Setting: Cockpit inside the Tracer

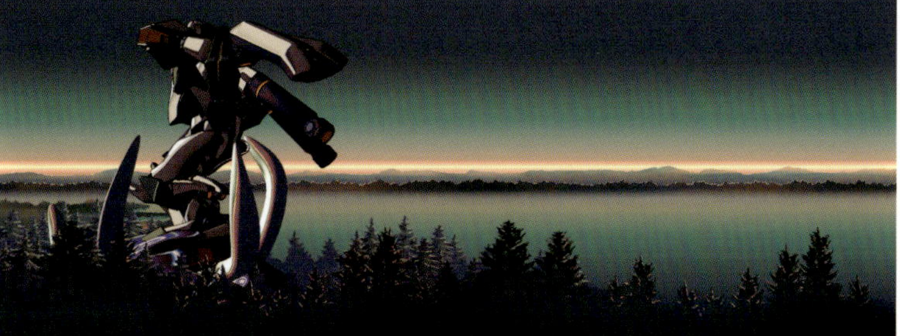

Voices of a Distant Star / CUT_I-04 / Setting: Surface of the planet Agartha

The cockpit of the Tracer in CUT_G-27 was rendered using simplified 3DCG, which was then used as a base for harmony cel elements. The final version included Mikako's character cel and the cockpit display. The Tracer in CUT_I-04 is also a 3DCG animation element. In CUT_I-35, the Lysithea was rendered in 3DCG, and lighting effects, etc. were brushed on top.

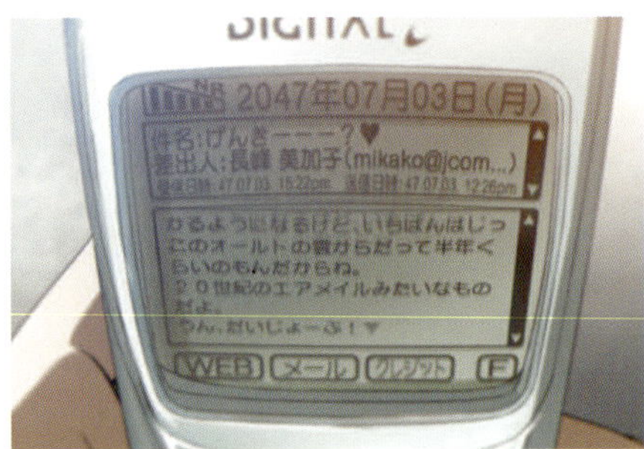

Voices of a Distant Star / CUT_D-21 / Cell phone

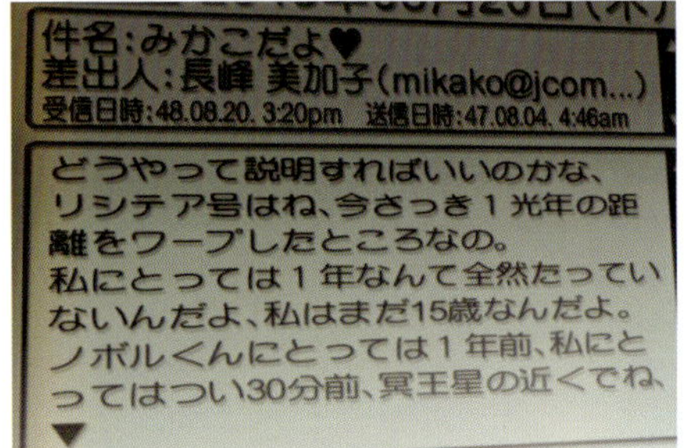

Voices of a Distant Star / CUT_F-12 / Cell phone

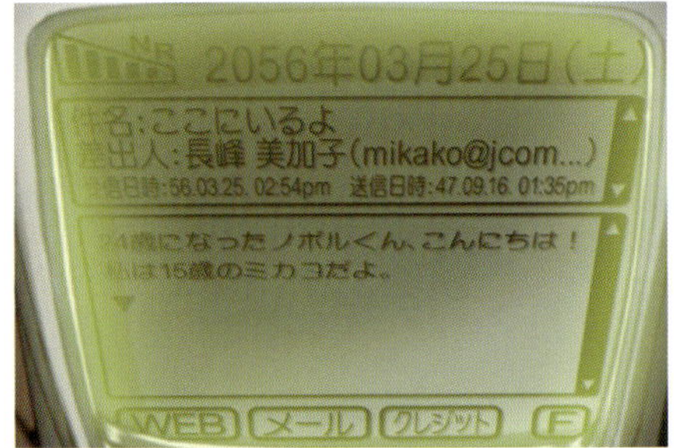

Voices of a Distant Star / CUT_H-16 / Cell phone

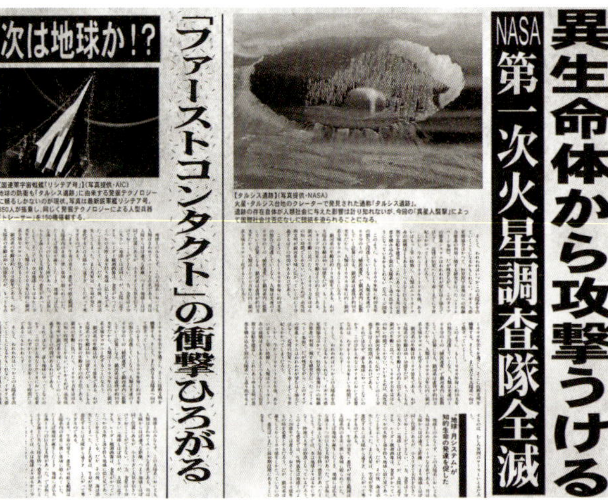

Voices of a Distant Star / CUT_C-18 / Newspaper

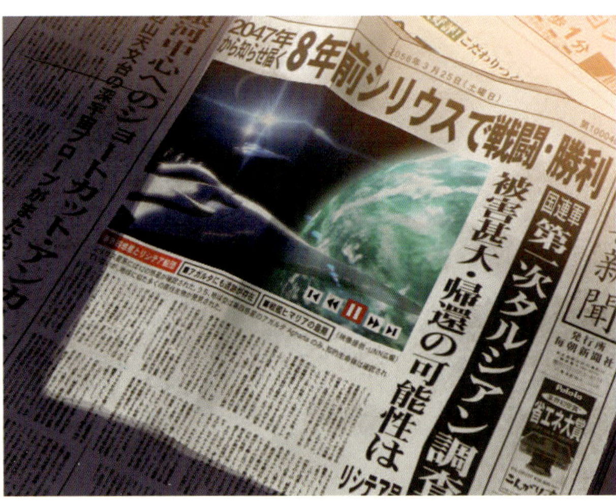

Voices of a Distant Star / CUT_H-03 / Newspaper

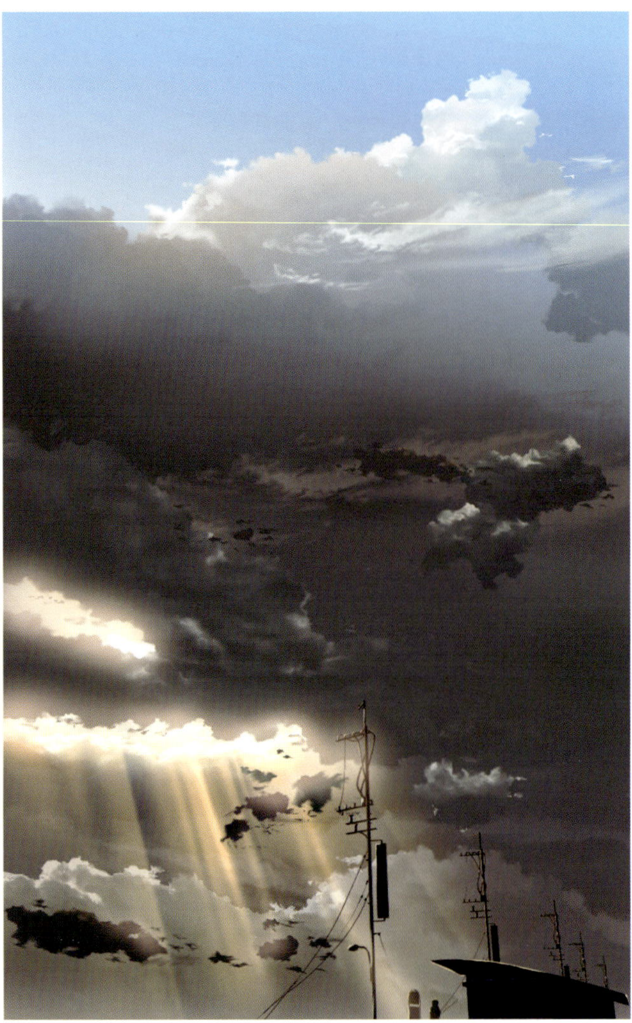

Voices of a Distant Star / CUT_I-45 / Setting: Bus stop at the top of a staircase, Saitama

CUT_D-21, CUT_F-12 and CUT_H-16 show cell phone emails that Noboru received. Please note how the characters on the LCD drop shadows onto the reflecting interface. The display was drawn on a separate layer, and a mask was used to create animation of the text scrolling along the screen. The color video part of CUT_H-03 was an animation element created separately that was then combined with the background art.

Both of these illustrations were used to promote the theatrical release of *Voices of a Distant Star*. The right illustration was created to announce the film's screening at the short film specialty theater Tollywood in Shimokitazawa, Tokyo. The left illustration was used in the announcement of the film's screening as part of the CG Anime Contest sponsored by Osaka-based Project Team DoGa. Both illustrations use cuts and layouts from the film that also include a sense of drama suitable for movie posters.

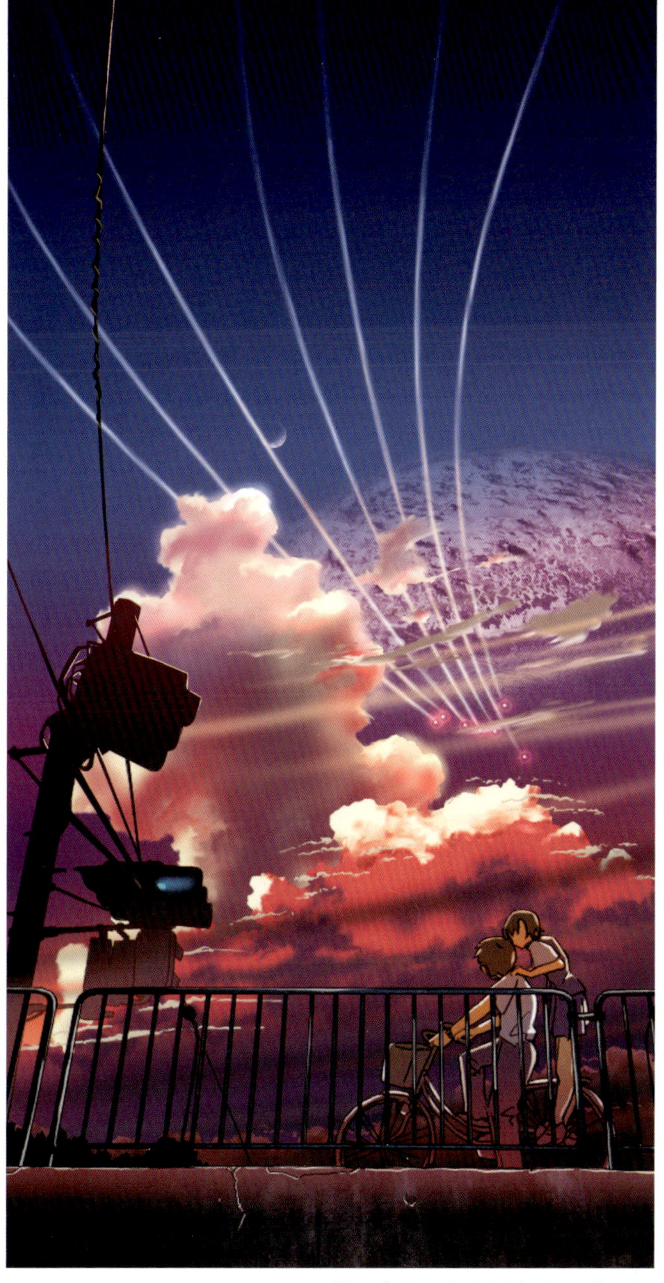

Voices of a Distant Star / CG Anime Contest illustration

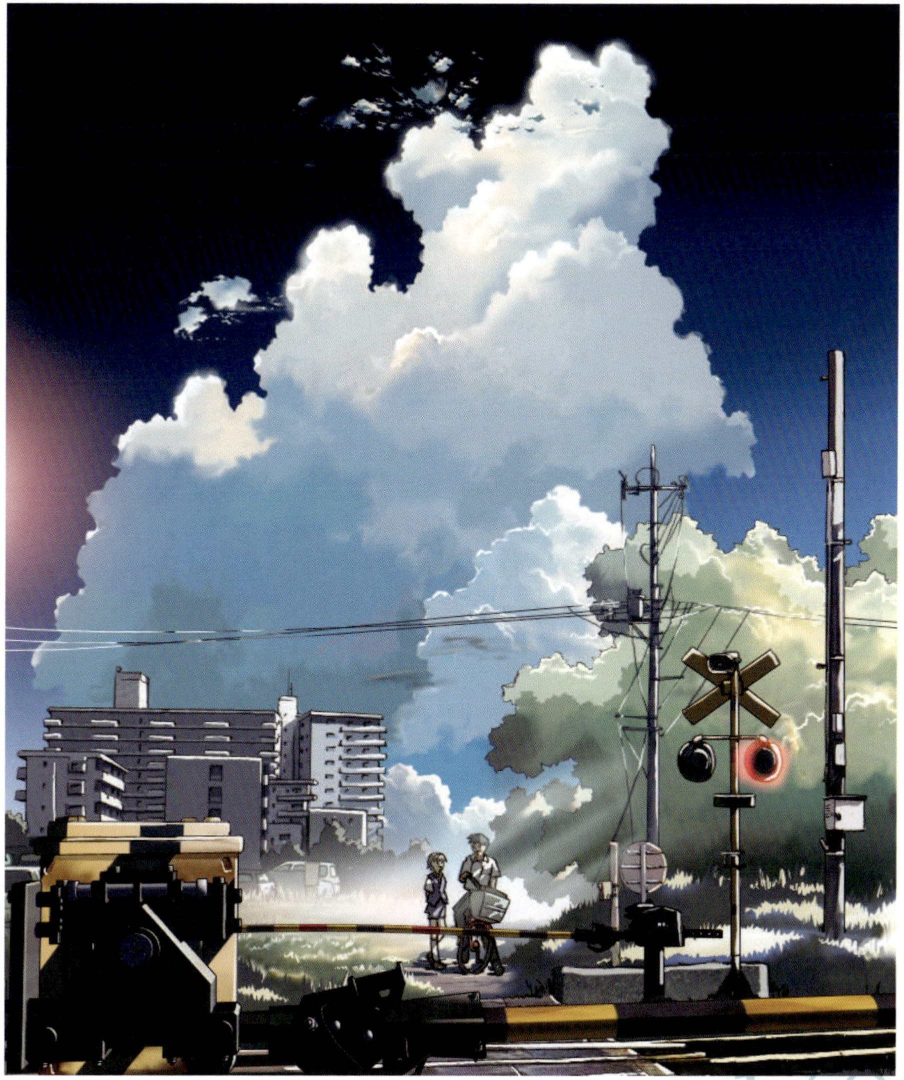

Voices of a Distant Star / Tollywood advertisement illustration

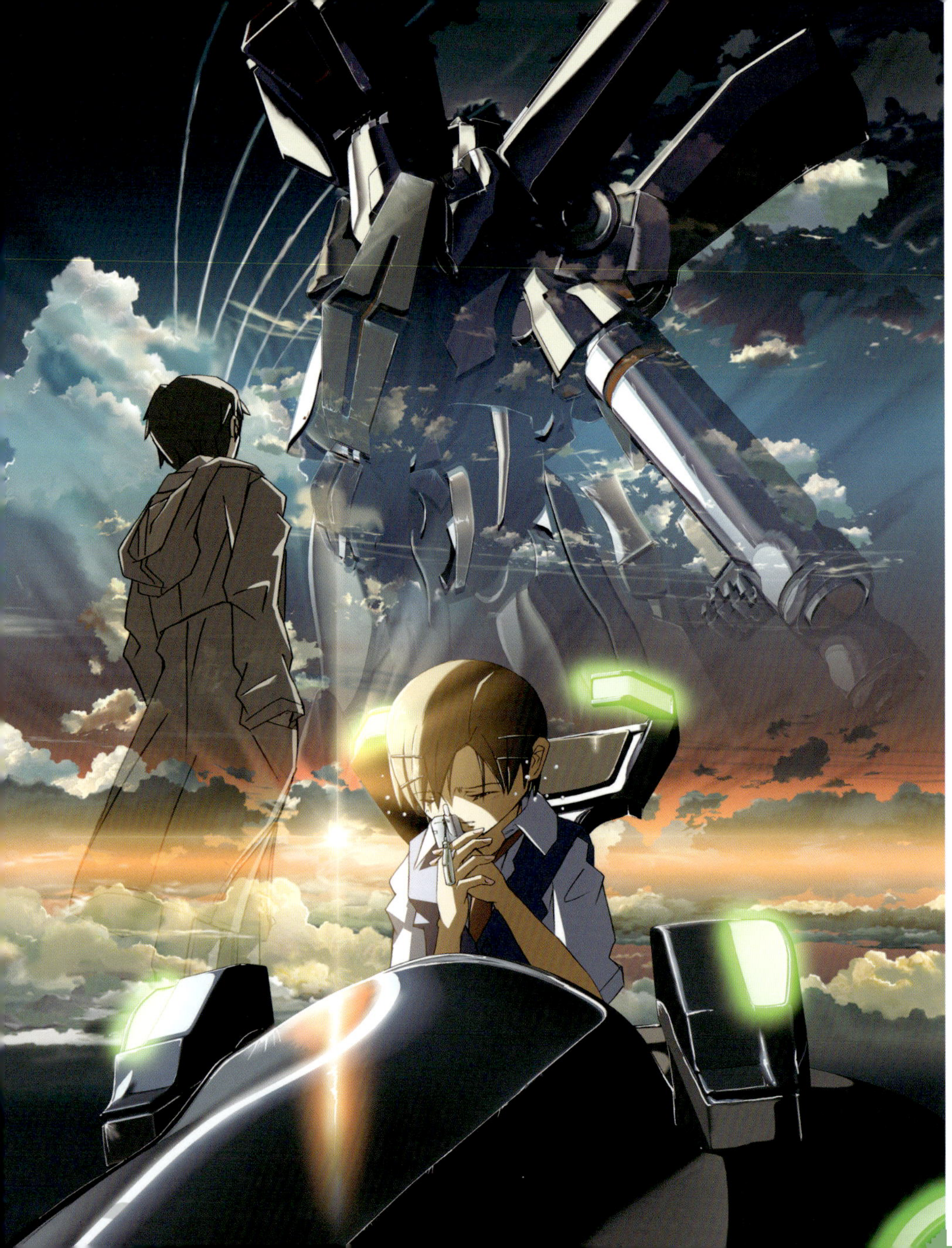

Key visual used for theatrical release posters and DVD packaging. The base of the Tracer was created using 3DCG, with additional details drawn in. As this image was used in printed materials, it was finished using Photoshop. It's a large-scale illustration, sized 10,100 x 13,500 pixels.

Voices of a Distant Star / Key visual for posters, etc.

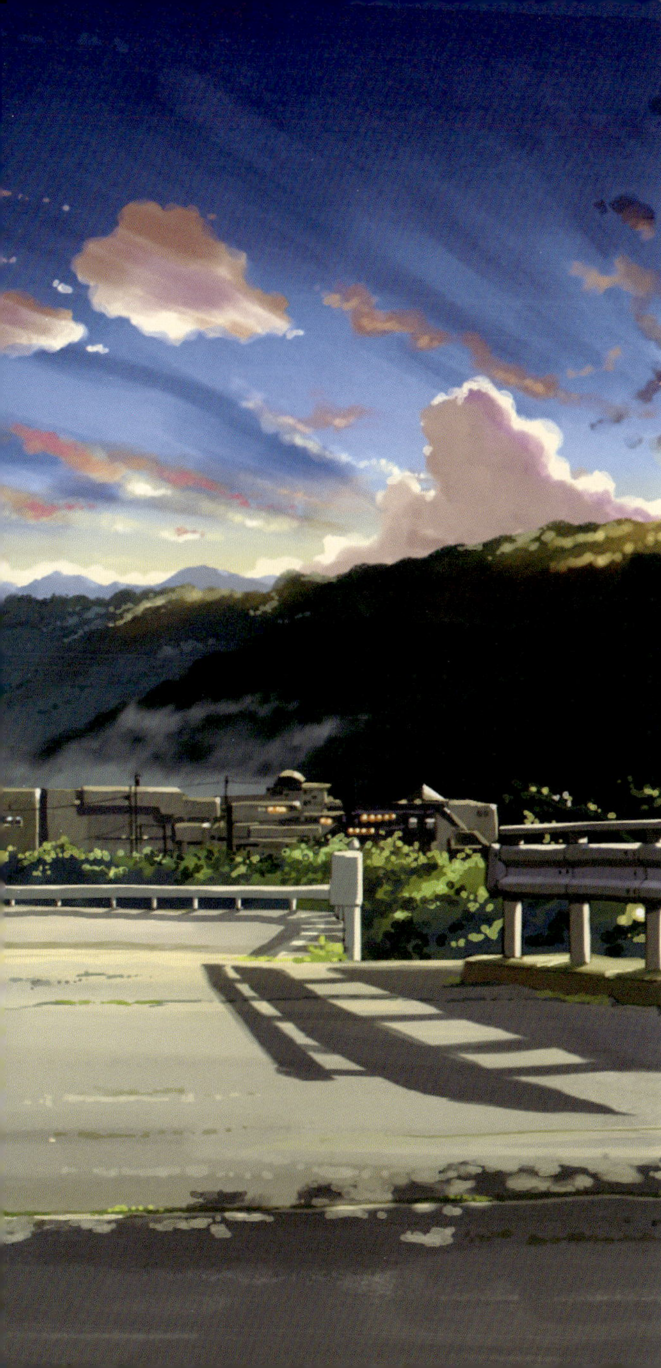

Say Something Important.

Shinano Mainichi Shimbun TV Commercial

On air: September 2007, on various commercial broadcasting stations within Nagano Prefecture, Japan
Running time: 15 seconds

Staff:
Storyboards, background art, 3DCG, photography: Makoto Shinkai
Original artwork: Takayo Nishimura
Music: Takako Tate

Cast:
Girl: Yoshimi Kondo

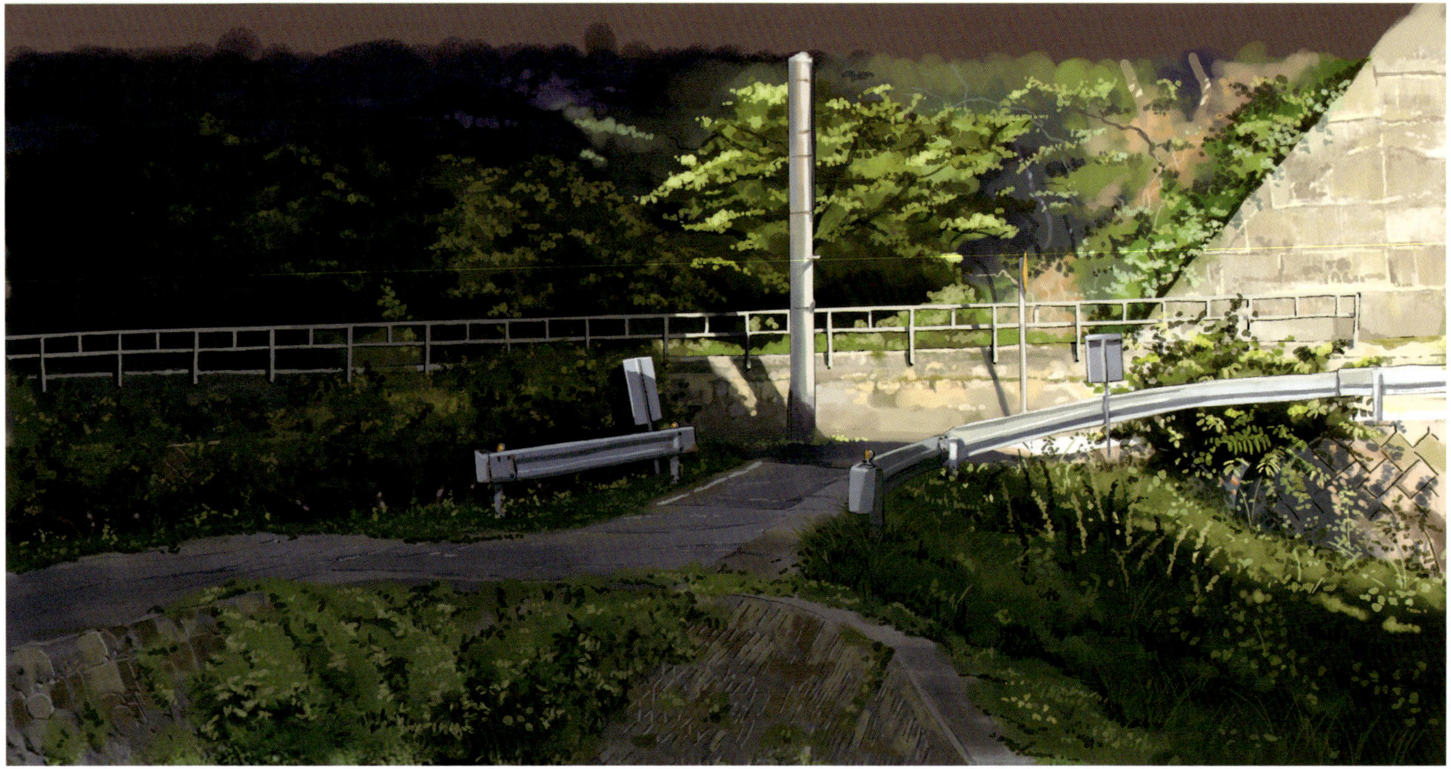

Background art for the scene where the girl chases after her father's train (a hybrid car on the Koumi Line), going from a farm road onto a highway. This is modeled on the area between Managashi Station and Koumi Station.

Shinano Mainichi Shimbun TV Commercial / CUT_001 / Setting: Koumi, Minamisaku District, Nagano

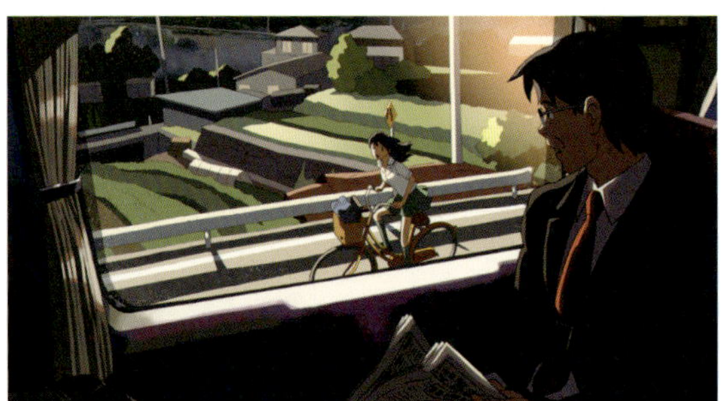

CUT_002 Final Version

The outside as seen from inside the train. The interior of the train and the distant background are background art, but the passing scenery is background animation. 12 frames were prepared for each second of footage. The parts hidden by the father's body and parts that move out of frame were not drawn.

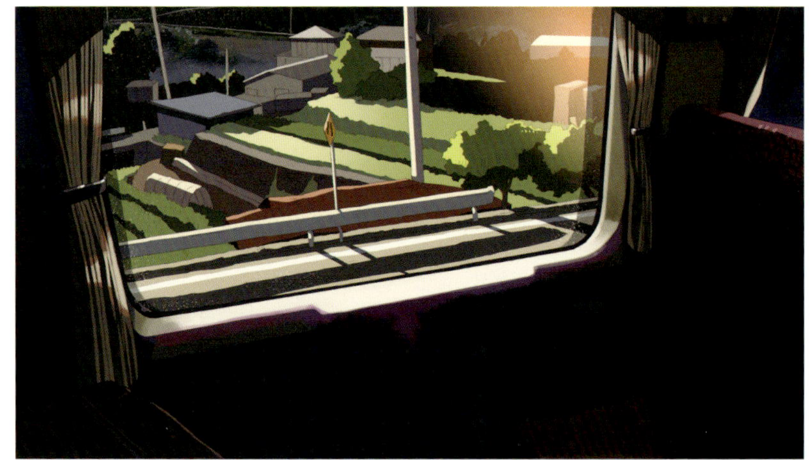

Shinano Mainichi Shimbun TV Commercial / CUT_002 / Setting: JR Koumi Station

Please note that the stone wall in the foreground is rendered with fine detail, while the background is drawn with far less density.
As the train is an extension of the background it was drawn on a harmony cel, and the reflections on the windows, etc. were created using video software.

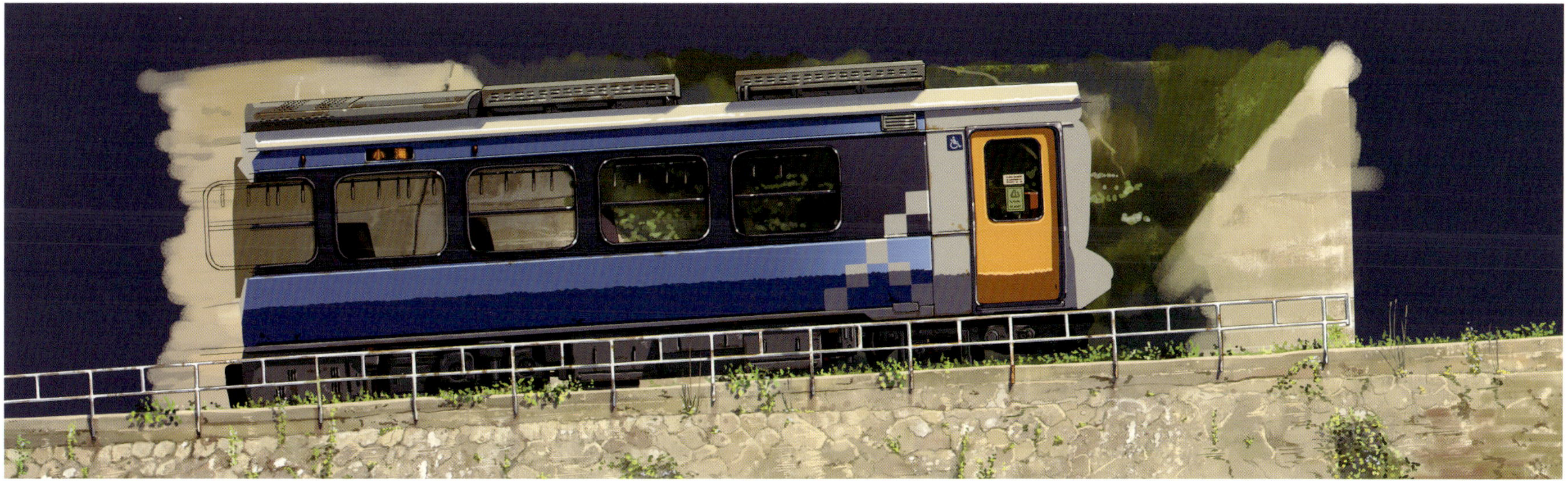

Shinano Mainichi Shimbun TV Commercial / CUT_003 / Setting: Koumi, Minamisaku District, Nagano

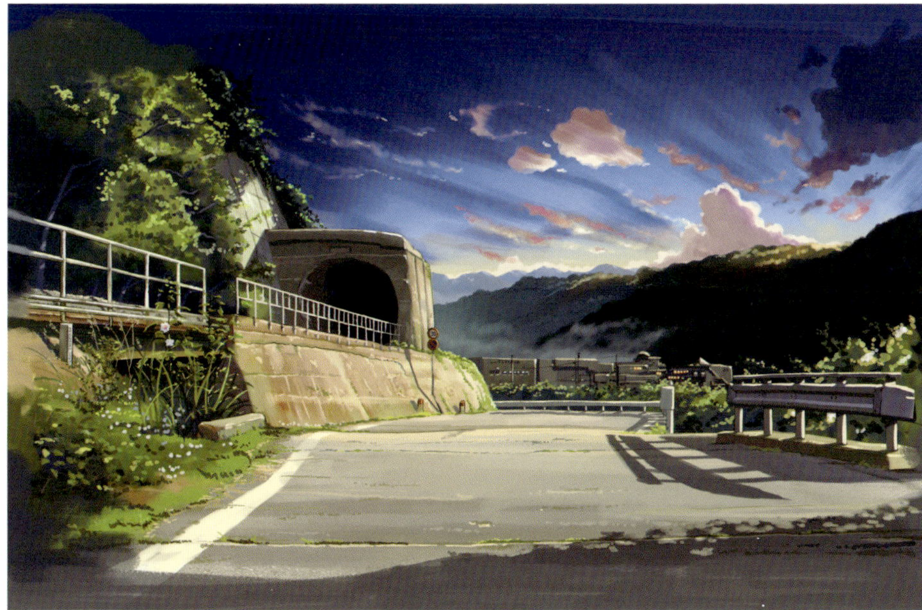

Shinano Mainichi Shimbun TV Commercial / CUT_005 / Setting: Koumi, Minamisaku District, Nagano

The tunnel seen in the final cut does not exist in the actual location that this is based on. The train that disappears into the tunnel was created using 3DCG. The butterflies that fly along the embankment are also 3DCG. By the way, CUT_004-1 (page 160) is comprised entirely of background animation rendered using 3DCG, so there was no concrete background art created for that cut.

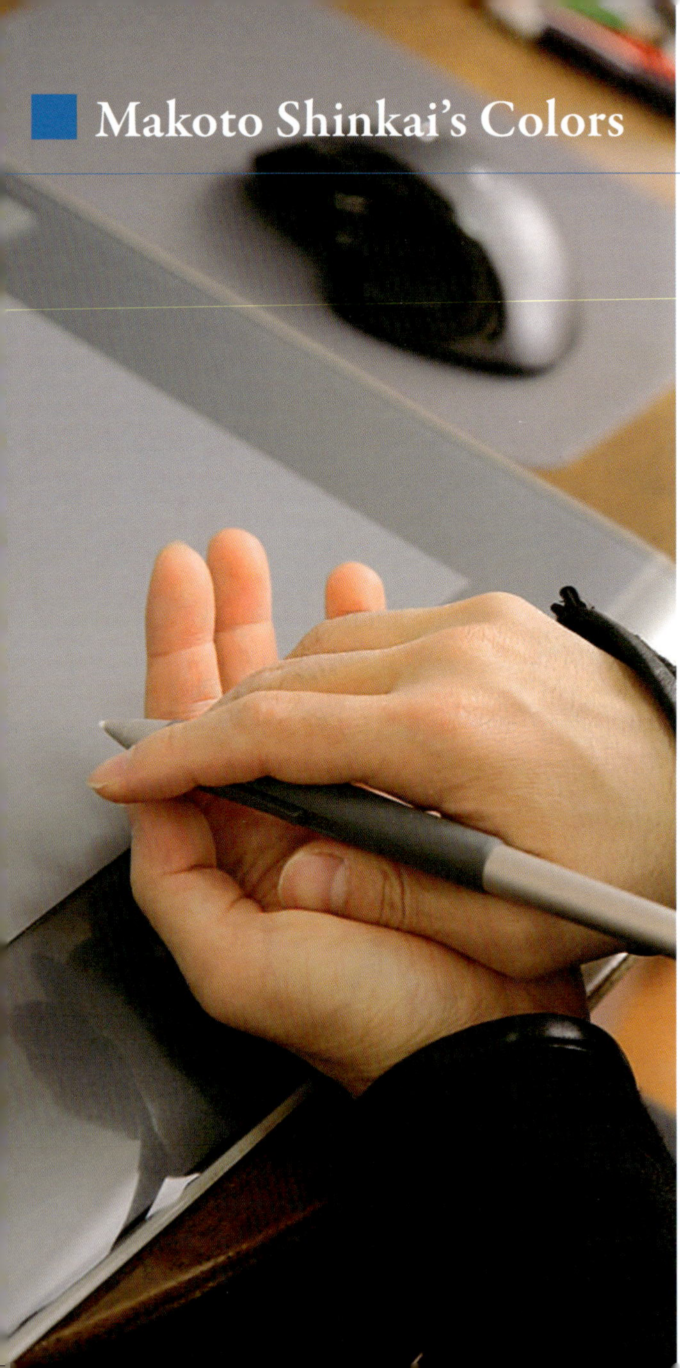

Makoto Shinkai's Colors

The rich color expressiveness in Makoto Shinkai's animated films is highly praised. By making free use of the special qualities of digital art tools in creating background art, the backgrounds become more than mere scenery for animation; they turn into elements of expression that produce the distinctive atmosphere of Shinkai's works, and so the background art is a major presence within his films. Here we'll break down the typical techniques found in Shinkai's works, using examples of background artwork from previous sections of this book, such as those from *5 Centimeters per Second*.

Work environment during the creation of *5 Centimeters per Second*

- Hardware specs:
  PowerMac G5 2.5 GHz Quad (8 GB RAM)
  + Apple Cinema Display (30")
  PowerMac G5 2.7 GHz Dual (8 GB RAM)
  PowerMac G5 2.0 GHz Dual (8 GB RAM)
  Several iMacs, etc.

- Operating system:
  Mac OS X 10.4.11

- Software specs:
  Video software: Adobe After Effects 6.5 Pro
  Image software: Adobe Photoshop CS2
  3DCG software: NewTek LightWave 3D 8.5

Makoto Shinkai's Desktops

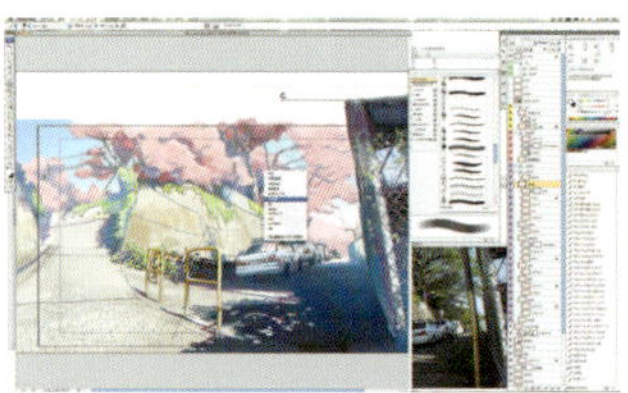

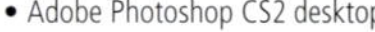

• Adobe Photoshop CS2 desktop

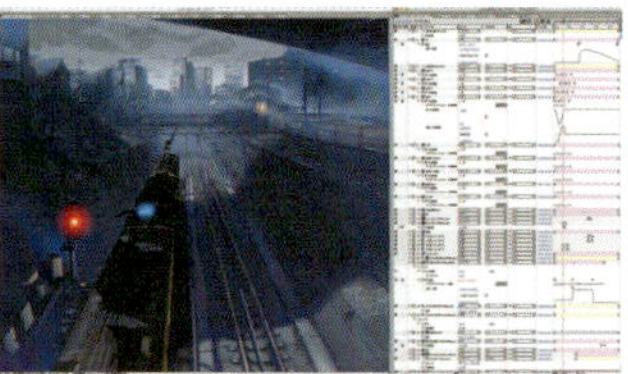

Adobe After Effects 6.5 Pro desktop

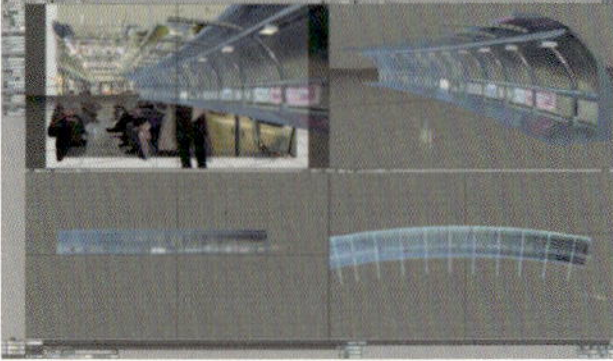

NewTek LightWave 3D 8.5 desktop

Mr. Shinkai mainly works on a genuine Apple 30" monitor and uses a 27" submonitor to display the files (sorted into folders) that are accessed during production. The programs used are Adobe Photoshop (to create still images), NewTek LightWave 3D (for 3DCG), and Adobe After Effects (for filming and editing). One time Mr. Shinkai tried using a different major brand's painting software, but it wasn't suitable for his art production needs, so he went back to working with Photoshop.

Makoto Shinkai's art production environment

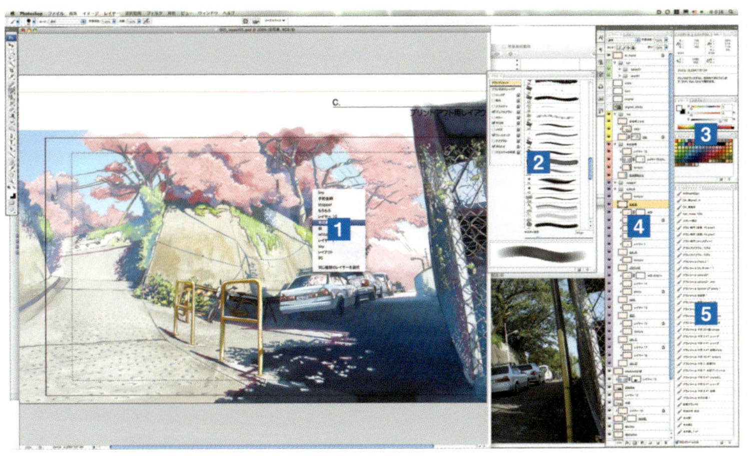

• Adobe Photoshop CS2 desktop image

In Shinkai's works, the background art is always created with the mindset that the backgrounds are "one of the materials used to create an animated film." For this reason, compared to typical illustration, the methods employed for using software applications differ greatly. Here we'll show you the drawing methods used, from Adobe Photoshop on the desktop (the main tool in creating backgrounds) to explaining Mr. Shinkai's work environment.

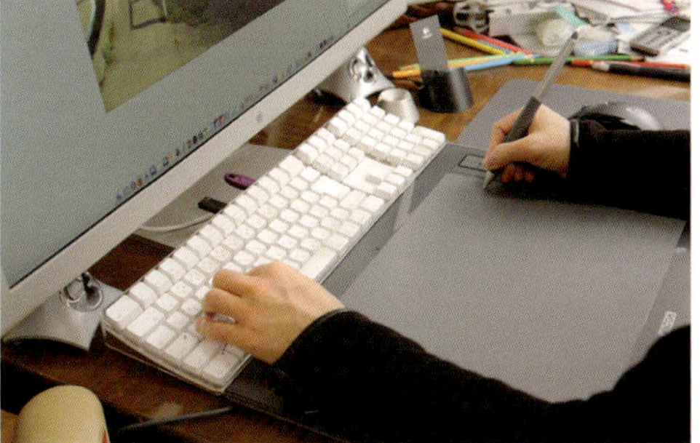

The input devices used are a Wacom pen tablet and an infrared mouse. As the pen tablet is the main device, it's placed in the center of the desk. Keyboard shortcuts are frequently used for speedier workflow.

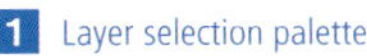

1 Layer selection palette

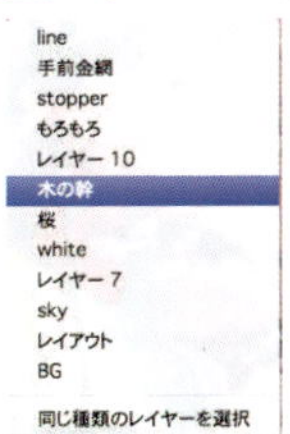

When working, artists frequently switch between layers, so they use a "select layer" window that pops up by the cursor, allowing for smooth workflow. A single background image can easily contain several dozen layers (at times over 100 layers), so the use of layers is very common, and having the ability to directly access layers while working on the image is indispensable.

2 Brush palette

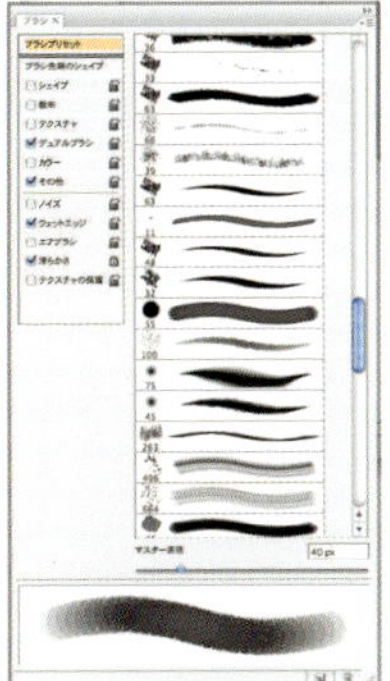

Brushes can be customized to create one that is appropriate for the image at hand. The brush shown at the very bottom (selected brush) was a customized brush created during the production of *The Place Promised in Our Early Days*, and has since been used by all of the art staff when creating backgrounds.

3 Color swatch palette

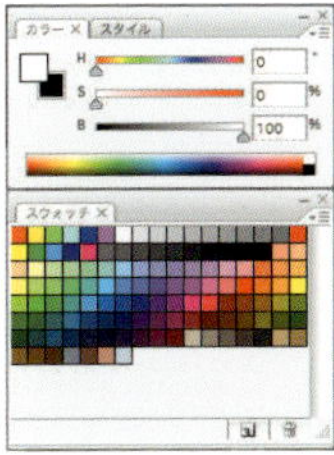

Colors are controlled by altering HSB (hue, saturation, and brightness), not RGB values. The color palette is the default palette in Photoshop, with no need to introduce custom colors, so all necessary colors can be created via adjustments to the HSB values.

4 Layer palette

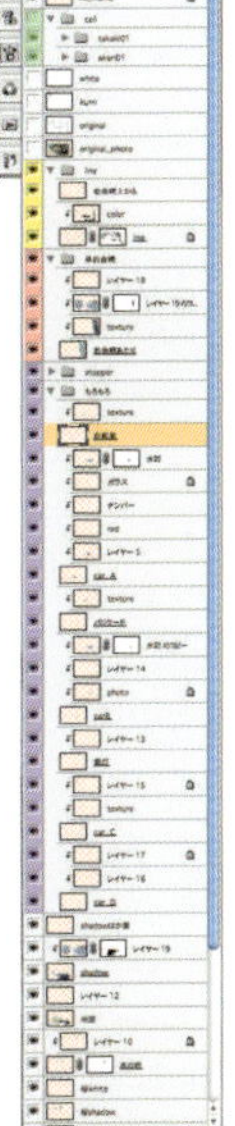

The palette that shows the layers in use during the creation of an image. In the final stages, layers are merged in accordance with Mr. Shinkai's direction, but during the creation process, numerous layers are created and arranged into groups for each object, which results in a large number of layers.

5 Tool presets

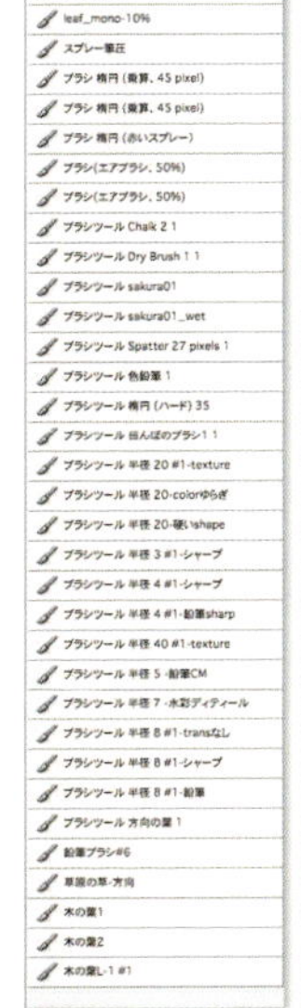

Frequently used brushes are loaded in advance to this palette, allowing artists to switch between brushes with a single click, instead of altering the brush settings each time. The background artists all use the same presets, which unifies everyone's work environments.

Fundamental techniques for creating background artwork

1

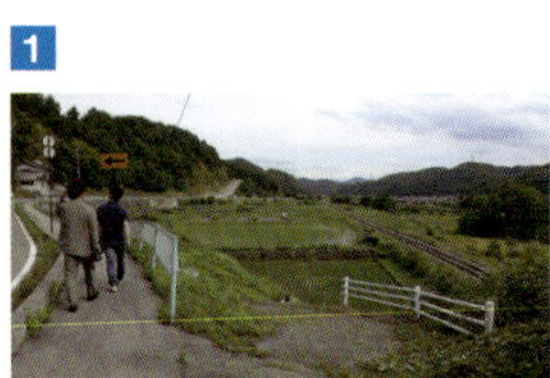

• Original photograph

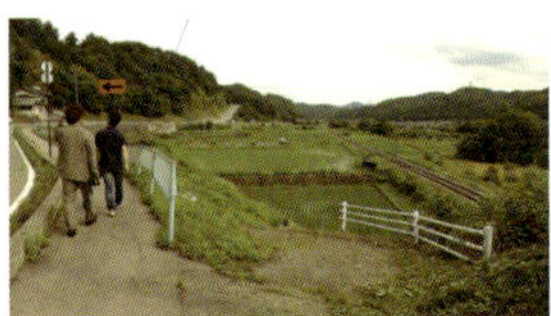

• After color adjustment

Using a location photo as the base, the hues and tints desired for the finished image can be determined by adjusting the color balance to change the overall color tone.

2

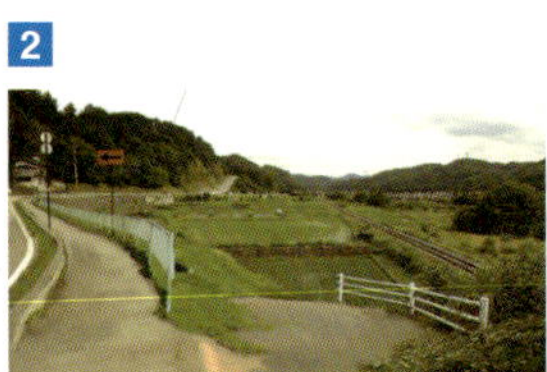

Use the dropper tool to pick up colors from the photograph. Paint over unnecessary elements.

3

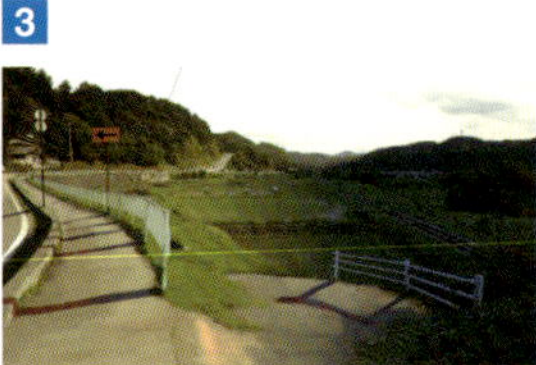

Determine the location of the light source (the sun). In this case, it's past the mountain range to the right. Draw in the shadows cast by the light source using shadow colors. Here we used blue tones on a layer with the blend mode set to "multiply" to build up shadow colors.

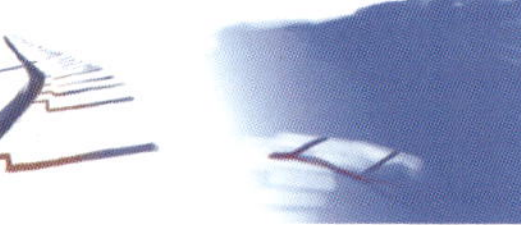

• Shadow layer only

4

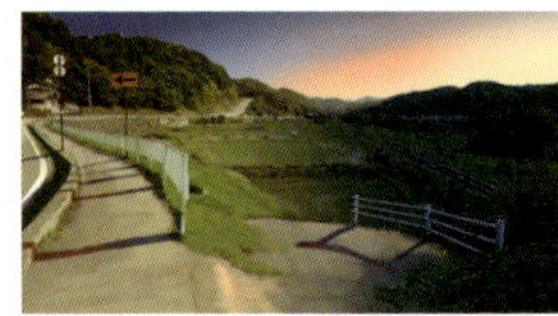

Cut out the ground sections of the image and place them on a separate layer. On a new layer, use the gradient tool to paint in the sky. As you use trial and error in the process of adding color, it's important to have in mind what the final image will be. Keeping a clear image of the final version in mind will allow you to work much more smoothly from that point on.

5

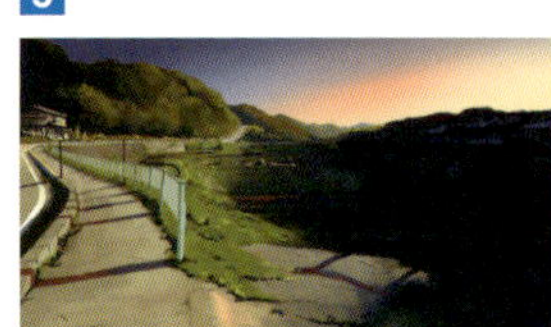

Add on colors in a way that paints over details from the location photo. Use customized brushes and take care to keep the overall feel from becoming too homogenous.

6

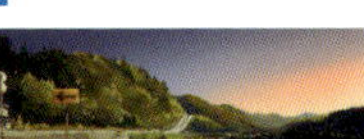

Draw in the details in the highlight sections (the areas that appear light), adding presence to the areas where you want to draw the viewers' attention. In this example, colors that represent the reflection of the setting sun are minutely added to the surface of the water in the rice paddies, on the metal railing and the railroad tracks.

On this page, we'll explain the process by which an image based on location hunting photos is colorized, using materials from workshops by Mr. Shinkai in the Middle East.*

One of the traits of the background art in Shinkai's works is that they are based on location photos, so they look realistic. Shinkai frequently employs certain methods because they allow a group of animators working together on a film to work quickly and efficiently in the pursuit of realism in animation. As it is necessary to finish off a massive workload during production, the ability to draw a great deal as quickly as possible is required. The method introduced here is one derived from experience developed during the process of creating animated films. However, as there are many situations where the use of photographs is not possible in the actual layout process (e.g., angles that are impossible to photograph, fictitious places, etc.), as with *5 Centimeters per Second*, cuts with images based on location photographs are limited to about 40% of the total. To create images that can't be based on photographs, the artists base their work on layouts created by the animators or the background art staff, as per usual. However, Shinkai says that whether or not an image is based on a photograph, the most important aspects in the creation of background art are always the colorization and the level of detail. While drawing all sorts of pictures in varying seasons, weather conditions and times of day, he creates a palette within himself, thinking, "In order to make it look like this, I have to use this drawing method," and devising unique patterns that then become the foundation in formulating his own visual world. Shinkai has repeatedly said that carrying a common pattern through an entire work is more important than the degree of perfection of each individual image. We would be very pleased if the examples illustrated on this page can become a guide in the creation of your artwork, dear reader.

*Digital art workshops sponsored by the Japan Foundation held in Jordan, Qatar, and Syria in January and February of 2008.

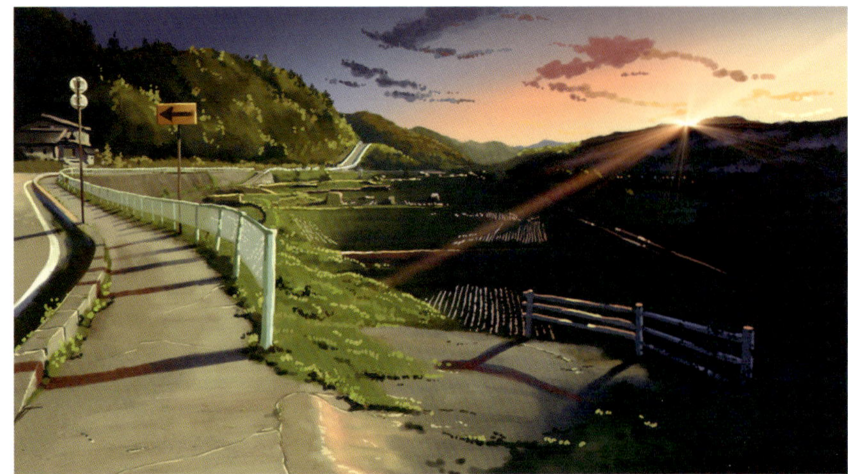

• Final image

Clouds are drawn in, and the setting sun is added in After Effects to create the final version. In the example image, as it was predetermined that a setting sun would be added, the mountain range on the right was painted using the darkest colors in the image.

Basic layer structure used in background art production

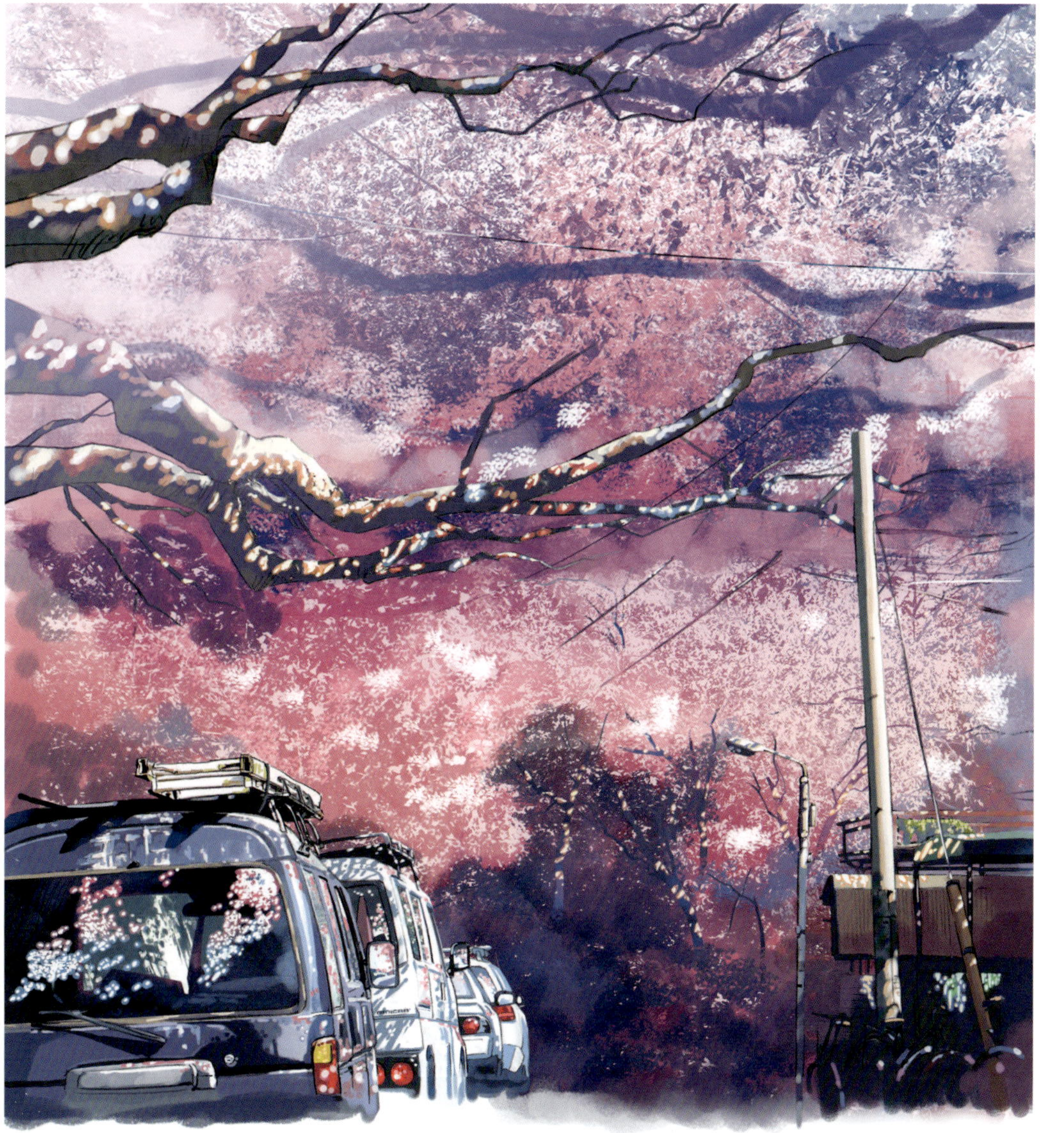

"Cherry Blossom" / CUT_009 / Setting: The road Takaki and Akari take to school

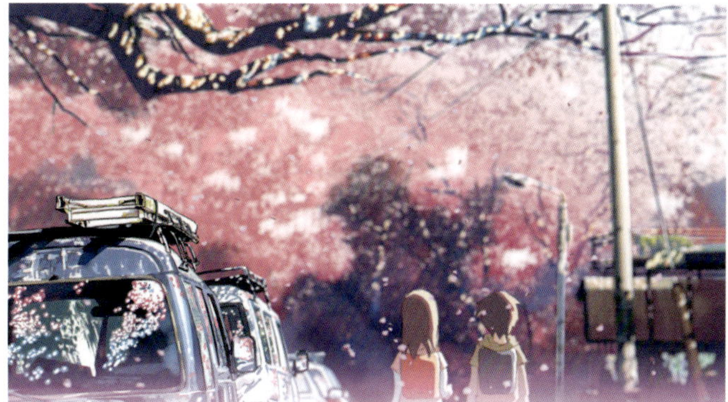

CUT_009 Final Version

This is the final image which includes visual effects and animation elements created in After Effects. Here you can see the elaborately detailed plan for creating this image while having the final version in mind.

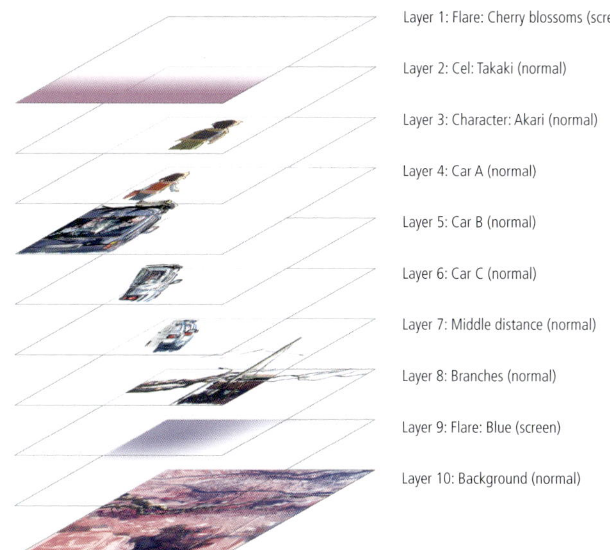

Structure of the layers used in CUT_009 (in fact, there were additional image adjustment layers not shown here). Individual elements were fine-tuned and animated in After Effects.

Methods for drawing buildings, etc.

- Example: CUT_118 from *5 Centimeters per Second*, "Cherry Blossom"

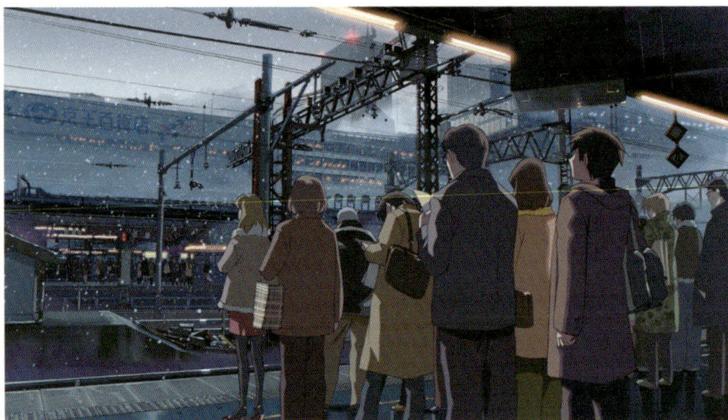

"Cherry Blossom" / CUT_118 / Setting: JR Shinjuku Station platform

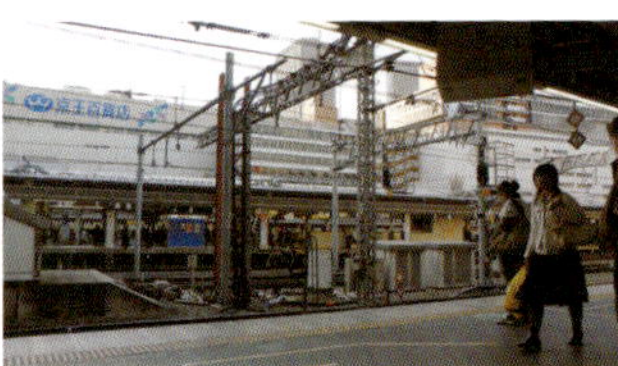

- Reference photo taken by Makoto Shinkai.

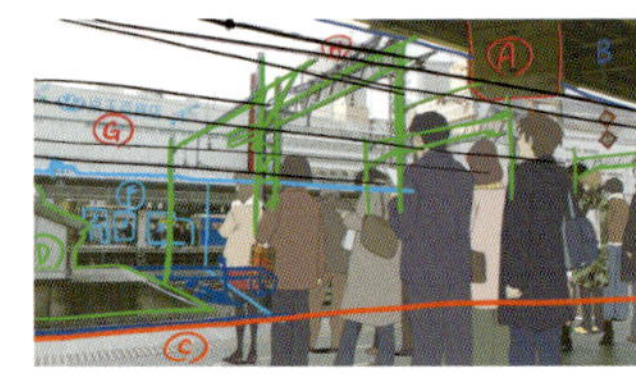

- Shinkai's directions for the division of layers.

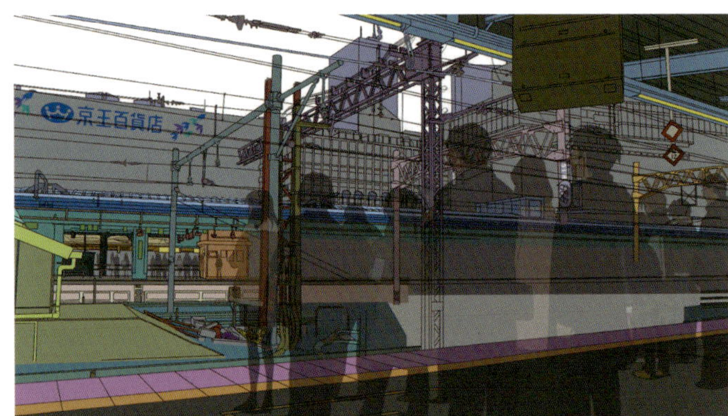

Line art view created by the background art staff. Following Shinkai's directions, the image is created with elements separated into different layers while observing the positional relationship of these elements.

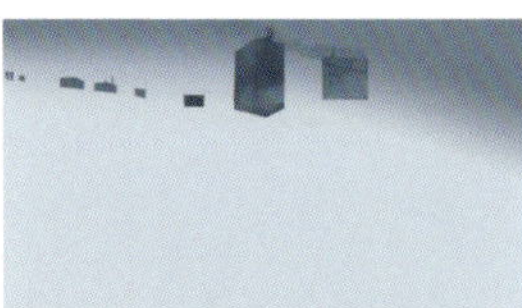

- Line art created by the background art staff

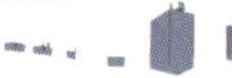

Shinkai colorizes and finishes the line art drawn by the background art staff. Note the buildings farthest back and the atmospheric perspective.

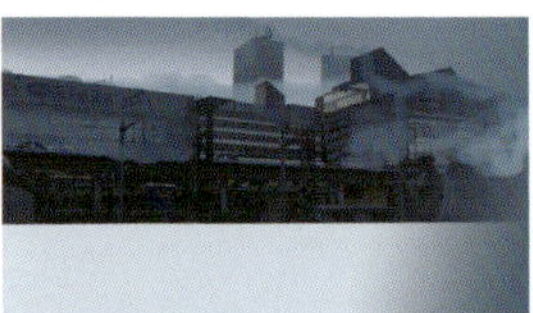

- Line art (background art staff)

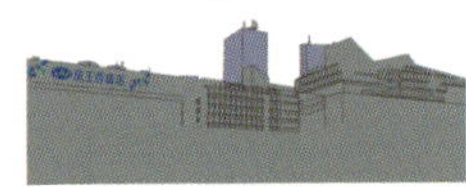

The department store building in the background and the platform on the far side of the tracks are based on the reference photo, and adjusted by erasing details. The overall density is also adjusted.

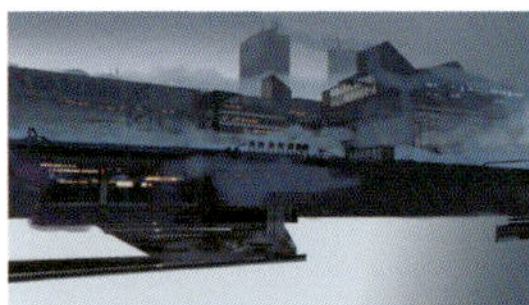

- Line art (background art staff)

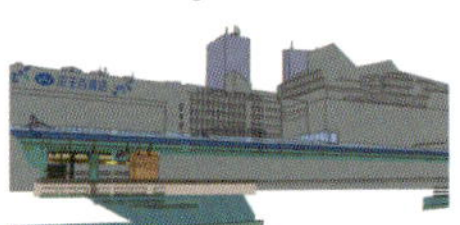

Artists use brushes to erase areas where the image is too dense. The lights on the platform and the far building are painted on (with brushes of different sizes), and adding varying levels of detail gives a lived-in feel.

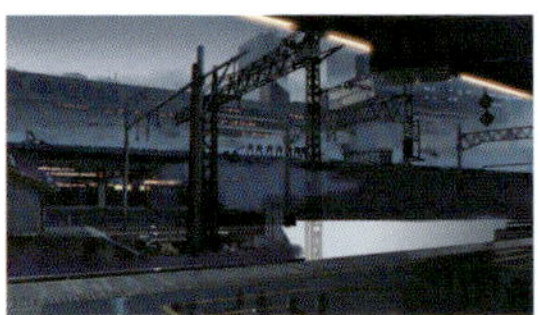

- Line art (background art staff)

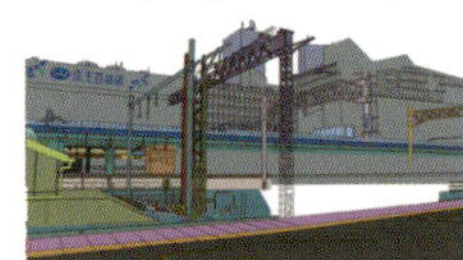

The closer platform is added. This increases the contrast of the foreground against the far background, to which animation of falling snow is added. The lighting effects are on a separate layer.

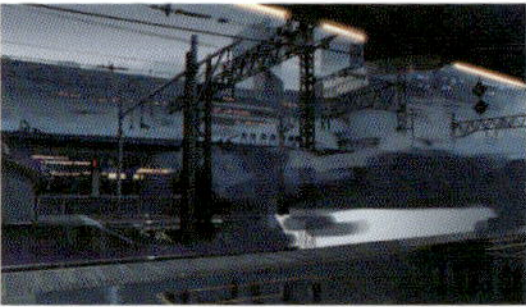

- Line art (background art staff)

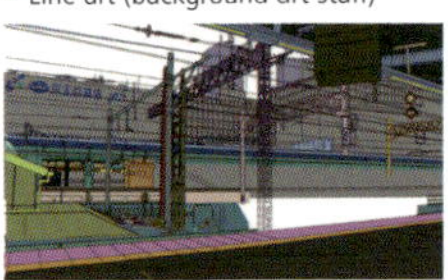

The overhead wires are added to complete the background art. The overhead wires are based on an adjusted version of the background artists' line art.

- Example: CUT_125 from *5 Centimeters per Second*, "Cherry Blossom"

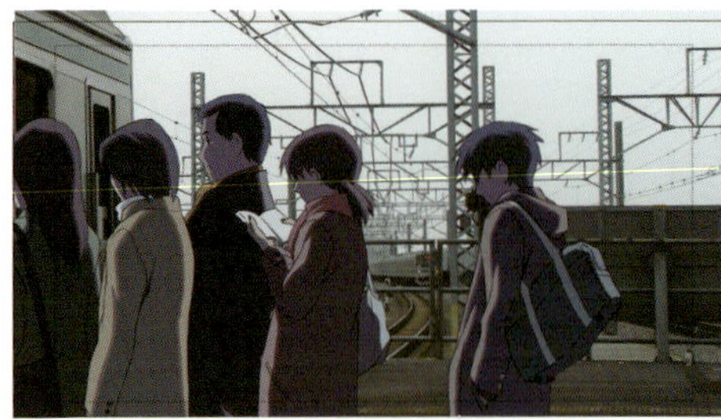

- Reference photo combined with character cels (Takaki, the crowd).

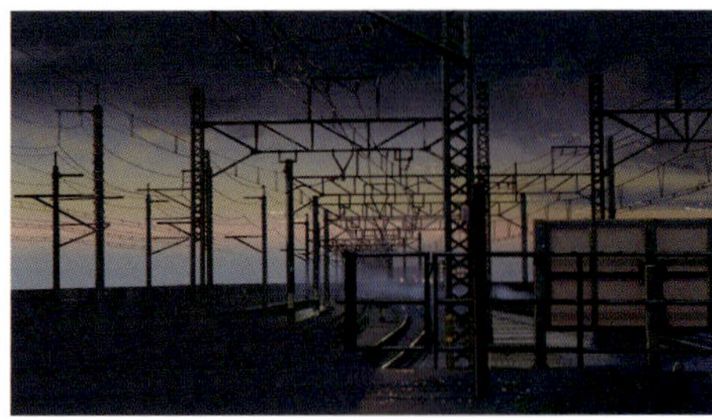

- The final background art.

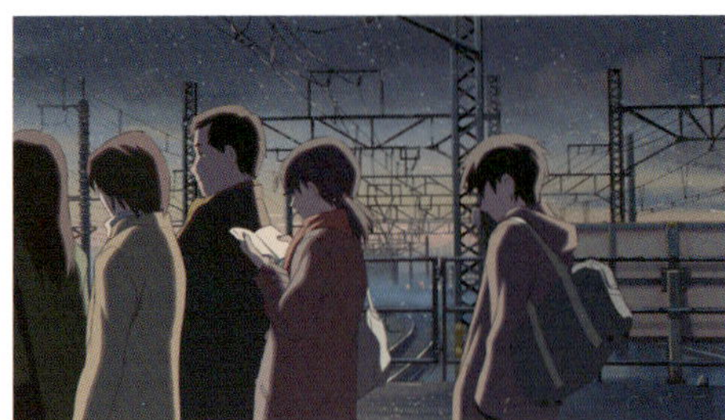

"Cherry Blossom" / CUT_125 / Setting: JR Musashi-Urawa Station platform

For CUT_125 of "Cherry Blossom," a test is done where the characters and a 3DCG train were combined with the reference photo as a base. In Shinkai's works, in cases where there is little variation between the reference photo and the finished image, the artists actively use the layout from the photo in creating the image. On such occasions, the greatest point of concern is the direction and strength of the sunlight.

Methods for creating background art using 3DCG

- Example: CUT_154 from *5 Centimeters per Second*, "Cherry Blossom"

"Cherry Blossom" / CUT_154 / Setting: View from a JR Utsunomiya Line train

In Shinkai's works, background animation elements are often created using 3DCG. In this cut, the countryside passing outside the window is created using 3DCG. The texture of the ridges and furrows of the snowscape has varying densities for the foreground and the distance.

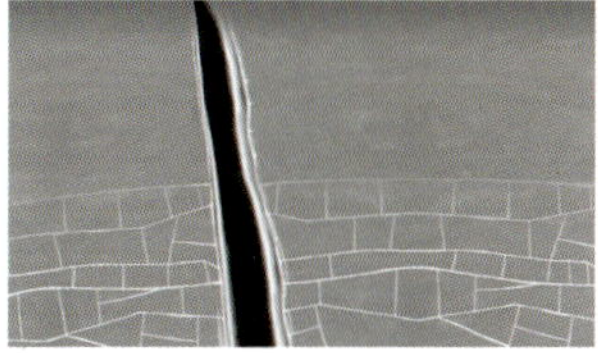

• Displacement map.

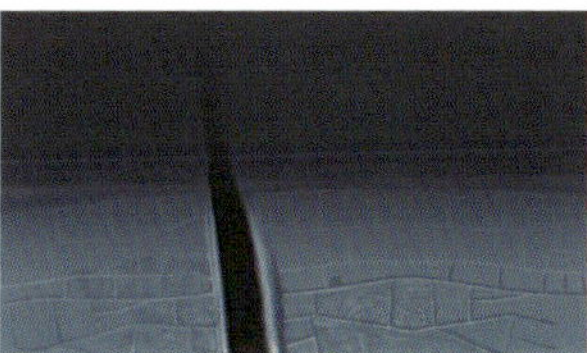

• Mapping texture image for 3DCG.

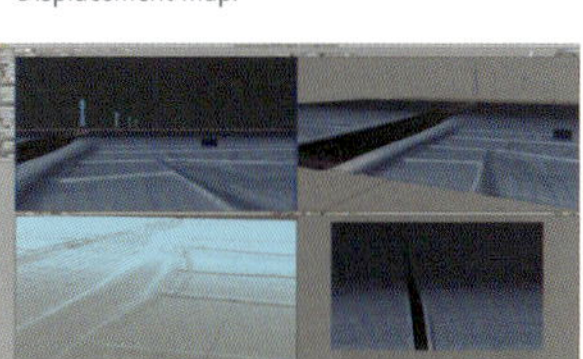

Rendering of the foreground (field) in LightWave 3D.

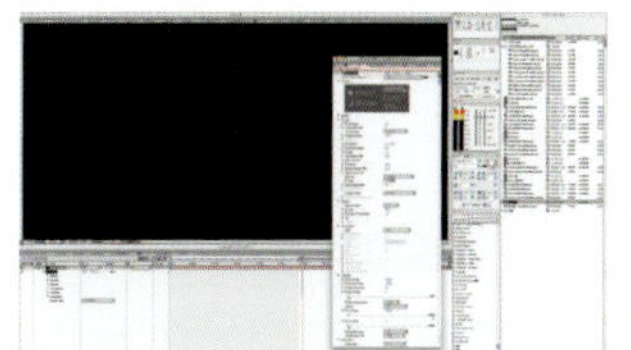

• Animation element of falling snow in After Effects.

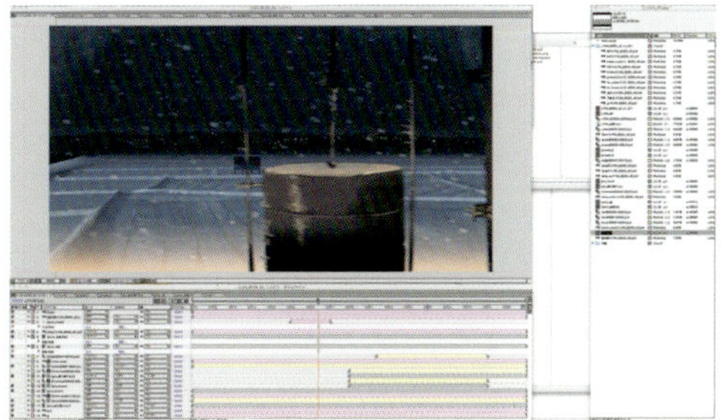

• Process of combining elements in After Effects.

- Example: CUT_078 from *5 Centimeters per Second*, "Cherry Blossom"

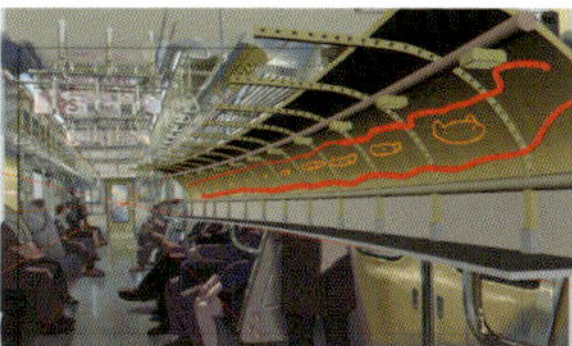

• Planning screen for image mapping.

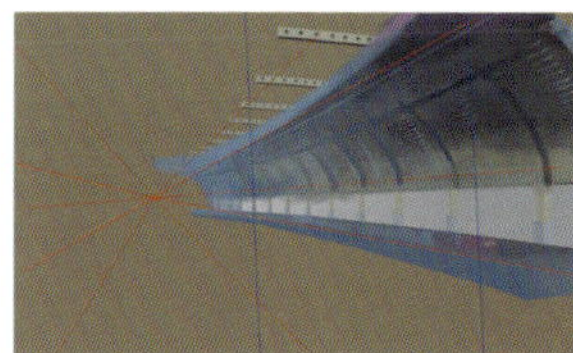

• Texture for the wall of the private railway line platform.

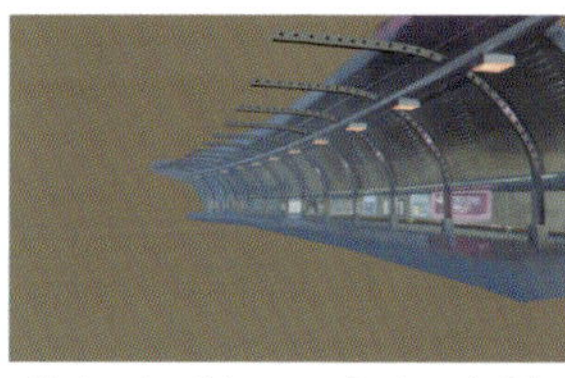

• Final version of the texture for the wall of the private railway line platform.

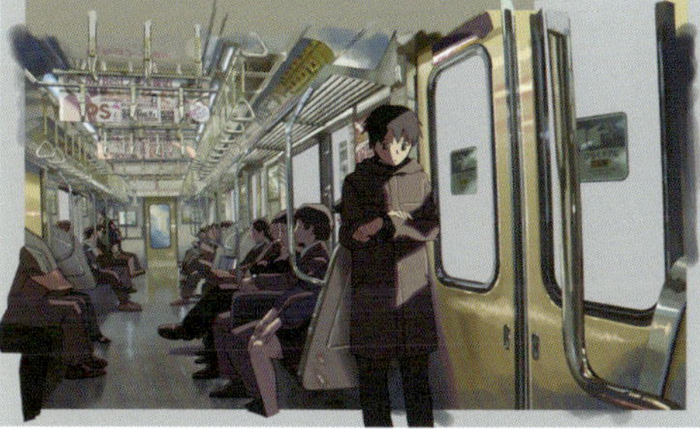

• The background art and character cels are tentatively placed to create a layout image for 3DCG work.

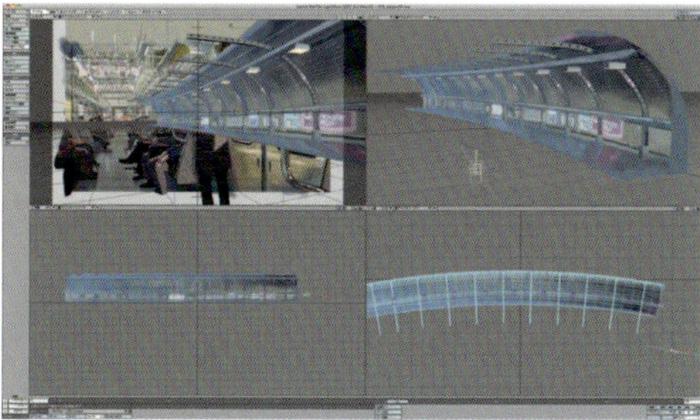

• Screen showing the creation of 3DCG animation of the private railway line platform in LightWave 3D.

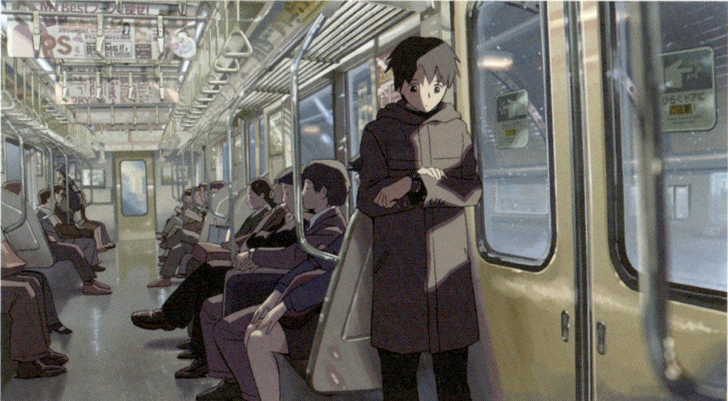

"Cherry Blossom" / CUT_078 / Setting: Train interior

The private railway line platform that passes by the window is made via mapping a texture in 3DCG and using it as background art.

Differences in expression using animated backgrounds

CUT_004 of the Shinano Mainichi Shimbun TV Commercial makes free use of various animation techniques. Varying methods such as "composite 3DCG/animated backgrounds" and "creating artwork as an animated background element" are used in scenes lasting less than a second, resulting in a dynamic visual effect on par with theatrical animated works.

• Example of composite 3DCG/animated background method

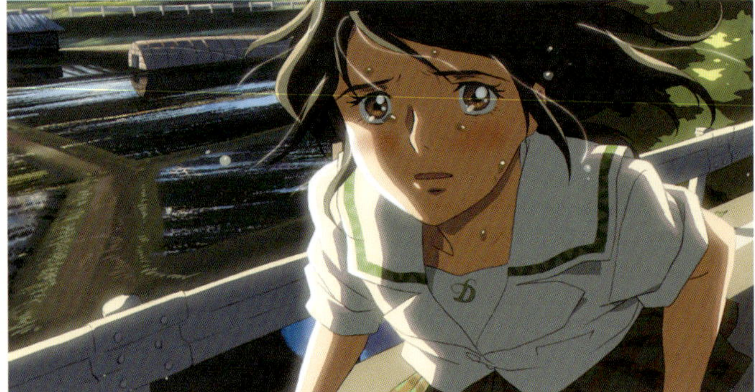

Shinano Mainichi Shimbun TV Commercial / CUT_004-1 / Setting: Koumi, Minamisaku District, Nagano

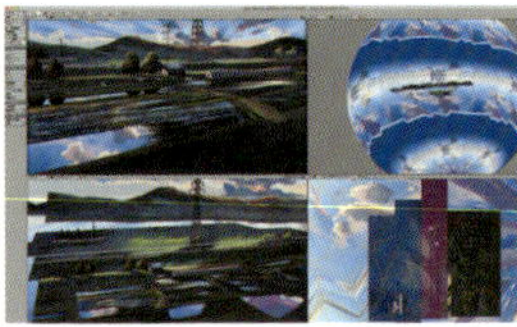

• Screen: creating animated backgrounds in LightWave 3D

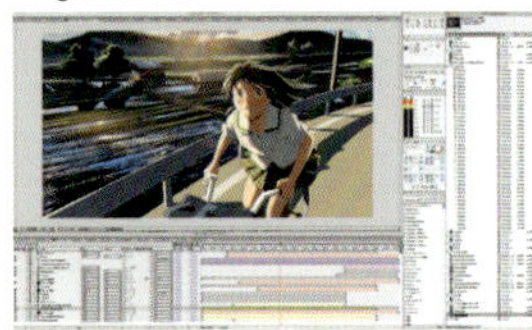

• Screen: combining animation elements and 3D elements in After Effects

In the scene where the girl chases after her father's train on her bicycle, first a test video was created using simplified modeling, and several movements and angles were selected to turn into keyframes. Based on those, the animators created animation of the girl, and the 3DCG animation of the background, including textures, was prepared by Shinkai. The sky reflected on the surface of the paddy field was created by opening holes in the texture, with the sky texture pasted on in a way that makes it look like it's peeking through from under the surface. The textures pasted in 3DCG are drawn with the same density and feel as the background art in other cuts, successfully bringing out the merits of both hand-drawn and 3DCG backgrounds.

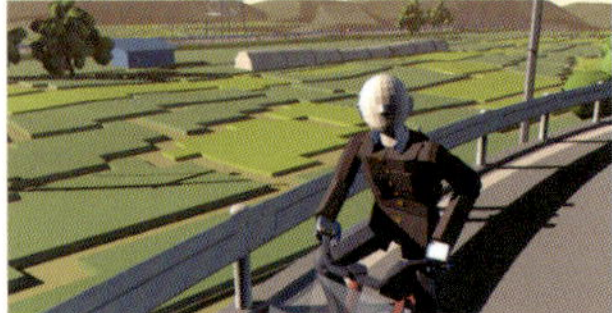

• Test video as an image creation guide in 3DCG

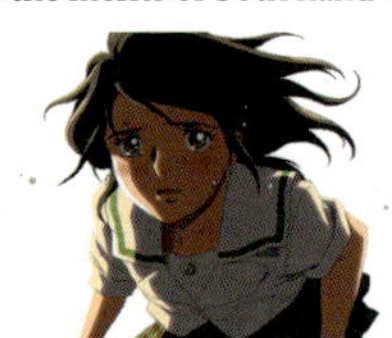

• Character cel (girl)

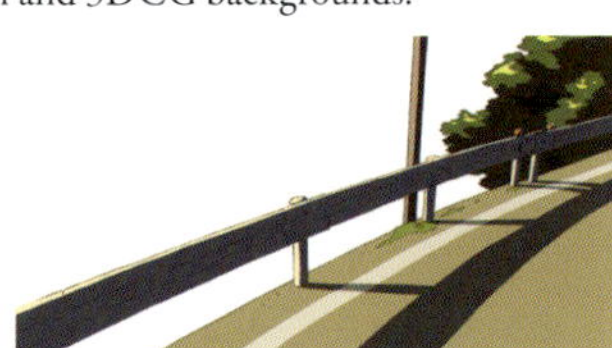

• Animated background (foreground) cel

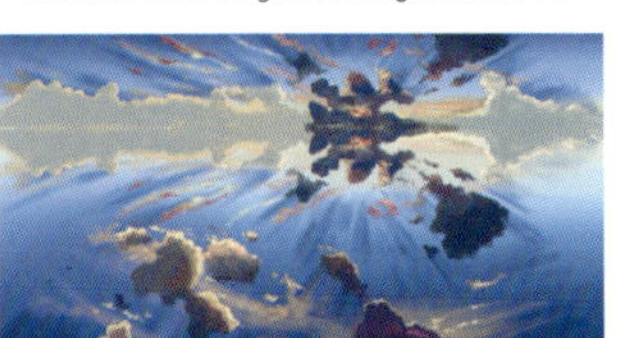

• Background texture image (sky)

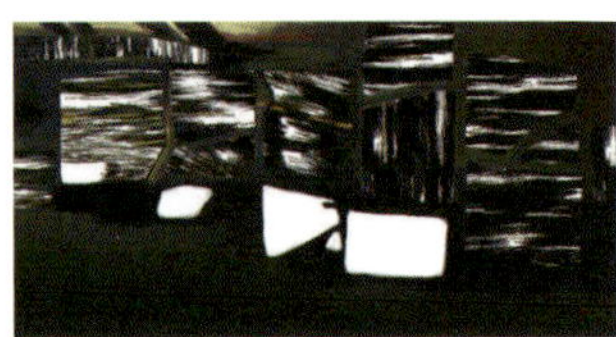

• Middle distance texture image (fields)

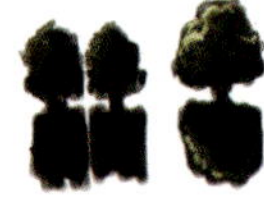

• Middle distance texture image (trees)

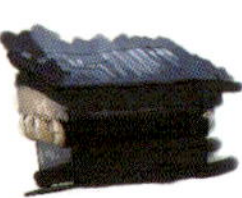

• Middle distance texture image (hut)

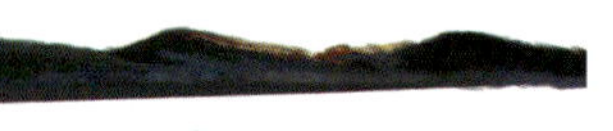

• Far distance texture image (mountains)

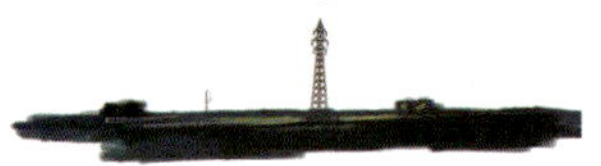

• Middle distance texture image (elevation)

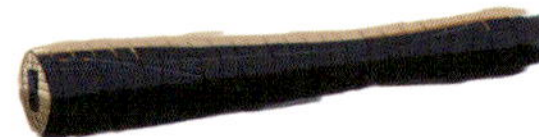

• Middle distance texture image (greenhouse)

• Example of an animated background

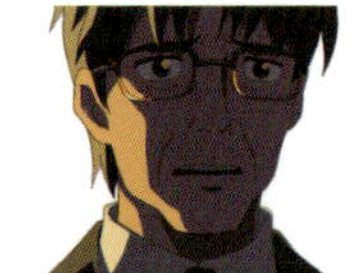

• Character cel (father)

• Background art (reflection of train interior)

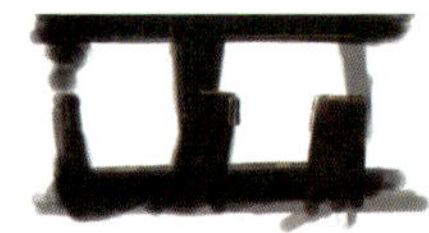

• Background art of the reflection of the train interior reflected in the opposite window

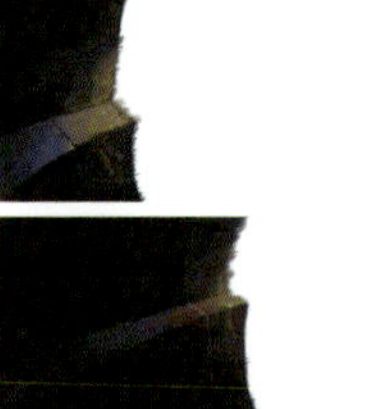

• Animated back-ground, 1st frame

• Animated back-ground, 2nd frame

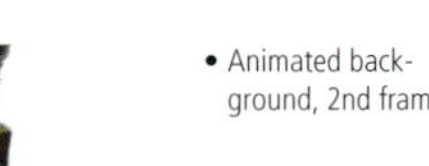

• Animated back-ground, 5th frame

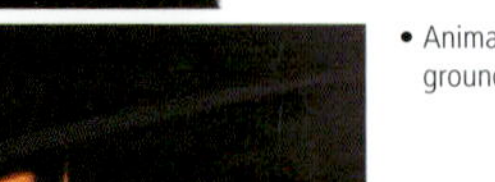

• Animated back-ground, 6th frame

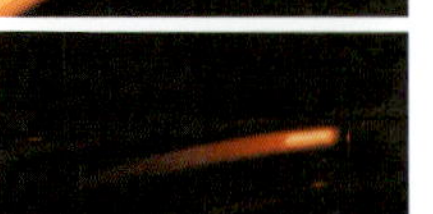

• Animated back-ground, 10th frame

The scenery of the tunnel interior that passes by the windows next to the seats is an animated background that uses artwork drawn by Mr. Shinkai himself. There are 13 stills used in the animation (7 of which were repeated), which are filmed on individual frames at a rate of 30 frames per second (character art was held for 2 frames each). The reflection of the train interior on the windows is added in After Effects after adjusting the transparency levels. The reflection of the opposite window is created by adding another layer of the train's interior, which creates a sense of depth.

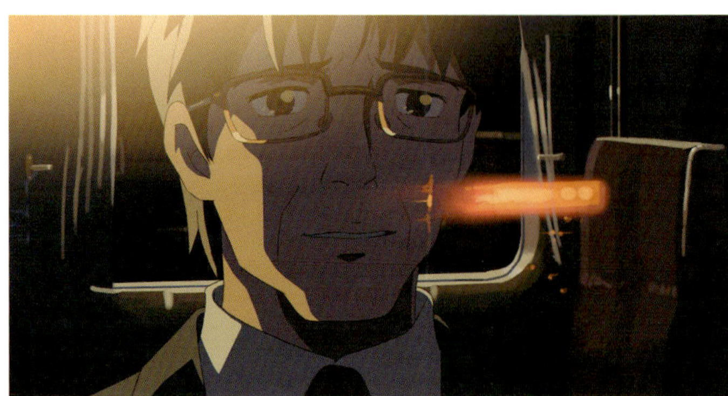

Shinano Mainichi Shimbun TV Commercial / CUT_004-2 / Setting: JR Koumi Line train interior

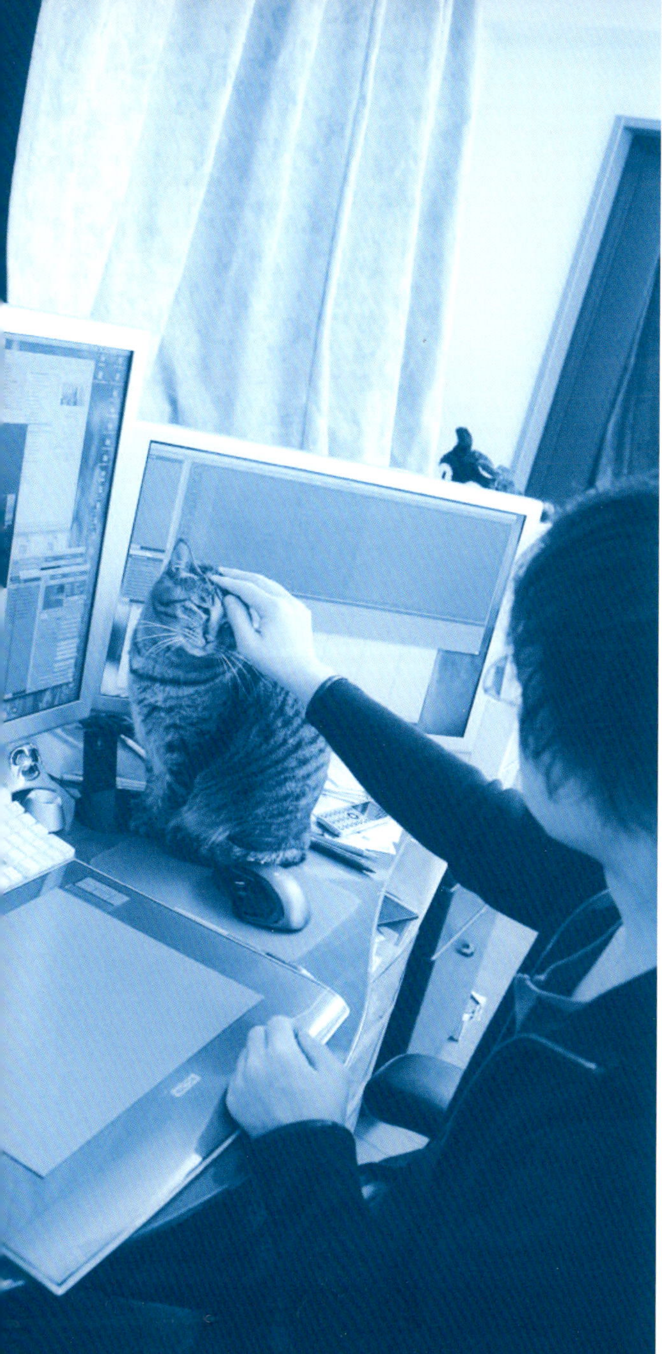

Testimonials of Makoto Shinkai's World

We begin with a long interview with Mr. Makoto Shinkai himself. In addition, we conducted interviews with the background artists that support his works: Takumi Tanji, Akiko Majima, Akira Hirosawa, Minako Shimada, Kaori Izumiya, Yoshitaka Takeuchi, Yumi Ishii, Tasuku Watanabe. We also interviewed character designer and animation director for *5 Centimeters per Second* and the Shinano Mainichi Shimbun TV Commercial Takayo Nishimura, as well as the on-site producer and creator of the Shinkai Team Koichiro Itoh. We "focused" on the man known as Makoto Shinkai, and tried to give a "close-up" of the feelings in his work and among his team.

Interview with Makoto Shinkai

Born 1973, in Nagano Prefecture. Graduated from Chuo University with a major in Japanese Literature. Began creating short animated films on his own while working at a video game company. Debuted the fully digital animated work *Voices of a Distant Star* in 2002, which garnered high praise and instantly launched his career as an animator. 2004 saw the theatrical release of his first feature-length work, *The Place Promised in Our Early Days. 5 Centimeters per Second* premiered in 2007. His works have won numerous awards both in Japan and overseas. Aside from animated works, Shinkai has also written novels and expresses himself in a variety of media.

○ What is the oldest memory of scenery you can recall?

I don't know whether this was something real or not, but in searching my memories, the oldest thing I can remember is seeing a steam locomotive at a train station as a child. I think, since I was a boy, I loved vehicles. My grandfather and grandmother would often walk with me to the station, holding my hands, to look at the trains. Back then, the station in my hometown, Koumi, was an old, wooden building, and there was a bridge of sorts from which you could look down onto the train tracks; the image of a steam locomotive stopped there and spouting smoke is the earliest memory I have. But I only thought to myself, "I love this sort of scene" when I was much older, when I began high school and would commute to and from school on the train. The trip from Koumi Station to the station where my school was would take about 30 to 40 minutes one way, and the train would run almost directly north to south, which meant the windows on either side would show due east and due west. Just like the scenery along the rail line shown in the Shinano Mainichi Shimbun commercial, in the mornings as I went to school, if I sat near the windows on the eastern side, I would be able to watch the sunrise the entire way, and on the way back, if I sat on the west side, I could see the sunset. It was while watching the shifting sunlight light up the scenery that I first had the clear realization that I loved looking at such views.

○ Do those sceneries influence those seen in your works?

I think there is a clear influence. For example, in Tokyo, there are no mountains, so you can watch the sun set until it's very low in the sky. The light weakens enough that you can look at it directly, and watch as it slowly sinks. But I grew up surrounded by mountains, where the sun would set behind the peaks at a rather high point. It would still be too bright to look at directly when it would suddenly slip behind the mountains. After I came to Tokyo, I remember feeling that something was off, that the setting sun should be much brighter. I'm often told that the sunsets in my works are extremely strong, but I think that's the influence of the scenery I saw as a child.

○ From your mainstream debut *Voices of a Distant Star* to *The Place Promised in Our Early Days* and *5 Centimeters per Second*, do you feel that you are moving away from the common selling points in mainstream animation such as robots and sci-fi settings?

That was a path that I was conscious of. Back when I was making *Voices of a Distant Star*, I was creating it with the knowledge that I would be leaving the job that I had at that time. My previous work, *She and Her Cat*, had already sold more than 5,000 copies, so I figured if I made a longer work and added the catchy element of a robot, I'd sell double that amount. Looking back now, that was quite naive of me. (laughs) In any case, I created the setting with sales in mind. However, I didn't go in with the awareness that I was twisting my concepts in order to make it more marketable. It's simply that, at the time, I didn't have a firm idea of what I wanted to express. So, when I made *Voices of a Distant Star*, it felt more like I was creating a cut-scene in a video game than a work of animation.

In the end, *Voices of a Distant Star* sold better than I had anticipated, and I earned a degree of recognition within an admittedly limited sphere. It was then that I realized that *Voices of a Distant Star*, which I had made as just a little cut-scene, was considered by a surprising number of people to be a full-fledged animation. In that case, I wanted to bring together a team in order to properly use animation as a means of expression for my next project, which turned out to be *The Place Promised in Our Early Days*. The actual production was incredibly difficult. We just barely managed to finish it. It went on to do decent business, but for me, it still has numerous issues.

After creating works in such a manner, when I considered what to do next, I had this thought: "It might not be possible to create a work that is 100% perfect. If that's the case, then for now, we should make something that we can confidently say that we alone are capable of creating." I wanted to leverage the recognition I had gained from my first two works, *Voices of a Distant Star* and *The Place Promised in Our Early Days*, remove the catchy elements that I had included in both of those works, and create something very simple.

○ Certainly, the decidedly commonplace characters and how their daily lives are depicted in a matter-of-fact manner in *5 Centimeters per Second* is something rarely seen in animation.

I discussed this in the video that was shot as part of the bonus features of the film's DVD, but even if you think that nothing so dramatic occurs in reality, I wanted to depict that sense of "nothing special" in a dramatic way. For example, even if nothing especially worth mentioning happens during your daily routine, by simply talking with someone you like during your commute, that alone might cause your emotions to really stir. I wanted to trace those stirred emotions. In order to get audiences to see such an animation, I had to make the images, music and direction far more powerful than my previous works. I think we got pretty close to my initial concept.

○ For *5 Centimeters*, you say that you wanted to create something simple, but the climax, set to Masayoshi Yamazaki's "One More Chance, One More Time" with scenes shown one after another, made a big impression. I'd go so far as to say that to merely layer images without a clear plotline with the intent of rousing the viewers' emotions was something that broadened the possibilities when it comes to expression in commercial animation.

I wavered quite a lot over whether or not to do that scene. I wondered if it was a good idea in a commercial film to use a technique that would leave such a large part at the end in the hands of the audience. For example, with a film like *Star Wars*, they created a fixed worldview, and the audience drops into that world for the duration of the film, and it's there that they enjoy the story that's given. That's a pretty general form of entertainment. But *5 Centimeters* is not that sort of film. If it had been, I would have chosen a different ending. The audience didn't drop into the world of the film to enjoy a story; instead, the film reached out into the audience and drew something out. It was for this reason that during the climactic scene I chose to hold the storytelling aspect in check and instead showed a collection of scenery that the audience would see on any ordinary day with a song playing in the background.

I think that scene was like a mirror that reflected each audience member back to themselves. Reactions were varied. Some thought it was great, others felt it was lacking. Some people cried, and maybe some people were angry. In any case, I still feel certain that the ending of *5 Centimeters* had to take that form.

○ Since *Voices of a Distant Star*, you have been both background art director and main director. Is there anything in your approach to background art that has changed between then and now?

From *She and Her Cat* and *Voices of a Distant Star*, the concept has changed bit by bit for each film, but I've never had a set preference for how background art should look. For *Voices of a Distant Star*, the backgrounds were created from a realistic requirement: how to draw the backgrounds within a limited amount of time so that they left an impression. The only reason we were able to add more detail to the backgrounds in *Early Days* is because I had other artists working with me. And of course everyone gave their all in drawing the backgrounds, but there were times when they might push back and say, "I wouldn't add that much detail to a background image." For *5 Centimeters* the issue of controlling variations in density of detail was always in my mind as we tackled each background. There were some cases of trial and error, but I never had the sense that I was pursuing some ideal of what an animation background should be. If anything, I felt that as I gained experience, I've become more moderate. In looking at other people's work, when I was younger, on occasion I might have thought, "I don't like that," but now, for most things I think, "Well, that works too, doesn't it?" or even, "I can't make such nice-looking backgrounds myself." (laughs)

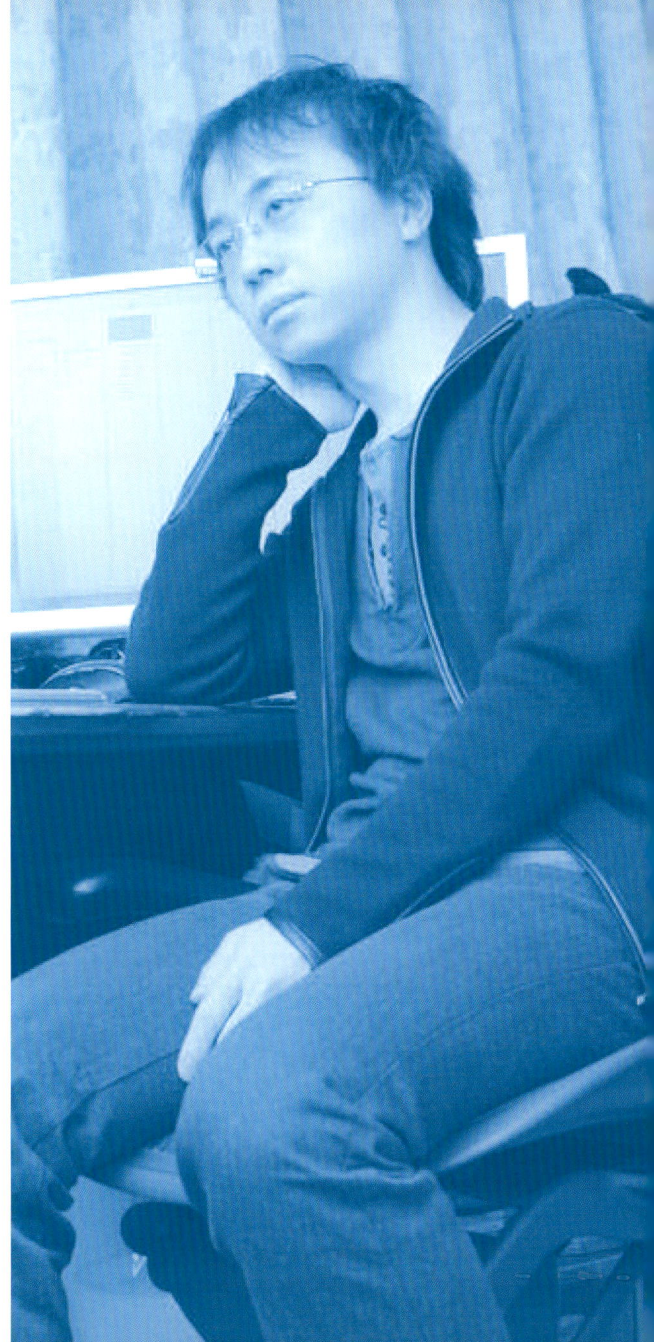

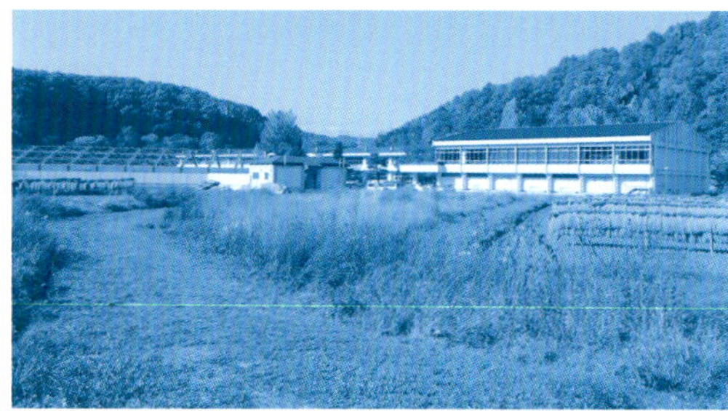

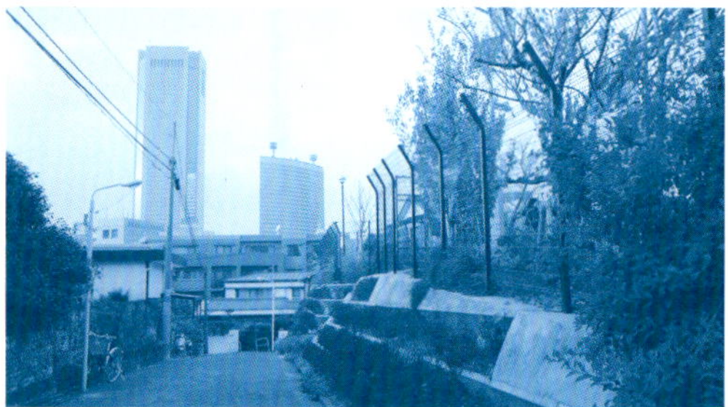

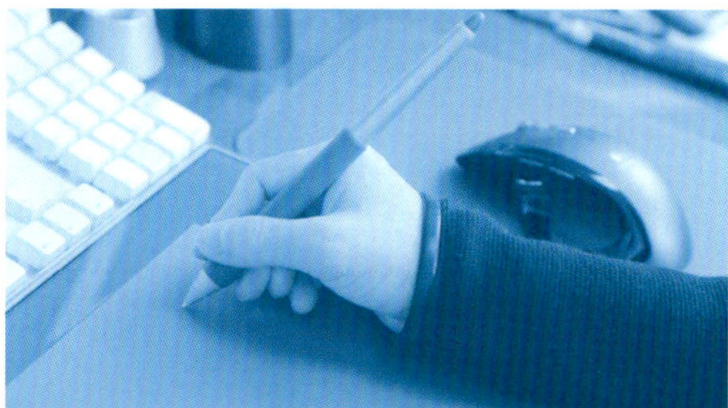

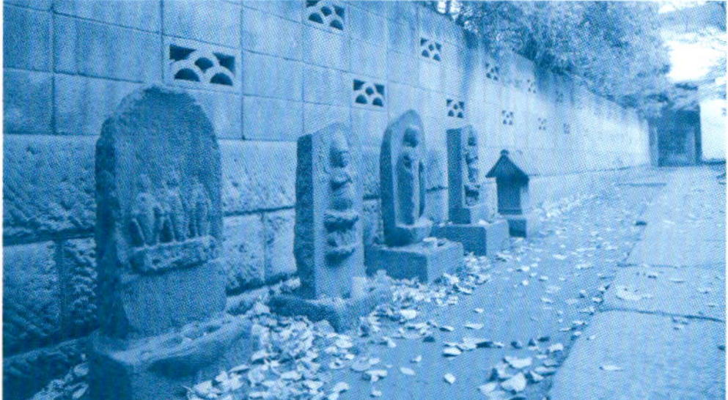

○ Viewers often mention the "Shinkai touch" and have all sorts of thoughts about your approach to background art, so it's interesting that you yourself aren't all that aware of it.

But I do have preferences, and when a staffer comes to me asking how to do something, I'll say, "Let's make it less this and more that" without hesitation. In that context, there are times when I am quite clear regarding how I want a background to look.

○ In mainstream animation, the characters seem to jump out from the background, but in your works, and especially in *5 Centimeters*, the characters seem to melt into their worlds.

In technical terms, for standard animation production, all characters get set palettes: colors for daytime, colors for nighttime, colors for evening. And in many cases, in scenes where the times are the same, they are painted with the same colors regardless of the tones used in the backgrounds. If the artists didn't do that, their work progress would be very slow. However, in the case of *5 Centimeters*, all the background art was created first, and for all 1,000 cuts, the color designs for the characters were modeled on the background art. In some cases where we just couldn't get the colors to work, we would alter the background colors instead, and so I have a real sense of accomplishment with regards to the color scheme in *5 Centimeters*.

What I want to draw isn't "just backgrounds" but scenes that incorporate people. I was especially conscious of this when drawing Kanae in Act 2: "Cosmonaut." Kanae was in love, hopelessly, and things never went the way she wanted, up to the very end. That part by itself would be an irredeemably sad story, but taking a step back and looking at it through a camera shows that she exists within a very beautiful scene. Even though it's a painful situation, as a scene it's very lovely, and I wanted to depict the pain she felt as a component of that beauty. I wanted to draw a scene where people can be saved by beautiful surroundings.

○ This year (2008) you're planning on studying language in London. Can you tell us why you made that decision?

These past few years, I've been able to create works in a truly blessed environment, which includes my staff and the relationship with my business partner, CoMix Wave Films. But in another sense, I wanted to experience once more all the various feelings including stress and negativity that I had within the business and societal restraints I was under when I made *She and Her Cat* and *Voices of a Distant Star*, which then became my motivating power. Of course I'd prefer to be in a comfortable environment, and I've sought that out when putting together all the projects I've done thus far, but conversely, in such a situation, I feel like I can't clearly see what it is that I need from the work that I will create from this point on. How do people deal with that chronicle of unease, loneliness and anticipation when they first move to Tokyo or start a new job? I want to stand still and properly devote thought to such things. I want to start with that thought and then connect it to my next project.

Background Artists

Takumi Tanji and Akiko Majima

○ What are the distinctive traits of Makoto Shinkai's art?

Majima: The colors.

Tanji: I think it's the colors too. With cloudy skies or the feeling of the sun, the way of using color to express temperature is connected to Mr. Shinkai's unique taste.

Majima: I also think the way he shows light and darkness is very distinctive.

○ I've heard that neither of you had drawn artwork using computers before working on *The Place Promised in Our Early Days*.

Tanji: Yes. I became involved when Mr. Itoh, the line producer, asked me to participate, and I'm certain that at first he told me that I didn't have to work digitally, that I could draw by hand, that they could simply scan in whatever I had drawn for the final stages. So for the first background, I drew it by hand, scanned it, then made adjustments digitally before handing it over. And then I was given the additional condition that all future backgrounds must be created digitally. (laughs) There wasn't time for me to make a few practice images, so Mr. Shinkai taught me how to use Photoshop as I created artwork for the actual film. But since I use computers in my work now, it turned out to be a very beneficial experience.

Majima: I had only ever used Word on a computer before, so I was surprised that it was even possible to draw artwork with Photoshop. But Mr. Shinkai and Mr. Tanji had already been working together for a while by the time I joined the team, so they had already established methods for drawing backgrounds. It took me a while to get used to it, but Mr. Tanji taught me all sorts of drawing techniques.

○ So there is a difference between drawing by hand and drawing with a computer?

Tanji: At first, painting in reality with a brush was much faster, so I felt a time lag until the image in my head showed up on the actual page, and that bothered me for a while. If I can't immediately recreate what I see in my mind, then I feel like the image slips away from me. I felt that I had to work as fast on a computer as I did with a real brush or I wouldn't be able to draw easily, so I mainly focused on learning shortcut methods.

Majima: I still feel it doesn't go the way I want it to with regards to the time lag it takes to recreate the image in my mind. In my case, that's also true when drawing by hand. (laughs) But nowadays I only draw using a computer, so I couldn't say what it would be like to draw by hand.

Tanji: You should draw by hand once in a while. I sketch by hand when creating my own work.

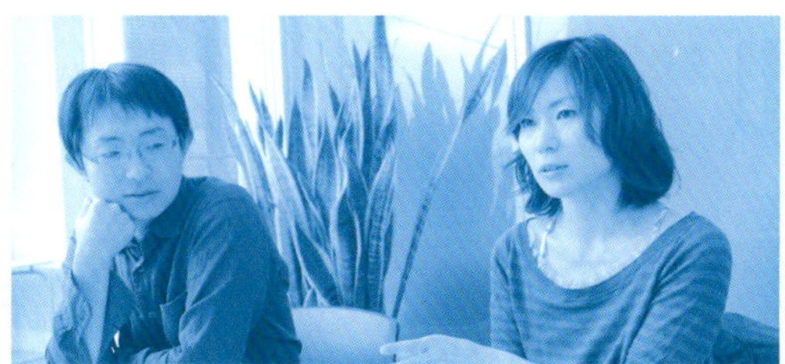

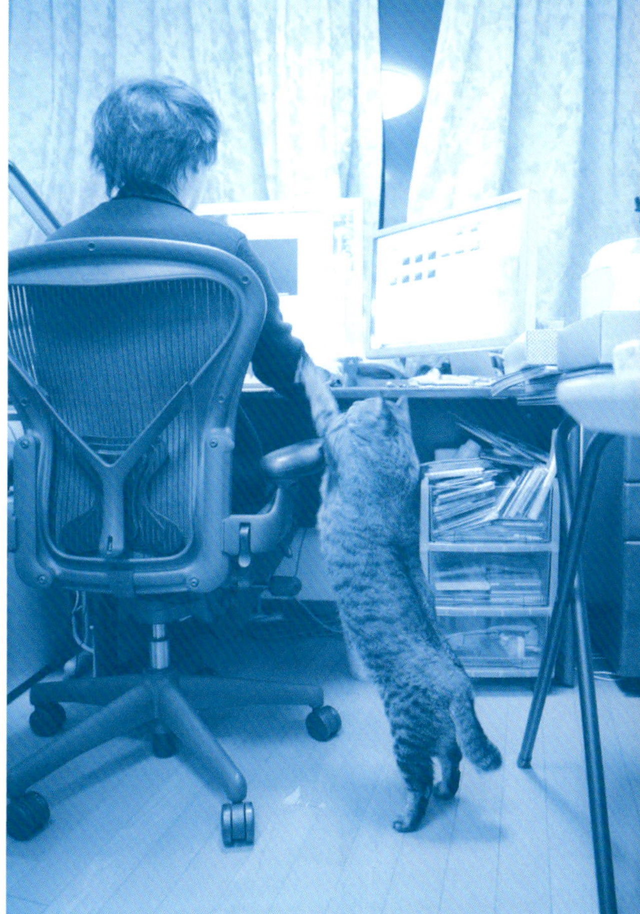

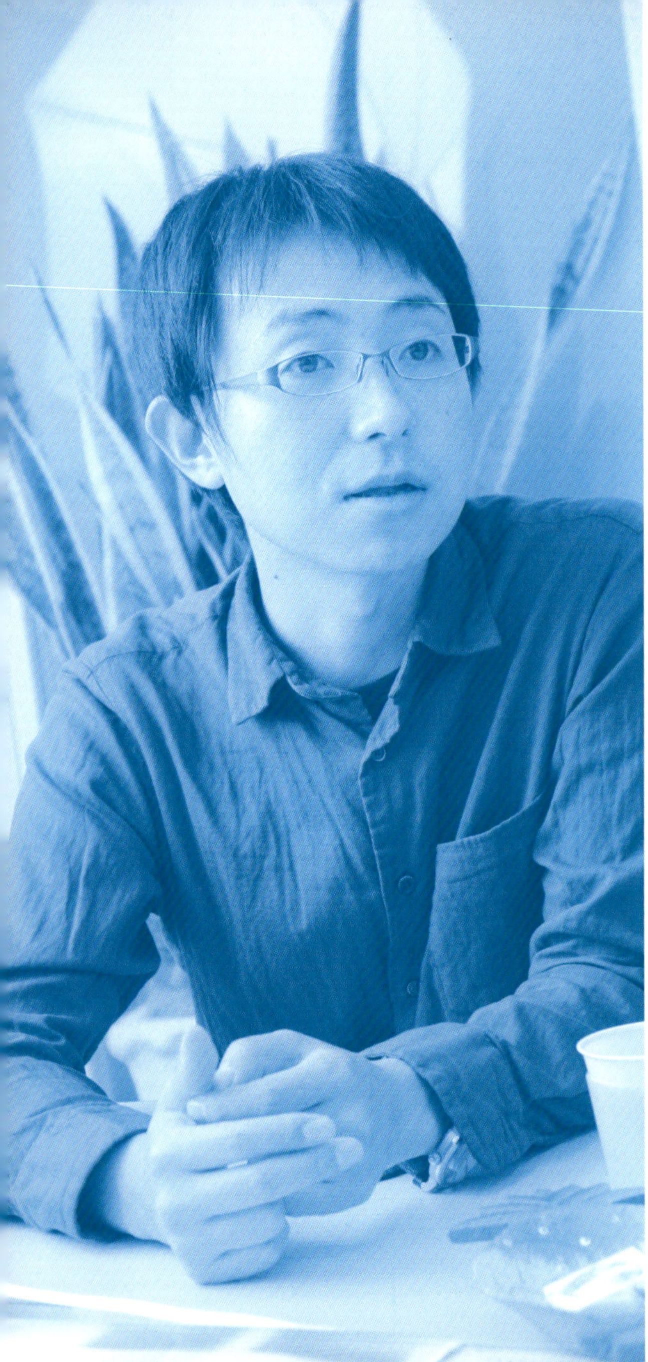

Takumi Tanji

Born 1974, in Fukushima Prefecture. Graduated from the Fine Arts Department of Tokyo University of the Arts with a major in painting. Has worked on a variety of projects as a freelance artist. Works include *Journey to the West, Japan Sinks* (2007), *CASSHERN, Azumi, Yomigaeri, Dragon Head, Calmi Cuori Appassionati, Shark Skin Man and Peach Hip Girl*, etc. Among Shinkai's works: *The Place Promised in Our Early Days, 5 Centimeters per Second.*

○ What was your first impression when you met Mr. Shinkai?

Majima: That he's child-like.

Tanji: I thought he was angelic.

Majima: I wasn't talking about his personality, I meant his looks. (laughs)

Tanji: He was wearing a white T-shirt, and his hair was brownish and gently flowing. That's why I said "angelic." Once we got talking, he was very polite and affable.

○ I've heard that the atmosphere during the production of *5 Centimeters* was very good.

Tanji: At the end of *Early Days*, we were really rushing to beat the clock, so many staff members would sleep over at Mr. Shinkai's place. The atmosphere wasn't strained, but we were all flustered. I think during *5 Centimeters* Mr. Shinkai took that into consideration and made the atmosphere as nice as possible. We had every weekend off, too.

Majima: Yes, it was a very pleasant workplace. Thanks to that, all the staff members became very close. I had fun during *Early Days*, too.

○ Is it possible that the softness of the background art in *5 Centimeters* is due to the relaxed mood during production?

Tanji: Mr. Shinkai himself said, "I want to create something that gives a softer impression than *Early Days*," and I think that extended to the atmosphere during production. As for the backgrounds, we didn't add too much detail, and where we did add details we varied the density.

Majima: Mr. Shinkai, at first, said he wanted all the line art for *5 Centimeters* to be drawn using pencils. He said even for the backgrounds we would trace everything in pencil, then scan it for use digitally.

Tanji: But by the time I joined the *5 Centimeters* team after finishing work on *Japan Sinks*, there was no sign of that.

Majima: Yeah, there are some cuts like that in the very beginning of Act 1, but we decided to stop doing it because it was so hard. (laughs) But if Mr. Tanji had been there from the beginning that method might have remained.

○ How far along was production on *5 Centimeters* by the time Mr. Tanji joined?

Majima: Around the end of Act 1, I think.

Tanji: No, it wasn't the end. (laughs) About halfway through?

Majima: That's right. About 1/4 of the total film. Once Mr. Tanji joined us, the pace suddenly quickened.

Akiko Majima

Born 1972, in Kanagawa Prefecture. Completed a Master's Degree in Painting in the Fine Arts Department of Tokyo University of the Arts. After studying abroad in Cuba, directed the short film *Distancias* which won the Cinematography Award at the Nazionale Cinema-Video Plaza Festival and the award for Best Screenplay at the CARACOL Festival. Among Shinkai's works: *The Place Promised in Our Early Days, 5 Centimeters per Second.*

○ What is your favorite artwork that you have created for Shinkai's works?

Tanji: I like the artwork showing the railroad tracks used in the poster for *Early Days*. At first, all the gravel looked the same, but partway through the process, Mr. Shinkai told me to make the gravel in the middle of the tracks look like they were covered in oil. The greenish sky was mostly drawn by Mr. Shinkai, and he made the final adjustments to create the overall tone.

Majima: I think my favorite is the pub, which was the first setting I painted for *Early Days*. It was the first thing I drew, so I didn't slack off at all, even when drawing the posters or small objects. (laughs) But I remember that when I saw it in the theater, the scene was longer than I had remembered and I nervously thought, "Please, hurry up to the next cut!"

○ What was the most difficult aspect of participating in creating Shinkai's works?

Tanji: For me, it was learning Photoshop when it was first decided that I would assist Mr. Shinkai. After that, I don't think I had much difficulty. I had fun! Though towards the end of *Early Days*, my hips hurt so badly that I couldn't sit, so I painted while lying down. It was like a severe case of back strain, and they had to carry me like that into the hospital, but I only dropped out at the very end.

Majima: My personality is such that I'm not good with drawing details. I like doing it, but with digital tools you can zoom in very far, and I lose sight of how much detail should be added. Especially when I worked on *5 Centimeters*, I had a pretty hard time of it until I understood the level of detail that should be used. Mr. Shinkai would always do the final corrections anyway, but I wanted to get it to a place where it would be easy for him to correct. Towards the end, I got the images about 80%? 70%? ...60%? done (laugh) by the time I submitted them to Mr. Shinkai. If I worried too much about making it look like something Mr. Shinkai would paint, it would end up totally different.

Tanji: Mr. Shinkai is actually very lenient, and if he likes something, he'll use it as-is. So there was never a sense that we had to make it look like his aesthetic.

○ Finally, if you were to compare Mr. Shinkai to background art, what sort of image would he be?

Majima: If you mean what sort of setting would be most suited to him, if he were placed in the recent Shinano Mainichi Shimbun commercial, then he would fit in very well.

Tanji: I agree, something like out of one of his works showing some man-made object sticking out in the midst of natural scenery, and that object is dirty or resembles some kind of relic. I think that might be Mr. Shinkai, or the image of his works. Hmm, it's pretty hard to compare him to a background.

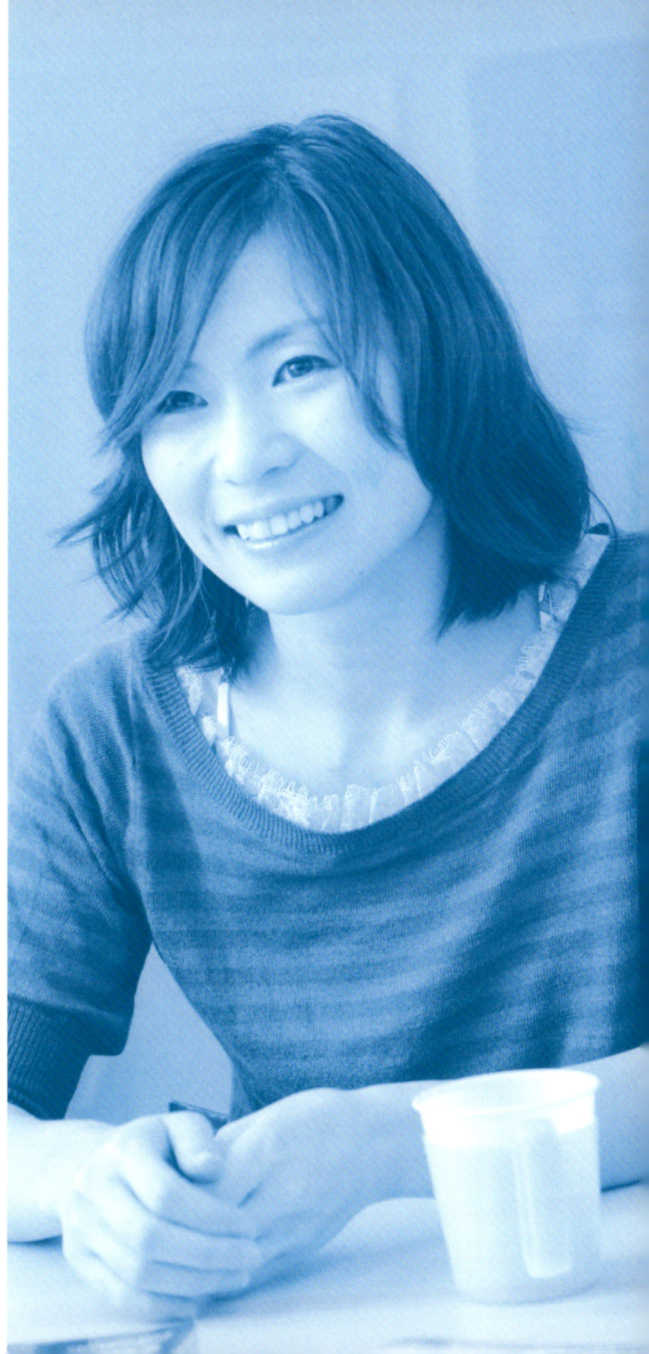

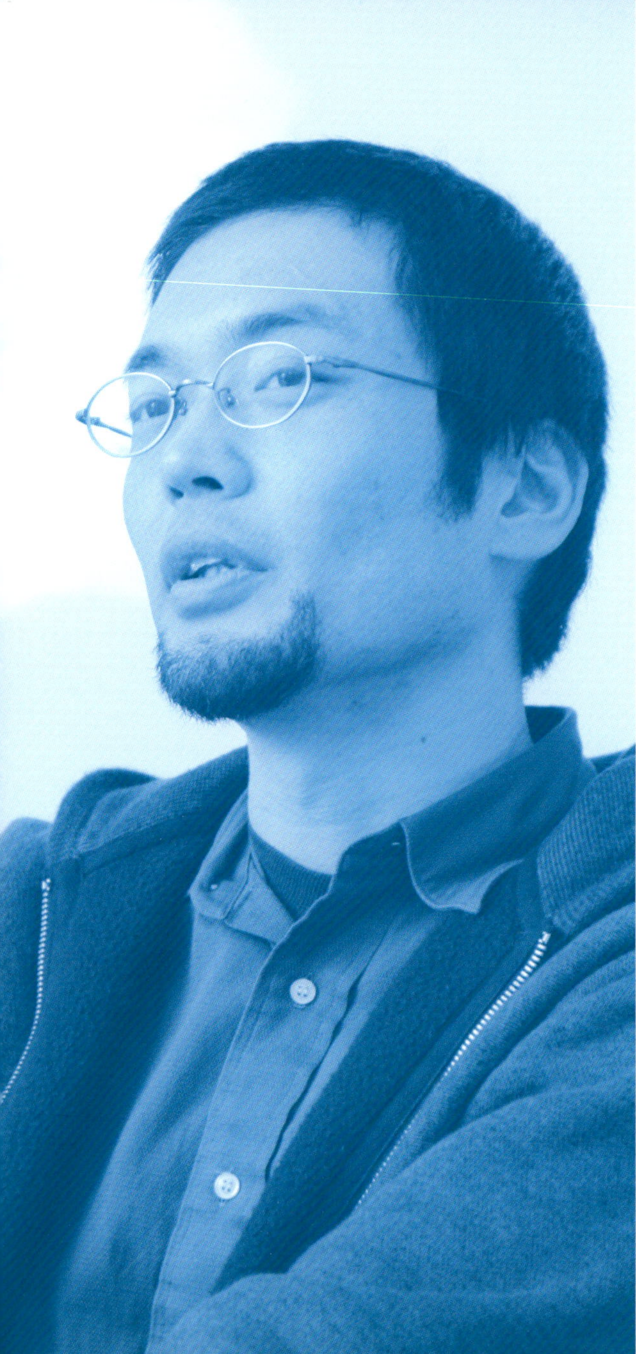

Background Artist

Akira Hirosawa

Born 1970, in Kanagawa Prefecture. Graduated from the Fine Arts Department of Tokyo University of the Arts with a major in Oil Painting. Holds a variety of jobs including teaching assistant at his alma mater, instructor at an art prep school, scenery painter for theme parks, and background artist for the film *Spy Sorge*, etc. Among Shinkai's works: *The Place Promised in Our Early Days*, *5 Centimeters per Second*.

○ Please tell us how you came to participate in Shinkai's works.

After I graduated from college I worked as an instructor at an art prep school and scenery painter while I was creating my own works. I also created background art for a live-action feature film, but that was only for a few months. I was brought in to work with Shinkai when Mr. Itoh went to my alma mater in search of people interested in painting backgrounds for animation, and the person at the school that he was in correspondence with happened to be a friend of mine. It was through him that I heard about the *Early Days* job. After joining the staff of *Early Days* I worked on other projects for CoMix Wave Films, which led to me working on *5 Centimeters*. For *5 Centimeters*, instead of commuting to the studio, my role was to assign artwork creation to staff artists who worked from home, then take their work and make adjustments before handing them in to Mr. Shinkai.

○ As that was your first time working on an animated work, did you ever feel lost or confused?

I was such a novice in the world of animation that that was the first time I'd ever heard Mr. Shinkai's name. At first, I couldn't even paint a single image. Using a computer to paint was even more difficult than I had imagined, plus having to make the images as close as possible to someone else's art style was something I'd never experienced before. I thought it was so impossible that I actually turned down the job at one point. I didn't want to simply quit though, so I introduced them to Ms. Majima whom I'd gone to college with. I had planned on leaving Ms. Majima with them and running away, but once I saw how readily she adapted to that environment, I had second thoughts and felt that I might be able to do the same. For the first three months, my pace was so slow that I could only complete two pieces per month. During that time, I attended lectures given by Mr. Shinkai, but he worked so fast that I couldn't learn anything. He made frequent use of keyboard shortcuts, which made it impossible to understand how he had done something. Even if I thought I had understood something during the lecture, when I went home, I found I wasn't able to do it anymore. That continued for some time. After a while, Mr. Shinkai was so busy that Mr. Tanji took over the lectures, and Mr. Tanji's work speed was perfect for teaching. Since we had attended the same school I felt comfortable enough to ask him to do something again, which helped a lot. Mr. Tanji, too, had only started using computers to create art when he first worked with Mr. Shinkai, so I think we had similar difficulties and questions. Once I was able to think of a computer simply as a tool, it became easier to paint. After that point, for *Early Days* and *5 Centimeters*, I worked at a pace of one piece per day.

○ What is a key point in undestanding the background art in Shinkai's works?

Color is a very distinctive trait. I keep in mind things like, Mr. Shinkai would make the brightness in this area like this, or add in blues or purples in the dark areas. Even so, for natural things like clouds or trees, I can never get close to his aesthetic, so after getting the image to a certain point I leave the rest to Mr. Shinkai or Mr. Tanji. The level of perfection that Mr. Shinkai seeks is far above what we're able to envision. As an artist, I have to respect his relentless pursuit of such perfection, and in fact, the artwork in *5 Centimeters* was more evolved that that of *Early Days*. Mr. Shinkai knows how to present each image, and we do our best to reach his goals. While it's difficult, I have fun creating the artwork.

Background Artist

Minako Shimada

Born 1980, in Tokyo. Matte painter for live-action films. Works include: *Kamen Rider Hibiki & The Seven Senki, Japan Sinks* (2007), *Akanezora, Heat Island,* etc. Among Shinkai's works: *5 Centimeters per Second.*

○ Please tell us how you came to participate in Shinkai's works.

I was working as a matte painter on live-action films when Mr. Tanji, whom I'd met at an art event, introduced me to Mr. Shinkai, and he invited me to work on *5 Centimeters.*

○ Can you tell us any struggles or memorable events that occurred during production?

I joined the team during the production of Act 2, and I was in charge of background artwork for Acts 2 and 3. In Act 3, there are a number of cuts that show cityscapes with buildings with lots of windows, which were difficult to create. We used Photoshop, which I knew how to operate, but the tools are different from what I use in matte painting. For live-action films, photographs are processed to create collages, so I had never created an image from a blank canvas using a computer before. The background art is created using brush tools, so there were a number of tools I'd never used. Mr. Shinkai very kindly explained the drawing process in a way that I could understand. I had the impression from his works that he was a high-strung type, but he's not like that at all. He's very good-humored and easy to talk to. When I started commuting to the studio, every day was so much fun. I got along very well with the rest of the staff, and we would take turns cooking meals each week. It was a feeling I'd never experienced at any other studio. I was working yet I was having fun. I think that was the most enjoyable work experience I've ever had.

○ Among the artwork you handled, were there any images that you liked, had trouble with or are emotionally attached to?

My favorite is the image of the mailbox on the road next to Akari's parents' home in the flashback sequence at the very end of Act 3. The one that gave me the most difficulty was also in Act 3, the cut showing a snowy city at night, with the pedestrian bridge in the foreground and the tower in the background. That was right around the time I joined the project, and I didn't know how to approach painting it. I was given directions to depict it slightly differently from the reference photos, but I just couldn't get it to work, so Mr. Tanji helped me out. Mr. Tanji would send back each corrected image and then explain to me what he had done, and also give me advice on how to do things, so I felt like I gradually learned how to paint the backgrounds. I think Shinkai's way of showing contrast is distinctive. Warm colors are used within cool colors, and such techniques make for pretty pictures. Also, I discovered many things during the artwork creation process, such as not over-drawing anything, or leaving areas that don't need to be illustrated with very little detail. My technical skills expanded via painting backgrounds, so I'm very glad that I was able to participate.

○ If you were to compare Mr. Shinkai to background art, what sort of image would he be?

The first thing that comes to mind is the snowy landscape shown in the poster for *5 Centimeters.* But not at night, and not with snow falling, just cloudy. There aren't many people around, and it looks a bit lonesome, yet it's not dark. The color palette is grayish and feels gentle.

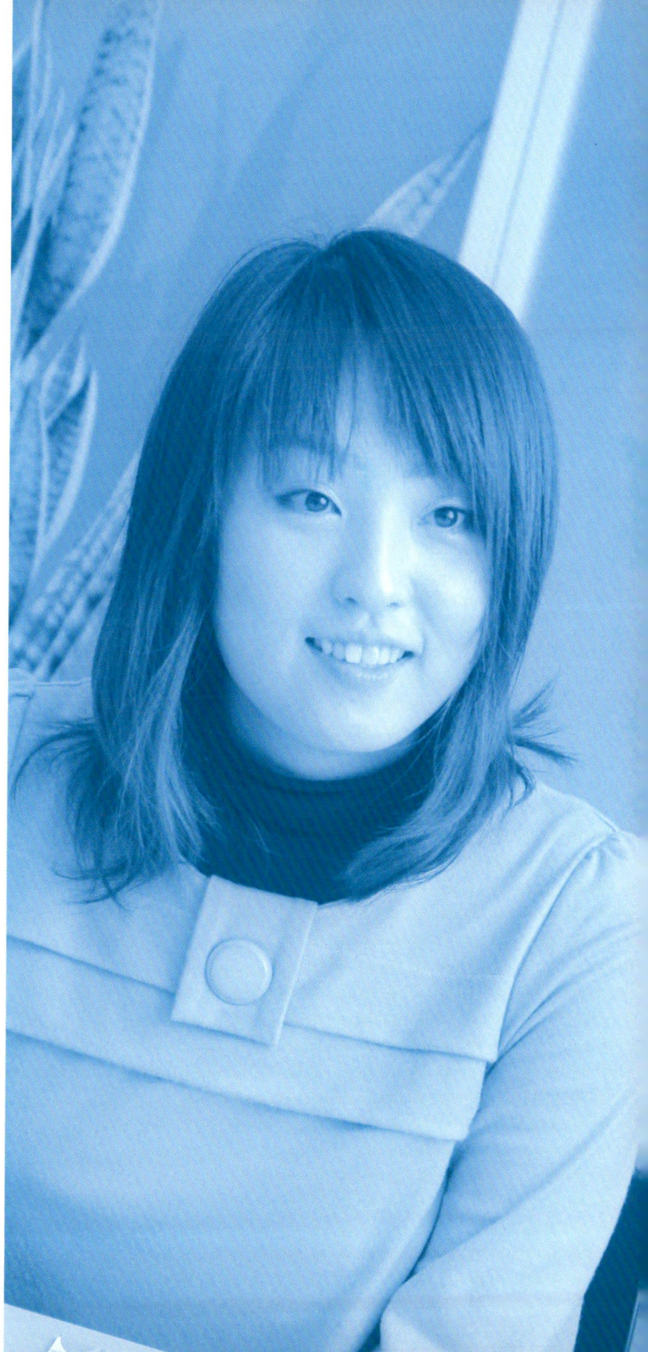

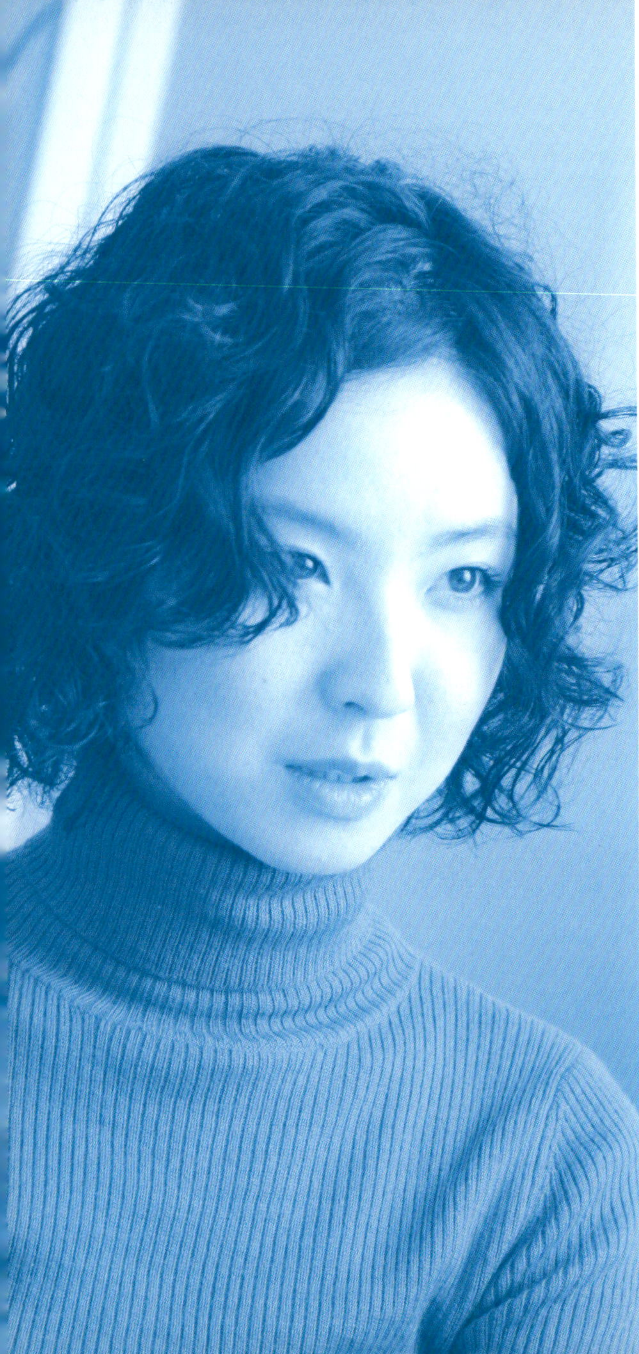

Background Artist

Kaori Izumiya

Born 1983, in Kanagawa Prefecture. Graduated from the Fine Arts Department of Tokyo University of the Arts with a major in Oil Painting. Among Shinkai's works: *5 Centimeters per Second.*

○ Please tell us how you came to participate in Shinkai's works.

I was working part-time while creating my own art after graduation, and on a trip back to the school to get my belongings I happened to run into Mr. Hirosawa, who invited me to join the production staff. Mr. Hirosawa was a teaching assistant at my college. If I hadn't gone back to school right then to get my things, I'd probably still be working part-time. I've always loved animation, so I accepted the invitation without hesitation. However, I'd hardly ever used a computer before, so I didn't understand how to work digitally, which made me worry. They had to teach me everything, starting with the definitions of "pixel" and "anti-aliasing." Mr. Shinkai is very kind, but he was dealing with a total amateur, so I'm sure I gave him a hard time. At first, in order to get used to using a computer, instead of painting backgrounds I spent a month coloring characters, then half a month scanning in key frames and inbetweens. For *5 Centimeters*, the line art just used the lines of the pencil sketches, which were then finished in Photoshop. It was a great way to get used to Photoshop, but was very mentally trying.

○ Among the artwork you handled, were there any images that you liked, had trouble with or are emotionally attached to?

During the creation of Act 1, I was assigned to finishing the inbetweens, so the first backgrounds I painted were a series of sunset scenes for Act 2. I was confused when it came to creating color palettes that suited Mr. Shinkai's style, so I had to have Mr. Tanji teach me all about it. I watched a fair amount of anime, but Mr. Shinkai's colors and hues are distinctive, like nothing I'd seen before. The contrast is very clear, and I feel that the saturation is very high. The artwork that I make independently is very low in saturation, so in many cases I had to use colors that I'd never used before. The last image I drew was the magazine rack in the convenience store in Act 3. There were so many details which were difficult to draw. I started off drawing too much detail, and there was just no end in sight. I'm slow, so I can't finish something in a day like the other artists can. Even so, I finished the image where you can see the magazine corner from the outside of the store within one day. I thought I would have a week to create the interior of the convenience store, but I was told to do it in three days, which was very hard.

○ Were there any memorable events that happened during production?

At the beginning of the day I start out listening to music on my headphones as I work, but towards evening my ears start to hurt so I take them off. I'm always muttering things to myself, but nobody ever comments on it. It was a place that really made me feel like I was at home. If there was something I didn't understand, I was able to immediately ask anyone around for help, and not a single person ever gave me an unpleasant look. Instead, they all kindly taught me what I needed to know. I'm really glad that I had the opportunity to learn Photoshop here. It's rare to get such a thorough education on something outside of a classroom.

○ If you were to compare Mr. Shinkai to background art, what sort of image would he be?

I think Shinjuku, more than some countryside scene. I mean the whole of Shinjuku, including Kabukicho and Shinjuku Park Tower. That's Mr. Shinkai. I might have that impression because the production studio was close to Shinjuku. He's from Nagano Prefecture, but I think he's a city person. He has a mysterious air, like a city where some things change and other things remain the same.

Background/3DCG Artist

Yoshitaka Takeuchi

Born 1985, in Nagano Prefecture. Currently enrolled in Tokyo University of Technology. While previously enrolled at a technical school, he worked as a background artist on CoMix Wave Film's *Hoshizora Kiseki*. Worked on both background art and 3DCG for Shinkai's *5 Centimeters per Second*.

○ Please tell us how you came to participate in Shinkai's works.

Mr. Hirosawa was an instructor at the technical school I attended before I enrolled in Tokyo University of Technology. One day Mr. Hirosawa asked if I would be interested in doing background art for CoMix Wave Film's OVA *Hoshizora Kiseki*. Sometime after that project was finished, I also joined the team for *5 Centimeters*. On *5 Centimeters*, at first I worked from home, but once summer break for college came around I had the time to commute to the studio. When I was in my junior year of high school, I'd learned that Mr. Shinkai was creating anime almost entirely on his own, which inspired me to pursue animation myself. That's why it was quite a surprise to find myself coming and going from the workplace of someone that I had admired. When I first met Mr. Shinkai, I felt that he was very easy to get along with.

○ You're in charge of 3DCG as well as background artwork, correct?

3DCG wasn't part of the conversation at first; when I was working from home I was only creating backgrounds. When I started commuting to the studio, I saw Mr. Shinkai making models for cels. The process took a long time, and he asked me to take over the job if I was able to do it. I made trains and automobiles, things that would be difficult to draw as cels, whereas the main aspect of 3D is the ability to save a lot of effort. The 3DCG trains made use of model data from previous CoMix Wave Films projects. Also, things like close-ups of watches are made to look like cels but are actually 3D. In some cases, backgrounds that appeared to be entirely conventional were in fact moving 3D images. For example, the snowy scene passing outside the train windows in Act 1 was made using 3D. In that case, the textures were created using background art methods. For most backgrounds, each element was placed on its own layer, part of which was created using 3D. Other places that were 3D without standing out as such include the upward view of the HII-A rocket launch scene in Act 2. The rocket subtly rotates, but it does't stand out at all. (laughs) I made the 3DCG elements using a program called LightWave 3D. I already knew how to use the software, but that was my first time making 3D images for a job, so there was some trial and error during the creation process.

I didn't draw that many backgrounds, but I did create a number of train interiors. After drawing a scene, Mr. Shinkai would touch it up to create the finished background. After looking at what he had corrected, I would take note of what was different or how something should be fixed, to gradually grasp his style. I'm not sure even now whether or not I actually comprehended it, but one thing I noticed was the subtle shifts in the colors used within shadows. I thought it was a very distinctive use of shadows. Other than that, I also made the moving screen on Takaki's computer. While I wouldn't make suggestions myself, I figured that no matter what I did it would be for my benefit, so if I was asked if I could do something, I would always answer, "Yes."

○ If you were to compare Mr. Shinkai to background art, what sort of image would he be?

I'm from Nagano, just like Mr. Shinkai, so I've seen the same sprawling paddy fields and scenery with falling snow. Mr. Shinkai is the season just after winter, when the snow has melted and the fields are damp. I think the scenery most similar to him is one at that time of year, in the morning, when it's growing warmer, and there's a sense of relief.

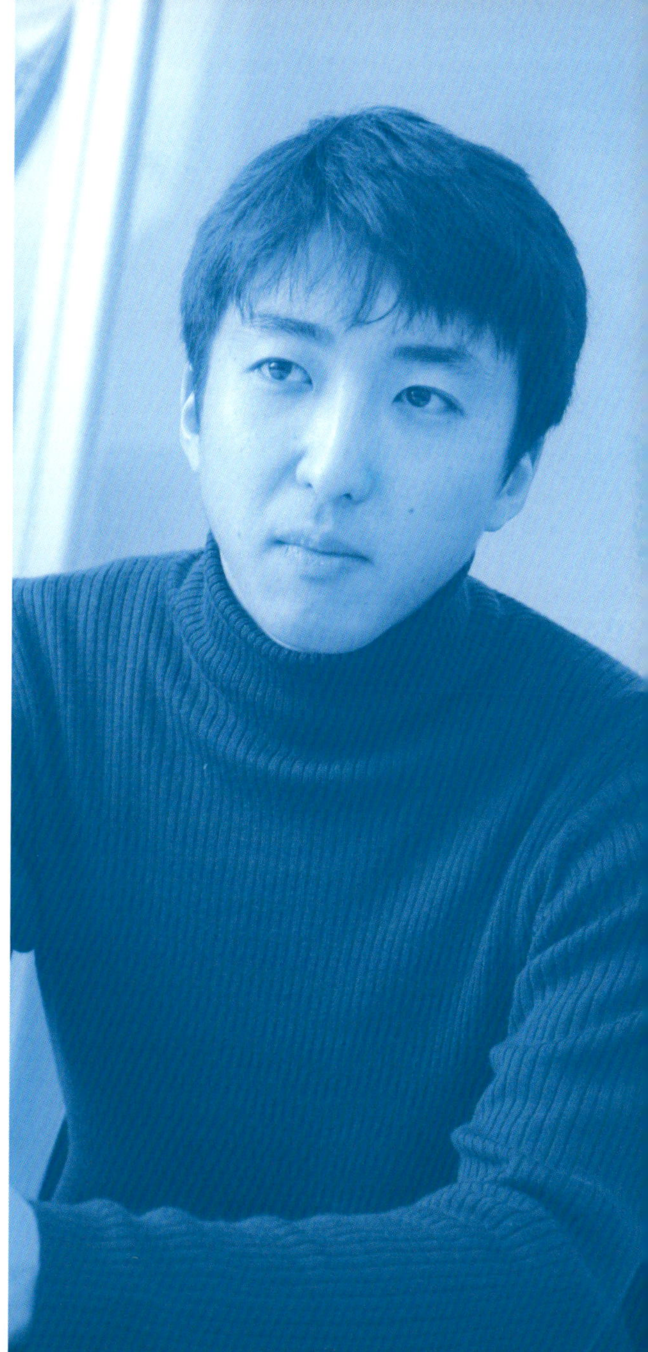

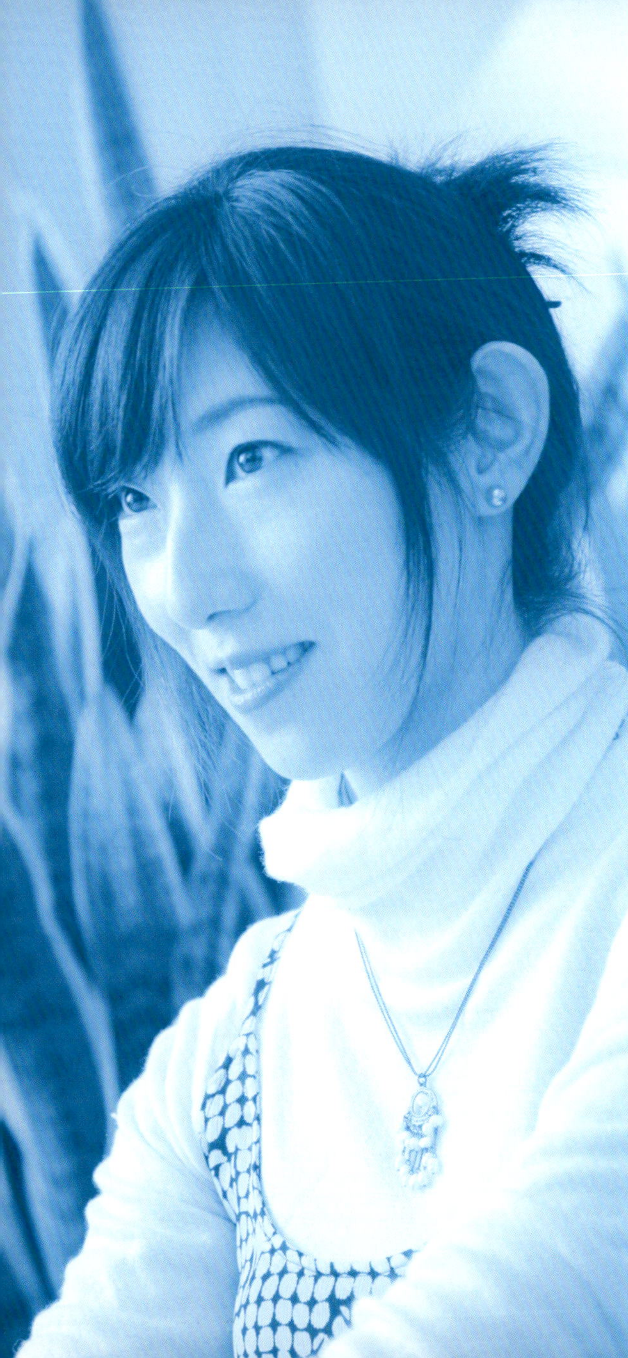

Background Artist

Yumi Ishii

Born 1980, in Tokyo. Graduated with a major in Painting from the Fine Arts Department of Tokyo Zokei University. Among Shinkai's works: *5 Centimeters per Second.*

○ Please tell us how you came to participate in Shinkai's works.

I was acquainted with Mr. Tanji. One time we both participated in the same gallery show in Yokohama, and he invited me to join the staff. But the art that I create on my own tends to be in physical mediums, which is in a totally different direction, so I wasn't really looking for work drawing animation backgrounds. I'd always liked anime though, and I thought the project seemed interesting, so I joined the production of *5 Centimeters* starting from Act 2. When I joined, I wasn't thinking very deeply about my future; I just wanted to do it. I had heard bits and pieces about Mr. Shinkai, but I'd never seen any of his films. I watched *Voices of a Distant Star* after talking to Mr. Tanji and before the job was offered, and was shocked to learn he made that all on his own.

○ Can you tell us any struggles or memorable events that occurred during production?

I had mainly used computers for email and the occasional retouching of photos in Photoshop. I had never used a tablet before, so having to learn everything from the very beginning was the hardest part. But Mr. Shinkai and Mr. Tanji were very precise when they taught me, which was a major help. I was in the same room as Ms. Majima, so I often asked her questions and am very much in her debt. As for the background art workflow, first Mr. Shinkai would meet with Mr. Tanji, and then with Ms. Majima. It wasn't like there were set groups, but Ms. Majima and I would get our instructions directly from Mr. Tanji. Mr. Tanji would make adjustments to my work, and then Mr. Shinkai would make the final corrections. Depending on the image, the hardest part would be understanding the initial direction. Of course there is the "Shinkai touch," but it was important that I arrange the image myself, by deciding how the light should look in a certain scene, etc. I've painted both artificial and natural things, and nature is by far more difficult. I worried over how to depict all sorts of things, from the growth of a tree to falling cherry blossom petals. But while it's difficult to draw things from nature, they're also interesting in their own ways, so I enjoyed thinking about such things as I worked. Mr. Shinkai's backgrounds are often based on photos, as if they're what you might see through a camera lens, so it's very easy to step into and get familiar with that viewpoint. Also, clouds are very distinctive. Just by looking at the sky normally I'll see shapes of clouds that look like they were drawn by Mr. Shinkai. But I never really see strangely-shaped clouds. I think the most memorable part that I created was the cherry blossom petals falling along the train crossing in Act 3. I was happy that that cut was used, but I wondered if it was good enough for the end. I drew that scene towards the end of the project, and I was thinking, "I don't want to have to say goodbye to everyone" as I worked. Looking back now, it was a very enjoyable workplace.

○ If you were to compare Mr. Shinkai to background art, what sort of image would he be?

Mr. Shinkai as a person isn't like the sky or the clouds. I think he's like a townscape, maybe because we only ever met in the city. I can't really imagine him relaxing out in the countryside, but I also see him as a small, sweet yellow flower blooming in an open field.

Background Artist

Tasuku Watanabe

Born 1983, in Saitama Prefecture. Graduated with a major in media design from the Design Department of Tokyo Zokei University. Among Shinkai works: *The Place Promised in our Early Days, 5 Centimeters per Second.*

○ Please tell us how you came to participate in Shinkai's works.

I was introduced by my instructor during summer break after my freshman year of college, and so I joined the staff of *Early Days* in the middle of production. It was from there that I learned of the world of animation background art, as I hadn't known anything about anime until then. I was a bit prejudiced, as I thought anime was something that only nerds watched. When my teacher first introduced me I was like, "Shinkai? Who's that?" But when I watched *Voices of a Distant Star* at CoMix Wave Films I was very moved. I realized that there were animated works like that, and I had to reconsider my stance and recognize anime as an art form. I wanted very much to help out with their work.

○ Can you tell us any struggles, memorable events or scenes in the films that came up during production?

I was still in college when I joined the staff for *Early Days*, so it was hard to manage both work and school life. It was a different situation from a normal part-time job, and I was mostly worried about how to create a work that would be shown to an audience without any compromises. As a result, I think it's regrettable that there are places in *Early Days* where, due to a lack of time or technical skills, I wasn't able to keep up. But all of the other staff artists were bright and friendly, and they would cheer me on when I was having a hard time managing work and school, so for me it was a positive experience. A memorable scene for me was Shinjuku Station in the cold open of *Early Days*. That was the image that I had the hardest time with, and it took me a week to complete. I drew everything including the title pattern, and both English and Japanese versions of the digital signboards. Shinjuku Station was one image, and then I drew countryside train station platforms. Mr. Shinkai chose who would create which backgrounds depending on each artist's particular knack. I tend to draw fairly dense images, so I was assigned images that required a lot of detail work, even if it took a while. Maybe it's just my subjective impression, but it made me happy to have someone expect something from me. I was someone that had only first used a computer at college, so I think learning on the job was a great way to absorb skills.

○ What are the distinctive traits of Makoto Shinkai's art?

To be honest, I don't think Mr. Shinkai's backgrounds are all that difficult. I simply look at his works and think they're beautiful. However, when I'm drawing backgrounds, I try to imagine that I have become Mr. Shinkai as I draw. I would think, "If I was Mr. Shinkai I would do this," for example. I think I have been especially influenced by Mr. Shinkai's works. I saw him in a TV interview once, saying, "I want to create works that influence people in some way," and I had the realization that "I am one such person that made it into this world after being influenced by Mr. Shinkai." Mr. Shinkai's films are like a signal to the heart. They have the power to directly communicate sadness, warmth, love and all sorts of emotions.

○ If you were to compare Mr. Shinkai to background art, what sort of image would he be?

I think Mr. Shinkai exists in a gap between the sky and the sea. There's the horizon, then the pure blue sky above, and he's standing on the surface of the ocean. Though, I think some clouds floating in the sky would be even more like Mr. Shinkai.

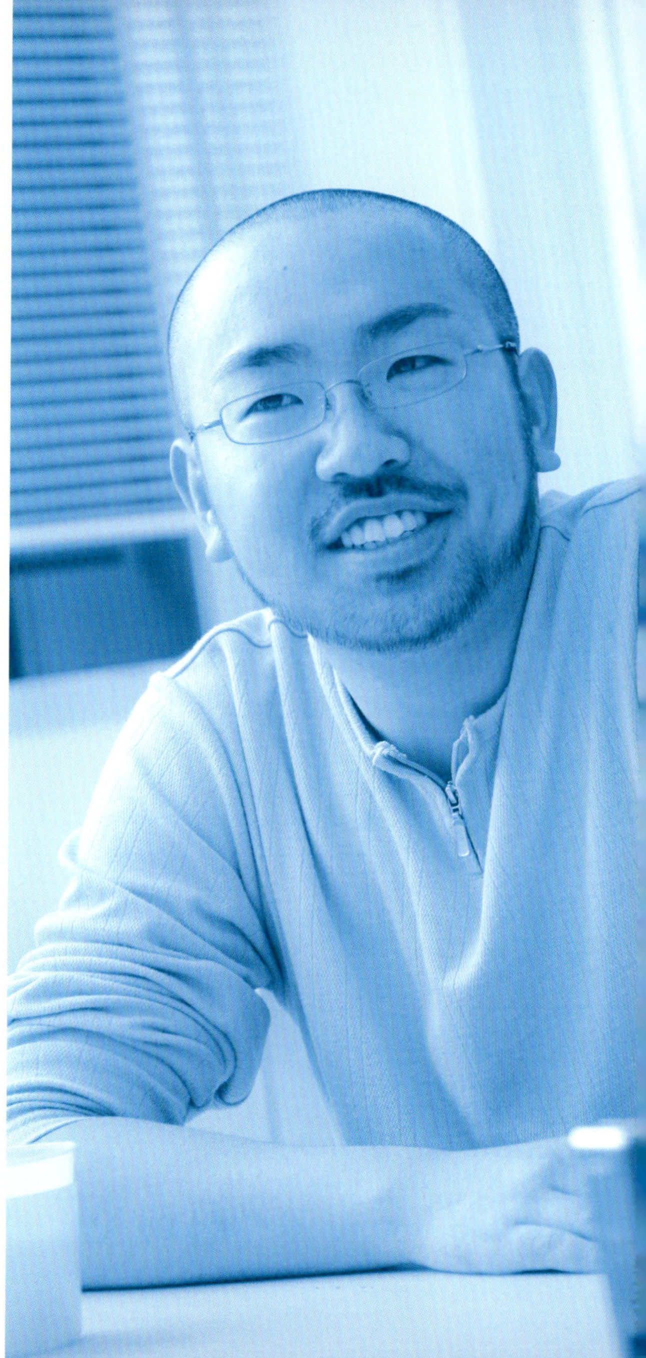

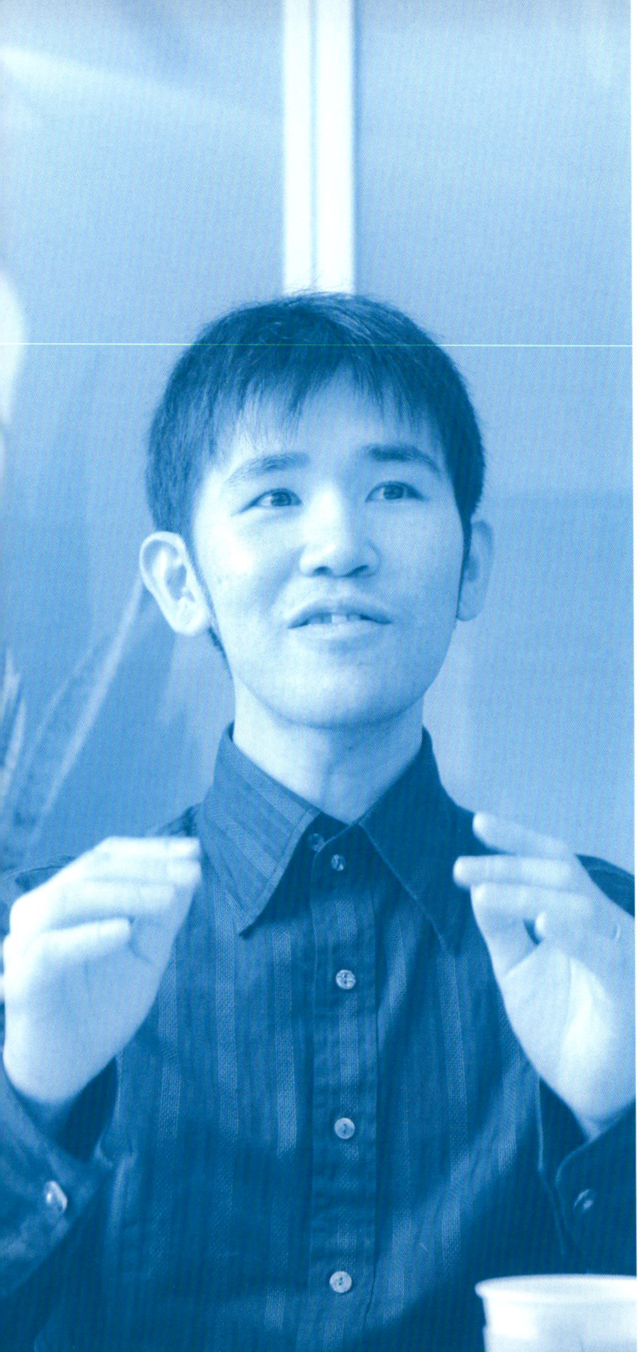

Character Designer, Animation Director, Animator

Takayo Nishimura

Born 1968, in Kanagawa Prefecture. Graduated from the International Animation Research Institute. Began his career as an animator at Studio Korumi before transferring to Disney Japan. Highlight work: *Lupin III Green vs. Red*, etc. First participated in Shinkai's works with *The Place Promised in Our Early Days.* Animation director and character designer for *5 Centimeters per Second.* Also created character designs and animation for *A Gathering of Cats*, which was part of Ani*Kuri 15 (NHK), and the Shinano Mainichi Shimbun TV commercial.

○ Please tell us how you came to participate in Shinkai's works.

After learning animation at a technical school, I was a key frame artist at an animation studio. I loved making characters move, and I wanted to create a lot of key animation, so I also worked on theatrical releases for Disney. One time when I happened to be between jobs, Mr. Itoh asked me to work on *Early Days.* I had participated in the production of anime that Mr. Itoh had produced for a prior company before joining CoMix Wave Films, so we were already acquaintances. When I saw the pilot for *Early Days* I thought the quality was very high, and that the backgrounds were lovely. I thought it would be worthwhile to add my drawings to these images, so I agreed to join the team. At first I was in charge of the climactic battle sequence, but since there was so much to do on the entire film, I became the assistant animation director when the workload got to be too much for Mr. Tazawa.

○ You were also in charge of character design in addition to acting as animation director for *5 Centimeters.*

A selling point of Mr. Shinkai's works is the sharpness of the art. I'm better at creating anime with soft lines, so to be honest, I wasn't sure that I would be right for the job. But when I saw the key frames for *Voices of a Distant Star*, though the shapes were sharp, the lines were very soft. I realized that the art was similar to mine, so I thought that I could mix the two styles as I created the characters. In *5 Centimeters*, we used a special technique where the lines from the key frames appeared directly on the screen. First we scanned the key frames, then made the lines of the inbetweens look similar to those in the key frames. For coloring, since the lines aren't connected, we can't use the fill tool. Instead we have to use the lasso tool in Photoshop to enclose a specific area. That's why the digital painters have the hardest job. Since they make use of the feel of the key frames, the varying strength of the lines comes through, which allows for excellent matching with the backgrounds. No matter what we do the quality will never be as good as the background art, but if we make up the difference with meticulous painting and movement, that will create a positive influence on the overall film.

○ Please tell us any memorable events that occurred during production.

5 Centimeters had many depictions of psychology, so we had many meetings about how to express them. In Act 2, Takaki stops Kanae's confession with his eyes. If that scene were in an ordinary anime, a lip-synch would have been persuasive enough. It would have been fine just like that, but by adding an extra bit of animation, it leaves more of an impression. I remember that Mr. Shinkai readily agreed to adding that animation at such-and-such timestamp. I was able to see something that I had drawn timed and placed into the film right there and then, and I was able to discuss things with Mr. Shinkai, so production was highly flexible. I think that workplace was very blessed when it came to furthering the quality of the work.

○ If you were to compare Mr. Shinkai to background art, what sort of image would he be?

I went to his parents' home when we took location photographs for the Shinano Mainichi Shimbun commercial. The land there is high above sea level, and the colors I saw when I looked at the scenery from the train were the same as the background art in his films. In my mind, Mr. Shinkai is the vividly-colored sunset of early summer and the sky reflecting in the paddy fields that I saw back then.

Line Producer

Koichiro Itoh

Born 1971, in Gifu Prefecture. Graduated from Niigata University. Left his position as an R&D engineer for a certain manufacturer to make films. Worked as a copy editor at Studio Hibari, an animation production company, and was in charge of TV animation production. Joined CoMix Wave Films in 2002 and has worked as a line producer for all Shinkai works starting with *The Place Promised in Our Early Days*.

○ Please tell us how you first met Mr. Shinkai.

Before I joined CoMix Wave Films, I had only known his name. Around the time *Voices of a Distant Star* was released I was working at a different company making TV anime. Someone bought the DVD of *Voices* and said, "He made this all by himself," and I thought that was amazing. I met him for the first time when it was decided that I would work on *Early Days*. My first impression was that he had a low profile and lacked that stereotypical anime industry aura. That's still unchanged to this day.

○ How far along was production on *Early Days* when you joined the crew?

At first, *Early Days* was planned as a 60-minute OVA, but when I read the screenplay, no matter which way you looked at it, there was definitely 90 minutes worth of material in there. When I asked how they would make it, the reply was, "Mr. Tazawa will draw the characters, and Mr. Shinkai will draw the backgrounds. That's all." (laughs) I think that was around spring of 2003, and they had completed 81 of 1,000 cuts. They said they wanted it to be finished by 2004, so I drew up a schedule and a budget, and rearranged the entire production. Of course it wouldn't have been possible for just the two of them to do everything, so we hired more people.

○ All the background artists that you gathered were people with zero animation experience.

I had the option of outsourcing that work to a background art company that I knew, but I decided that doing so wouldn't suit Mr. Shinkai. Besides, many of Mr. Shinkai's methods deviate from the industry's customary practices, so I figured they'd turn us down even if we asked. I discussed the possibility of bringing in people who were outside the animation industry with a friend who worked in film, and he introduced me to Mr. Tanji. He told me that he had never drawn images using a computer, so at first I was worried, but Mr. Shinkai taught him how to use Photoshop, and from the second image he was suddenly very adept. I learned that, so long as someone is very good at drawing, they can work in animation even with no prior experience, so after that I asked Mr. Tanji and Mr. Hirosawa to introduce people they knew.

○ Your title is line producer, but it seems like you built the production studio from scratch.

Yes, well, there's quite a disparity between the methods used by preexisting animation studios and Mr. Shinkai's methods, so while we employ the best practices from both sides, we fumble around and use trial and error to find new methods as well. There was also the thought that it would be a waste to dissolve the team we had gathered after the project was done, so we tried to keep as many staff members as possible for the next project. We acquired other projects until the start of production on *5 Centimeters* in order to keep the staff on board. As a result, we have a set team of trustworthy members, each of whose skills has only improved, and I'm hoping that one way or another, we can continue to work with them on future Shinkai projects.

○ Please tell us your thoughts on the Shinkai works you've produced thus far.

There's a misconception that Shinkai's studio is carefree and untroubled, but the truth is that everyone worries and suffers for the sake of creating a great film, so the atmosphere is very positive. The most interesting aspect for me as an on-site producer is when I bring two people together and they work together very well. After introducing Mr. Tanji to Mr. Shinkai for *Early Days* and Mr. Nishimura for *5 Centimeters* those works went on to be successful, and that to me is the greatest joy.

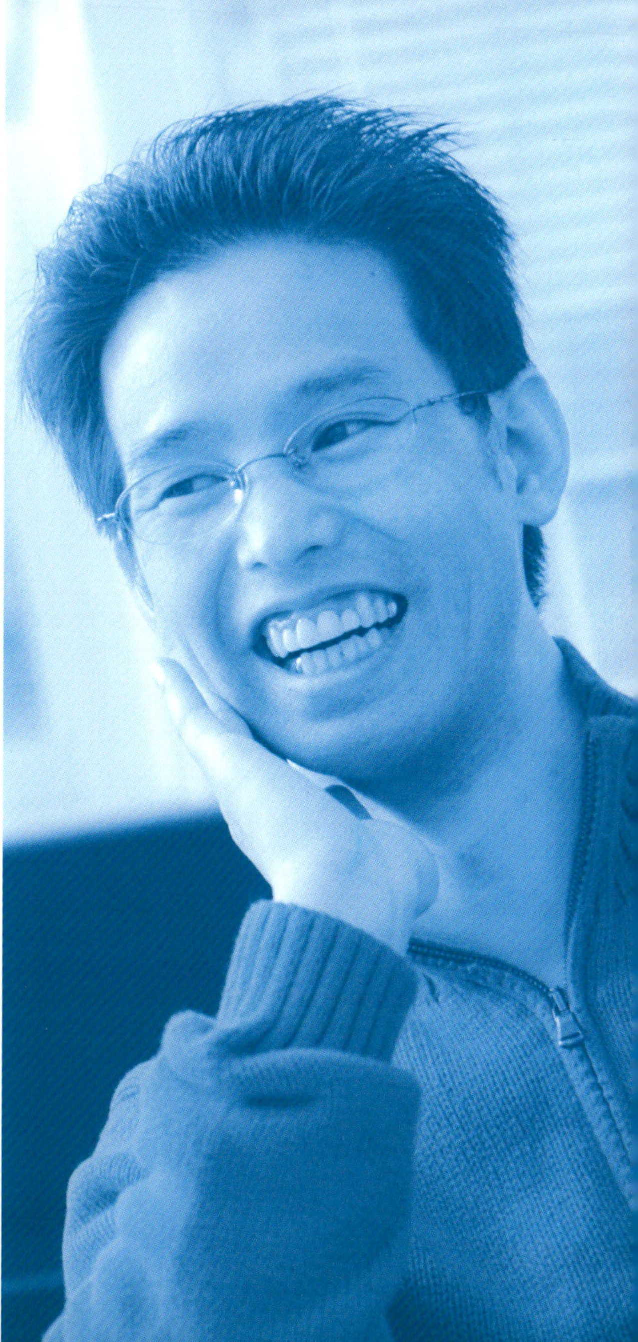

~a sky longing for memories~

The Art of Makoto Shinkai

Translation: Maya Rosewood
Production: Grace Lu
Vetting: Carl Li

First published in Japan in 2008 by Kodansha Ltd., Tokyo.
Originally published in Japanese as *Shinkai Makoto Bijutsu Sakuhin-shu Sora no Kioku*
Publication rights for this English edition arranged through Kodansha Ltd., Tokyo.

ISBN: 978-1-941220-43-6

Printed in Canada

First Edition

Seventh Printing

www.kodansha.us

Photographs:
Hiroshi Saitoh
Kou Yonezawa

Support:
Makoto Shinkai
Takumi Tanji
Takayo Nishimura
Akiko Majima
Akira Hirosawa
Minako Shimada
Kaori Izumiya
Yoshitaka Takeuchi
Yumi Ishii
Tasuku Watanabe
Noritaka Kawaguchi / cwfilms
Koichiro Itoh / cwfilms
Hiromichi Nakajima / cwfilms
Koumi Public Elementary School, Koumi City, Nagano
CoMix Wave Films, Inc.
NIITSU GUMI

Makoto Shinkai's Official Website
https://www.shinkaiworks.com/